We will Remember Them

with best wishes,

Colin Pendrill

9 Dec '17

And We Were Young

Here dead lie we because we did not choose
To live and shame the land from which we sprung.
Life, to be sure, is nothing much to lose;
But young men think it is, and we were young.

More Poems xxxvi
A.E.Housman

This book is dedicated to two more 'lads' who did not return from the Great War, two great-uncles unknown and unknowing.

Cecil George Hewson, a sorter in the London Postal Service and a private in the Post Office Rifles. He was killed in action near Les Boeufs, on the Somme on 8 October 1916, aged 21.

Robert Anderson Morgan, a clerk with McVities Biscuits in Edinburgh and a private in the Cameron Highlanders. Seriously wounded at Kemmel Hill, near Ypres, he died in the Maricolen Military Hospital, Deinze in Germany, on 10 May 1918, aged 22.

And We Were Young

Oundle School and the Great War

Colin Pendrill

Helion & Company Limited

Helion & Company Limited
26 Willow Road
Solihull
West Midlands
B91 1UE
England
Tel. 0121 705 3393
Fax 0121 711 4075
Email: info@helion.co.uk
Website: www.helion.co.uk
Twitter: @helionbooks
Visit our blog http://blog.helion.co.uk/

Published by Helion & Company 2017
Designed and typeset by Mach 3 Solutions Ltd (www.mach3solutions.co.uk)
Cover designed by Paul Hewitt, Battlefield Design (www.battlefield-design.co.uk)
Printed by Short Run Press, Exeter, Devon

Cover: All images save the photograph of the bust are from Oundle School Archive. The bust was sculpted by Henry Chen, photograph taken by Jeremy Oddie.

ISBN 978-1-912174-19-5

British Library Cataloguing-in-Publication Data.
A catalogue record for this book is available from the British Library.

For details of other military history titles published by Helion & Company Limited contact the above address, or visit our website: http://www.helion.co.uk.

We always welcome receiving book proposals from prospective authors.

Contents

Acknowledgements

I am hugely grateful to Oundle School Archive for permission to print pictures and written material stored therein. All pictures used in the book are from this archive, unless otherwise stated. I am also grateful to Michael Leventhal at Greenhill Books for permission to quote from *Sagittarius Rising* by Cecil Lewis. Other quotations, especially regimental diaries came from regimental websites. Map of the Somme battlefield courtesy of the Commonwealth War Graves Commission. And many thanks go to Duncan Rogers and all the staff at Helion and Company for their care and hard work in publishing *And We Were Young*.

Foreword

When I joined Oundle as a Berrystead boy in 1967 the Chapel loomed large in my life, and in the lives of my contemporaries. With its vast magnificence, separated from any other building in a no-man's land of lawns and pathways, it commanded our attendance, filled to the brim with startlingly large boys, every weekday and Sunday. Chapel set the tone for a school day crammed with places to be and things to do. I was not then very conscious that this was the school's living monument to a conflict that had swept away generations of its young leaders and that its routines and disciplines in an earlier building had trained generations of boys for the slaughter of the Western Front. Yet even so, that was a war to which in the 1960s we could still feel very connected. My father had served through the second war in the RAF; my parents' was a war marriage, and my oldest sister was born in 1944. One granny had a mysterious first husband, presumed to be a casualty of the first war. In the Berrystead the splendid housemaster, Colonel Anderson, was a further reminder of an age when any military service commanded respect.

Now, fifty years later still, it is an honour to be asked to contribute this short foreword to Colin Pendrill's compelling account of Oundle at war. The focus is quite rightly on those who gave their lives in active service, lives which at Oundle were crammed with rugby and cricket, the debating club, and winning scholarships to university that some would never live to take up; leading to an often too brief period of active service before becoming a casualty of war. But we also never lose sight of the war in Oundle itself: the annual round of speech day, the eager pitching in for the war economy, the growing lists of the fallen in the Laxtonian; most of all the ever looming presence of the absent, a reminder of the inevitability that so many of those still happily doing battle on the playing fields were destined to give their lives for their country.

The Oundle Colin Pendrill describes in this book must seem worlds away now, but not so much in the 1960s. The dreadful food, OTC, cross-country running, unheated dormitories – all of this rings true, as does the obsession with ceaseless activity ('apathy' seemed to be a word specifically invented to be brandished about by schoolmasters). Most of all, in an age before social media and the mobile phone, we shared with this earlier generation the almost total separation from home; and we lived, as they did, exclusively in a society of boys. In my schooldays writing letters provided the only link with distant family; we still wrote letters, and home still wrote to us. This, as it turned out, was the tale-end of the age of correspondence so vividly evoked in Colin Pendrill's volume, and a cornerstone of any study of the First World War soldier. We read the first, optimistic pledge of allegiance and bright-eyed enthusiasm for the anticipated quick victory; the tales of trench life, first jaunty, later less so; the cautious education of the home front to the realities of war; the dreadful letters of comfort to grieving families of the deceased, penned with great sensitivity by exhausted company officers; the painful, riveting letters of goodbye prepared before a fatal attack. I recently read my own father's 'read after dying' letter to my mother, and was astonished by the gentle eloquence called forth by extreme circumstances; the wisdom, generosity and humanity that could be summoned in times of extraordinary stress and pain. We all know this as the age of the war poets, and truly great poetry emerged from the trenches. But the everyday prose of these letters is in many ways as impressive, and even more moving for the lack of conscious art.

The Western Front generated a mass of post: it is generally acknowledged that the Forces Postal Service was one of the unalloyed triumphs of the war. It was the junior officer's responsibility both to distribute the mail and to censor his men's outgoing replies. For the sleep-deprived junior officer this can hardly have been a welcome duty, but for many young officers, generally sons of professional families and schooled among their own, this was an awakening to a world of which they knew nothing: the life of the urban working class. It is no accident that the two future Conservative prime ministers to have experienced the war as junior officers, Anthony Eden and Harold Macmillan, came out of the trenches as One Nation Tories, with a lifelong commitment to bettering the standard of living of the men with whom they served and their families. And it is one of the tragedies of the war that so many of those who might have used these experiences to ameliorate the harsh divisions of interwar society never lived to make their contribution to the necessary work of rebuilding society.

In 1914 Oundle was a school of around four hundred pupils, though this represented a rapid increase over previous years. This was a tribute to the energy of its greatest pre-war headmaster, Frederick Sanderson, appointed in 1892. Sanderson was a controversial choice: the first non-cleric to lead the school and a northern scientist to boot. But he made Oundle distinctive, with a strong emphasis on practical subjects, science and engineering. The workshops were a characteristic Sanderson innovation, and came in very handy when war broke out. When as a ten year old I was practising racing changes on the high power lathes (the term 'health and safety' had not the same resonance then) I had little idea that the ancestors of these machines had been turning out munition parts during the Great War. The manufacturers, inspecting the boys' work, were generous enough to say that these parts were of higher quality that those produced in their own factory (as reported in *The Oundle Munitions Gazette*). Thanks to Sanderson, Oundle also had agricultural land that could immediately be turned to boosting home food production.

Innovative and imaginative though Sanderson may have been, he shared the general public school confidence in the character-building qualities of the Officers' Training Corps. Founded in the wake of the British army's humiliations at the hands of Afrikaner irregulars in the Second Boer War (1899-1902), the OTC played an essential part in the life of any public school. Though not compulsory, to have opted out would have produced evidence of the lack of 'moral fibre' that the OTC and the whole structure of school life were meant to develop. Some schools would not allow boys to represent them in competitive sports until they had passed their OTC shooting test. The importance attached to the OTC and its status in the school meant that when the call went out for volunteers in 1914, the OTC delivered a ready-made cohort of officer material: indeed, the name of your school was regarded in itself as proof of capacity to lead. The playwright R.C. Sherriff, who poured his own experience of combat into the classic dramatic account of trench life, *Journey's End*, records the humiliation of presenting himself for officer training only to be told that his school was not on the list. It mattered not that Kingston Grammar School had been founded by Queen Elizabeth I in 1567. Forced to enlist in the ranks, Sherriff eventually made his way to a commission.

Brutal though this may have been, it seems to have worked. The graduates of the public schools were fit and strong, inured to hardship by the boarding school regime and trained to a leadership role. They were also, on average, an astonishing five inches taller than their men. In the harsh regime of the trenches, a natural air of command and self-confidence were priceless assets, and qualities the men clearly valued. The young second lieutenant was generally a respected figure, particularly as, to a larger extent than in other armies, junior officers were expected to pitch in with their men. The officers who experienced the most difficulty gaining the respect of their platoon were often those who made their way up through the ranks filling the gaps left by the punishing casualty rate. Such officers were known as 'temporary gentlemen' a single phrase that sums up so much about the army, British society and the idiocy of war.

Though officers were not supposed to take part in the physical work of trench digging (and in the smarter regiments could be disciplined for doing so), many did help out with hauling and carrying; sometimes on marches they ended up carrying not only their own pack, but another for an exhausted private who would otherwise have fallen behind. Patrols into no man's land, or the perilous work of repairing the wire, were always led by officers. The German army consigned these tasks to NCOs, which is one reason their casualty rates among junior officers were less brutal. Obliged to lead their men over the top, vulnerable to German sniper fire, the freshly minted junior officers were the most vulnerable of all to the scarcely understood perils of trench warfare. Later in the war officers would be instructed to dress in the uniform of a private soldier, to make them less recognisable (though they still carried the distinctive service revolver). But that was too late for the Oundle generation of 1914, who had answered the call to arms with such cheerful enthusiasm, along with similar cohorts from the English public schools.

The chaos of battle, and the arbitrary sorting of death and survival, brought many teenage soldiers to still more demanding responsibilities. In battlefield conditions subalterns often found themselves in charge of a large mixed mass of men from different units, whose own officers had been killed. The wonder was that so few broke under the strain. Young officers, it has been said, had the psychological buoyancy of corks, but many came to hate the war, and some began to say so openly. When Siegfried Sassoon wrote a letter to *The Times* criticising the war, its publication caused something of a stir and Sassoon was bundled off to hospital for psychological rest. He later 'recovered' and returned to the front line. Most young officers felt they had no choice but to go on, not least for fear of the shame attached to any other course of action. The fear of letting down friends, or family, or England, was palpable, to which one can add the fear of letting down one's old school. When Second Lieutenant Gerard Manning was killed leading his men out of the trenches on the Somme in November 1916 his last words to his NCO were to tell Uppingham that he did all right. It was only when the NCO reported this exchange to the company commander that he realised that the dying man had been referring to his school.[1]

The terrors of hand-to-hand combat, of defying a wall of machine gun bullets, were real enough, but for many the worst of trench life was the waiting: waiting to go over the top, to take out a wiring party, for friends to return from patrol, for a shell to burst nearby; or simply just waiting. The High Command's not unsympathetic response was to fill the day with work, checking soldiers' rifles or feet, writing reports, killing rats. But since so much of the work of patrols or checking sentries took place at night, this could mean a whole twenty-four hours, or sequence of days, without sleep. Only frequent rotations out of the front line allowed some respite for recuperation and preserved some semblance of sanity and combat effectiveness. The resilience of the boy officers is, in retrospect, quite astonishing. Few were invalided out by exhaustion or simple incapacity to go on. But just as few smokers die of Alzheimer's, few subalterns were in the front line long enough to feel the long-term effects of trench life: they were either dead or wounded back to Blighty. Many indeed prayed fervently for the wound that would provide for an honourable retreat from the Hell that was Flanders. But even a wound had to be nicely calculated; anything less than permanent invalidity could mean patching up to return to the front line to fight again, and often to die.

Oundle pupils in the 1970s were nothing like as well travelled as they are today. Few of us holidayed abroad as a matter of course, and a theatre outing to Leicester was considered exotic. But I did enjoy the privilege of a week-long tour of world war battlefields, culminating in a largely undiscovered extension of the Maginot Line, at which we were the only visitors. It was almost totally unmarked; the only damage was the bullet holes inflicted when the storming of the redoubt was re-staged for the benefit of the German news-reel cameras. The whole edifice had been a huge, ruinously expensive, pointless folly. In the event it was my father's generation that paid the price

---

1   This story and many of the insights in this brief foreword comes from John Lewis-Stempel, *Six Weeks. The Short and Gallant Life of the British Officer in the First World War* (London: Weidenfeld & Nicolson, 2010). See also Anthony Seldon and David Walsh, *Public Schools and the Great War* (Pen & Sword Military, 2013).

of the failure to find peace in the two decades after the Great War. Ultimately the greatest tragedy of those who had given their lives in the 1914 conflict, often without hesitation or a backward glance, was that 'the war to end wars' was anything but. But consider this. Oundle boys died all over the Empire, though curiously few in the Royal Navy. But the Navy was in many ways the greatest monument to the Imperial ideology that sent so many schoolboy soldiers off to die with bright countenance and shining eyes. And in 1940, with German armies unchallenged in continental Europe, and Britain bruised and apparently broken, it was the Royal Navy's command of the Channel that persuaded Hitler to abandon the invasion of Britain that would have extinguished resistance. From this decision was built the fightback that eventually rescued Europe from tyranny and dictatorship and created the modern democratic Europe that today we take for granted.

Professor Andrew Pettegree O.O.

Preface: In Memoriam – *Haec monumenta suis posuit pia mater alumnis*

> They carry back bright to the coiner the mintage of man,
> The lads that will die in their glory and never be old.
>
> **A.E. Housman**

And they were young. In the picture of the Dryden House OTC platoon taken in the summer of 1912, there are 34 boys from a House of 41. The other seven are not there probably because they were too young to join. Those in the picture are aged between 14 and 18 and they are ready for war. As they gaze out at us, do they see the coming conflict? Eleven of them – one in three – would be killed in the carnage which engulfed their world between 1914 and 1918.

Dryden House OTC Platoon, summer 1912. Numbering from left to right, the following were killed during the War: Back row: **4** and **7**; Row 3: **3, 5, 6, 7, 9** and **12**; Row 2: **3** and **5**; Front row: **1**.

Over 1,200 lads from Oundle School and Laxton School answered their country's call. Of those, more than 90 percent had left school after 1900, meaning that the vast majority of Oundle's servicemen were under 30 when they went off to war. The average age of those killed in the conflict was just 23 years and some 65 percent of Oundle's fallen were aged between 18 and 24. John Savage, shot down by German air-ace Max Immelmann in the summer of 1916, was just 17 years old when he gave his life for his country.

And the death rate amongst the servicemen who had once been schooled at Oundle or Laxton was very high. Nearly one in four of them – 260 old boys and four members of staff at the last count – perished in the conflict and at least as many again must have been wounded. The Dryden House of 1912 fared even worse. It lost 14 of its boys to the fighting, some 34 percent of the House. The high death rate amongst Oundelians, at least twice the national average, is easily explained by looking again at the Dryden photograph from 1912. At public schools like Oundle, boys received military training in the Officers' Training Corps. Up and down the country, these units were established at schools after the Second Boer War (1899-1902) had laid bare British military weakness. With OTC training under their belts, Oundle boys who volunteered were able to gain commissions as second lieutenants. As junior commissioned officers, it was their job to lead their men 'over the top'. And from the earliest days of the war, German soldiers, especially snipers were told to target these young officers as a first priority.

And they were mostly volunteers. They volunteered to fight for their country in great numbers. Looking again at the Dryden House OTC picture from 1912, all but four in the picture joined up and all seven Dryden boys not in the picture also played their part in the conflict, so in total 37 boys from the Dryden House of the summer of 1912 (90 percent) 'did their bit'. At first glance, the volunteering spirit of Oundelians, might appear to be less marked than at some other public schools. In the 2013 volume, *Public Schools and the Great War*, Anthony Seldon and David Walsh indicated that the number of Oundelians who joined up was less than three times the number of boys in the school in 1914. This compares unfavourably with some other major public schools where the number of boys going off to war was four, five and occasionally six times the immediate pre-war school population. However, in Oundle's case such comparisons are misleading since the two schools grew so rapidly in the 20 years before the war. The *average* number of pupils at Oundle and Laxton in that crucial period was only 230 boys, not the 400 in the schools in 1914. So 1200 fighting Oundelians represents five times the pre-war average school population.

And they knew why they went. Geoffrey Vickers who left Sidney House in 1912 and three years later won Oundle's first Victoria Cross, explained the volunteering spirit in these terms: "In August, Germany invaded Belgium, we had a treaty with Belgium, so we all stopped what we were doing and went off to war. It was as simple as that." For Oundelians in 1914, as for so many other young men of the time, there was no agonizing about the rights and wrongs of the war. They were, after all the sons of the British Empire, the largest empire ever seen. Strong patriotism and pride in their country as a force for good in the world came entirely naturally to these boys. In addition, the German threat to the European balance of power was clearly identified in the years before 1914, so Oundle boys knew who the enemy would be. With their privileged position in society, education, ethos of service to their country and community – particularly strong in Sanderson's Oundle – the volunteering tide became a flood. And, as one Oudelian, Eric Yarrow, wrote, it was because they were young and privileged and without dependents that they were the obvious men to go. It was also a matter of honour. Housman reminds us that these lads "did not choose to shame the land from which they sprung." Perhaps it was also to do with love. As Cecil Spring-Rice put it so movingly in *I vow to Thee, My Country*, written during the war: "The love that never falters, the love that pays the price, the love that makes undaunted the final sacrifice."

And Oundelians went off to war cheerfully. So many letters to grieving parents insisted that their boys were always cheerful, even in the thick of the fighting and the very worst of living conditions.

And the boys themselves wrote home with optimism and reassurance, recalling exciting adventures, talking up the prospects of victory and asking for all manner of home comforts. Their wartime letters to their parents are written in same tone and style as their earlier letters from school. Most Oundelians were officers, so they had to encourage their men and, like prefects in boarding houses, they had to maintain discipline. They had to set an example of unconcerned courage and fortitude. Perhaps the most telling letters of sympathy to grieving parents are those from the NCOs who served these Oundle boys, who spoke so feelingly of their courage and good humour at all times.

And they came from across the empire. Oundelians from Australia, New Zealand, Canada, India, South-Africa and the West-Indies all joined up. And they died across the globe, on land, at sea and in the air. Most of course on the Western Front, nearly 75 percent, but others in Gaza and Gallipoli, Portuguese as well as British East Africa, Italy and India, Mesopotamia, Malta and Macedonia, Jutland and Coronel and even one in the Russian Civil War, long after the Armistice of 1918. Ninety boys (34 percent) have no known grave including five lost or buried at sea. Surprisingly perhaps, twenty-one Oundelians (8 percent) are buried at home in Britain.

And the dead became glorious. On war memorials up and down the country as well as marble tablets, stained glass windows and wooden plaques, Oundle names are inscribed – a fitting testament to the extraordinary courage, resilience and fortitude of these young men who gave their lives for their country. And they are all recalled in this book.

In recent years at Oundle, it has been the custom to gather staff and pupils together in the School Cloisters, little changed since the war, to mark the Armistice which finally ended the long years of suffering. At the 11th hour and with Union Jack fluttering from the tower, the two minute silence is observed, the last post is played and Binyon's familiar words intoned:

> At the going down of the sun
> And in the morning
> We will remember them.

A century after the conflict, it is still a very solemn and moving occasion, touching young and old alike. But in truth, we have only been able to remember them in general terms – Oundelians as part of a generation lost; names inscribed on memorials. This book is mainly concerned with and dedicated to the boys who perished in the conflict, piecing together their deeds at school as well as their deeds in the war; hearing what they have to say about the world around them and seeing their faces, in peace and in war, at home and far away. Now we shall remember them more fully.

The job of bringing these boys back to life could not have been done without the written and pictorial traces they left behind. Luckily their school has preserved many of the records which allow us to see and hear them even at a distance of one hundred years. The School's Memorial Book published in 1920 has been the most important source for exploring the lives of Oundle's fallen. It has citations for all the boys who died and in addition, and so importantly, it has photographs of most of them. Those photographs, mostly head and shoulders, mostly in military uniform and often sporting an officer's moustache are vital in visualising these young men. The School's archive also holds many splendid pictures of the same boys in team and house photographs and you can see exactly where they were taken around a school many of whose buildings are little altered since their day.

In addition, the families of several old boys published their letters and diaries or deposited them in the archive. The wealth of material we have for some, makes us more aware of what is missing for others. School publications of the period, particularly the termly Laxtonian magazines have also been hugely valuable. Here they are as schoolboys, writing about their experiences at Oundle, with all the enthusiasm that schoolboys can muster. There are the witty articles poking fun at the world and the people around them, reports of debates and academic lectures. There are the many reports of sports fixtures – very many! And then there are the poems, some extremely funny and others terribly moving, including a hugely touching poem, rediscovered in the course of these researches, written by a housemaster, himself on active service abroad, on hearing the news of the death of one of his boys. And the boys wrote so well and with a sense of style that makes even their reports of the humblest house match a joy to read. Add these personal memorials created by the boys themselves, to the memorials raised to them after the war and we can really begin to measure and describe the impact of the Great War on the two Oundle schools.

I am indebted to Quentin Thomas, Director of Music and Chris Pettit, sound engineer, for the splendid music from wartime Speech Day concerts, which will be available on the school website, as current Oundelians 'do their bit' to commemorate their predecessors. I also thank my classical colleagues, Tim Morrison and Nic Aubury for help with some tricky Latin and Greek and Keith Hannis for help with some tricky English. Likewise, Elspeth Langsdale, school archivist and Leigh Giurlando, school librarian for their valuable help and support in my researches. Ivan Quetglas, school photographer has laboured hard to improve the quality of some of the photographs, as has SDS Group with their super scanning equipment. Two great ladies were crucial in inspiring me to undertake this particular labour of love. My good friend and one-time colleague, Sue Smart produced the captivating story of Gresham's School and the Great War, *When Heroes Die*, as long ago as 2001, while Avalon Eastman, determined to honour the memory of her uncle, Avalon Hutchins, ended up visiting the graves of nearly all the Oundle boys buried at home and abroad, and published an updated and less unwieldy version of the School's Memorial Book. My good friends in the History Department at Oundle School, once so ably led by Max Habsburg, have remained a constant inspiration. In particular, Philip Pedley, with whom I have discussed the First World War and the School on so many occasions, has been a real source of encouragement for this project, as befits a schoolmaster who served Oundle so well for more than 36 years.

The impact of the war has much to tell us about the importance of family. My family have helped me more than they will know – Sue and Jan, Hilary, Rebecca and Matthew and, of course, Ella.

C.R.P
History Department
Oundle School
13th February 2017

Prologue: Speech Day 1914

I cannot help thinking that war is imminent.

The Coming of War – the final Armageddon

In the Michaelmas Term of 1912, 17 year old Justin Willis, in his last year in New House at Oundle School, in rural Northamptonshire, penned a series of exciting and remarkably prophetic letters to his parents. It all started with some history lessons:

> "We have been doing some very interesting lessons lately, one on Frederick the Great and another on the war in the Balkans. My Daily Mail War Map came the other day, it is jolly good. I still think there is a considerable chance of there being a general mix up between the Powers, the final Armageddon…As Austria is one of the Triple Alliance and Russia one of the Entente-Cordiale with France and ourselves, if war should break out between Austria and Russia, the war would become general throughout Europe."

And Britain's enemy in a future war is made explicit. Later in the same letter, young Willis referred to "the rotten Germans" and in a missive sent the next month to relations staying in Berlin, he says: "I hope the Germans don't declare war on us whilst you and Joan are in Germany." In yet another letter, that same term, he returned to his favourite theme of why a war with Germany was a real possibility and concluded by saying: "My arguments are probably rotten but still, I cannot help thinking that war is imminent."

In the autumn of 1912, no doubt many of the excitable schoolboys at Oundle would have agreed that war with Germany was a distinct possibility. But while the prospect of war with Germany was no doubt uppermost in the thoughts of many schoolboys in these years, by the summer of 1914, the chances of war in Europe had apparently faded. The Second Balkan War had ended the previous year and it seemed as though the Powers had once again steadied the ship. Major-General Birkbeck, who would inspect the School's Officers' Training Corps on Speech Day 1914, later wrote to the Headmaster in these terms, reflecting on the unexpected outbreak of hostilities: "We little thought when I spoke to those boys of yours how near we were to our trial." On Speech Day 1914 then, Justin Willis' war looked unlikely.

Speech Day 1914

Oundle School's Speech Day in 1914 was held on Saturday 4 July, some four weeks before the end of term and just six days after the assassination of Archduke Franz Ferdinand and his wife in Sarajevo. But a double murder in far off Sarajevo could do little to dampen Oundle spirits and the School was in bullish mood. The festivities began on the Friday evening with a series of scientific experiments which parents and other visitors could inspect. Such experiments, demonstrated by pupils of course, had become a staple part of Speech Day celebrations under headmaster Frederick William Sanderson. The editor of the school magazine, the Laxtonian, reported that in 1914, the experiments were "more successful than they have ever been." In the gymnasium, there were experiments on mechanics, sound and electrical induction, while in the physics laboratory, seniors explored optics and juniors took on natural history and biology. All told there were eight rooms and corridors given over to scientific experiments, including, naturally enough, the famous school workshops.

These displays of scientific prowess went under the name of *conversazioni* a term coined by Sanderson to stress both the explanation of the experiments by boys but also as an exposition that might lead to further discussion, questions and answers. As if the varied *conversazioni* weren't enough, on that Friday evening, 3 July 1914, visitors and boys had the opportunity to see "the school film and some scientific films shown at various times in the Great Hall."

The next morning, 4 July 1914, amidst glorious sunshine, the Commemoration Service was held in the parish church and afterwards Major-General Birkbeck CB CMG (who would later send his three sons to School House) duly inspected the school corps on the field. He was driven up to the cricket field, which doubled as a parade ground, in the Headmaster's car. According to young Alexander Crawford, who had just joined Sidney House that May, the Major-General "in full dress uniform" was "an impressive figure, the plume of his cocked hat flying in the breeze." After the ranks had been inspected, the school battalion "marched past in column of platoons and marched back again in 'close column', finally advancing once more in 'review order'." The Major-General made a speech in which he naturally alluded to the danger of war. Young Crawford was doubtful. It was a beautiful sunny day in Oundle and he thought that "in the context of those halcyon days, the very idea of a major European war seemed unthinkable."

After lunch in houses, prize-giving took place in the Great Hall. The Headmaster gave his annual review of the School's activities, in glowing terms no doubt and, as was customary at a school run by the Grocers' Company, the prizes were given away by the current Master, J. R. Drake. He then made a speech and the vote of thanks was proposed by the Dean of Peterborough and seconded by Mr Monckton and Sir Ryland Adkins MP. The ceremony closed, according to the Laxtonian editor, with "the usual cheers given with the usual heartiness."

After the prize-giving and speeches, the Headmaster's wife, Mrs Jane Sanderson hosted a garden party in the grounds of School House, rendered all the more enjoyable by "the perfect weather" and the playing of the Wellingborough Band, conducted by the School's Bandmaster, Charles Clayson. In the evening, back in the Great Hall, a concert was given, with most of the music supplied by the boys. Sanderson was keen on music and would later introduce the radical idea of 'whole school' singing. As we shall see, music making by a dedicated team working together to produce harmonious results was very much a reflection of his social and educational ideas. The Laxtonian editor concluded that the concert on Speech Day 1914 "was one of the most successful the School has given," though he was worried by its excessive length!

As well as items by the School Orchestra, Chorus and the Junior School Singing Class, there were a number of solo items. Ironically, two of the soloists were of German descent. Roland Keiffenheim played the serenade from Gounod's *Faust* on his flute. The Laxtonian noted that it was "quite expressive and nicely played." Meanwhile, on the violin Ernest Weintraud played a *scène de ballet* by de Bériot. Weintraud was described as "a most capable violinist" who "revealed his powers in an excellent performance." By contrast, Charles Storrs did not do quite so well on his violin, as he allowed "his natural nervousness to spoil his performance." Pianist Thomas Bowen however, played well. He "made his debut and played with refinement and musical expression." The Laxtonian correspondent noted that "he has an excellent touch" but described "his technical equipment" as only "satisfactory". Other soloists on the night were Frank Berrill and Harold Walkerdine who sang songs and won "well-deserved applause."

All six soloists in the Speech Day concert of 1914 would fight in the war, which unknown to them just weeks away. Charles Storrs and Tom Bowen both joined the Royal Engineers and survived apparently unscathed. The singers were not so fortunate. Harold Walkerdine was badly wounded serving in the Royal Flying Corps and Frank Berrill, who joined the Royal Field Artillery, was invalided home for the winter of 1916-17 with gas poisoning and was then killed in France in September 1918. The two boys of German descent were also killed. Roland Keiffenheim changed his name to Roland Trubridge, for obvious reasons, in September of 1914. He joined the Royal Flying Corps and died of wounds in May 1918. Ernest Weintraud became Winton at the outbreak of hostilities, joined in the Royal Garrison Artillery and was killed in France in December 1917.

As was traditional, the Speech Day concert concluded with the singing of the school song *Carmen Undeliense* composed by the music master Clement Spurling and published in 1912. The acquisition of a new school song, (replacing *Floreat Undelium* of 1864), written in Latin, and composed by the music master of more than 20 years standing, was another mark of Oundle's increasingly realistic claim to be a public school of national significance.

Speech Day 1914 then, saw an Oundle School which was 'on the up'. The number of pupils in the school had reached 350, nearly four times the figure when Sanderson had arrived as headmaster in 1892. While not as big as Uppingham with 450 or Rugby with 555, let alone Eton with over a thousand pupils, Oundle was clearly 'the coming school'. The School's reputation was nationwide, masters and pupils were purposeful and high achievers and on Speech Day 1914 even the glorious weather played its part to underscore Oundle's success and self-confidence.

The School in 1914: Two schools not one

By 1914 there were seven senior boarding houses at the School. The oldest was of course School House, with the Headmaster in charge. Then in order of longevity came Dryden, Laxton (now called Fisher), Sidney, Grafton, Crosby and New House. All were in their current positions, except for Dryden which, naturally enough, then occupied the building that is now called Old Dryden in North Street. In addition, in 1901, the School had opened the Berrystead as a preparatory house and the number of boys in residence there had grown in an encouraging way.

But in 1914 Oundle School was two schools not one. In addition to Oundle School with its boarding houses, there was also Laxton Grammar School. This was the successor of the original medieval guild school in the town, which looked set to close after the attack on the guilds and chantries by Protector Somerset in reign of the boy king, Edward VI. This school was dramatically saved, on his death-bed, by one of the guild school's most successful old boys, Sir William Laxton. He had attended the school as a boy and, armed with an education and the links that the Oundle guild already had with the Grocers' Company in London, went to the capital and made his fortune as a 'grocer', becoming Lord Mayor of London as well. Dying of plague in 1556 and with no children of his own, Laxton left some of his properties in the city to re-found the school in Oundle which had given him such a good start in life. At first the Grocers' Company was hesitant about taking on the burden of running a provincial school in Northamptonshire and some of Laxton's relatives disputed the will and started a court case. Eventually, in the reign of Queen Elizabeth, some 17 years after Laxton's death, the Wardens of the Grocers' Company took formal possession of their new school. Destroyed by the grasping regime of Edward VI, the School survived by the skin of its teeth, thanks to Laxton's generosity, to become the Laxton Grammar School offering a free education to local lads.

By the late 19th Century, Oundle was a well-established provincial grammar school and had a number of boarders, but had little chance of joining the ranks of the elite English public schools. In class-conscious times, it failed to attract enough pupils on the boarding side, and the feeling was that middle class parents were unwilling to send their sons to a school whose main focus was still the free education of local boys.

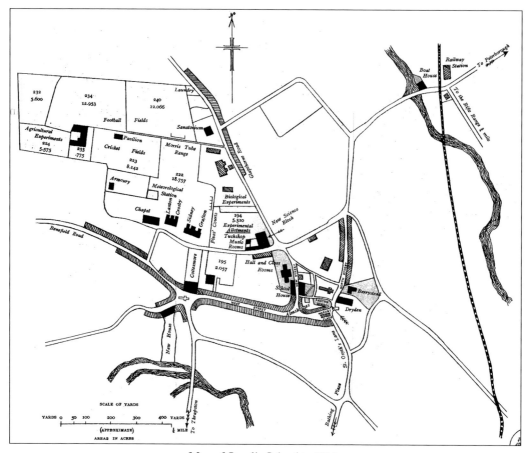

Map of Oundle School in 1914.

In 1876, to remedy this problem and to set Oundle on the way to becoming a public school of national standing, the Headmaster, Henry St. John Reade, persuaded the Grocers' Company to divide the School into two 'twinned' schools. The first would be Laxton Grammar School, advertised now as "a Modern School for sons of farmers, tradesmen etc. resident in Oundle or its vicinity." This was the original foundation in a new guise, providing a tuition free education for local boys. In fact, as well as day boys, Laxton Grammar School also had some boarders, to generate more income. Alongside Laxton Grammar School – and sharing the same headmaster – would be a new Oundle School which would be mainly for boarders and any 'day boys' whose parents were prepared to stump up the fees. This school was advertised as "a First-Grade Classical School." The division of the School into two went well at first. Numbers increased and new school buildings were erected facing onto New Street. Reade, a Tonbridge boy himself, put more emphasis on games and he introduced a school magazine, the Laxtonian in December 1876. Printed by Mr Alfred King, it would appear once a term.

However, in 1882, six years after the invention of Oundle School, Reade proposed to raise the fees payable by day pupils in the Modern School. This seemed clumsy and high-handed, particularly as he had not apparently informed the Grocers of his intention. Local parents and townsmen, worried that their children's rights to a good and free education, as established by Sir William Laxton's will, were being eroded took their protests to the Grocers' Company in London. This led to Reade's resignation in 1883. The next headmaster, Rev Thomas Fry resigned

Laxton and Crosby Houses c1914.

New House (on the left) c1910.

because of ill health after just four terms. He was followed by Mungo Park. In his time numbers at the schools fell sharply and after seven years at the helm and with his health in decline, he like Reade and Fry resigned prematurely. When Park resigned then, there were only 90 boys in the two schools. This was actually fewer than under Headmaster Stansbury (1848-76) in the 1850s and 60s, when there was only one school in Oundle. By 1892, when Frederick Sanderson was appointed to succeed Park, it seemed as though the bold experiment to create a public school in Oundle to rival Uppingham and Rugby had failed. Yet the basis for a great public school had been laid. The division of the Schools in 1876 was pivotal in the long-term, as was the fact that the income from the London properties left to the School by Sir William Laxton had seriously increased in value by this time.

Financial prosperity

Financially, one particular reform, under Sanderson, was to be crucial to Oundle's future prosperity. From the earliest days, there had been boarders at Oundle School but they paid their boarding fees directly to the housemaster – usually the headmaster. In the years before 1914 however, Oundle, like other schools moved to a 'hostel system' whereby housemasters were paid a higher salary, commensurate with their responsibilities but the boarding fees went to the School, so that profits from boarding and from the expansion of boarding could be re-invested in new buildings and more staff. By 1914, the Houses as hostels were paying some £2,000 a year into the School's Building Fund.

Even before Sanderson's arrival, the increasing wealth of both Oundle Schools accompanied by financial backing from the Grocers' Company had allowed for the creation of new school buildings. The Cloisters building fronting onto New Street opened in September 1883 as new classrooms for Oundle School and in 1885 the old guild house by the churchyard was completely rebuilt and

School Cloisters on New Street in 1910.

enlarged to become the main building of Laxton Grammar School. Also at this time, the new School House buildings went up opposite the Cloisters, replacing the original 'school house' at the west end of the churchyard. With rising income and new buildings, all that was then needed to create a great public school was a visionary and dynamic headmaster with exciting new views on education. In Frederick William Sanderson, the School found such a man.

Sanderson and educational reform: Widening the curriculum

Sanderson himself had been a controversial appointment in 1892 but because the School was at a low ebb, the Grocers decided that a young and energetic science teacher was what Oundle needed. Up until then most Oundle headmasters had been clergymen, most were prosperous middle class men and classical scholars. Now the Grocers appointed a non-clergyman from the working classes, who was not really interested in games, who spoke with a 'geordie' accent and who espoused left-wing politics! Sanderson was an ardent reformer but found it hard to communicate his new ideas and had a fierce temper, so that his early years were very difficult, with staff and boys often hostile to the new Head. His view of the staff he found at Oundle was hardly complimentary. He thought they were insufficiently industrious and hostile to change. One of the first things he did was to close down their Common Room! "I have been surprised to find," Sanderson wrote in his first term at Oundle, "that the assistant Masters, with hardly an exception, have no idea of what hard work means." This was not entirely their fault, he conceded but it resulted in boys who were "not being pushed forward" and who displayed "a very low standard of energy." He realised that, "it will undoubtedly take some time to infuse a spirit of work throughout the school."

Unsurprisingly, a number of staff left or were asked to resign and Sanderson brought in more energetic men. Henry Ormsby Hale, (known as 'Tally' or 'H$_2$O') who had been one of Sanderson's colleagues at Dulwich, arrived at Oundle with him in September 1892. Then there was H. M. King (known as John and notorious for keeping classes in over morning break), who had been taught and enthused by Sanderson at Dulwich. By 1914, the number of teachers had grown to 26 and they were all believers in Sanderson's educational ideas. This dedicated body of men were ranged behind Sanderson on Speech Day 1914 and at the forefront were his housemasters. Llewellyn Jones ('Jug' or 'Juggie') in charge of Dryden, Albert Nightingale ('the Major') in Sidney, Sammy Squire in Laxton, Francis Norbury, an old boy, in Grafton, George Tryon in Crosby, Henry Hale in New House and the Reverend Malcolm Brown in the Berrystead.

Aided by these impressive and energetic men, Sanderson had introduced a number of pioneering education reforms at Oundle which gave the School a growing national reputation. By 1914, the success of these reforms was clear to see. The range of subjects on offer was widened to include engineering, Russian, Spanish, biological sciences, botany and agriculture, while traditional subjects, particularly classics were re-invigorated by the appointment of new staff. The most notable change in the curriculum was the introduction of engineering and the setting up of workshops in the Cloisters. Other schools did teach science of course but few if any went in for engineering and woodwork. Such practical, dare one say 'dirty subjects', smacking of the shop floor and the industrial working classes, were seen by most public schools as much inferior to Latin and Greek, which they saw as the proper domain of gentlemen and scholars. At Oundle, the new emphasis on giving boys practical experience of engineering and manufacturing gave the School a special reputation and niche in the education marketplace, so that many industrialists, in particular, would decide to send their sons to Oundle.

And Sanderson did not want the boys to merely play at engineering, he was determined to give them the proper instruments and machines needed to do the work properly. Robert Bragg, who arrived in Dryden House in 1909 at the age of 16, when his father moved from Adelaide in Australia to take up a professorship at Leeds, was suitably impressed by this aspect of Sanderson's

Sanderson and his staff in 1899. From left to right: Rev. Malcolm Brown, Llewellyn Jones,
Edward Hansell, Albert Nightingale, J. Mercer, Henry Hale, W. G. Grace Jnr., 'John' King,
Clement Spurling and J. Hornstein.

workshops. After a few weeks he wrote home enthusiastically: "I have to have a slide-rule…we must have one the head says. Don't they use grown-up things here, ones that I would never have dreamt of using until I went to university at least, yet every small boy has one and knows how to use it." A month later he was equally impressed when the workshops acquired another new piece of heavy equipment: "A new planing machine has just arrived at the school, it is an enormously solid affair, the bed is about 12 or 14 feet long and it must have cost a fabulous amount." What struck him as well was the reaction of the boys who had been at Oundle somewhat longer than the new Antipodean: "there is no particular excitement about it, in fact it seems that everyone is quite used to new pieces of machinery arriving like this."

The expansion in science and engineering was not however at the expense of more traditional subjects. Sanderson wanted merely to raise the profile of science, so that it was seen as equal to classics and not inferior. By 1914, there were ten teachers of science and engineering at Oundle but also eight classicists and five teachers of what were described as 'modern' subjects – English, geography and modern languages. Boys at Oundle would broadly follow either the classical side or the science and engineering sides. While there were nine science forms from Fourth Form onwards, there were still seven classical forms as well. And in the thirty years of Sanderson's headmastership, Oundle boys won just as many Oxbridge scholarships in classics as they did in science. Sanderson believed that with such a range of subjects on offer, every boy could find his passion and no boy would be seen as dull and unimportant.

From 1909, the School also moved into practical farming and horticulture. In that year, experimental work was started on some land turned over to allotments. Amongst boys in the middle and lower school, there was the opportunity to analyse plant growth in the allotments, backed up by research in the laboratories. By 1911, agricultural work was further developed with the help of agreeable local farmers, so that boys could take advantage of experiments on a larger scale and have a more practical impact in terms of local food production. By 1914, the School had its own farm, some 13 acres given over to experiments not only in crop growing and crop rotation, but also to experiments in the breeding of livestock. At the same time, Sanderson developed links between Oundle and the Rothamsted Agricultural Institute in Hertfordshire – clear evidence of Oundle's willingness to look beyond its own portals in the search for real education. In 1912, Sanderson appointed young George Olive to the staff as an agricultural expert. Olive further developed the work of the boys on the plots, encouraged local farmers to come to his Science Society lectures and also started a miniature Kew Gardens with interesting specimens. With all these developments in agriculture, Oundle would be ready to answer the nation's call for improved food production in wartime.

Amongst traditional subjects given greater prominence under the energetic Sanderson was music. In Clement Spurling, the Head had an inspirational and loyal music master, who served throughout Sanderson's 30 years at the helm. It is notable that the Blue Books (school lists) of the period give special priority to musical matters. The first lists in these volumes are not the house lists or the form lists but the music lists. On average seven pages in each booklet name all the boys in

Sidney House 1914 with Housemaster 'the Major' Albert Nightingale, Head of OTC.

the Chapel Choir, the Choral Society, the Orchestral Society and the Drum, Fife and Bugle Band. The numbers involved were impressive. The Chapel Choir by 1914 consisted of 156 boys some 44 percent of the School and some 130 boys (37 percent) had instrumental lessons.

Pupils teach themselves

While enlarging the curriculum was a key innovation, Sanderson's second major innovation was to introduce the idea of pupil research. Instead of being taught everything by their teachers, Sanderson wanted boys to find out for themselves, engaging in project work, which they could then communicate to their fellows. It was vital to do away with the deadening impact of rote-learning and a wholly teacher-centred educational experience. Instead boys would be free to explore and experiment for themselves. Only in this way would they gain an enthusiasm for their studies, a genuine academic curiosity and, probably most important of all for Sanderson, a willingness to think for themselves. In biology, Sanderson claimed that his boys "are often attracted by the wide field of research which is opened to them in school". Boys would, "devote themselves to research, some to the service of medical research, others to the claims of agriculture and related industries." In mathematics, as in other subjects, the School proclaimed the end of passive, teacher-centred learning. As the Oundle School Commemoration booklets, which appeared on Speech Day each year, often proclaimed:

> The object of the new method is to give a boy the opportunity of acquiring a body of practical information, and of gaining the capacity for making use of his knowledge. In carrying out this method an attempt is made to look upon a class as a staff of workmen actually engaged in some "live" work. In this way mathematics will come in incidentally, and be learnt as the need arises. [A boy] is not simply a passive being to be taught something…he is an active worker called upon to do something.

In addition, there was teamwork. Just as good citizens and workers should work together in a spirit of co-operation, so too should schoolboys. This would replace the competition between boys in school which led to too much individualism and left so many boys feeling inferior to their more able fellows. Parents, staff and boys were told that the new method of teaching "makes use of the principle of co-operation. The boys work as a staff of workmen engaged in the regular work of the shop. Each boy is a member of the staff and has his definite part of the work to do, and he finds that his own part is of importance to the whole." In this way every boy's contribution was important: "each boy feels that his work is not done for himself alone and that carelessness or failure on his part spoils the work of the whole form."

And it was the same in English literature. Though he would later wonder whether it was time "to give Shakespeare a rest" in favour of more modern (and socialist) authors such as Ruskin, Wells, Shaw and Galsworthy, before the war, Sanderson instituted a new approach to performing Shakespearian scenes. These were enacted where each character was assigned to a group of boys. As the Commemoration booklet for 1913-14 commented:

> Every term a play of Shakespeare, previously adapted for the purpose, is selected and each character is assigned to a small group of boys. This grouping is one of the essential features of the scheme, the idea being that the more backward boys, finding that they are supported, learn confidence and often develop quite unexpected abilities.

The writer also noted that the boys learnt the language and meaning of Shakespeare, "not by the Master's instruction but by reciting and acting." One old boy from Sidney House remembered a school production of *A Midsummer Night's Dream* where each part was played by three boys:

It was a truly splendid affair. Lesser generations can scarcely imagine what a court scene in Athens, for instance, looked like when you had three actors doing each part. A dense crowd filled the entire stage, which groaned dangerously. There was Theseus, all three of him and there was Helen of Troy – of which I was the third – and there were what looked like thousands of courtiers all milling around in a sort of ordered confusion. It was superb.

Outside the classroom

At the same time and in a similar way, Sanderson was keen to take boys out of classrooms as often as possible. He thought that they should "be taken frequently from the ordinary class-room and spread out over a large space in workshops, laboratories, testing-rooms, drawing offices, machinery halls and parts of the school grounds."

Under Sanderson, much emphasis was placed on speaking and singing in foreign languages. Junior boys were taught singing in English, French and German, whilst amongst the seniors, "French and German recitations are learnt with assistance of the gramophone and dramatic performances are given twice a year in English and French." A further device, acquired before the war to help improve pronunciation, was the dictaphone – a phonograph with a recording apparatus. A boy could actually record his voice and his errors "can thus be made more apparent to him and can be contrasted any number of times with a correct rendering from a previously made record."

In a similar vein, all forms had regular library periods to carry out their own reading. However this was not a free-for-all. The boys were given detailed schemes of work devised by the staff. These 'research' periods were often used to carry out inter-disciplinary work, to show that timetabled subjects all related to each other. In history, for example boys were given lists of English novels grouped according to the period of history in which they were set. Boys could each read different novels, write up their research and then present their findings to the rest of the group. And then, boys could go to the art room to find portraits and other pictures to help them "visualise the persons and reconstruct for themselves the events in which they are interested." At Oundle then, boys were teaching themselves and each other – it was all terribly modern!

Conversazione

The showpiece of Sanderson's reforms was the *conversazione*. At the end of the Lent Term, boys of all ages would put on displays, build models, draw maps, sing songs, deliver dramatic recitations, demonstrate experiments – there really was no limit to what they could do! The junior *conversaziones* of March 1918, give a flavour of what was on offer from the boys. Form C.VB2 (the second form in the Fifth Form on the classics side) produced a plasticine map of Syracuse and its environs at the time of the Athenian siege in 414BC; a map of Hannibal's march from Spain to Italy and models of three different Roman siege engines – a ballista, a catapulta and an onager. Meanwhile, Form C.VB3 exhibited outlines and interactions of French and Italian history 1815-70; Caesar's campaign against the Belgae, together with recitations from *Twelfth Night* and Tennyson's poem *To Virgil*. Meanwhile junior French sets sang French songs and produced "especially difficult Proses with original English." These *conversaziones* could then easily form the basis for the experiments and displays for Speech Day.

Boys being busy

Sanderson also placed huge emphasis on the need for boys to remain busy at all times and Oundle was one of the first schools to organize activities throughout the day. As Sanderson explained:

After making liberal allowance for sleep, meals and school work, there remain some fifty hours [in the week] not filled up. These hours form a very important part of the life of a boy at school, as they afford an opportunity for him to develop his own particular tastes and character in a way it is impossible for him to do when in school. It is now generally recognised as one of the duties of a school to provide occupations for these 'free' hours.

One big part of these free hours was taken up with games of course but there were also a range of clubs and societies on offer. The Choral and Orchestral Societies met on Saturday evenings, there was much debating, a Science Society and a Classical Society, lots of OTC naturally, together with 'voluntaries' in the workshops and science laboratories and even a Dancing Society from 4:45 – 6:30 on Saturdays with an attendance of about 100 boys! All these extra-curricular activities were needed to fill up the boys' time. For half the school year, early school began at 7 a.m. each day, so there were plenty of hours to fill!

No such thing as a dull boy

Sanderson's widened curriculum plus pupil-centred research, not to mention his left-wing politics, made the Oundle Headmaster a genuine educational pioneer with a growing national reputation. At the same time, Sanderson and his staff were not only interested in boys who showed real academic promise. "There is no such thing as a dull boy" was one of Sanderson's more famous sayings and he believed that many boys appeared dull because of regimented and dull teaching methods, allied to a narrow syllabus. "Every boy must find his passion", was another of Sanderson's mantras and he enjoyed taking on boys who were often seen as difficult and limited by their prep schools.

When the mother of Reginald Secretan saw Sanderson with a view to sending her son to Oundle, she explained: "How backward Reggy was as regards book-learning and that the masters at his preparatory school had found him difficult to teach." She was surprised by Sanderson's kindly face and his response: "Send him here," he said "I have had many such boys, and their parents have been astonished at their progress, there is a lot to interest him here." And he was right. Mrs Secretan later wrote: "His words came true, for the boy revelled in the splendid engineering shops. I feel we can never be grateful enough to Oundle, no other school could have provided him with such interesting work, and thereby made a man of him."

Taking in boys of all abilities fitted nicely into Sanderson's idea that schools should be a new world in microcosm. Out would go the competition between individuals which drove the free market of capitalism; instead workers in industry, whatever their standing, like his boys at Oundle, would work together in a new way to end industrial disputes between owners and workers, creating a more harmonious society where all workers could enjoy the value and fruits of their labour. Ultimately, Sanderson saw the development of a new type of education, with Oundle School as the prime example, as an engine of social reform.

Another key to the success of Sanderson's methods was that he was a great publicist. Details of everything the boys were doing were published in the annual Commemoration booklet for Speech Day; the termly publication of the school journal, the Laxtonian, and also the publication of the researches undertaken by junior and senior *conversaziones*. Sanderson saw the importance and value of getting his message across in black and white.

No beating?

One other educational reform also needs to be investigated to absorb the true flavour of the Oundle School in Sanderson's time. In his later years, Sanderson used to claim that corporal punishment, in terms of beatings, was used only rarely at Oundle, unlike other notable public schools. In fact, this seems to have been something of a myth. One old boy, who arrived in Oundle in 1913, pointed out the difference between the official view and the reality: "To the eye of the average 'worm', crawling through his first year in the Oundle of 1913, 'old Beans' (Sanderson's nickname amongst the boys) was not great at all: he was just peculiar and rather alarming. Peculiar because you never knew what would happen next; alarming because when it happened it was apt to be drastic." He recalled how, in the summer of 1913, Beans had gone off the deep end during one of Clement Spurling's singing practices:

> One fine day in the summer of 1913, a choir practice was being held and 'Beans', as he often did, had chosen to be present to see that all went well. Unfortunately, that day all was not going very well and Mr Spurling, the music master, was having trouble with the trebles. Suddenly 'Beans' who liked plenty of action out of his choir, decided that the trebles were just a lot of idle little lay-abouts who were not really trying. This was too much to be borne. He flew into a splendid rage, accused them of sabotaging the practice and ordered them – all fifty of them – to go across to the gym and there await his pleasure. They all trooped over and when the great man arrived hot on their heels, he flogged the lot of them!

As the writer concluded, Sanderson was clearly capable of double-speak when it came to corporal punishment at Oundle:

> One of the most extraordinary things about Sanderson was his apparent conviction that there was virtually no beating at Oundle. The truth was that practically everybody in authority beat, especially the prefects. As far as wielding the cane went, the place was a sort of glorious free-for-all. Yet in public and in private, Sanderson used to maintain that at Oundle the cane had been abolished.

The abolition of beating was clearly one educational reform that Sanderson had not introduced.

A boy's-eye view

Yet if the School was officially doing well, what was the view from the boys? If Robert Bragg was typical (and he probably wasn't) then all was well with the pupils. In one of his first letters to his parents after his arrival in 1909, he was hugely enthusiastic about his new school. The services in chapel were clearly inspiring: "all the boys in the school sing like anything and in harmony too!" Lessons were exciting as well:

> I think the English will be very interesting because he lets us order books to read in our spare time and also he gives us decent books to do in school. The chemistry I like far and away the best. It is nearly all practical. Today he showed us how to extract the pure metal from an ore and we are going to do it ourselves next time in little muffle furnaces – it will be great fun.

School books were similarly inspiring – no dusty old tomes for Oundelians: "We have very nice books to work from, mine look so interesting being new." Pre-war food was also scrummy – at least in Dryden House:

> For breakfast we have either porridge, bread and milk, sausages or smoked fish and 'jims' [bread and butter] and marmalade always. For dinner we always have 1 hot joint, 1 cold one and generally a stew to choose between. Then we have two hot puddings. For tea we have 'jims' and marmalade and anything else we like to take in ourselves, as they will do you eggs if you provide them.

And if Bragg and Co. were still hungry at bed-time, which was at 10pm, there was always cake to be had: "The school cake is just great, another boy and I partake of it just before going to bed." And he loved his surroundings too: "Oundle is such a pretty place. There is a very pretty old church [the parish church] over the road. Lots of tombstones have Todd on them – isn't that funny." Even his Housemaster, the venerable Llewellyn Jones, who set much stock by classics, rowing and the OTC was actually a very nice man:

> I have spoken to 'Jug' about Cambridge and the Greek and he has awfully decently lent me a Greek book and is going to do Greek with me on Saturday nights. Don't you think that is awfully good of him? I went to see him last night and felt such a brute because he was so comfortably settled with a book before the fire with his feet on the mantelpiece but he seemed very pleased that I had come and kept me up 15 minutes after all the others had gone to bed.

One can see that young Bragg, who clearly loved the idea of extra Greek on a Saturday night, was possibly an unusual pupil but, luckily, he did have a few gripes as well. He noted that the days were very long: "half past 6 to quarter past 10 and that 6 days out of the week." In addition each day started "with an icy bath." However, his biggest complaint was about Sanderson's extra scripture lessons on a Sunday evening: "Isn't it a nuisance. Beans gave out yesterday that all fellows who want to be confirmed must attend his classes from 7-8 pm on Sundays and also that those who had never attended any of his classes must come also, so I have to waste an hour on Sunday evenings. I feel so annoyed about it."

Spaciousness

By 1914 then, Oundle School was clearly on the up. With its beautiful location and buildings, spread around a charming market town, together with the ability to acquire new land and buildings, Oundle could achieve the 'spaciousness' which Sanderson thought was such a crucial factor in giving young minds the right environment in which to fulfil their potential. In this particular quiet market town, he could develop and expand the School in an environment which would also appeal to prospective parents. In Reade's time the Grocers' Company had shown that they were aware of Oundle's attractiveness as the site of a great school. In an early prospectus, they noted that "the quaint and almost collegiate character of the town, the peculiar beauty of the Church and the antiquity of the School [are] of no small value for educational purposes." This was why, in the years before the outbreak of the Great War, Oundle grew and prospered, laying the foundations for a school that would be able to contribute more than most to the coming war-effort.

New buildings under Sanderson

On Speech Day 1914, Sanderson and his staff could also look back on years of expansion, particularly after 1900 which had been dramatic and exhilarating. 1901 had seen the establishment of the Berrystead in North Street as a preparatory house. There followed the building of four new purpose-built boarding houses on Milton Road. Sidney and Laxton were moved from other buildings in 1899 and 1900 respectively and Grafton and Crosby, added as new houses in 1902 and 1905, then moved to Milton Road in 1905 and 1907. In that same year, New House was established in its old buildings on Stoke Hill. Later, School House was also expanded, adding to its pupil capacity and a new private side was built for Sanderson and his family in 1910.

In 1899 new laboratories were built in the Cloisters on the site of the old fives courts. In 1904 a new stone building appeared on the Church Lane side of the Cloisters to house the new workshops which would include four screw cutting power driven lathes and a milling machine.

On Speech Day in 1907 the foundation stone of the Great Hall was laid by the Master of the Grocers' Company. The Great Hall was opened in 1908 and two years later, two wings were added which housed classrooms in the north wing and an art museum, with the new library above it, in the south wing. In 1910, the Great Hall acquired its familiar wood panelling and an organ was erected there in 1912.

One of the important centres of school life were the workshops and engine room in the Cloisters. All boys on the engineering side attended workshop classes in school hours and there were also voluntary classes on half-holidays in the two winter terms. By 1914, the School employed ten skilled men in the 'shops', who taught and carried out maintenance work and repairs on school buildings. They also made much of the new furniture the growing school needed. As the Commemoration booklet for 1913-14 noted: "The patience care and exactness shown by these men in their work has a great influence, often an unconscious influence, on the work of the boys."

The Great Hall before the addition of the wings.

School Cloisters in 1905.

By the outbreak of war, the School also possessed an engineering laboratory, a museum, a forge, foundry, observatory and biological gardens. Then there were extended playing fields, boat houses and a new cricket pavilion in 1895. The original fives courts in the Cloisters were removed in 1899 and rebuilt behind Laxton and Crosby, then moved again in 1905. The gymnasium was built in the Cloisters in 1896 and enlarged a year later. A new laundry, to keep the boys looking clean and smart was built in 1906.

The spiritual needs of the boys had also found a new home under Sanderson. Formerly the boys attended ordinary Sunday services in the parish church (mornings) and the Jesus church (afternoons). In 1902, a new chapel was built on the field near Laxton House. Affectionately known as the 'Tin Tab' because of its corrugated iron roof, it was always seen as a temporary structure. As the Commemoration booklet of 1914 opined, the Chapel "has been of immense value to the School, but it is not in keeping with the other buildings; a permanent building is a hope for the near future." Ironically it would actually take the war and the contributions of many a grieving parent to build that new chapel.

By Speech Day 1914, the latest new building was nearing completion across Milton Road from the Great Hall. This was the new Science Block. In November 1913 Sanderson wrote: "The new Science Block is making rapid progress. It will give great opportunities, and will enable the School to develop methods of education on lines which would appear at the present moment to be much needed." Rather proudly he added: "The block will, as far as I know, be unique in public schools: and the building of it marks another epoch in the history of Oundle." The Science Block would provide four lecture rooms, a standardising laboratory, a teaching museum with aquaria, physics, chemistry and biological laboratories, a drawing office and a machinery hall. The erection of such a notable and, in public school terms, pioneering structure just as the war broke out was further testament to Oundle's unprecedented growth and prosperity on the eve of the Great War.

Interior of the 'Tin Tab', the School Chapel in 1905.

The Great Hall and the Headmaster's House in 1914.

Development of the OTC

Justin Willis, who wrote those letters about the chances of a European war, was a very keen OTC man. In his last year, he was in the new army class and his letters home are full of his military activities including five pages on the Field Day at Ampthill! He also had to take company drill:

> In the afternoon, on the field, we had the company drill. My turn came last so I had the deuce of a time in which to get nervous. Heaton and Lyon Hall made rather a mess of the things they had to do. When my turn came I felt quite alright, quite calm and collected, and I got on jolly well. I didn't give one wrong command for a wonder. But I was damned glad when it was over.

By contrast, another pupil, young Bragg from Dryden, who loved his extra Greek lessons and bedtime cake, was worried about the unyielding corps boots: "I think I had better get a pair of very thick socks to wear because the corps boots are most awfully solid things and on the one day I wore them [Field Day] they wore a great hole in my heel!"

The OTC was another notable innovation of Sanderson's time, and was to assume much greater importance when war broke out in 1914. In 1902 it began life as the Rifle Corps. The Commanding Officer was W. G. Grace junior (son of W. G. Grace senior, the famous cricketer) with Mr Nightingale as the senior lieutenant. Nearly every boy took part and fierce rivalry developed between the different house platoons. One hundred rifles were soon acquired and the boys received military uniforms with a red stripe down the trousers. The official title of the corps thus formed was the Oundle School Cadet Corps. Originally attached to the Northamptonshire Regiment, in 1908 it became an Officers' Training Corps, with 112 boys as members and was under the direct control of the War Office. There were weekly training sessions and drills, inspections on Inspection Day and Speech Day, two field days per term and also annual summer camps, where Oundle boys would mix with cadets from other public schools.

Oundle School OTC parading in New Street c1912.

In 1905, a 500 yards shooting range was constructed at Elmington and a year later an armoury appeared on the school field. Membership of the OTC was voluntary but practically every boy who was old enough joined. The boys' participation in the School's OTC meant that Oundelians would be at the front of the queue for commissions in the New Army developed after the destruction of most of the British Expeditionary Force by the end of 1914.

Masters and Boys on Speech Day 1914

It was not only the boys of Oundle who would soon be on their way to war but also some of the masters who taught them. Two of the housemasters ranged behind Sanderson on the Great Hall stage on that fateful Speech Day of 1914, Francis Norbury and George Tryon, together with George Williamson, a young classics master would all join the Kings Royal Rifles and all would perish in the conflict. So too would Maurice Miskin, another young classicist and cricket coach.

And what of the boys on that Speech Day of 1914? As they listened to the Headmaster's address and some received prizes, what were their thoughts on that sunny Saturday afternoon? For the 75 or so leavers no doubt the usual thoughts that leavers have. Some sadness at departing from Oundle for the last time but also excitement at the prospect of a new life away from the classroom. Those not leaving would be looking forward to the long summer holidays, though they were still nearly a month away. None of the boys assembled in Great Hall that day would have thought that within weeks their hopes and dreams would be derailed by the outbreak of the greatest conflict the country had ever seen.

Nineteen of the seventy-five leavers, that year, more than a quarter, would be killed in the war and a further fourteen wounded. Head of School, editor of the Laxtonian and secretary of the Classical Society, was Frederick Milholland of New House. Next term he would win an exhibition in classics and a Rhodes Scholarship to Balliol College, Oxford but would never take up residence there. He was gazetted to the Yorkshire Regiment as soon as he left Oundle and was killed in February 1918. John Line of Laxton House was no doubt looking forward to taking his place at Downing College, Cambridge where he too had won an exhibition in classics. He went up to Cambridge that October but left to join the North Staffordshire Regiment in December and was killed in 1916. John Russell of School House would leave Oundle in December 1914 having won the Senior Classical Scholarship at University College, Oxford. He would be killed on the Somme in July 1916.

The Commemoration booklet issued on that particular Speech Day reported with pride on those Oundelians who had moved on to army careers the year before. The prophetic Justin Willis and his friend James Ricketts had passed the entrance exam for the Royal Military Academy at Woolwich. Both would be killed in action in 1918. Five others had won places at Sandhurst and went on to serve in the war. John Jackson died in 1915, when he contracted meningitis while recovering from serious wounds. George Needham joined the Lancashire Fusiliers and was killed at Gallipoli, that same year. Edward Betts became a lieutenant in the Wiltshire Regiment and a prisoner of war. Victor Jungbluth, a second lieutenant in the Royal Field Artillery was wounded in the war and George Lloyd, an officer in the South Wales Borderers, survived.

Of the 325 boys in the senior boarding houses gathered together on Speech Day 1914, some 266 or 82 percent would join up, most within weeks of leaving school. Fifty-seven of these would be killed and forty-five seriously wounded by the terrible conflict that lay ahead, a casualty rate of nearly 40 percent. Laxton House and New House, the worst affected houses amongst the boys who attended the School in the school year 1913-1914, would have casualty rates of 46 percent, while Crosby House would suffer just 27 percent killed and wounded. Only three Crosby boys in the audience that Speech Day were killed but Sidney would lose 10 and Dryden and Grafton 11 each. A quarter of the Dryden boys assembled in the Great Hall for Speech Day in 1914 would not survive the coming conflict.

Last rugby match before the War

Perhaps Sanderson and some of the senior boys present on Speech Day 1914, recalled the last match of the Michaelmas Term in that school year. Both of Sanderson's sons, Roy and Thomas played for the OOs that day – 29 November 1913 – so Sanderson almost certainly went to watch. It had not been a vintage season so far but the XV had notched up six wins and just three defeats against useful opposition, including four Cambridge colleges. In the most important match of the term, the Laxtonian rugby correspondent reported on a win for the OOs by 37 points to 25, commenting that in a day of high wind "the School defence seemed to break down altogether and though the forwards held their much heavier opponents, they forgot to get back and help their three-quarters."

Amongst the scorers for the OOs that day was Ivor Davies who kicked the goals, one of Sanderson's sons scored a try, possibly Roy, but the star of the show seems to have been the captain from the previous year, Eric Yarrow. Playing in the three-quarters, he scored three tries that day to ensure victory for the Old Boys. Eric Yarrow, Ivor Davies, Roy Sanderson, James Dixon, Thomas Warner and Douglas Armitage – six of the OO team that day – would perish in the war which was then, unknown to them, less than a year away. Three of their opponents, Alan West, Donald Ramsay and Frederick Milholland, current Oundelians playing their last match before the outbreak of hostilities, would also fail to survive the coming storm.

The last XV before the War. Frederick Milholland, Donald Ramsay and Alan West would all be killed in the conflict.

Cricket XI 1914

And what of the cricketers gathered together on Speech Day 1914? The Laxtonian commented that the team of 1914 "was certainly above the average." Unfortunately a number of matches were cancelled but the School had an unbeaten season, winning three and drawing five. Of the drawn matches "three would easily have been easily won if we had had another quarter of an hour's play." The batting was very successful on the whole and the side was only bowled out twice during the season. The star batsman in 1914 was probably Brian Sundius-Smith who "showed himself, when set, to be in a class by himself." However some inconsistency in his efforts meant that it was Ithel Owen who headed the batting averages for the season. He was also a good steady bowler and set an excellent example in the field as captain. Altogether he was "the best all-round player in the School." The coming losses in the war for this XI would be three. Alan West, who of course also played for the XV, John Line and Hugh Davis.

Laxton School in 1914

As there were two twinned schools at Oundle at this time, there were also two speech days. We do not know exactly when Laxton School held its Speech Day in 1914. In the years before the war, it was generally held in December but by 1917, it was held in the summer. Whenever it was held in the School year 1913-14, it was clearly an important occasion. The Grocers' Company turned out in force for "the annual Speech Day of the old Foundation School of Oundle," as it was termed. In the summer of 1917, the Master of the Grocers' Company, two of the three wardens and 10 members of the court and the clerk were in attendance, so it is probable that the same officials attended in 1914. Also there, of course was the Headmaster, Sanderson, who had always shown a keen interest in his other school. After his speech and probably a short musical programme, the prizes would be distributed by the Master, who would round off proceedings with another speech. With a brief vote

Laxton School in 1905.

of thanks from the Oundle vicar, the Rev. Smalley Law, there would be cheers for the Master, Mr and Mrs Sanderson and for the master-in-charge of Laxton Grammar School, Mr Thomas Ross. In 1917, and so probably in 1914 as well, the Grocers were then shown round parts of the School and retired for "a bountiful tea" on School House lawn, followed by an organ recital in the Great Hall from the music master, Clement Spurling.

In July 1914, there were some 52 boys at Laxton School and exactly half of them, surprisingly, were boarders. Most of these were fairly local, based in Kettering or Stamford or Thrapston but three were Londoners and one – Henry Blower – had the distinction of living in the Crown Prince's Palace in Athens! Numbers at the School had declined in the last two years, from highs of 84 and 85 in 1910-12. Sanderson himself thought that 60 was about the ideal number. Certainly, Laxton School had enjoyed renewed vigour since 1900. After 1898, Laxton School boys had lessons on Saturday mornings, did games in proper games kit and now had a straw hat to wear on Sundays! Class singing became popular amongst them and the academic profile of the School improved as boys were entered for the senior, junior and preliminary examinations, set by the Cambridge Local Examinations Board. One further development helped to raise the School's academic standards, which in turn attracted more boys to the School. In the past, most Laxton boys had left school at the age of 15 but before the war this was raised to 16 and senior boys, staying beyond this point could be taught in Oundle School forms and thus exposed to a high standard of specialist teaching. The first to win an Oxbridge award from Laxton School was James Foulds, who won a science scholarship to Sidney Sussex College, Cambridge in December 1908. He was one of an increasing number of Laxton boys who straddled the two schools. The best example of this was Douglas McMichael. As a very talented student, he remained as a 'leader' in Laxton School in the Sixth Form but attended Oundle School classes. When he won a scholarship to Clare College, Cambridge, both schools claimed him as their own and this continued in death. He was killed near Ypres in April 1916 and his name, uniquely, appears on the official war memorials of both schools.

Boys and Staff of Laxton School in 1914.

As well as Speech Day, Sanderson and his wife always attended the Laxton School Sports Day and Mrs Sanderson usually presented the prizes. Symptomatic of the growing confidence and pride of Laxton School was the creation of an Old Boys' Club complete with annual journal in 1908. In 1909, 68 Old Laxtonians attended the annual meeting, followed by dinner, speeches and entertainments in the Talbot Hotel. Sanderson was present, acting as chairman and stressed the importance of Laxton Grammar School as the original school in the town out of which Oundle School had grown.

At the same time, Laxton School, though relatively small in numbers, maintained thriving association football and cricket teams, each of which played 10 or 12 fixtures in a season. A troop of boy scouts was formed just before the war and although less overtly military than the Oundle School OTC, it did drilling and had a summer camp. The two original patrol leaders, Edward Hunt and Joseph Baxter would both be killed in the coming conflict. Further evidence of growth came with an increasing number of evening lectures, the development of a nature club and in 1910 the founding of a debating society. In many ways then, Laxton School was imitating its larger twin and was enjoying a period of growth and achievement. As Sanderson remarked, Laxton School, as the only secondary school between Wellingborough and Peterborough, "could look forward to a bright future."

Amongst the 52 boys, attending the last Laxton Speech Day before the war, six would be killed in the ensuing conflict. Amongst them was the younger Foulds boy, Maurice, whose brother had done so well at Cambridge. He would leave the school in 1915 and be killed just two years later. His friend and fellow boarder from Kettering, John Anderson would also be killed in October 1917 at Passchendaele. Also amongst the fallen were the day boys, Jesse Wallis, Henry Curtis, Hugh Turnill and Herbert Markham; the latter dying one day before the Armistice that put an official end to hostilities.

Laxton School Cricket Team 1910.

End of Summer Term 1914

It is not clear when term ended for Oundelians of both schools in 1914. Oundle School's Blue Book for the Summer Term of 1914 declared that the Schools would close on Tuesday 28 July but in his diary, John Binder, a local grocer and baker claimed that it was not until Saturday 1 August that "the Boys of the Laxton Grammar School and the Grocers' Company School went away for their holidays." At the start of the holidays, many Oundelians would normally have been going on the annual army camp. Ironically, the OTC camp for 1914 was cancelled. John Binder noted in his diary: "In connection with the Grocers' School there is an Officers (Army) Training Corps which usually goes into Camp with the regular army. But this year, they are not to do so as measles have been very prevalent in the School." Perhaps this outbreak of measles was the reason for the delayed end of term in 1914. As it was the boys went home on Saturday 1st August, the very day that Germany declared war on Russia.

Four weeks earlier, on Speech Day 1914, few would have guessed at the horrors to come. Instead, Sanderson and his staff, the boys and their parents, inspired no doubt by their Speech Day experiences would have been celebrating the prosperity and achievements of this once provincial grammar school, without an inkling of what lay ahead. There had, of course been talk of a 'show down' with Germany particularly since the naval race which began in earnest in 1908 when Germany built four dreadnoughts in one year but in fact the 10 years before 1914 had been relatively quiet in terms of Anglo-German relations. The murder of the Austrian Archduke and his wife in far-away Sarajevo six days before Speech Day had certainly grabbed the headlines but everyone quickly assumed that the problems thus created between Austria and Serbia by Gavrilo Princip's two shots would soon be settled as neither country wanted a war. Even if the double murder led to a broader Balkan crisis, few people in Britain could see how problems in that region or even an Austro-Serbian war could possibly lead to a general European conflagration.

By the time that term ended, however, matters were very different. On 28 July 1914, Austria declared war on Serbia. Two days later, Tsar Nicholas II ordered a general mobilization of Russian forces towards Russia's borders with both Austria and Germany. Germany responded to what she saw as a threat of a war on two fronts, by declaring war on France as well as Russia. To defeat France before turning their full attention to the Russians, the German 'Schlieffen Plan' dictated that German troops should reach France by advancing through neutral Belgium. On 4 August 1914, German forces invaded Belgium. Britain and the Oundle Schools went to war.

1

Year 1 Away: Training and Fighting – August 1914 to March 1915

I am so bucked. I am a real soldier at last.

Enthusiasm for war

The number of boys from Oundle School, who served in His Majesty's armed forces during the war is recorded, in the School's Memorial Book published in 1920, as 1044. According to one source about 150 Laxton boys also served making a total of around 1200 Oundle boys, who played their part in the conflict. While a number were already in the armed services before 1914 and still more were in reserve or territorial battalions, the majority of these boys who served were volunteers not regular soldiers. They flocked to the colours in 1914 and afterwards, with patriotic enthusiasm, not wanting to miss out on the great adventure that the war offered. By November of 1914, 420 Oundelians had enlisted and this number had reached 657 a year later. However enthusiastic they were, they also knew that war was about death and destruction. From the earliest weeks of the conflict, British losses were severe and by the end of 1914, many of those in the British Expeditionary Force of 100,000 men were casualties and the stalemate of trench warfare had developed on the Western Front. All those Oundle boys who volunteered after August 1914 knew what to expect.

Reports of early fighting – the Western Front

For some Oundelians in different parts of the world, the reality of fighting was an almost immediate experience. Those Oundelians already serving in the army or in reserve battalions would find themselves quickly in action as the power and speed of the German advance into Belgium and France became clear. One anonymous Oundelian in the British Expeditionary Force told of his experiences in the first weeks of the war. He disembarked at Le Havre, moved up river to Rouen, took a train to the French/Belgian border and so marched up to Mons where he spent the night. From there the retreat began which took him right back to Paris. Writing for the school magazine, the tone of the letter is jaunty and the war is portrayed as a great and thrilling adventure. Describing his reactions to the Battle of Le Cateau, he remarked that "this was the first time I was under fire. I was not very pleased with it then, but don't mind it at all now!"

His battalion had also had an exciting encounter with a German aeroplane: "We shot a German aeroplane and fetched it down, and chased some Uhlans [German cavalry] but got 'stymied' in barbed wire and they escaped." And the adventure continued as the Oundle boy took his first prisoner: "I got a wounded officer, and have as trophies a rifle, carbine, helmet, sword etc. and hope I shall be able to bring them back to show you when this holiday is over." Meanwhile, the Germans themselves were portrayed as cowards: "After the Marne, we caught 40 prisoners who came in like lambs." At one place on the Front he claimed that "the Germans could have cut the lot of us to pieces if they had had any guts." Britain's enemies were also wantonly destructive: "Near St. Quentin, I was going to a farm just off the road for food, when the Germans put four shells into it, which was silly, for there were no troops in it." At the same time, his belief in an imminent British victory was clear: "When we get to Germany things will be much more lively. I only hope the Russians will not spoil the whole show for us…We are looking forward to our tour in Germany, which I am told, is a very pretty country. France is nothing out of the way, in these parts at any rate."

Commenting on the terrible conflict on the Aisne, the Oundle correspondent treated it with his customary understatement: "On the Aisne, we had some very exciting times, and I nearly got 'had for a mug' more than once." Even the awful German shells, it seems, merely added to the excitement:

> German heavy shells are funny old things, and we call them 'whistling Willies', because you could hear them coming miles away, and they were so slow about it. They burst with a terrific crash and the mud goes miles, but as a rule they do little damage. They make a terrific noise, and the heavy ones dig great holes from four to five feet deep and the bits travel several hundred yards.

But German shells could easily be dodged: "At the bridge, we had to wait till a shell burst, then rush across before the next one came."

Meanwhile, life behind the lines was, apparently, delightful: "We were billeted on a bourgeois, who entertained us like kings." However one particular Frenchman, with whom they were staying aroused suspicion: "He spoke German, and I am wondering now if he could have been a spy, for he wanted to know a lot and his house was very clean." And, as might be expected, this Oundle correspondent had suffered only one minor injury and even that was self-inflicted: "So far I have been extremely well, and one tooth is my only casualty. Fortunately it is not right in front; my horse fell with me when I was jumping a ditch, and I knocked it out."

No doubt letters home of this type were very much appreciated by the Oundelians who read them. Here was war of dash, bravado and adventure, right out of the comic books of the time. Such letters were a feature of the early months of the war but later the tone changed as the terrible scale of the British casualties became clear. A letter from Lieutenant Frederick Drake, a London boy who had left School House back in 1907, painted a more realistic picture of the fighting, especially the retreat from Mons: "We used to fight all day and dig trenches at night. We got no sleep at all, we never shut our eyes. During the long retreat we found that the Germans were not very good as regards the use of the rifle but the field gunners were extremely good." He and his men got lost and were forced to hide during the day in hen houses or cellars or woods and were shot at several times. Here is the first report of deaths in the war. Drake tells his schoolboy readers: "The first two of our fellows to be shot were the doctor and his orderly. They were binding up a man who had been wounded and the Germans came up within twenty yards and shot them dead."

Here too the first mention of the terrible impact on soldiers of machine guns combined with barbed wire. Drake and his men tried to get away across country but they were "caught up in barbed wire" and the Germans "turned two machine guns on us." On approaching the village of Honcourt they were "being shot at from behind and in front, and there was barbed wire on both sides of the road." The destruction wrought by the Germans on French villages is also clear. At one point Drake was hiding in a wine cellar and "the Germans came and burnt down the house above us."

While Drake somehow escaped unscathed, Lieutenant Charles Irvine, who left Grafton House in 1910, was not so fortunate. In that same retreat from Mons, in August 1914, he was seriously wounded and captured by the Germans. He was then taken to Bavaria where apparently, he was well looked after. He eventually recovered from his wounds but remained a prisoner of war. His war was over after a few weeks.

Oundelians join up

While some Oundelians were involved in the fighting from the start, many others now rushed to join up. For many this was straight-forward enough. All had OTC training and some were already enlisted in territorial or reserve battalions and so could expect immediate call up. Robert Bragg, who left Dryden in 1911 had joined a territorial unit called King Edward's Horse whilst at Cambridge but with the war in its third month, he decided to try for a commission with the Royal Field Artillery. It was all pretty straightforward: "Another man and I went straight to the War Office…and at last got to Major Tatham's room. He came out and saw us and was most awfully nice. I asked him all about the R.F.A. He said that he could almost certainly get me in and in fact that I might order my kit straight away!" The only problem then for Bragg was getting measured up for his new uniform: "I get £30 for my kit and another £7.10 for my field kit i.e. sleeping blankets etc. We went to Wybro and Walker and I was measured there. I thought he would be too expensive but he wasn't. We also tried Harrods and Burberry's. Harrods was rotten and Burberry's too expensive."

For other Old Oundelians, joining up was more problematic. Eric Yarrow had left Grafton House in 1913 and had completed his first year at Cambridge, but his father, Sir Alfred Yarrow, like many parents no doubt, hoped that his son would not go off to war. He thought that Eric should join the work force at his shipyard on the Clyde, doing vital war work there and thus be spared active military service. On 1 September 1914, Eric wrote to his father asking his permission to join the army. While stressing that he would not do anything which might upset his father, he argued carefully and thoughtfully in favour of enlistment:

> There is undoubtedly an urgent need for young men of all classes to come forward to serve, and it would appear that those who, by their social position, are able to do so with the least sacrifice, should be the first…My being at the works is an excuse for not doing what…appears to be the duty of all young men.

It seems that Sir Alfred gave his permission and Eric gained a commission with the 7th Battalion of the Argyll and Sutherland Highlanders in the autumn of 1914. The Cambridge correspondent for the Laxtonian was quick to comment on Eric's joining up: "You will, I am sure, be pleased to hear that the kilt suits Second Lieutenant Yarrow very well; he has been over to ask our opinion on the hang of his sporran." Promoted lieutenant on leaving for France in December 1914, Eric presented all 50 men in his company with a woollen shirt, under-vest, mits and gloves. Their departure for France was not without mishap. Having boarded the Oxonian, an old cattle boat, he and his men had to disembark when "it was discovered that coal in one of the bunkers had caught fire!"

While most Oundelians joined up quickly and got stuck into their training, others found it hard to get started. Reggy Secretan of Sidney House left school in the summer of 1914 and was desperate to join up. His mother recalled: "On the outbreak of War, he dashed up to London on a motor cycle belonging to a friend who was abroad, and tried to enlist in the first lot of Dispatch Riders…He tried eight or ten times to enlist, but was always rejected for eyesight." By December however, he had been accepted by the Motor Transport Army Service Corps. He wrote home immediately: "I am so bucked! I am a real soldier at last."

Early Casualties: Colonial adventures

The December 1914 issue of the Laxtonian which made light of the war, also reported on the first Oundle fatalities. The first death occurred not on the Western Front, nor indeed in Europe but in Africa. On 14 August 1914, the British gunboat Gwendolen fired upon the German gunboat von

Wisserman on Lake Nyasa (now Lake Malawi) where British East Africa bordered on German East Africa. The German ship was taken completely by surprise and the German captain, Berndt, was taken prisoner. Unlike his British counterpart, Berndt was quite unaware that his country and Britain had been at war for the last 10 days. He and his British opposite number, Captain Edmund Rhoades had been on good terms up to now and when his friend launched this surprise attack, he assumed that Rhoades was drunk! "Afraid not old chap," replied the sober Rhoades, "our countries are at war. Best thing you can do is surrender!"

It was in this context – a colonial war between Britain and Germany in East Africa – that the first Oundelian to be killed in the conflict came to grief. He was **Samuel Frank Edmonds**. Born in Northampton in 1878, he came to Oundle and Laxton House in January 1893, staying until summer 1898. His father, Rev. Francis Samuel Edmonds was vicar of the nearby village of Harringworth. Sam captained the School's Cricket XI in 1898, was a forward in the Rugby XV and was also a school prefect. A leading member of the Science Sixth, he won numerous school prizes for science, was on the committee of the recently founded Oundle School Science Society and won a scholarship to Sidney Sussex College, Cambridge. He took a first in Part One of the Natural Sciences Tripos in 1901 and rowed in the college 1st boat.

After a year as a school master at Bradford Grammar School, Sam Edmonds joined the navy, training at the Royal Naval Colleges at Osborne and Dartmouth. For 10 years, much to Sanderson's delight no doubt, he was a science instructor at the latter. At the end of 1912, possibly in search of adventure, he left Dartmouth for what was then known as the British East African Protectorate (modern day Kenya). At the outbreak of war, he immediately enlisted as a private in the East African Mounted Rifles. He was killed, aged 35, just 7 weeks later on 25 September 1914, when his platoon, just 30 in number, attacked a force of some 35 Germans and 150 African natives which

had crossed the border from neighbouring German East Africa. The German force had two maxim guns and after a sharp encounter both sides retreated, the British force having lost eight men killed and four wounded. The official history of the skirmish concluded that the action in which Samuel Edmonds died was a victory: "Since the enemy had abandoned his enterprise, which was directed presumably against the Magadi branch railway, the East African Mounted Rifles had every reason for satisfaction."

Sam Edmonds died in good company. Two of the other victims were also public school men – one from Eton and one from Bedford. He is commemorated on the British and Indian memorial in Nairobi (Kenya), as he has no known grave. The central panel of the memorial is inscribed with these words: "Here are recorded the names of officers and men who fell in East Africa, to whom the fortune of war denied the known and honoured burial given to their comrades in death." Like many another Oundelian, whose bodies, even if found, would not be repatri-ated, he is also remembered on a stone plaque

Samuel Frank Edmonds, Laxton House 1893-98.

in his local church. In his case this was Foxton church in Northamptonshire, where his father was vicar. The memorial ends with the words: "They counted not their lives dear unto them."

The war in East Africa would continue for the next four years. The German commander, Paul von Lettow-Vorbeck was determined to tie down as many British troops as possible away from the Western Front. Even after being forced out of German East Africa, he continued the fight from Portuguese East Africa, where his forces would account for another Oundle boy as late as July 1918. He did not finally surrender until two weeks after the Armistice that November!

Further east, in Singapore, another Oundelian who died defending the Empire in the early stages of the war, was **Captain Moira Francis Allan Maclean**. He came up to School House in January 1897, played for the XV in 1899 and left school in July 1900. Unlike Sam Edmonds, he was determined to follow a career in the army and, after training at Woolwich, he joined the Garrison Artillery and was posted to a battery at Colaba in India. After 13 years in India, he was appointed to command the Mountain Battery of the Malay States Guides with the rank of captain and by early 1915, he and his men were in Singapore. With the outbreak of war against Germany, he was anxious to join the conflict in Europe and his recall had just been authorized when the Singapore Mutiny broke out.

The 1915 Singapore Mutiny, also known as the Sepoy Mutiny, involved some 400 Indian soldiers or sepoys, who rose up against their British officers in Singapore in February of that year. The mutiny lasted nearly seven days and resulted in the deaths of 47 British soldiers and local civilians, before being crushed. The origins of the mutiny went back to the founding of the *Ghadar* or 'Rebellion' Party in 1913. This largely sikh organization

Moira Francis Allan Maclean, School House 1897-00.

aimed to oust the British from India. With the outbreak of war in 1914, it targeted Indian regiments with anti-British propaganda.

In Singapore, the British had just replaced the King's Own Yorkshire Light Infantry, which had now been ordered to France, with the 5th Light Infantry Regiment of the Indian Army from Madras. Unusually, it was an entirely Muslim unit. These men were upset by the promotion of Lieutenant Colonel Martin to command of the regiment, even though he was unpopular with his fellow officers and inspired little respect from the men. In addition, the entry of Turkey into the war on the side of Germany in 1914, meant that the Sultan of Turkey, Mehmed V, had issued a *fatwa* against the British, which further alienated those Indian soldiers who were Muslims. Added to this, the discontent of the sepoys was underpinned by a belief that they were about to be moved to the killing grounds of the Western Front. Others were convinced that they were to go to Turkey to fight against their fellow Muslims. In fact they were about to be sent to Hong Kong.

In the afternoon of 15 February 1915, 100 men mutinied. Old Oundelian, Captain Moira Maclean was probably one of the two officers killed by snipers that afternoon trying to regain control of the troops. After the crushing of the mutiny, more than 200 sepoys were put on trial by court-martial. As a result, 47 were publically executed, 64 were transported for life and 73 were sent to prison. The public executions, witnessed by a crowd estimated at 15,000 people, took place at Outram Prison. The sepoys who did not mutiny were then shipped off to German East Africa, where Oundle's war had started. Moira Maclean lies buried in Bidadari Cemetery in Singapore. He was 31 years old at the time of his death.

Oundle's war at sea

In 1914, the strongest part of Britain's armed forces was her navy. The fleet was vital to the defence of the Empire as well as the country but the early encounters in the war at sea showed that Britain's ruling of the waves could not be taken for granted.

Albert Evelyn Fairfax Kynaston was not a front line sailor but a ship's doctor. He died of enteric-pneumonia in Dunskaith House in Cromarty, Scotland while on active service and was laid to rest in Cromarty parish churchyard. He entered Laxton House, where he would have known Sam Edmonds, in January 1895 and left just three years later at the age of 17. Tragedy had already struck the family when his father was killed in a riding accident. His horse was 'spooked' by the sudden emergence of a pheasant from the undergrowth. Dr Kynaston was thrown and the horse fell on top of him. Determined to emulate his late father, in terms of his profession, Albert Kynaston went to Guy's Hospital and qualified as a doctor. He then worked for 7 years in the unglamorous but worthy surroundings of the Poplar and Stepney Sick Asylum. The asylum was rocked by scandal in 1908 when 6 members of the Board of Guardians were found guilty of defrauding the rate-payers!

In the first week of the war, Albert Kynaston joined the Royal Naval Reserve as a temporary surgeon and was sent to join the

Albert Evelyn Fairfax Kynaston, Laxton House 1895-98.

crew of the armoured cruiser HMS *Devonshire*. Just two days after the war began, the *Devonshire* saw action, capturing a German merchant ship. After several weeks of intense work with sick sailors, Kynaston became ill. Tragically, he refused to take sick leave until it was too late. He died, aged 33, in Dunskaith House in Cromarty (which had been converted into a naval hospital) on 13 October 1914. The cause of death was enteric-pneumonia, a disease which was easily spread in the cramped quarters of a warship. A friend from his days at the asylum wrote of Albert Kynaston: "Everyone who worked with him got to love him."

The next Oundelian death at sea was altogether more dramatic. Just two days after the death of Albert Kynaston, another Oundelian, who had also joined the navy, this time as a sailor, was drowned after a U-boat attack. **Arthur Erskine Gurney Coombs** had been a Day Boy at Oundle School. His parents paid fees for their son to attend lessons at Oundle School rather than receiving free tuition at Laxton School. He was killed when his 'protected' cruiser HMS *Hawke* was sunk off Aberdeen on the morning of 15 October 1914. The *Hawke* was one of the oldest ships still in service. When war broke out, she was put on blockading duties but by mid-October, she was protecting a troop convoy from Canada. Coombs' ship, 80 miles off Aberdeen, was sunk by a single torpedo from a German U-boat. The torpedo struck amidships near the magazine, thus detonating a second deadly explosion.

At the time of her sinking, the *Hawke* had moved away from the other British ships in the convoy to collect mail from another boat. Therefore she was not steering a zigzag course, which was standard procedure as protection against U-boat attack and she was not moving at top speed. 524 officers and men were killed including the Captain. There were only 70 survivors. Apparently Arthur Coombs, who was the Navigation Officer, stayed on the bridge with the Captain as the ship went down. Aged 26, his body was never recovered.

Arthur Erskine Gurney Coombs, Day Boy 1898-1902.

The captain of the U-boat which sank the *Hawke* (the U-9) was Otto Weddigen. For this action and for sinking three more British ships, the *Aboukir*, *Hogue* and *Cressy* in the previous month off Holland, he was awarded the *Pour le Mérite* which was Prussia's highest military decoration. Weddigen was commanding the U-29 the following year and was killed when his submarine was rammed by HMS *Dreadnought*.

Lionel Bernard Ray Wansbrough of Grafton House was rather further from home than Arthur Coombs when he was killed in action. Aged 25, he drowned in the Pacific Ocean off the coast of Chile when his ship was sunk by a German cruiser. Born in Bristol in 1889 and raised in Derbyshire, he was in Grafton for only five terms, leaving in 1905. He immediately joined the navy, training for three years at the Royal Naval Engineering College, Keyham in Plymouth. Afterwards he worked at the naval college at Osborne (Isle of Wight) up to the outbreak of war. He was a very able rugby player but, leaving

Lionel Bernard Ray Wansbrough, Grafton House 1903-05.

Oundle before his sixteenth birthday, had no chance to find a place in the XV, which was clearly Oundle's loss. In the navy, he appeared frequently for the United Services XV but his greatest day as a rugby player came on 7 March 1914, when he represented the Royal Navy in a match against the Army, played at the Queen's Club in London. King George V himself was in attendance that day but unfortunately, Wansbrough and the Navy went down to defeat 26-14.

At the outbreak of war, he was posted to HMS *Monmouth* and he was killed when his ship was sunk by the German light cruiser *Nürnberg* on 1 November 1914 in the Battle of Coronel, off the coast of Chile. The battle was Britain's first naval defeat since 1812 and British overconfidence may have been an important factor in the unexpected outcome. It took place partly by accident as neither admiral expected to come across the other in full force. The British squadron led by Rear Admiral Sir Christopher Cradock was made up of largely obsolete or under-armed vessels, most crewed by naval reservists of limited experience. By contrast the German East Asia squadron under Vice-Admiral Maximilian Graf von Spee consisted of five modern ships, with officers hand-picked by Grand Admiral Alfred von Tirpitz himself.

Despite being outnumbered and outgunned, Cradock believed he should make haste to engage the enemy. In the ensuing battle, two British armoured cruisers the *Monmouth* and the *Good Hope* were sunk with the loss of 1,600 officers and men. The *Monmouth*, with Lionel Wansbrough on board, was badly damaged by the superior guns of the German armoured cruisers and was slowly sinking but still moving when the German cruiser *Nürnberg* approached and invited the British ship to surrender. When surrender was declined, the *Nürnberg* opened fire. All 735 officers and men were drowned as the seas were too rough to attempt any rescue mission.

Although the Germans had won, von Spee refused to celebrate knowing that his inability to replace the ammunition used up in the battle and the Royal Navy's strength in depth would lead to the destruction of his squadron in due course. When presented with flowers in Valparaiso harbour in Chile after the Battle of Coronel, he commented, "these will do nicely for my grave." He was to die with most of his men in the Battle of the Falkland Islands just one month later. Here a new naval task force under Vice-Admiral Sturdee destroyed von Spee's squadron and revenged the deaths of Lionel Wansbrough and his colleagues.

The last loss at sea in the first year of the war also had links with Chile but was quite unlike the other three, as this Oundelian was still a civilian. **Charles Ralph Buckmaster** was the only son of Charles and Lucy Buckmaster. His father was a JP and at one time Chief Inspector of the technical branch at the Board of Education. The younger Charles came to Oundle in September 1905, entering Sidney House at the age of 14. While at Oundle, he was prominent on the football field, where he was a promising half-back. On the river, he was a keen oarsman but he failed to make the School Crew.

After Oundle, he spent a year at Göttingen University in Germany and then went up to Lincoln College, Oxford. Unfortunately he failed to take his degree, partly because he spent so much time rowing, improving Lincoln's position on the river. He went on to row for his college at Henley and was a member of the London Rowing Club. At the outbreak of war, he was working on a 'nitrate

Charles Ralph Buckmaster, Sidney House 1905-08.

estate' in Chile and decided to return to England in order to join up. Tragically, the Italian ship bringing him home, was driven ashore on the Shetland Islands by a terrible storm and all aboard perished. Charles Buckmaster was 24 years of age at the time of his death on Easter Sunday, 4 April 1915.

The Western Front and the First Battle of Ypres 1914

By far the worst area for Oundelian deaths in the first year of the war was, of course, the Western Front. The first four deaths in this sector, in October and November 1914, were near Ypres, a town whose name would burn itself into the memories and griefs of the entire nation. In the first school year of the war, 'Wipers' as the soldiers called it, would claim 13 Oundelians and they were the first of many more whose lives would be ended in the defence of plucky Belgium. The first to fall was **John Greville Hobart Bird**. Born in Wolverhampton, he left the School in April 1903, having resided in Laxton House for just one term! After Oundle, he returned to his home town of Wolverhampton where he attended King Henry VIII School. After school, he was engaged in tea-planting in Ceylon but was always intent on a soldier's life. He joined the Queen's Own West Surrey Regiment and was gazetted as second lieutenant in May 1913. His battalion was in South Africa when the war began on 4 August 1914 but three weeks later, they were aboard HMT (His

John Greville Hobart Bird, Laxton House 1903.

Majesty's Transport) *Kenilworth Castle* and docked at Southampton, having stopped off at St. Helena on the way, to pick up more troops from the British garrison there.

On 5 October John Bird and the West Surreys sailed from Southampton and landed in Belgium. Twelve days later they were strengthening and improving trenches near Zonnebeke, beyond Ypres. Second Lieutenant John Bird was killed on 26 October 1914 when his platoon was sent to reinforce the Yorkshire Regiment. Under severe enemy fire, and whilst trying to help one of his men, he was hit by a shell and died instantly. He was 25 years old. The Laxtonian of December 1914 noted that "His short army career was one of much promise." Posthumously promoted lieutenant in May 1915, John Bird is commemorated on the Menin Gate in Ypres. Carved on the walls of the Gate are the names of more than 54,000 officers and men who have no known grave. John Bird would be the first of 10 Oundle names to appear there.

The First Battle of Ypres, in which he and three other Oundelians died, was a ferocious encounter between the remnants of the British Expeditionary Force (BEF) and the Germans in the autumn of 1914, when it looked as though the Germans might turn the British flank in what became known as 'the race to the sea.' The extraordinary tenacity of the BEF in the face of repeated German assaults saved the city of Ypres for the British. The Ypres Salient then became the scene of further carnage in 1915 and again, more famously, in 1917, with the Third Battle of Ypres, always known as Passchendaele.

Just two days after Bird's death, Ypres claimed its second Oundelian. **James Booker Brough Warren** was in Grafton House from September 1903 to April 1907 and would have known Lionel Wansbrough well. He arrived at Oundle just as the Officers' Training Corps was being founded and entered the army soon after leaving school, through the Special Reserve. This was a body of about 64,000 men who were part-time soldiers enlisting for six years. They had six months of training in the first year and four weeks a year thereafter.

At the end of July 1914, James Warren's battalion of the Border Regiment was sent to Southampton and on 8 October they sailed to Zeebrugge in Belgium. After a series of forced marches, they arrived at Zillebeke a week later, having shot down a German plane in the process. But tragedy struck when one of James Warren's fellow officers, Lieutenant Egerton, was unfortunately shot by his own sentries. He had gone ahead to inspect a more advanced post and lost his way in fog on the way back.

James Warren was killed on 26 October 1914 at the village of Gheluvelt near Ypres as a result of a sudden German counter-attack: "Front-line trenches held by A and B Companies were taken – 70 survivors were driven to the rear. Captains Anderson, Cholmondeley, Lees and Lieutenant Warren killed." Lieutenant James Booker Brough Warren was 25 years old at the time of his death and his name is also inscribed on the Menin Gate.

Another Oundle name recorded there is that of **Philip Chabert Kidd.** He came from Otley, Yorkshire, entering Crosby House in September 1905 and leaving in December 1906 at the age of 14. He then became a professional soldier and held a commission in the Alexandra, Princess of Wales's Own Yorkshire Regiment, also known as the Green Howards. He joined them in October 1911, aged 19, and was promoted to lieutenant on 27 October 1914, just three days before his death. His battalion – the 2nd Battalion of the Yorkshire Regiment – was sent to Belgium at the outbreak of war and also saw action in defence of Ypres.

The battalion diary makes clear the intensity of the fighting in the Ypres salient that autumn:

James Booker Brough Warren, Grafton House 1903-07.

Philip Chabert Kidd, Crosby House 1905-06.

On 29 October [1914] the Germans had a chance of victory. They gathered together all their energies to make that chance assured. They strove to batter the Yorkshires out of existence, via continuous shell fire. Next day, in an attack of overwhelming numbers of infantry and appalling bombardment, Colonel King was killed among very heavy losses of officers and men.

After a week of heavy fighting, Kidd's battalion had been reduced from 1,000 men to less than 300. Among the fallen was the Oundle boy. He was killed on the second day of the German attack. This was just four days after John Bird, who died, as we have seen, attempting to reinforce "the Yorkshire Regiment." Philip Kidd was just 22 at the time of his death.

Even younger, indeed four years younger, was the next Oundle lad, who fell in the vicinity of Ypres. **Gervase Thorpe Spendlove** of Sidney House died 18 days after Philip Kidd. Leaving Oundle in July 1913, he joined the motor section of the Legion of Frontiersmen. This unofficial organization had been set up by a British veteran of the Boer War in 1905. The 'Fontiersmen', essentially a paramilitary force, were concerned that Britain and its Empire was not ready for a future war.

When war broke out in 1914, Gervase Spendlove took the most direct route to the fighting. He and three friends travelled on motorbikes to the British General Headquarters in France, with a letter of recommendation for Sir John French himself, Commander of the British Expeditionary Force. Gervase and his friends were immediately attached to the Royal Engineers as dispatch riders holding the rank of corporal. When an appeal was then made for men with OTC training, Gervase Spendlove took a commission and was attached to the 2nd South Lancashires. He had served with them for just three days when he was killed by a shell on 17 November 1914 near Ypres. Unlike

Gervase Thorpe Spendlove, Sidney House 1909-13.

the other Oundle victims at Ypres that autumn, young Spendlove has a known grave. He is buried in Ypres town cemetery, which was used by the British until February 1915. It contains the remains of 142 British soldiers. There is also a plaque commemorating him in Beeston Baptist Church in Nottinghamshire, erected to his memory by his grieving parents. At 18, Gervase Spendlove was the youngest victim of the war so far. His life after Oundle had lasted just 15 months.

With the onset of winter, there was some let up in Oundle deaths on the Western Front. But as the new year of 1915 dawned, the School suffered a doubly tragic blow with the death of an old boy who had also been Grafton Housemaster until the war intervened. This was **Francis Campbell Norbury** and the circumstances of his death were even more poignant than usual as he was killed by a British shell.

He was from Stratford-upon-Avon, and entered Laxton House with a classical exhibition in September 1896, the start of Sanderson's fourth year as headmaster. A serious illness and a subsequent operation prevented him from sharing in many of the ordinary games for a greater part of his boyhood but he won a place in the Cricket XI in his last year and he was one of the best fives players the School had produced. In his last year, he was also one of nine senior boys who were chosen as school prefects, four of whom were in Laxton House.

Francis Norbury was a gifted scholar and won an exhibition in classics to St John's College, Cambridge and then returned to teach classics and history at his old school in 1904. He was assistant housemaster in Grafton House in his first years and in January 1910 became housemaster. Old Graftonians of his time praised his unselfish devotion to the House and his unwearying influence for good. He was also secretary of the Old Oundelian Club organizing a range of meetings and dinners in Oundle, Cambridge and London. He had received military training whilst at Cambridge and naturally joined the newly formed OTC when he returned to

Francis Campbell Norbury, Laxton House 1896-01.

Oundle and became senior captain. Under his guidance the OTC flourished and won glowing reports on its annual inspections.

On the outbreak of war, he was much torn between his allegiance to the School and his duty to his country. In the end, he returned to Oundle in September 1914 and stayed until arrangements could be made for his work at Oundle to be covered by others. He believed that in the present crisis, it was, as he said, "his plain duty to give his services to his country." He joined the Reserve Battalion of the King's Royal Rifle Corps in October 1914 and left for France the next month. Before his departure, the boys in the House presented him with a revolver and a flask as some slight memento of the debt they owed him. How they got hold of a revolver is not recorded! In one of his last letters, he wrote to George Olive, who succeeded him as Housemaster of Grafton: "Just a line to say goodbye in case of accidents. Good luck to you and the House. I'll drop you a line from the other side when possible. Please say goodbye to all my friends."

He was killed near Béthune on the 8 January 1915, when a shell burst in his dugout. The report of his death in the Laxtonian made clear the true nature of the tragedy: "one of our own shells burst short, killing him and two others." Local grocer John Binder heard the story on 13 January and made a note in his diary: "The circumstances under which Captain Norbury was killed I have heard today are quite pathetic. He and several of his men were asleep in the trenches when a shell fired by one of our guns fell short and dropped into the trench, killing three of them instantly and wounding several others."

Francis Norbury's Commanding Officer said: "I cannot tell you how well and gallantly he commanded C Company of my battalion. He had made himself a most brave and capable officer. I feel his loss most deeply." The Laxtonian commented that he was "unpretentious, willing, companionable, never physically very strong, yet never anxious to spare himself and universally popular." He was affectionately nicknamed 'the slave' by his contemporaries. This appellation came from a Greek saying, which he, as a classical scholar, would have been very familiar with:

He who wants to be the first amongst you, is the slave of all.

Captain Francis Campbell Norbury was just 32 years old at the time of his death.

Four days later, Eric Yarrow, complete with kilt and sporran, was beginning to acclimatize to life in the trenches. Choice of footwear was very important and it seems that his father had the answer:

> The kind of boots to adopt is a most difficult question. Father seems to have solved it by sending some leather gum rubber boots which are very sound. Coming up to the knee as they do, I was able to walk along the trenches the other day in places where the shorter ones would have filled with water. There is so much water in the trenches that the men have taken off their kilts.

However uncomfortable and damp and rat infested the trenches were, Yarrow also noted that the policy of soldiers on both sides seemed to be one of 'live and let live':

> Owing to the mutual truce which existed between the rival parties here, there was very little sniping going on and this was a good thing because the regiment that had been in before us had the sandbags taken off the top of the parapet to make it less wet underfoot and it was very difficult to take cover for one's head.

At the front, Yarrow also ran into a captain who had witnessed the unofficial and apparently spontaneous Xmas truce on the first Christmas Day of the war: "The Captain told me that on Christmas Day, he was in front of the trenches inspecting when out of the mist he ran into a couple of German Tommies. One of them told him he had been at the Shaftesbury Avenue Hotel for ten years and

Grafton House Junior Cricket Team 1911 with Eric Yarrow (back right).

sent a message via the Captain, to the manager who was a great friend of his." Eric's diary entry for that day also told of the impact of the war on French civilians. He wrote that he was "now billeted with three other officers in a ripping house owned by a rich man who is at present living in the basement with his caretaker, his family all having been sent away."

Training the Troops

For most Oundelians, however, the war experience began not with immediate front line fighting but with military training. As many had OTC experience, some found themselves acting as instructors. One Oundelian writing to the Laxtonian in the autumn of 1914 from Coventry, in an article entitled *From Kitchener's Army*, caught a mood of amused detachment. Recalling his military training at Oundle he said: "I must not give you the impression, my dear Mr Editor, that I undervalue the military training I had at school, but Time, with his healing hand, had caused me to forget much of it by last August." He admitted that "Until some weeks ago my conception of the life military was composed of confused memories of marches past, right sections to the front, railway journeys to Cambridge, cocoa and ham sandwiches." Now, by contrast, he noted that matters were rather more serious: "I have not only to recollect how to march myself past, but also to learn the intricate art of forming fours, than which there is no more effectual method of annihilating the enemy."

In the same vein our unknown Oundelian claimed that "I am now in a position to understand the use of the eye-glass by army officers. It is to enable them to preserve a fierce expression and to prevent any facial contortions due to laughter." The standard of raw recruits he had to work with did not impress him: "There is one type who is particularly objectionable. A figure slouches into the room, cigarette in mouth. 'Do you wish to enlist?' you ask. 'Might as well, gov'nor; carnt get no work. Don't seem nothink else going!'"

Another article in the same issue of the Laxtonian came from an Oundelian who had joined the University and Public Schools' Brigade. Stationed in Surrey, they were first taken to billets by special constables. There the main task of the men was to build their accommodation: "Each battalion has a week of fatigue work, which is officially called 'Hutting'…the chief work was hammering i.e. nailing roofs on and putting floor-boards down." Once again the tone was one of quiet amusement: "It is quite an amusing sight to see about a dozen men on top of the roof hammering away like mad and a whole platoon nailing the boarding down inside." A visit by the King was one special highlight of the building work: "It was during our first visit to Woodcote that the King came round. Of course everyone started working with unwonted energy, and one man who was hammering and watching the King at the same time, drove his hammer right through the roofing board!"

On their second tour of duty at Woodcote Park, this Oundelian's platoon "were converted into navvies and dug trenches for the mains." This was a skill which would be very useful in the future and as the Oundle correspondent noted: "To some who were not used to hard work (as all OOs are) it came as a bit of a shock." Daily routine at the newly built camp consisted of three parades a day. The first, before breakfast was for "physical drill" when the company was "put through it by a sergeant-major." The other parades in the morning and afternoon were devoted to extended drill, route marches, field work and musketry. They now had a drum and fife band and their own news sheet called *The Pow-Wow*, with its column of wit and humour, "without which Life would be dull." Most importantly, the writer says that the weather has been good all through "or else training would have been – well, unspeakable."

By contrast, Justin Willis, who foresaw the coming war so clearly, found the weather in Chatham where he was learning to shoot, rather irksome. "I should think that Shornmead is about the coldest place in the British Isles. The range itself is on the banks of the Thames and is below high water mark. In consequence there is generally a damp mist about. All last week there was a raging north-easterly gale which added to the cold." Despite the inclement conditions, Willis was very keen to get to the Front:

> We have just heard that in all probability we shall get out to the front on 1st March [1915]. The first new army is going out then and the second on March 30th; and then the Germans will have to hook it back like hell. I was so braced about this good news that I promptly went and got a first-class in lamp reading, a thing which only one other fellow, Simpson, was able to do.

By the end of January 1915, young Willis' training as a signaller was running at full tilt:

> On Friday we had a Scheme. I was Signal Officer which, of course, is my job and I had to run an Army Corps Headquarters Signal Office, which is no joke I can tell you. We had to transmit about 250 messages in about two hours, which is no joke, especially when the Colonel goes and cuts all the wires to see what you will do. I think I was reasonably successful as Signal Officer especially as it was my first time. It is a fearfully harrowing job at any time, but when the instruments go wrong and the wires get cut, it is positively bloody.

A few weeks later, Geoffrey Donaldson, a Cambridge scholar who was two years above Willis in New House, found himself stationed near Colchester. He was a musketry instructor with the Royal Warwickshire Regiment and recalled some of the difficulties in training the men how to shoot: "Of all the muddles which the new unit in these days had perforce to encounter, assuredly that General Musketry Course was the worst. Shortage of time, shortage of rifles, shortage of range accommodation and in consequence shortness of temper and lack of training and keenness."

Oundelians always valued 'keenness' but sometimes the enthusiasm of the higher ranking officers or 'Great Ones' as Donaldson called them, could lead to embarrassment. At the firing range, an inspecting officer "took it into his head to give an exhibition of shooting." Donaldson thought that this was unwise. "I have always held," he noted in his journal, "that it is much better for musketry instructors not to shoot – the results are apt to bring about lack of confidence!" On this occasion however, the officer insisted on exhibiting his skill with predictable results:

> Bang! No response from the butts, 'your marker's a little slow. What?' from the recumbent expert. Bang! Again no responses. And yet again. Full of fiendish joy I turned to the telephone man. 'Ask them to signal the shots on No.1.' The telephone was actually working and the response was 'none'. By this time all the instructors were standing round the great man. 'None' I said in as low a tone as I could. The expert expressed surprise mingled with expletives. 'Ask them where the shots are going,' was his first coherent remark. This was duly done, but the markers had no idea as to the direction of the shots. Much surreptitious smiling and nudging amongst the NCOs on my reporting this. 'Perhaps, Sir,' I suggested with great deference, 'you have not set your sights correctly.' Which was indeed the case!

Surely, OTC instructors at Oundle never suffered such embarrassment but this incident must have reminded some of those present of their school days!

And there seems to have been plenty of fun and larks during training. Geoffrey Donaldson again noted that his CO was surprisingly cheery and easy going: "He was capable of laughing as heartily as any junior subaltern, when the greater part of the mess hurtled round him in some rag, smashing the furniture, and as often as not nearly pushing the Great Man himself into the stove." Later he recalled many a "rowdy evening together" and "many sore heads the next morning." Presumably incidents such as these did not remind young Donaldson of his days at Oundle.

By March 1915 then, only 10 Oundle lads had died in the conflict. Hundreds of others had by now joined up and most of those were still engaged in training, serious and not so serious. But with the coming of spring, Oundle School would begin to learn the true cost of a war which had been very far from over by Xmas. Fourteen more of her sons would die in the three months between March and May 1915.

2

Year 1 Away: The Battles of 1915 – March to September 1915

> By George, I'll have a good sleep when the war is over.

> By Jove, what a lot I shall have to tell you when I get back.

The Battle of Neuve Chapelle, 10-13 March 1915

By the spring of 1915, the British High Command was determined to make a break-through on the Western Front. The subsequent attack in the Artois region of France, west of Lille and close to the Belgian border, was originally planned as a joint offensive with the French but they were forced to pull out because of problems elsewhere. The new British offensive was prepared in great secrecy and the terrain was mapped out carefully with the help of the Royal Flying Corps. The first day of fighting brought tactical success with the capture of the village of Neuve Chapelle. However the advance could not be exploited partly because of a breakdown in communications between the artillery and the front line troops. Although the land gained was consolidated, the attack at Neuve Chapelle provoked a huge German counter-offensive which put paid to British hopes of further progress. Stalemate was reborn.

The commander of British forces at Neuve Chapelle was Douglas Haig and the initial artillery barrage was more intense, per yard of German front, than that at the Somme in the summer of 1916. Neuve Chapelle showed clearly that an artillery barrage followed by an advance across no man's land might enable the British to break into German defences but would not allow them to break through. Ironically, Haig had experienced the defensive power of trenches in the Boer War and would witness the futility of massed attacks again at Loos in the autumn of 1915. Nonetheless, he would employ exactly the same tactics again and again on the Western Front. At least the Battle of Neuve Chapelle was mercifully short, lasting just four days. Nonetheless it would cost the British nearly 12,000 casualties including the lives of five Oundelians, two of them contemporaries from Crosby House.

Lieutenant Edward Maurice Williamson was born in Newcastle in July 1893 and entered Crosby House in September 1906, leaving five years later. He captained Crosby's rugby team in his last year, playing at full-back but they were knocked out in the

Edward Maurice Williamson, Crosby House 1906-11.

first round of the competition by Laxton. He was a corporal in the OTC and a good shot. Two of his older brothers, also Oundelians, followed their father's career, training as doctors and served as naval surgeons during the war. Young Edward, by contrast, was determined to join the military. Entering Sandhurst in 1912, he was later gazetted to the 1st Battalion Notts. and Derby Regiment, which was always known as the Sherwood Foresters. Having joined his regiment in Bombay in September 1913, he returned to England in October 1914 and the battalion proceeded to France the next month. Promoted to lieutenant in December 1914, he was killed on 1 March 1915 near Laventie, as British troops prepared for the Battle of Neuve Chapelle. He was shot by a German sniper when he was crossing a road to visit a detached platoon. He was hit in the chest through a screen which had been put up specifically to hide an unprotected part of the line. The Germans apparently often shot through the screen on the off-chance of scoring a hit and on this occasion they were lucky.

"He was a most excellent subaltern," wrote his Company Commander, "if he had a fault it was that he was almost too daring. Had he lived, he must have received some recognition at the end of the war." His sergeant, displaying a compassion and admiration typical of NCOs for their young military superiors, later wrote: "If ever there was a gentleman, it was Mr. Williamson. He was one of the few officers who knew how to treat his men as men." One of Williamson's comrades remembered his boxing prowess, probably picked up at Oundle: "He was a good boy and plucky. He gave me a black eye last week, boxing, and I shall miss him as a sparring companion. I wish we could get more like him."

He was buried in the Royal Irish Rifles Graveyard outside the village of Laventie in France. The graveyard now holds the remains of over 800 men killed in the war, 350 are unidentified. Edward Maurice Williamson was 21 years old at the time of his death.

Second Lieutenant Duncan Hepburn Gotch, who left Sidney House in 1910, was killed ten days later during the battle itself. At the outbreak of war, he had joined the Artists' Rifles and as early as November 1914, he sailed from Southampton to Le Havre having been posted to the 1st Battalion of the Worcestershire Regiment. By January 1915 he was gazetted second lieutenant and his battalion went into action at Neuve Chapelle on 10 March. After three days, they had lost 19 officers and over 400 men. Amongst the officers killed on 11 March 1915 was Duncan Gotch who was just 23 years old. His younger brother, Davis Ingle Gotch, also a Sidney boy, joined the Northamptonshire Regiment, was mentioned in dispatches and became a prisoner of war.

A Northamptonshire boy from Kettering, Duncan Gotch was at Oundle for five years and left in July 1910. In his last year, he helped Sidney to win the house rugby title, beating Dryden 35-0 in the final. He was a very promising scholar and whilst at Oundle, he developed a passion for the study of insects. In his last term, he gave a talk to the Science

Duncan Hepburn Gotch, Sidney House 1905-10.

Society on moths and butterflies. He duly gained a scholarship in natural sciences at Caius College, Cambridge and took his degree just two years later. In 1913, he was appointed to the Imperial Bureau of Entomology in South Kensington. The Head of the Bureau wrote of him: "His cheery enthusiasm and charm of manner endeared him to all who had the pleasure of working with him and his place will be hard indeed to fill." He has no known grave and is commemorated on the memorial erected in the village of Le Touret, close to the scene of the battle.

The next day at Neuve Chapelle, two more Oundelians were killed. **Lieutenant Ronald Christian Sundius-Smith** was three years younger than Duncan Gotch. He entered New House in September 1909 but in May 1910 he transferred to School House, where he helped them win the Senior Cricket Cup in 1911. He left Oundle in July 1912, aged 18 and like Edward Williamson, he decided on an army career. He won a prize cadetship to Sandhurst and started his training there in December 1912. He then entered the Indian army, joining the Indian Army Reserve of Officers but at the time of his death, he was attached to the West Yorkshire Regiment. Ironically he was killed during this battle where Indian troops played such a distinguished role in the capture of the village from the Germans and where more than 4,000 became casualties.

Ronald Christian Sundius-Smith, New House and School House 1909-12.

Ronald Sundius-Smith was killed on 12 March 1915, aged 20. He has no known grave and his name is inscribed on the Neuve Chapelle Memorial built after the war. He is also remembered in a stained glass window, erected by his grieving parents, in his local church, St Andrews in Portslade, just outside Brighton.

John Sherard Veasey lived not far away in Surrey. He was at school in Potters Bar and Gosport, before coming to Grafton House in May 1904. He left school just two years later and, like Williamson and Gotch went to Sandhurst, which he entered in January 1908. Like Gotch too, he received a commission in the Worcestershire Regiment and was promoted lieutenant in June 1912. By the time he arrived at the Front, he was Adjutant of his battalion.

British losses and casualty rates in the battle of Neuve Chapelle were severe. Veasey's battalion lost 19 out of 26 officers and 420 out of 870 men. In the official regimental history, John Veasey was described as "a brilliant young officer." Like Duncan

John Sherard Veasey, Grafton House 1904-06.

Gotch and Ronald Sundius-Smith, John Sherard Veasey has no known grave and his name joined that of Duncan Gotch, on the memorial in the nearby village of Le Touret. He was 26 years old at the time of his death.

Two days later, the Battle of Neuve Chapelle swallowed up one further Oundelian. **Second Lieutenant Randall Stewart Mason** was another Northamptonshire boy who joined up as soon as the war started and was given a commission in the Special Reserve. In September 1914, he joined the 6th Battalion of the Rifle Brigade. He went out to France in December, was home briefly on leave at the end of February 1915 and was killed at Neuve Chapelle on 14 March.

Randall Stewart Mason, Crosby House 1907-12.

The Chairman of Rushden Council referring to the heroic death of the son of their Town Clerk, Mr Mason, said he was sure he was expressing the feelings of every member of the Council and also of the officers when he said how deeply they sympathised with him in the terrible loss he had sustained in the death of his only son at the front. That sad event brought home to them all very much the dreadful nature of war and the sacrifices that were being made and would have to be made before it came to a conclusion.

Randall Mason entered Crosby in May 1907, a year below Edward Williamson. While at Oundle he was prominent on the cricket field and played for the XI in 1911 and 1912. Like Duncan Gotch, Randall Mason was a Cambridge man. In October 1912, he went up to Jesus College and a letter in the Laxtonian of December 1912, reported that he was enjoying his golf. Randall Stewart Mason was just 20 years old at the time of his death and was buried in the churchyard at Neuve Chapelle.

Two weeks after his death and not far away, two Oundle men bumped into each other – possibly the first of many chance encounters between Oundelians on the Western Front. One of the men was Captain Arthur Elliott OO, the school doctor and the other was Sergeant Crowley from the School's OTC. A few weeks after that, while billeted in a cottage with a machine gun officer, Dr Elliott met a member of the Oundle teaching staff, Maurice Miskin, only appointed in September 1914 and teaching for just one term before joining up. Promoted to the rank of major, he would be killed in October 1918. Not long afterwards, Dr Elliott met yet another Oundle old boy. He shared a billet with John Jones once of Dryden and heard about Hugh Barwell, who was in the same battalion as Jones but was currently on leave. Dr Elliott saw Barwell, once of Sidney, in June 1915, when he returned. John Jones would survive the war apparently unscathed while Hugh Barwell would be shot down and killed in the spring of 1918, after transferring to the Royal Flying Corps.

By April 1915, Eric Yarrow, once of Grafton and Captain of the XV in 1913 was leading a pretty settled existence, behind the lines and seemed a long way from danger. He had two very close friends – Gifford Moir and Jack Barr – and the three of them did everything together, becoming known as 'the three musketeers'. There is no doubt that this type of comradeship helps to explain how young, inexperienced soldiers coped with the dangers and privations of life in the trenches. In March 1915, Yarrow's Commanding Officer had written to his father, giving a glowing account of the young Oundelian: "He [Eric] is very smart and intelligent. He is absolutely cool and energetic…He is in the best of health and is as happy as the day is long."

However, when Yarrow moved into front-line trenches in April of 1915, his demeanour changed. He was most upset by news of strikes by munition workers and others back in Britain: "I consider the strikers' action is far more ignominious than that of the Germans, because they run no risks themselves and, at the same time, deliberately prolong the war and consequently will be the cause of a great deal of bloodshed. To my mind, the moment they strike, they cease to be patriots." Just a few days later, his letter appeared in the Glasgow Herald, under the headline: OUTPUT OF MUNITIONS – SOLDIER'S POINT OF VIEW. Whether Eric knew or approved of this use of his letter is not known but his father was clearly seeking to shame the strikers in Glasgow back to work. Elsewhere in this letter, Eric revealed the dangers and difficulties facing the troops at the Front and explained why letters home always painted an unrealistic and unduly cheerful picture of the soldier's life there:

Eric Yarrow in the uniform of the Argyll and Sutherland Highlanders.

> During the day, we get what sleep we can, sometimes there are dugouts, other times the dugouts are uninhabitable owing to the smell of rotting human remains… It is consistent with the British character to be cheerful under all circumstances, and it is this spirit which prompts the men to write those cheerful letters to ease the anxiety of their families.

The letter then became even more strident in tone:

> If we out here can be cheerful and work hard, risk our lives and our limbs, and exist under most uncomfortable conditions and with little money, why on earth cannot those at home 'do their bit' and do the utmost in their power to help those who are fighting for them…I could put into words what we feel towards the Germans, but no words will express our feelings for those who fail us at home.

Ironically, Yarrow's diary reveals that outside the front line trenches, behind the lines and in reserve trenches, officers could enjoy a fairly comfortable lifestyle. As a commissioned officer, he even had a servant called Evans to help out. His daily routine here was orderly and perhaps not so unlike the routines of life back in Grafton:

7.30   Evans calls me with a cup of cocoa.
7.45   Evans calls me again, bringing my boots.

8.00	Evans calls me again with hot water.
8.30	Breakfast.
9.00	Go to headquarters, men's billets, meet other officers etc.
9.30	Go out for route march; area somewhat limited as German trenches are all over the countryside.
12.15	Return to billets.
1.00	Lunch.
2.00	Post arrives.
2.00-4.00	Do odd jobs, pay the men, censor letters and write letters.
4.00	Tea. Write or read.
7.30	Dinner.
8.30-10.00	If not in bed, play cards, write or read.

You can see from the above that we do not lead a very strenuous existence.

But 'strenuous' times lay just ahead for Eric Yarrow and his friends. It was the calm before the storm.

Meanwhile, the Battle of Neuve Chapelle was not quite finished with Oundelians. Although officially, the battle had come to an end, there was still fighting in the area. And the next Oundle lad to die in the war, co-incidentally, worked in the Yarrow shipyard in Glasgow, which belonged to Eric's father. In early May 1915, **Arthur Templeton Railton** yet another Crosby boy was killed at the neighbouring village of Vieille Chapelle. A Lancastrian by birth, he spent his early years in Manchester and then Buxton. He came to Crosby in 1906, the same year as Edward Williamson. Leaving in December 1909, he secured a place at Glasgow University where he studied for 4 years and took a BSc in naval architecture. This training got him a job at Yarrow's shipyard on the Clyde in Scotland. In August 1914, he was given a commission in a Scottish regiment, the Seaforth Highlanders and after training in Bedford, he arrived in France in November 1914. He survived Neuve Chapelle but was killed on 9 May 1915 at the Battle of Aubers Ridge, east of the village and was buried at Vieille Chapelle.

One of his fellow officers, Arthur Hope, an Old Rugbeian noted in his diary for 9 May: "The Seaforths actually reached the enemy trenches, but they were forced to fall back...Railton was pretty badly wounded at the very start but was missed by stretcher bearers somehow and a couple of days later, a small party went up to look for him, but they found him dead, killed by shrapnel." He lay just a few yards from the German lines. An officer wrote of him: "He had made himself a

Arthur Templeton Railton, Crosby House
1906-09.

great friend of officers and men; hardworking and brave, he never spared himself, and in him we have lost a very capable officer." His Commanding Officer was even more fulsome in his praise: "He fell, as I am sure he would have wished, at the head of his men, who may and probably did equal him in gallantry and bravery but could not possibly surpass him in either." Arthur Railton was 24 years old at the time of his death and survived his employer's son, Eric Yarrow by just one day.

More Oundelians in Action

In a series of letters to the Laxtonian, published in July 1915, the glamour and adventure of the war were still apparent. There was plenty of dering-do, thrilling moments and sporting metaphors, all of which were to be expected in letters written for publication in the school magazine. No doubt the boys back at Oundle found it exciting reading.

Gilbert Meakin, once a member of the XV who had left New House in 1912 joined the RFC and later became a prisoner of war. Now he reported on a series of dog-fights with three German planes. While one of the German planes, an Albatross, had a specially mounted machine gun, Meakin "had only a machine-gun which we used from the shoulder like a rifle, over the edge of what is called the fuselage." With 25 minutes of "loosing off" at the German machines, Meakin had "never had such an exciting time" and "quite expected to be hit, and the machine crash to earth. Never have I had such excitement. It is a ripping day here now, and I'm absolutely OK as regards health."

In March 1915, the ex-School House boy Mordaunt Mauleverer Parker, who would go on to become an important British artist, was aboard the mine sweeper HMS *Sagitta* and reported back to his *alma mater* from his ship. They were sweeping for mines off the Belgian coast, near Nieuport which was under attack from the Germans. There was great excitement as he watched the British ships being attacked by German bombers: "The enemy proceeded to fly over one of our paddle sweepers at a great height, and I actually saw the bomb leave the aeroplane and followed it right down." "That," he commented, "was a truly thrilling moment." He went on to describe the character of the conflict:

> The mode of fighting (on shore) was as follows: First one side, say the British, would fire a star shell over towards the enemy lines…Then almost immediately we would see the flash of the British guns, followed almost immediately by the flash of a bursting shell in the enemy's trenches…Once during the night I went down below for a moment, when all of a sudden the ship gave a big jar and there was a noise as though she had grounded on a hard rock…A mine had exploded in our sweep wire…Next morning a destroyer found and exploded another seven mines in the same area of sea so we had good luck not to strike any of them. It was a night I shall long remember.

Parker concluded in classic terms for his no doubt eager readers: "it was good sport that night and such a colossal cheek on our part – sweeping away German mines right in front of their batteries. Lucky we were not caught."

Meanwhile a correspondent identified simply as JW, probably Jeffrey Walker, formerly of School House and now a lieutenant with the Royal Warwicks. wrote in from France. In April 1915, he recorded his experiences on being taken up to the trenches in France with the platoon he commanded. There was lots of mud of course. Walking up to the trenches, he talked to the Captain showing them the way: "How far are we from the firing line? Oh, about 500 yards. Could we get hit here? Oh yes; as a matter of fact just here is a dangerous spot; most of the sniping bullets settle here." Walker gulped and changed the subject. "Just as I was getting the men closed up under the wall, three bullets spluttered close to my feet: it didn't seem to worry me." He was then taken round the trenches and found everything rather interesting: "The men were mostly sitting round fire-buckets, making tea and singing. When we had visited most of the trenches, I was taken out with a party to dig a new trench…It was very interesting."

> I had coffee and herrings for breakfast – excellent. Afterwards we crept to the trenches and saw things by daylight. Of course you cannot put your head over the parapet by day, so a periscope is essential…One thing that was very interesting was one of the old trench mortars. They are wonderfully dangerous…First you load the gun, then you set the bomb, drop it down the muzzle, and run away quickly. If it doesn't go off, you approach the thing cautiously, light the bomb, then quickly light the gun, and run for your life.…We had chops for lunch.

But while he found lots to interest him, Walker later revealed something of the horrors of the situation and the war weariness of the men. He even gives the impression that he might share the men's sentiments:

> A dreary succession of days and weeks of muddy and apparently aimless digging, without excitement, hope or interest, one's only thought centred on how to get home to a wife and family, into a warm and comfortable house – this was the spirit of the men and most of the officers of the battalion whom we joined for instruction in the trenches.

Another School House boy, Leslie Rundell, who would be killed in December 1917 near Bapaume on the Somme, reported on his experiences a few days later: "We succeeded in driving out the enemy (such as did not surrender) as far as the communications trench." Proceeding further however things took a turn for the worse: "the cunning devils opened on us with a couple of machine guns. Then followed the warmest minute or two I have ever experienced…To this moment I cannot understand why we did not have more than one man hit, as the shots were ploughing the ground all round us." Yet another old boy, probably George Teal a captain in the Lincolnshire Regiment, was commanding a company of 150 men by July 1915:

> There is always lots of work to be done in the trenches, building up with sandbags, laying down floorboards, putting out wire and cutting grass… A sniper had a shot at me earlier this morning but only succeeded in scattering earth over me from a sandbag…I don't know if this will interest you, but it gives some idea of the life we are leading. I am writing this from the place where I first landed but how different it now looks.

Meanwhile, in the spring of 1915, Reggy Secretan, once of Sidney House, was having a wonderful time. He was attached to GHQ in France as a dispatch rider: "We are all merry and bright out here," he wrote, "we always seem to have a good joke on the whole time. The weather is awful and the roads are worse." And he soon found that the natives were friendly. He was invited to spend his evenings with a local cobbler called Monsieur Castenoy. The latter employed an interpreter to write to Reggy in English in the following terms: "As we know that it is not easy for you to have some clean water for cleaning your face and hands when you are working in the day time, do not worry about it. When you have finished your work, do come here and we will be pleased to supply you with clean water, soap and towel." After Reggy's death in July 1917, the same cobbler wrote to his grieving mother thanking her for sending a framed picture of her son:

> Thank you very much for having sent me and my family this precious souvenir. This photo-graph will remind us each day of the features of a friend who made a short stay amongst us, but whom we shall never forget. Your son was to us 'un bon ami,' whom we loved and we feel his death as if he had been one of ourselves.

In early 1915 though, even Reggy Secretan was beginning to see the darker side of the war. Though still a dispatch rider, now with a car rather than a motorbike, he had seen a churchyard ruined by shell fire. "I got the shock of my life when I went to see a church one day. The grave yard had been literally ploughed up with shells. Shell holes full of water, coffins sticking out of the ground, gravestones, skulls and bones all over the place – it was terrible – and all as still as death." While his mood changes between and indeed within letters, it is also clear that he felt homesick at times. In February 1915, he wrote home saying, "I shall soon be home again, it's almost over I'm sure." Though he might wish for the war to be over, he had no truck with pacifists or conscientious objectors. He wrote to his mother in these terms: "Please tell the COs and the rest of their kind that we should like to see them in our billet for a few minutes! We would make them swallow their words, even if we had to ram them down their throats!"

While Reggy Secretan was upset by conscientious objectors, Eric Yarrow, now in Belgium, took aim at the drinking of alcohol as another cause of inefficiency and discontent among the all-important war workers back home. In a letter to his eldest sister, Ethel, he took her to task for claiming that the importance of 'the drink question' was exaggerated:

> We know that a considerable number of the heads of firms manufacturing munitions of war have definitely stated that drink is delaying [sic] the efficiency of their work; that is to say the war is being prolonged, our chances of victory decreased, more men will be killed….To say that the drink question is exaggerated in the face of this is indeed amazing.

Warming to his theme, he suggested that drastic steps may be needed. On the alcohol question he thought that the government should enforce a 'Total Prohibition'. With strikers, his solution is even more severe: "Out here, a main who refuses to fill a sandbag is liable to be shot….why, therefore, should excuses be made for those who wilfully refuse to work at home?" If he sounds unduly censorious, he explains that he has been hardened by the miserable sights he has seen – the devastation of homes and property, the terrified mothers and the children with their "serious, frightened and haggard expressions."

The Second Battle of Ypres, April-May 1915

And Eric Yarrow did not have long to wait for his chance to be in the thick of the action. In the late spring and early summer of 1915, the centre of British operations on the Western Front moved back to Ypres, for the second battle of that name, a battle which would last over a month, would claim nearly 60,000 British casualties including seven more young Oundle lives. The battle was started by the Germans and involved their first use of poison gas, as yet another weapon of mass destruction. Now locked into a war on two fronts, the German objective here was not so much to gain ground as to wear down their British opponents. It was a classic battle of attrition and the Germans would use the same tactic, on a much larger scale against the French at Verdun in 1916. At the end of the battle, the British, while still holding the Belgian city, had lost ground and the danger of being driven out of Ypres would spur Haig on to mount a huge offensive here in 1917 – Passchendaele. The losses on both sides in the 1915 encounter were staggering but seemed to justify the German's decision to launch the attack. German casualties were in the region of 35,000 but British, French and Belgian losses were nearer 90,000. During the first school year of the war, the Ypres Salient alone would devour nineteen Oundelians.

Basil Herbert Watts like Sam Edmonds, the first Oundelian to die in the war, was the son of a vicar, Rev. J Watts of Allingborough Rectory, Wellingborough. In Sidney House from January 1894, he was a good sportsman, and a half-back in the XV of 1896, described in the Laxtonian as "full of grit and never beaten. With more weight he would be a first-rate half-back." Basil Watts was also a useful bowler in the Cricket XI of 1897, where he played alongside Sam Edmonds. In the cricket match against the Masters in that year, Watts was out for 6, being caught by Grace junior, bowled by Grace senior – Grace senior being the legendary W. G. Grace, a friend of Sanderson's, whose son was a master at the School. In his second season with the XI in 1898, Watts sometimes opened the batting but it was one of the least successful seasons in recent years, with the XI not winning a single match and being saved from defeat on at least two occasions by the weather. As well as rugby and cricket, Basil Watts was also involved in soccer, gymnastics and boxing. In the Sixth Form he specialised in engineering, being taught by his Housemaster, Henry Hale and winning workshops prizes in his last two years.

When the war broke out he was in Canada and so joined the Canadian Infantry. He was amongst the first detachments to arrive in England in October 1914 and from there they were deployed to Belgium, just north of Ypres. He lost his life probably on 19 April 1915, just

Edwin Walter Saunders, Crosby House 1906-10.

before the official start of the Second Battle of Ypres. It is believed that he died of pneumonia, possibly brought on by the German gas and was taken back to Quebec for burial. He was 36 years old at the time of his death and he is one of only a few fallen Oundelians for whom there is no picture.

Lieutenant Edwin Walter Saunders, from Whittlesea in Cambridgeshire, was killed in May 1915, also near Ypres. Another Crosby boy (1906-10), we know little of his school career, except that he won a form prize on Speech Day 1908, when he was in the Fourth Form. He left just two

years later and took up farming. Before the war, he held a commission in the Territorials (army reserves) in the Cambridgeshire Regiment and so was fast-tracked to the Western Front in February 1915. He held the rank of lieutenant, survived the fighting at St. Eloi, but fell at Hill 60, near Ypres, on 5 May 1915. His Commanding Officer wrote of Edwin Saunders: "The Regiment will miss him very much, for he had been doing splendid work the whole time we were at the front." Aged 22, he has no known grave and is commemorated on the Menin Gate.

The next day, **Walter Montagu West** was also killed in action. He was brought up not far from Edwin Saunders, in Wisbech and fought alongside him in the battle outside Ypres. The son of Mr and Mrs W.W. West of Needham Hall, Wisbech, he came up to

Walter Montagu West, School House 1910-13.

School House in September 1910. He helped his House win the senior cricket in 1913 but was on the losing side of the senior rugby final against Dryden. He left Oundle in December 1913 and 3 months later, like Edwin Saunders, joined the Cambridgeshire Territorials. Soon after the war broke out, he was promoted to lieutenant and his unit was sent to France. The men sailed from Southampton and landed at Le Havre in February 1915 and marched to the Front north-west of Ypres. West was wounded on 5 May 1915 and died the next day. He was just 19 years old at the time of his death.

Two days after the death of West, Oundle lost a boy, who has posthumously won lasting fame since he would give his name to a permanent war memorial in the school grounds – Oundle's so-called 'Temple of Vision', now known as the Yarrow Gallery. **Eric Fernandez Yarrow** was born in Blackheath, London on 5 January 1895, the second son of Sir Alfred and Lady Yarrow. He attended prep school at St Andrew's, Eastbourne and entered Grafton House in 1909. Although originally placed in the lowest form on the engineering side, he went on to do very well academically. In July 1910, he passed the Lower Certificate examinations in arithmetic, additional mathematics, mechanics and physics, gaining a first class in each subject. In his last year at the School (1912-13), he was Captain of the XV and the Laxtonian magazine claimed that he had "developed into a splendid attacking forward, who made good openings for the three-quarters and scored tries." He also won the Lyveden Challenge Cup for athletics in his last year, coming first in the 100 yards sprint and in 'putting the weight', with a second place in the quarter-mile. Whilst at Oundle, he was particularly keen on the sciences and in his final year, he delivered a paper to the School Science Society on the rise and progress of steam navigation. In October 1913, Eric went up to Trinity College, Cambridge, to read mechanical sciences but, keenly interested in ideas of social reform – no doubt encouraged by Sanderson's ideals – he was planning to take up political economy in his second year. This plan was interrupted by the outbreak of war in August 1914.

Despite some pretty forthright opinions about strikers and alcohol, most of his letters home from the Front abounded in optimism, with comments such as: "We were a very merry party" and "We had a great time on the whole." A letter home of 21 April 1915 concluded: "One hears about the war ending soon, so I will be back ere long." But the war did not end soon and Eric would not come home.

The day after he wrote that letter, the Second Battle of Ypres began in earnest. Three days later, on 25 April, his two closest comrades and fellow lieutenants, Jack Barr and Gifford Moir were killed. Eric personally retrieved Barr's body and dug his grave. Two days later, he wrote a six page letter of condolence to Barr's mother:

> Jack was killed leading his men into the thickest part of the action. Those who saw Jack say that he led his men brilliantly and with great courage. It is characteristic of his stout heart that though wounded, he continued to lead his men until they, with him, fell victims of the machine gun which killed them instantly. Late at night, amid the shriek of shells passing overhead, the groans of the wounded and the noise of men passing to and fro, we laid Jack's body to rest and erected on his grave a small cross which was lit up by the light of a burning farm.

The letter, like so many others written by officers and comrades, is a most moving threnody of grief and pride:

> I knelt down beside his grave and prayed for those who loved him, that they might suffer the minimum of sorrow. I prayed for myself too that I might follow his deeds and lead the same pure and upright life that Jack did…In my heart I have many remembrances, these will remain with me always. Sad though they must be, the sadness is accompanied with an intense admiration and love; love of one of the bravest and noblest of God's sons.

Two days later he wrote to Gifford Moir's parents, this time quoting Wordsworth:

> Gifford, I am certain, went into action conscious of the fact he bore the characteristics of the 'Happy Warrior' of whom Wordsworth says:
>
> 'This is the happy warrior, this is he,
> Whom every man in arms should wish to be.'
>
> In this fact I hope some comfort may be found. Regrets intensify one's sorrow; where a life has been lived in which there were no regrets, the loss of that life should lessen the grief of those who loved him.

The deaths of Barr and Moir, affected Eric deeply. He told Sergeant Alexander Hunter afterwards that he didn't care whether he was killed because "the devils had killed his two best friends." This may help to explain Eric Yarrow's extraordinary courage and apparently reckless heroism on 2 May 1915, just one week after their deaths, when he led his men over the top amidst a German gas attack. Sergeant Hunter reported: "Our gallant Lieutenant Yarrow took the lead, waving aloft a knife, his only weapon and shouting 'Come on Argylls'. On reaching the German trenches, Lieutenant Yarrow got on to a machine gun and accounted for a great many Germans that day. There is no doubt that his heroic deeds saved the situation." Five days later, having survived this intense fighting, Eric wrote a reassuring letter to father: "I hope you will not worry about me as I am well and safe but I fear you will have been having an anxious time. No doubt this is or has been a most intense time of the war and I think

Eric Fernandez Yarrow, Grafton House 1909-13.

that the worst is over." The next day, 8 May 1915, with the worst of the German assaults on British lines apparently at an end, Eric Yarrow was struck by a German shell and killed instantly. The last of the three musketeers had perished.

Grief at his death was universal. One witness reported that the event had "cast a gloom over the whole battalion." Sanderson, describing his death as "calamitous news," wrote this appraisal:

> My great pupil gone. Friend he was for he and I were in close touch and sympathy in all kinds of things, and views of life. A great loss to us – to me irreparable. Life cannot be the same...Dear kind soul, thou art gone. And yet though so young, we can truly say, and I who knew him so well can say, that he is not gone away. 'He will live again in minds made better by his presence.'

One of his former teachers spoke of Eric's "beautiful altruism and optimism." The Headmaster of his old prep school in Eastbourne wrote in these terms to his father: "I am more grieved than I can tell you. I never had – or could wish to have – a better boy; nor could you have a better son or our country a better citizen." Frederick Weintraud up at Clare College, Cambridge wrote about their time together in Grafton: "At Oundle – as I once told the Head – Eric was the moving spirit, the heart and soul of every wholesome movement. His marvellously contagious happiness, backed up as it was by an in-born sense of reasoned justice, gave him a tremendous influence for good. As an opponent – generous and just; as a friend – glorious." Eric Yarrow was just 20 years old at the time of his death.

In the memoir compiled by his father, he included a poem called *A Lieutenant* by the Daily Mail poet, Touchstone, who, after the first day of the Battle of the Somme in 1916 would pen one of the most famous poems of the war about the Surreys 'playing the Game.' In *A Lieutenant*, he takes up Eric Yarrow's theme in his letter to Gifford Moir's parents – that death in a noble cause should evoke pride rather than sorrow:

> Somewhere in Flanders he lies
> The lad with the laughing eyes;
> And I bade him good-bye but yesterday!
> He clasped my hand with manly grip,
> I can see him now with smiling lip,
> And his chin held high in the old proud way.
>
> Weep but the wasted life
> Of him who shrinks from strife,
> Shunning the path that the brave have trod;
> Not for the friend whose task is done,
> Who strove, with his face to the morning sun,
> Up and up to his God.

And still the fearful Second Battle of Ypres continued to take its toll.

One week later, **Captain Robert William Pearson** of Dryden House, also died. He attended Oundle between 1894 and 1897. In his last year he coxed the Dryden boat which lost narrowly to Laxton in the house final. He was also a useful rugby player but Dryden also lost in the final of the house rugby competition that year. After Oundle, he became an analytical chemist and worked in a hospital in Darlington, county Durham, where his brother was a surgeon. At the time of his death, he was a widower as his wife died tragically after only one year of marriage.

He was killed in action in Flanders on 15 May 1915. He had been a keen Volunteer and Territorial and became the senior captain of his battalion in the Durham Light Infantry. The battalion diary noted at the time: "We had a number of casualties including Captain R. W. Pearson who was killed by a stray bullet. His death was a great loss to the Battalion, with which he had served since 1905." He was buried

Robert William Pearson, Dryden House 1894-97.

in the Ypres Reservoir Cemetery. There are now over 2,600 Commonwealth servicemen of the First World War buried or commemorated there. Robert William Pearson was 34 years old at the time of his death and thus one of the older Oundelian casualties of the conflict.

A rather better sportsman was **Frederick Alfred Trenchard** who was killed nine days after Robert Pearson. Coming to Oundle in September 1902, he was in Laxton House and in his last year he was a school prefect and Captain of Rowing. He was also a forward in the XV for several years, and was a very good athlete, setting a school record in the hurdles. He sang in the School Choir and had a part in the school production of *The Taming of the Shrew*.

He went up to Trinity Hall in Cambridge in 1906 and was elected to the committee of the Old Oundelian Club. The Cambridge correspondent for the Laxtonian magazine noted that Trenchard was enjoying his time. "One Trenchard of the Hall," he noted, "thinks that life is a bed of roses." Sadly, he was prevented from rowing for his college because of a weak heart. He graduated from Trinity Hall in

Frederick Alfred Trenchard, Laxton House 1902-06.

1909 and despite his heart problems, represented Cambridge in the sports of 1910, winning a half-blue for throwing the hammer. He also played rugby occasionally for Rosslyn Park.

From Cambridge, he was gazetted to the Royal Field Artillery and was sent to France with his battery in September 1914. He was mentioned in dispatches in November of that year and wounded in December but remained with his men. He was killed in action on 24 May, aged 27, the last but one day of the 1915 Battle of Ypres. He was forward observing officer during very heavy shelling and was in the top room of a house, carrying out his duties. He was speaking to his Major on the telephone, when the building was hit by a shell, killing him instantly. He was buried in La Brique Military Cemetery No. 2 not far from Ypres. He left a widow, Frances, having been married less than a year.

Herbert Edward Hobbs from Northumberland came to Laxton House three years after Frederick Trenchard had left, in January 1909 but stayed only until the following December. In September 1913, he went up to Keble College, Oxford and was a member of the university contingent of the Officer Training Corps. He joined up in August 1914 and was a second lieutenant in the 2nd Battalion of the Northumberland Fusiliers. He was only 20 when he was killed in action at Hooge, east of Ypres on 25 May 1915, officially the last day of the battle. His body was never recovered.

Herbert Edward Hobbs, Laxton House 1909.

In Flanders Field – June to August 1915

Arriving in Oundle in 1909, at the same time as Herbert Hobbs but staying rather longer was **Frederick Maxwell Waite**. A Grafton boy, he was a keen member of the OTC and a good all round sportsman. At U16 level he won the 75 yards swimming race and the half-mile running race. In 1912, he was one of the losing Grafton team in the senior fives matches, where he played alongside Eric Yarrow. He left Oundle after only three years and was articled to a firm of chartered accountants in his home town of Newcastle. He joined the army as soon as war broke out in August 1914 and went to France early in March 1915 with the 4th Battalion of the Leicestershire Regiment. He received a commission as second lieutenant and was killed in action on Messines Ridge, south of Ypres on 7 June 1915. Like Herbert Hobbs, he too was just 20. He was hit by a sniper while his battalion was dug in on Messines Ridge. An officer wrote of him: "He was always cheerful and was a real leader of men; he did not know what fear was; always a soldier and a gentleman, and beloved by all about him,

Frederick Maxwell Waite, Grafton House 1909-12.

ready for work or fun, each in its own place. His men would do anything for him and would have followed him anywhere."

But not far away from the carnage and destruction around Ypres, other Oundelians were experiencing a different kind of war. Reggy Secretan, the dispatch rider, was less than 30 miles from Ypres but in a different world. In May 1915, he wrote to his mother about his kind landlady: "The lady where I am billeted is awfully nice, she only charges three francs a week and that includes hot baths, and coffee at night and in the morning, so you can see we are doing pretty well up here. They are awfully good to us. I call her ma mère pour la Guerre." In June, he had his first experience of being under shell-fire but re-assured his mother that "I was more curious than nervous, one can't feel afraid with all the fellows around taking no notice of it a bit." A week later, five days after the death of Freddie Waite at Ypres, he wrote home from the village of Hinges. He regaled his mother with tales of a glorious sports day organized by the officers. His enthusiasm and tone show that it must have reminded him of all the sporting encounters he had enjoyed at Oundle: "We entered for the five-legged race and carried off five prizes." He was less happy however about the swimming race, accusing others of ungentlemanly conduct:

> I was first in the water and back again, straight into clothes dripping wet, then I stopped to do up braces and buttons as instructed, but some other fellows never did up a thing, awful swindle, as I could easily have been first!…Is it not extraordinary that all this took place within five miles of the trenches which we can see quite easily with our glasses.

Meanwhile he had time to look forward to his twentieth birthday. Perhaps remembering such occasions at Oundle, he wanted, "a nice large hamper for my birthday, full of cakes and eatables to make a spread for the fellows here who have been awfully good to me." And he was in luck. When he got back to his lodgings after tea on the big day, "there were nine parcels all stacked up against the walls!…So I had an awfully nice birthday out here."

Whilst Reggy Secretan opened his splendid 20th birthday presents, **John Montague Hammick Jackson,** once of Crosby House and also 20 years old was seriously wounded at Ypres. But he did not find a grave in a foreign field. He died two months later in a London hospital and was buried at home in Devon. Like many another Oundle fatality, he was an only son. He spent a full six years at Oundle, first in the Berrystead and then in Crosby. Having enjoyed his time in the school workshops, he went on after Oundle to the Armstrong Engineering College in Newcastle. In August 1914, he obtained a commission in the 5th Oxford and Bucks. Light Infantry and went out to France in May 1915. The next month, he was seriously wounded in the head when leading his platoon in an attack on a German redoubt near Ypres. He was in hospital in France and then in London and seemed to be making excellent progress until, in August 1915, he was struck down by meningitis with fatal consequences. One officer later commented: "His men will never forget his bravery and devotion to duty to the last." He was laid to rest in the churchyard of the 13th century church of Saint Margaret and Saint Andrew in Littleham, in Exmouth, Devon. It was in this village that John Jackson had spent his happy childhood.

Another Berrysteader to suffer in the Ypres Salient and the fourth in a quartet of 20 year olds was **Ivor Theophilus Davies.** He was killed in action on the 22 June 1915, the same day that John Jackson was seriously wounded and Reggy Secretan enjoyed his 20th birthday. Ivor Davies had a long and distinguished Oundle career, entering the recently opened Berrystead in September 1905 at the age of 10 and moving to Laxton House two years later. While at Oundle, he was yet another keen and able sportsman. He played in the school fives team alongside Eric Yarrow and Frederick Waite and in 1913,

John Montague Hammick Jackson, Berrystead and Crosby House 1907-13.

Ivor Theophilus Davies, Berrystead and Laxton House 1905-13.

they beat the Masters 274-139 – no mean feat. All six of the school team went off to fight in the war and four were killed. In the Masters' team that day, two housemasters would fall in action – Francis Norbury and George Tryon.

Ivor Davies also helped Laxton to win the senior fives competition; stroked the house boat; appeared in the house shooting team and was commander of the house platoon. He was also a school prefect and Head of House and was first choice as scum-half for the XV of 1912 but had the misfortune to break his collar bone in the first match, which ruled him out for the rest of the season. By the summer, he was fully recovered and played for the Cricket XI. "He plays forward nicely at times," opined the Laxtonian but his defence as a batsman was seen as rather "unsafe." This resulted from "looking down at his toes and not enough at the pitch of the ball." In truth, his contribution to the team was limited. Apart from a plucky 24 against the Masters' XI, he averaged only 7 with the bat and does not seem to have bowled in a team where West and Owen dominated with the ball.

After the disappointments of the 1912 rugby season, he was able to return the next year, playing scum-half for the OOs as they beat the School 37-25 in the last major match of peace time. In the Sixth Form, Ivor Davies enjoyed science and went up to Caius College, Cambridge to study medicine. He left the college after just a year to do his bit in the war. Like John Jackson, he was given a commission as a second lieutenant in the Oxford and Bucks Light Infantry and with them he journeyed to France and to the Western Front. He was killed in action at Bellewarde, near Hooge on 22 June 1915, as the Allies attempted to expand the Ypres salient. Unusually, he was actually buried by the Germans but his body was not found when the war ended and so his name is now inscribed on the Menin Gate.

Also killed near Hooge on the eastern edge of the Ypres salient, was **Evan Wilmot Harley Russell.** He came to Sidney House in May 1907, where Mr. Nightingale was the Housemaster. Leaving just two years later, he joined the Great Northern Locomotive Works in Doncaster, where he also became a part-time soldier, when he joined the Yeomanry, with the West Yorkshire Dragoons.

When war came, he was in London at the King's Cross Railway Works and from there joined the Honourable Artillery Company. He went to France in December 1914 and remained there for six months. By June 1915, Evan Russell had decided to take up a commission and he and five others were posted to Staff Headquarters, out of the firing line, awaiting orders to return home. When the British attack outside Hooge began and realizing that casualties were heavy, Evan Russell volunteered as a stretcher bearer and was killed instantly when hit by a shell while rescuing wounded men. The village of Hooge would later be captured by the Germans in July 1915 when they introduced their new flamethrowers.

Evan Wilmot Harley Russell, Sidney House 1907-09.

An officer wrote of Evan Russell: "He was highly esteemed by us all, he was always cheerful and willing to sacrifice himself for others."

Also killed not far from Ypres was the first of those Oundelians who had attended Speech Day in July 1914 and the first of the Dryden platoon of 1912. **Thomas Stanley Newell** entered the Berrystead in September 1906 and transferred to Dryden House in September 1909. He was interested in engineering, not surprising given that his father was Chief Engineer of the Mersey Docks and Harbour Board. He was a sergeant in the School's OTC and the Laxtonian, in his obituary, noted that Thomas Newell "was one of the keenest NCOs that the Corps was every lucky enough to possess. Unfortunately debarred from the usual games, [presumably through ill health], he devoted all his time to the OTC and was mainly responsible for Dryden's success in the House Competition in 1914." Even though he was unable to participate in 'normal team games', Thomas Newell twice represented Oundle at fencing in the national competition held in Aldershot.

Thomas Stanley Newell, Berrystead and Dryden House 1906-14.

On 15 August 1914, just 11 days after the declaration of war and on his 19th birthday, he joined the Cheshire Regiment. He was sent to the Western Front in March 1915 and stationed near Ypres. Writing on 6 June that year, he gave some impression of his experience of war, recalling the all too grim realities of life under fire:

> We went along the railway for about two miles. Then six large shells full of gas burst about 20 yards in front of the column. These of course gassed several men and killed and wounded several. I myself got a good mouthful of gas, which made me very sick. Then one of my men who had been badly gassed, collapsed with his arms around my neck...We no sooner showed our noses above the bank than they plastered us with shells of all kinds. I did not stop but ran on shouting 'Come on, boys.'...

> Again the shells fell around us like hailstones...We then made a rush for it. The Germans shot us down like rats. I ran from shell-hole to shell-hole, sometimes crawling, other times rolling, and every hole I got into was full of wounded and dead...I can tell you I do not wish to spend another Bank Holiday in this way.

At first he was laid up in hospital as a result of his injuries, but just days later, on 3 July 1915, he was back in action and was seriously wounded at Dickebusch, south-west of Ypres. He was out in advance of the British lines with a special working party when he was wounded by a shell. Typically he is said to have remarked, "I think this is a ticket for Blighty, Sergeant." He died in a dressing station two days later and was buried in the nearby cemetery of Bailleul across the Belgian border in France. His father would contribute the handsome sum of £50 towards the building of the new School Chapel built to honour the boys who gave their lives in the Great War. His own 'boy' was just 19 years old at the time of his death.

Two years older was **Second Lieutenant Alan Godsal**, killed in action on 30 July 1915. Like Thomas Newell, he came up to the Berrystead aged 11 and later transferred to School House.

He was born in New Zealand but his family later re-located to Blackheath and then to Wokingham in Surrey. Godsal was a good gymnast and a keen shot, making it to the Shooting VIII in his last year. He was a prefect in Sanderson's House and sang bass in the School Choral Society.

Just a year after leaving Oundle, he was gazetted to the 7th Battalion, the Rifle Brigade, at Aldershot and went with them to France in April 1915. They were positioned in the line to the east of Ypres. He was then promoted to the Colonel's Staff as Battalion Machine Gun Officer and his Colonel described him as "quite my most promising officer." In late July 1915, his battalion was relieved of front line duty but had to return at once in order to retake British trenches which had just been lost to a German counter-attack. Heroically, Alan Godsal recaptured one of the German machine guns and used it against the enemy until the ammunition ran out. He was last seen in Sanctuary Wood using his revolver. One of his men said of him: "I shall never have such an officer again. All of us loved him."

Alan Godsal, Berrystead and School House 1905-13.

Charles Bailey Boucher, the next to fall near Ypres in the summer of 1915, arrived at Oundle at the same time as Alan Godsal but was two years older. He entered Sidney House in September 1905 and left in December 1909, having been a member of the Cricket XI in his last summer at the school. In the autumn of 1910 he passed the entrance examination for Sandhurst and obtained a commission in the York and Lancaster Regiment in 1912. Two years later he was promoted lieutenant. He served on the Western Front and like Herbert Hobbs and Evan Russell was killed in the fighting near Hooge (not far from Ypres) on 9 August 1915. On that day, he led his men into action and was twice wounded before crawling back to the British lines. He was having his wounds bandaged when he was killed by shell fire. His name is inscribed on one of the windows of St. Andrew's Church in his home town of Wiveliscombe in Somerset. Charles Boucher was 24 years old at the time of his death.

Charles Bailey Boucher, Sidney House 1905-09.

The final victim of the conflict near Ypres in 1915 was the first Laxton School boy to be killed in the war. Without OTC training, of course, Laxton boys necessarily took longer to be readied for the battlefield. **Henry Berry Stranger**, the son of Charles and Elizabeth Stranger, was born in Warwickshire but by 1901 the family were living in Barnwell, close to Oundle. He came to Laxton School in April 1903 at the age of 12 and left four years later in April 1907, going on to work on his father's farm alongside his elder brother, Charles. Soon after the outbreak of war, like many of his fellows from Laxton School, he joined the Northamptonshire Yeomanry and was killed at Poperinge near Ypres on 9 August 1915 aged just 25. Two other Oundelians were killed on that day, Charles Boucher at Hooge and John Newman in far off Gallipoli, making it the worst day of the war so far for the two schools. Henry Stranger was buried in the New Military Cemetery in Poperinge close to where he fell and he lies not far from another Oundelian, Edward Spofforth who would be killed

Henry Berry Stranger, Laxton School 1903-07.

there in March 1916. In his home village of Barnwell, Henry Stranger's is one of 16 names from this war on the War Memorial Cross erected in the churchyard.

Meanwhile, reviewing the destruction wrought by the Second Battle of Ypres, even Justin Willis' powers of cheerful endurance were being severely tested. Last heard of in April 1915, near the French/Belgian border, the intrepid signaller's mood was now rather darker. A letter home written probably in the summer of 1915, comments on the destruction of Ypres, during the battle:

> The fighting has been pretty fearful, sort of hand to hand effort, with plenty of gas thrown in, or rather blown in. At the present moment we are sitting down in front of a well-known town, or rather the remains of it, in Belgium. I should think more gore has been shed round this town than in any other town in the world. The place is absolutely blown to hell. The stench is godless...We have had the very devil of a lot of work to do, with very little sleep and an awful lot of worry. While the actual fighting is on, eighteen or nineteen hours on duty out of twenty-four is quite common. By George, I'll have a good sleep when the war is over.

Oundelians at Gallipoli, Summer 1915

By the time of Henry Stranger's death, in August 1915, the British had added another name to the war's killing grounds – Gallipoli. Fourteen Oundelians would die there during the course of the campaign, six in the school year 1914-15. Unable to break the stalemate on the Western Front, Churchill's plan was to deliver a crushing Allied victory against the Turks. As Germany's ally and the so-called 'sick man of Europe', Churchill believed that they would prove an easier foe to defeat than the Germans and the attack would allow the British to deploy their strongest weapon, the navy, in a meaningful way. In Oundle, John Coleman Binder, local grocer and baker, thought the attempted invasion of Turkey by British forces a master-stroke. In early March 1915, he wrote: "One cannot but admire the genius that conceived this stroke in the Dardanelles, and evidence is given that it has been carefully planned. It opens up such immense possibilities. It will probably mean the end of the Turkish Empire in Europe, but as to what will be done with Constantinople is a ticklish question..."

In fact, the plan was hopelessly ambitious and hopelessly flawed. The navy would be used to force the straits between the Mediterranean and the Black Sea and capture Constantinople. When this plan duly failed in April 1915, a second plan was dreamed up involving landing hundreds of thousands more men from France, Britain and her Empire on the Gallipoli peninsula, who would then take the overland route to the Turkish capital. After the initial failure to force the straits in April, this second plan had even less chance of success. By August 1915, when the troops were landed, the Turks were ready and waiting. As a result, British forces often had difficulty getting ashore and when they did, they found themselves engaged in the trench warfare, they had hoped to escape. In addition, unlike the Western Front, the troops in Gallipoli had no allied hinterland to support them and were totally dependent on the navy for all their supplies. Furthermore, they had very little reliable intelligence about Turkish positions and defences; they were fighting at the height of the Turkish summer and in terrain which was also very difficult and of which they had no reliable maps. In their efforts to escape the disasters of the Western Front, the Allies managed to create another disaster but this time thousands of miles from home.

Captain Walter Lionel Paine, was not only an Old Oundelian but also the first Housemaster of Crosby. He attended Mr Mallinson's school in Dulwich and came up to School House in 1894, two years into Sanderson's headmastership. Two years later he won the prestigious Senior School Scholarship and was Captain of the School 1899-1900. He stroked the School Crew until, unluckily, he was diagnosed with a heart problem and was forced to give up strenuous sports.

From Oundle he went up to Sidney Sussex College, Cambridge with a scholarship in classics. In 1903 he returned as a classics master, took a year off to study French at the Lycée d'Amiens and in 1907 was

Walter Lionel Paine, School House 1894-1900.

appointed the first Housemaster of the new Crosby House. He left Oundle two years later and went to Whitgift School in Croydon, possibly to be closer to his mother.

At the outbreak of war, he failed to gain a commission and so he enlisted as a private in the Grenadier Guards. His talent and ability led to rapid promotion. In December 1914, he was given a commission as a lieutenant in the King's Own Royal Lancasters and just one month later was promoted to captain and adjutant. In May 1915, he was sent to Gallipoli, being by then attached to the 1st Lancashire Fusiliers. They famously landed at Helles on 25 April and won 6 Victoria Crosses in one day – the so-called '6 VCs before breakfast.' Aged 34, Captain Walter Paine was killed leading his men in the ill-fated advance of 4 June at Cape Helles and was buried in Twelve Tree Copse Cemetery, close to where he fell.

A month later, Robert Bragg, once of Dryden House, wrote to his father, as he arrived in Alexandria, en route for Gallipoli. The excitement of the adventure and the beauty and bustle of the scene made a deep impact on him:

> It was a glorious day not a cloud in the sky, the sea deep blue with shadows of dark cool green under the cliffs and piers. The boat went right into the harbour and was immediately

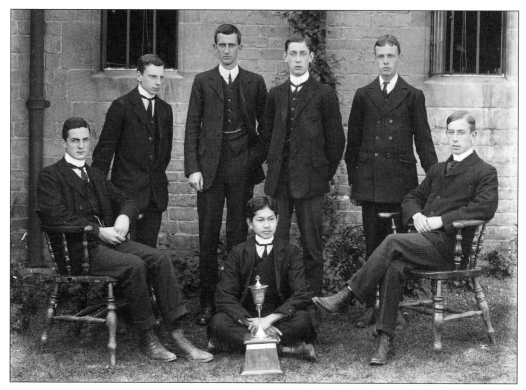

Crosby House Swimming Team 1909 with Old Oundelian, Walter Paine (with watch chain) as Housemaster.

surrounded by rum boats full of lusty voiced boys who dived for pennies and sold oranges. Imagine above this sea a sun-baked, shadowless city straggling up the hill…We met another big transport in the harbour with some of the infantry on board, also 8 of the subalterns of our brigade who couldn't fit into our ship. We signalled to them gaily most of the time we were in port and some of them came on board. By Jove what a lot I shall have to tell you when I get back.

In fact, this was to be one of his last letters home and Robert Bragg would not get back after all.

A month after that letter was written another Oundelian fell under Gallipoli's unrelenting sun. Also in the Lancashire Fusiliers in Gallipoli that summer, like Walter Paine killed in June, was **Captain Arthur James Goodfellow**. A Mancunian, he came up to School House in January 1902 and left just 2 years later, having played for the XI in his last Oundle summer. After leaving, he became a keen territorial officer and was promoted captain with the Salford Fusiliers in 1911. In September 1914, his battalion was sent out to Alexandria in Egypt to guard the Suez Canal. By May 1915, he was in Gallipoli. He took part in the Third Battle of Krithias in June 1915 but was killed on 7 August, when his battalion was driven out of recently captured Turkish trenches by a ferocious counter-attack. He was buried in Pink Farm Cemetery, near Helles. He was later mentioned in the British commander, Sir Ian Hamilton's dispatch of November 1915. A fellow officer wrote of Arthur Goodfellow: "Quite fearless himself, he made his men a resolute lot, and was always devising some new expedient. He is a real loss to those of us who knew him." Aged 28, he left behind a widow, Doris. They had been married in Cairo just seven months before his death.

A third member of the Lancashire Fusiliers on that ill-fated expedition to Turkey was **George Geoffrey Needham**. Like Arthur Goodfellow, he was from the Manchester area being born in

Oldham in July 1895. He came up to School House in May 1907, three years after Arthur Goodfellow's departure. He became Head of House under Sanderson and left Oundle at Xmas 1913. Two months later, he entered Sandhurst, quickly rising to the rank of cadet-sergeant. In October 1914 he was gazetted second lieutenant in the Lancashire Fusiliers and was later sent out to the Dardanelles.

Writing to the Laxtonian editor early in May 1915, aged just 19, he outlined their landing at Gallipoli at the end of April:

> I expect you have already read an account of our landing last Sunday: I wonder if the account was at all accurate. It was the most awful and exciting day I have ever been through....Almost as soon as we left the pinnaces, the enemy on the cliffs opened a terrific rifle fire on us...I jumped out first and fell into a hole and was totally submerged twice. (I believe that this fact probably saved my life, as most of the men were hit as they were getting out of the boats)...We were all so flabbergasted that we lay inactive for about five minutes, with the enemy peeping over the top and picking us off.

Arthur James Goodfellow, School House 1902-04.

George Needham's landing at Cape Helles on Sunday 25th April 1915 went down in the history of the war. That was the morning of the '6 VCs before breakfast'. But they came at a terrible price, over 700 men from the regiment were killed in a couple of hours.

On the following Thursday, Needham found himself with a few men, well ahead of the rest of the British infantry. "We decided to make a run for it...I shall never forget that run...The enemy must have wasted 500 rounds of ammunition on us in that run: the bullets were flying all round." He was so "done up" that he was given "two days sleep in."

He was wounded a few days later and was awarded the Military Cross for his gallantry in operations south of the village of Krithia. There followed more than two months of hard fighting, during which he celebrated his

George Geoffrey Needham, School House 1907-13.

twentieth birthday. He died of wounds on 22 August and was buried in Hill 10 Cemetery, close to where he fell.

His Company Commander wrote to his grieving parents: "Your son was in my company, and during the short time I saw him in the Peninsula, he made himself a name, in and out of the Regiment, for dash and cheery humour." His Commanding Officer from his training days back in England wrote simply: "He had every quality that makes a good officer."

Along the coast from Cape Helles, in Suvla Bay, **John Sherwood Newman** enjoyed rather less fighting than George Needham. Aged 21, he was killed just three days after landing on the peninsula. Attacking Turkish lines on 9 August 1915, he was shot in the head. At first he was reported missing but was later presumed to have been killed in action. He has no known grave and his name is thus inscribed on the Helles Memorial alongside the names of over 21,000 other British soldiers.

Born in York, he came to Oundle in September 1908, first to New House and was then transferred to Grafton in September 1909. He left Oundle in the summer of 1912 and, just a month after the outbreak of war, obtained a commission with the East Yorkshire Regiment and trained with them at Grantham and Witley for the next ten months. He left England with his battalion in July 1915 bound for Gallipoli. They landed first on the Greek island of Lemnos and then moved to Imbros. Early in August, they left the safety of Imbros heading for Suvla Bay. In his last letter home, written the day before their departure for Gallipoli, he wrote with patriotic enthusiasm: "I am gladder than ever that I came here and not to France – you realize what the fleet is to England here, where we eat, sleep and fight and do everything absolutely dependent on the fleet."

Another Oundle name on the Helles

John Sherwood Newman, New and Grafton Houses 1908-12.

Oswald Coke Winstanley, Sidney House 1901-04.

Memorial is that of **Oswald Coke Winstanley**, killed in Gallipoli probably on the day after John Newman. He was the third son of Mr. and Mrs. George Winstanley of Crackley Hall, Kenilworth in Warwickshire, born on the last day of 1887. He came to Sidney House in Oundle in May 1901 and left in December 1904. He then joined his brothers in business. In November 1914, he enlisted in the Royal Warwickshire Regiment and three months later, won a commission as second lieutenant in the Welsh Regiment and went with them to Gallipoli in July 1915. He was reported missing on 10 August 1915 and his death was presumed to have occurred on that date. Aged 27, he was the fourth Oundelian to die in the ill-fated Gallipoli campaign.

Another Oundelian sent to Suvla Bay in early August 1915 was 31 year-old William Angus once of School House. Academically talented he left Oundle in 1903 having won a science scholarship at his Headmaster's old college, Christ's in Cambridge. By the summer of 1915, he was a doctor in the Royal Army Medical Corps and in his diary, he recorded the chaos surrounding the landings at Suvla.

Their attempt to land at Anzac Cove had to be aborted when no lighters came to take them to the shore. So they moved on to Suvla Bay, where matters were no different: "It was dusk when we got to Suvla and there were no lighters. All that day, we lay out at sea in the bay at Suvla and watched and watched, aching to be on shore where we could see that we were needed." From his boat, he realized that troops who had already landed were pinned down on the beach by Turkish artillery: "Every time that a body of men reached a certain spot, which we learnt to know to a nicety, a Turkish shell would burst as it seemed in the very middle of them." And there was a further threat in the air: "Overhead there was an enemy aeroplane which dropped bombs, 2 of which came very near us with a horrible screeching whine." Once ashore, Angus described a hastily constructed dressing station:

> The whole place was very dirty with sand and dust, and dressings were littered about, and at the back was a table with morphia and iodine and one wash hand bowl of very dirty water. I was told that we must not use more than two candles because there was no prospect of getting more and besides, the light was unsafe, it tempted snipers too much.

As if the conditions were not bad enough, young Angus of course, had to deal with lots of wounded soldiers, rather too many for his team to cope with: "Wounded were being brought down to the dressing station and when that became crowded, they were put outside to wait and gradually the area covered by the stretchers grew and grew until there was a lane some 200 yards long." Other wounded men were taken straight to the little pier, "waiting for a boat to take them away." The horror however continued. At the pier:

> there was a similar area, dead, dying, dressed and undressed all lying together, some waiting 72 hours for evacuation. Many of the cases had been lying out all the previous day in the August sun before the stretcher bearers could get to them. While they waited some were dying and some were hit afresh by rifle and machine gun bullets.

At the same time, William Angus was outraged at the cavalier and callous attitude of some of those in charge:

> The Officer Commanding turned up about 9 having had quite a good night and a capital breakfast and a wash and a shave. I hardly saw him all that day. I remember only two things he did that day. Once, when I was carrying a stretcher he told me that there were men to do that work. I carried on. Once he said that I should immediately go and attend to an officer who was in urgent need of surgical aid. I was very busy at the time and had recently seen a boy, shot through the spine and lung, in some pain and rapidly dying. I had given him as much morphia as I dared short of a lethal dose and put him out of the sun. I told this to the officer and he left me with this parting shot, 'Well, the message was from the Colonel.' A little later, the boy was dead.

A few days later, not far away, another 'boy' died. **Percy Edmund Burrell** was killed on 21 August 1915 in an attack on 'Chocolate Hill'. His Commanding Officer wrote: "He was creeping down a trench to help the wounded under heavy fire….He proved himself an excellent officer in every way; keen, brave and full of energy." A fellow officer noted: "He was a splendid officer, popular with his men, cool and courageous under all circumstances, his first thought always for others." For his unfortunate parents his death was just the beginning of their sorrows. Percy was the first of three sons, all Dryden boys that they would lose during the war. He had come to Oundle back in 1896 and left three years later. Afterwards he spent some time in the Canary Islands, later joining his father's firm where he was appointed managing director. Then, in 1909, he joined the Honourable Artillery Company and was promoted sergeant in the 2nd Battalion. In February 1915, he accepted a commission in the South Wales Borderers and arrived in Gallipoli in May of that year. Percy Burrell was 33 years old at the time of his death and has no known grave, being commemorated, like so many others, on the Helles Memorial, close to where he fell.

Percy Edmund Burrell, Dryden House 1896-99.

One day later, back in Oundle, John Coleman Binder remained optimistic about the chances of British success in the Dardanelles:

> Again I am compelled to re-iterate that I believe the Dardanelles to be the supreme interest in this war. Once we force the passage [the straits] I am convinced that we will see great change. We are constantly assured that we shall force this passage and that before long…There seems to be some idea abroad that next month will show great changes and that a supreme effort will be made to conclude the war before winter…I hope this may be so…

But it was not so. Binder's words show a nation in the grip of wishful thinking. Out in Gallipoli there would be no break-through and the casualties would continue to mount.

Another Dryden boy who became a casualty in Gallipoli was **Second Lieutenant Robert Charles Bragg**, the boy who enjoyed extra Greek lessons with his Housemaster on Saturday evenings and had responded poetically to the sights and sounds of Alexandria back in July. Now, seeing action for the first time, the realities of war caught up with him. He was born in 1892 in Australia where his father was Professor of Mathematics and Physics at Adelaide University. He came to Dryden in May 1909, already 16 years old and stayed until December 1911. He was Head of House in his last year, a member of the XV and Captain of Boating, much to the delight of Llewellyn Jones his Housemaster, who ran rowing at Oundle so well for so long. Bragg went up to Trinity College, Cambridge in 1911 and in November 1912, he joined a territorial regiment called King Edward's Horse, which had seen service in the British Empire. When war broke out, he joined the Royal Field Artillery and was duly sent to Britain's new 'Middle Eastern Front'.

On 6 September 1915, his parents received the telegrams they dreaded. The first prepared them for the worst: "Regret to inform you that 2nd Lieutenant R.C.Bragg, Royal Field Artillery was dangerously wounded 1st September. Further news will be telegraphed as soon as received." The second telegram confirmed their worst fears about the fate of their younger son: "Deeply regret to inform you that 2nd Lieutenant R.C. Bragg died of wounds at sea on 2nd September." Unlike so many of his fellows, Robert Bragg did not die leading his men into action. He and a colleague were censoring letters home in their dugout when they were hit by a shell. As chance would have it, Bragg lost both legs, while his colleague escaped with a slight wound on his elbow. Robert Bragg, aged just 22, was buried at sea and is now remembered on the Helles Memorial. A few weeks after his death, his father and older brother Lawrence shared a Nobel Prize for Physics.

Robert Charles Bragg, Dryden House 1909-11.

Robert's Housemaster, Llewellyn Jones, who had retired from Oundle to North Wales by this date, wrote of his former Head of House in glowing terms, recalling his Australian heritage: "Bob was one of the most loveable boys I ever had in Dryden and I had the warmest regard for him. He had all the extra virility of the colonial combined with the refinement of the English gentleman."

Headmaster Sanderson wrote to Robert Bragg's parents with these words when he heard the news:

> The blows are falling with terrific force. We in schools are losing all the best of our old boys. We are distressed to see in the papers today that your dear boy has passed away. I trust that he was spared much suffering…A fine boy he was, who would have done good work in the world.

Noel Campbell Kyrle Money, unlike Robert Bragg, was a professional soldier, the third son of a colonel, born in India on 6 December 1882. He came to School House in 1897 and left in the summer of 1900, having played for the XI in his final term. He passed through Woolwich and spent 7 years in the Royal Garrison Artillery, before being transferred to India with the 22nd Punjabis.

Noel Campbell Kyrle Money, School House 1897-00.

Letter from Sanderson to the parents of Robert Bragg. (courtesy of the Royal Institute Archive)

He was home on leave when the war broke out and transferred to the Connaught Rangers that same month. Promoted to major in December 1914, his battalion was sent to Gallipoli early in July the next year. Major Noel Money was wounded in the head on 2 September, was taken down to a hospital ship but never recovered consciousness, dying at sea near the Island of Malta five days later. He was buried in the Pieta Military Cemetery on the island.

Noel Money had a further important connection with Oundle. In 1912 he married Dorothea Stansbury, daughter of Dr Stansbury, Headmaster of Oundle 1848-76. After his death, Noel Money was awarded the Distinguished Service Order, and was mentioned in dispatches for his gallantry in the Dardanelles operations. Major Noel Campbell Kyrle Money was 32 years old at the time of his death.

Beyond Gallipoli

But Noel Money was not the only Oundelian who died on 7 September 1915. That same day, **Basil Montgomery Coates** was killed south of Ypres by a sniper, whilst going to the aid of a wounded colleague. His Colonel wrote with dismay: "He was out patrolling with a corporal, crawling about in the crops when he was seen by the enemy and killed. He will be an irreparable loss to the battalion, as he was our best scout and absolutely fearless." Another colleague also commended his courage and his popularity: "Coates is a tremendous loss to us, there was nothing in the world to frighten him. He was always in very high spirits and very popular with everyone."

Basil Coates was a Cambridge lad from birth as his father was the Bursar of Queens' College. He was educated at the Perse School and came to New House, at the age of seventeen in 1910, leaving just two years later. He went up to Queens' in September 1912, just months after the sudden death of his father, to study medicine. Here he joined the University OTC and won a place in the University Athletics team which secured the International Cup. On the outbreak of war, he received a commission in the Rifle Brigade and went out to Flanders in the early summer of 1915. As with so many, his active service lasted just a few weeks. Basil Coates body was never recovered and he is remembered now on the Ploegsteert Memorial, together with over 11,000 other men. He was just 21 years old at the time of his death.

His sister Kathleen Wallace wrote a number of moving poems about the war, remembering her brother. In *Chestnut Sunday* she pictures him waking to see the chestnut blossom he loved in Cambridge:

Basil Montgomery Coates, New House 1910-12.

> Oh in your dreamless sleeping dear
> I know, I know you see me here,
> Between the voices and the sun
> And petals pattering, one by one.
>
> I never feel you watch me weep,
> Nor din of battle breaks your sleep
> But I am sure you wake this hour
> To see the chestnut trees in flower.

By contrast with his fellows in Gallipoli or on the Western Front, **John Egremont Thimbleby**, once of Laxton House, did not die in action or even on active service. Though serving in the Lincolnshire Regiment, his unit was part of a so-called second-line division, which was held in reserve and first saw action in 1916 in Ireland, when they helped to quell the Easter Rising. Instead of death in action, John Thimbleby was killed in a motorcycle accident near St. Albans, in August 1915. He had recently been appointed Machine Gun Officer, and his Colonel described him as "a splendid officer

John Egremont Thimbleby, Laxton House 1902-06.

and worshipped by his men." He was buried in the cemetery of his home town of Spilsby in Lincolnshire. He was the second son in the family and came to Oundle in September 1902, leaving after four years, having been a member of the XV. He had no apparent interest in the military and took up his father and grandfather's profession as a solicitor. Nonetheless, when the call came, he joined up as soon as he was able, determined, like all the others, to do his bit.

By the start of the school year 1915-16, thirteen months into the war, Oundle School and Laxton School had now lost 42 old boys. The war had spread to the Middle East but the Gallipoli Campaign had resulted in a stalemate to match the one on the Western Front. It was just the beginning. The war would last another 38 months.

3

Year 1 Home: Oundle School 1914-15

Another gone! The well-known name,
And then, the all too brief career,
His home, his School, athletics fame,
"In action – in his nineteenth year."

In February 1915, the newly enlisted Geoffrey Donaldson, who had been in New House three years earlier, found himself based in Northampton and he took the opportunity to visit his old school. "The Old Man [Sanderson] was preoccupied and depressed," he wrote. "He had always been anti-militant. On one occasion in Scripture class, he came to the passage *Those who take the sword shall perish by the sword*. 'Ah boys,' said he, 'I wonder what Lord Roberts [retired Commander in Chief of British Armed Forces] would have to say to that'." But now masters and boys alike were being trained to take the sword and by the end of the school year would mourn over 40 boys who had 'perished by the sword'. And for the boys still at school and on the verge of leaving, attitudes to the war were often ambivalent. Alexander Crawford, who would be too young to fight, remembered divided opinions amongst the senior boys he knew:

> Some were keen to join up 'while the fun lasted,' as one of them put it, others were not. At least two spoke to me of their premonitions that they would not return from the front. Sadly they were right. The name of one was Ainley, the other Hollick who, at the end of his last term, said to me 'The next you will see of me will be my photograph in the Roll of Honour'.

Both boys would be killed in 1918.

OTC

Training to take out the sword meant that the School's OTC assumed greater importance than ever before. By the end of the school year, the Commemoration booklet could report that some 90 percent of ex-cadets from the years 1909-13 were now serving in some capacity. In December 1914, the first Laxtonian magazine of the war years reported: "One result of the war has been an emphatic justification both of the Territorial (Reserve) Force and the Officers' Training Corps. They have supplied men and officers at home, in India, Egypt and in the fighting line, without whom the military situation might have been almost desperate." Numbers in the corps naturally rose. From September 1914, the school magazine also reported that "almost every available boy has been taken into the Corps as a private."

There were now parades three or four times a week as well as extra "small field days and night marches." At the same time there were instructional classes for NCOs twice a week and boys practised "a fair amount of trench digging." A semaphore signalling class was established which had by the end of term "considerable proficiency." Apparently "plenty of keenness" had been shown by the boys, meaning that the military efficiency of the corps had been raised "in every direction." On 6 November 1914 a Field Day was held in Cambridge though, for some reason, it took the boys over three hours to reach their destination. Oundle's young soldiers, over 250 strong teamed up with the Cambridge OTC and there were manoeuvres against enemy forces which were deemed a success. However the Oundle boys were not too pleased to hear that this was not the end of their efforts. Just as they were eating or "attending to the needs of the flesh" as the Laxtonian correspondent put it, there was a heavy downpour and they were told to advance against another enemy force across open and very wet fields. Overall though, the day was judged a success and credit was given to "the smaller members of our corps for the cheerful way in which they accomplished the return march over heavy fields."

Set against this overall success in raising standards, the OTC had to contend with the loss of half the School's rifles, requisitioned by the government in November 1914. This was seen as "a great disadvantage." By July 1915, the house drill competition was seriously handicapped by the continuing shortage of firearms. As might be expected in time of war, new rifles could not be obtained but even the dummies which had been on order for six months had not yet arrived and would not be acquired until the following November.

As well as the loss of half the rifles, Oundle's OTC also had to deal with the loss of its top officers. Early in the year, two members of staff, Captain Norbury and Captain Tryon joined the Special Reserve Battalion of the King's Royal Rifles and by the end of term, Lieutenants Williamson and Miskin together with a number of the senior cadets went off to join "Kitchener's Army". By the spring of 1915, Captain Norbury had been killed and Captain Tryon wounded. The departure of experienced OTC officers was mitigated by six members of staff volunteering to take their places and as the Commemoration booklet for 1915 made clear, they made "a willing sacrifice of their holidays in order to make themselves proficient in their new duties." By the Lent Term 1915, helped by Captain Tryon, who was recovering from his wound back in Oundle, trench digging had become rather more sophisticated. The boys had dug "quite creditable firing, support and communication trenches." They were also becoming more expert at bayonet fighting. This particular type of combat "has been practised with enthusiasm that at times became almost too realistic." In July 1915, Sergeant Curley came to Oundle for the day to judge the bayonet fighting and to give "a little instruction in the art." One Oundle boy, Sidney Savage recalled that the boys had to charge straw-filled sacks representing Germans. The difficulty he remembered was not so much stabbing the sacks, though they dangled from ropes, but rather extracting the blade from the sack afterwards. "We had to hold the 'German' with our left boot as we withdrew the blade," he later wrote.

Just like games, the Oundle OTC was to be affected by the premature departure of senior boys to play their part in the world of real soldiers. Furthermore, by the end of the Summer Term 1915, tensions within the OTC were becoming clear. Lack of rifles and "the claims of cricket" meant that field operations had been curtailed and the senior NCOs and experienced shots refused to give the necessary coaching and help to the junior boys with their shooting, resulting in nearly half the corps "failing to classify".

Workshops

One area where Oundle was better placed than most schools to contribute directly to the war effort was in the making of munitions and other materials needed in time of war. With the expansion of the School's workshops before the war, Oundle already had the means to answer the nation's call. Work for the War Office began in earnest at the start of 1915. In May 1915, local grocer John Binder noted the importance of the workshops in his diary: "Some of the boys at the Schools here are helping to turn parts of shells. Their carpentry shop has been cleared and new machinery

Grafton House in 1905. Francis Norbury, killed in January 1915, is seated second from the right.

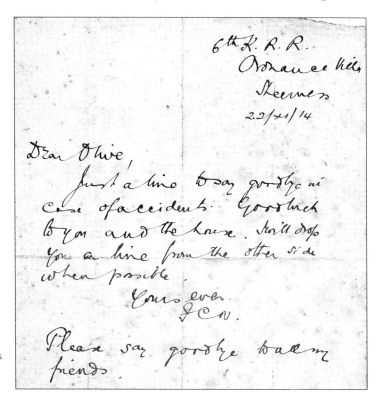

Francis Norbury writes his last letter before leaving for France.

installed at a cost of £600 (it is said the Headmaster bore the expense of this) and here 40 boys are working for several hours daily on this manufacture of shells." By the summer, workshops were seen as "the great feature of the term," by the Laxtonian magazine. By May 1915, Fifth and Sixth Formers, more than 200 of the 359 boys in the School, gave over one day each week to the shops, working from 7:00 a.m. to 5:30 p.m. in groups of 35-40.

The importance of workshops' production to the war effort was underlined by the decision to continue working in the summer holidays of 1915. According to John Binder: "The Boys of Oundle School have broken up...but about 65 are remaining behind to continue the manufacture of Ammunition. They will remain 14 days, and will then be replaced by another contingent...At present the boys are engaged in making parts of Bombs or Mines..." The holiday work seems to have been a great success and the boys even produced two issues of *The Oundle Munitions Gazette* to record their deeds. The boys, old boys (including the Head's son Roy Sanderson), masters and visitors (some from other public schools) were divided into two shifts. The first worked from 6 in the morning until 1 in the afternoon with a one hour break and the second operated from 2 until 7.30 with the same break time. On 29 July 1915, some of the finished items were taken to the firm which had commissioned them, Brotherhoods of Peterborough and the Works Manager, "expressed his complete satisfaction" claiming that the work done by Oundelians "was really better than that done by the firm itself." At the same time, three new machines were secured for the shops to increase capacity.

Of course it was never a case of all work and no play for Oundelians employed in holiday work. Tennis was popular out of hours and new courts were prepared on the cricket field. On Saturday

Grafton House Fives Champions, Lent 1915. Edward Stevens, standing on right,
would be killed two years later.

31st July, at the end of the first week, an excursion and picnic to Fotheringhay was organized. Mrs Sanderson produced one of her famous teas on the Bank Holiday following and there was an evening dance in the Great Hall. In between, there was time on the Sunday for a musical recital in the same building. For Sanderson, the whole holiday munitions programme must have been a wonderful example of a purposeful industrial society, filled with productive and joyous workers, showing that the School was not just a preparation for life but was life itself.

Food Shortages

From the start of this school year, Oundelians began to complain about rising food prices. In the Laxtonian of December 1914, there appeared a poem entitled, *the War (an excuse)*:

> Though prices are often alarming
> In shops that perforce we frequent
> The shopman's politeness is charming
> When annexing the cash that is spent.
>
> He gives an excellent reason
> For jam costing more than before,
> Which is not that the fruit's out of season,
> But the pressure he feels from the war.

As well as rising prices, Oundelians also had to cope with limited supplies of things such as sweets. It was not until the spring of 1919 that the Laxtonian noted the occasional re-appearance of chocolate at the tuck-shop as a clear sign that the war was actually over. In 1914 however, food shortages and rationing lay in the future but by the end of the first year of the war one concerned Oundelian, thinking of what he might do to help Asquith and Kitchener, wondered if he should "knock off marmalade, or eat one egg at tea instead of two." In fact, the supply of food at Oundle in the first year of war was pretty much as normal. There would be more difficult days ahead. Alexander Crawford in Sidney House spoke of the food situation in 1916: "The school authorities gave us enough to eat although the diet, naturally, was restricted and unattractive, we had molasses on our porridge rather than sugar and dripping instead of butter on our 'slogs' [thick slices of bread], marmalade was very scarce." Nonetheless, Oundle was less affected by food shortages than the cities. "Towards the end of term," Crawford noted, "our parents used to send us some money with which we bought butter, eggs, sugar etc. to take home with us."

Agriculture

Since 1909, the School in its go-ahead fashion, had encouraged boys not just to grow crops but to carry out agricultural experiments. In 1910, they had grown new types of wheat – "Professor Biffen's new-bred hybrid wheats and a recently imported French wheat." The next year there were more wheats and "the measurement of the yield and sugar content of sugar beet" grown on school land. Five different types of oats were grown in 1912. The main agricultural experiment of 1914 measured the effects on potato yields of three different preceding crops. In the spring of 1915, all nine acres available for these experiments were sown with Essex Conqueror wheat, a British pedigree wheat which previous experiments indicated did well in Oundle soil.

At the same time, junior boys in the classical forms, were encouraged to cultivate and tend small allotments, near the new Science Block. Here the boys might find "the means of learning about the natural world through Nature herself." The herbaceous border here was developing nicely with the printing of a plan giving the names of all the plants. Orchids were doing well in the 'marsh' and there was an area adapted for growing plants of the seashore. A greenhouse was in operation to grow seedlings and there was a plan to create a fernery in the future.

In June 1915, Sanderson issued a public notice offering the services of Oundle boys on local farms:

> If any farmer of our neighbourhood is hard-pressed in time of hay-making and cannot get sufficient labour, the boys of Laxton School and the younger boys of Oundle School (the older boys are occupied in war-work) will be glad to give what help they can. We can send boys out in sets. Each boy can give one whole day per week, and the regular work of the School will be provided for at other times or in other ways. Should any farmer think that we can thus be of service, I shall be glad if he will apply to me or see me.
>
> F.W. Sanderson

Whether any farmers applied for help is unknown and John Binder thought it unlikely because the hay crop that year had been so light. One wonders if the boys were consulted on the issue!

Appeals

In the first year of war, Oundelians were the object of various direct appeals to help a range of good causes linked to the conflict. In the spring of 1915, boys were asked to contribute to a fund which might be thought to be close to their hearts, namely to supply the troops with tobacco. This was the Sailors and Soldiers Tobacco Fund which claimed that our troops, numbered now at some two million men, would need 28 tons of tobacco just to give them half an ounce each! The Laxtonian of December 1914 also recorded other acts of charity. The School had sent £100 to the Prince of Wales's Fund, £50 to the official committee to help Belgian victims of the war, £20 for Princess Mary's Fund and last (and least) only £5 for the Northants. Regiment Tobacco Fund!

Similarly in 1916 there was an appeal from the British Red Cross and the Order of St. John War Library based at Marble Arch which asked for games, magazines and 'novelettes' for wounded troops at home and abroad. Apparently these organizations had already sent and shipped 20,000 such items a month to the sick and wounded since the outbreak of war in places as far afield as "East Africa, India, Mesopotamia, Egypt, Salonika and Malta." The same charitable bodies supplied reading materials to 180 hospitals in France and nearly 2,000 hospitals in Britain.

The war was naturally at the forefront of everyone's thinking and this was re-enforced by lectures given by outside speakers, which centred on aspects of the war effort. In October 1914 for example, the School heard a lecture from Stephen Paget on "Surgery in War" with slides of hospitals old and new. He emphasised the importance of cleanliness in surgery and the development of antiseptics.

Debating the War

At the same time, the School Debating Society clearly had the war in its sights. In October 1914 the motion before the house was that "Might is Right, especially in relation to international politics." The future Captain of the School, Mr Rissik, proposing the motion, denounced "modern sentimental notions of honesty and trust as mere hypocrisy." He argued that if Britain had trusted in the good faith of other nations and disarmed, then she would have lost the current war. Similarly, he suggested that if England had crushed Germany when she had the chance then "there would have been no war." The opposite point of view was taken up by the current School Captain, Frederick Milholland who argued that while a German Empire, which demonstrated the theory of Might is Right would have brought peace, it would have been at the expense of the freedom of the individual. After a lively debate from many boys which drew praise from Sanderson, the motion was lost.

Perhaps it is rather a surprise then that in February 1915, the motion before the House was that "Germany is justified in the violation of Belgium, and in using any means she may think will help her to win." Charles Bingham, who seconded the motion declared that he was still "a great admirer of Germany, who would not undertake such an important enterprise without justification." For England and its government he had nothing but contempt. England, together with her ministers was "no better than a hotbed of hypocrisy." These were strong words indeed and perhaps exaggerated for effect but what is interesting is that, while the motion was lost, some 19 boys voted in favour. Perhaps it is not surprising therefore that a later motion that "the call for conscription is to be condemned" was carried. Even in time of war, Oundelians tended to be free thinkers.

On a lighter note, the Debating Society in March 1915 considered "the value of cabbages in war." Hector MacDonald expressed his opinion on cabbages in a forthright manner declaring that such vegetables were "perishable, cheap, unpleasant to the palate and did not incite to battle fury." In July of that year, the motion was that the pen is mightier than the sword. Here Alan West opposed the motion observing that in recruiting fresh troops, "a zeppelin is more effective than a poster." Even the French Society, whose meetings were conducted in French of course, debated whether voluntary military service was better than conscription and whether or not England needed to fear a German invasion.

Music

The advent of war also meant that patriotic and military music was more in vogue at Oundle School. In the first term of the conflict, the Orchestral Society learned Elgar's military march, *Pomp and Circumstance No. 4*, not played at school since 1908. At the end of term concert in

Housemaster's Study. H. M. (John) King in his study in Laxton House in 1908.

December 1914, Elgar's stirring music was accompanied by the playing of the national anthems and songs of Britain's allies, France, Russia and Belgium. The treble choir sang *Hearts of Oak*, *Men of Harlech* and *John Peel* while other offerings included *The Empire Flag*, *Follow the Colours* and *It's a long way to Tipperary* – fast becoming a wartime favourite. Wartime favourites were less in evidence however in the midsummer concert given on 3 July 1915 but *La Marseillaise* survived as did *Follow the Colours*, which topped the bill just before a no-doubt hearty rendition of the school song – *Carmen Undeliense*. By the end of the year, the patriotic and military flavour of school music was unmistakeable. The house concerts held on 16 July 1915 were inundated by patriotic melodies. Dryden had the *Marche Militaire* and *Four Jolly Sailormen*, Laxton and New House featured *The Yeomen of England*, Grafton had its own 'Dreadnought Orchestra' and nearly every House had a rendition of Ivor Novello's wartime anthem, *Till the Boys come home*, no doubt with all the boys joining in. On the other hand, the coming of war meant the temporary suspension of the School's Drum and Bugle Band. Sergeant-Major Clayson who was in charge, joined up in August 1914.

Wartime Cambridge

The Laxtonian magazines of the period also show that Old Oundelians at Cambridge were thinking much about the war: "We think and talk of nothing else, and even this ancient seat of learning is not exempt from general war fever." The writer who signs himself only as O.O.Cantab. goes on to report that "we spend our time in drilling and being drilled… and when we find time to snatch a moment for coffee and a pipe, we proceed to draw up and demolish plans of campaign, worthy of the great von Kluck himself." Perhaps this admiring view of the German commander reflects the relative novelty of the war and sense of adventure or perhaps it indicates the public schoolboy's natural respect for his sporting opponent.

And the Cambridge correspondent also reports on a town where many have already joined the forces: "All, all are gone…the old familiar faces." Oundelians who are left, like Marr, Catterall, Harvey and Little "are seeking commissions while they and others such as Barrell and Davey are very busy in the university OTC." At the same time, other varsity men who have already joined up, have found time to visit their old school friends. In this category we find Threlfall and Yarrow, who, apparently, looked good in his kilt, though worried about "the hang of his sporran". The writer's jaunty tone and benign view of the war is underscored by his final comment, wishing everyone a peaceful Christmas, "free from German raids and similar treats."

By the spring of 1915, Cambridge was a rather gloomier place. Thousands of Territorials were being lodged in the town and an enforced blackout for fear of Zeppelin raids left Cambridge "blacker than Erebus." In addition, by this time, there were now relatively few Oundelians left to report on.

Cecil Lewis and Maynard Greville decide to leave school

Meanwhile back in Oundle, some of the boys were becoming restive and wanted to join up as soon as possible. In the spring of 1915, two study-mates, aged just 16, were discussing the matter in front of the School House studies. One of the two was the Honourable Maynard Greville, second son of the Earl of Warwick, no less. His mother, the notorious Daisy Warwick, who had an affair with the late King Edward VII, was apparently one of the great attractions for mothers on Speech Day. They used to remark on her heavy make-up! Now her son Maynard decided to leave school as soon as possible. He told his friend Cecil Lewis, son of an Anglican vicar, that while you had to be 18 to get a commission in the army, the Royal Flying Corps would take young lads at 17.

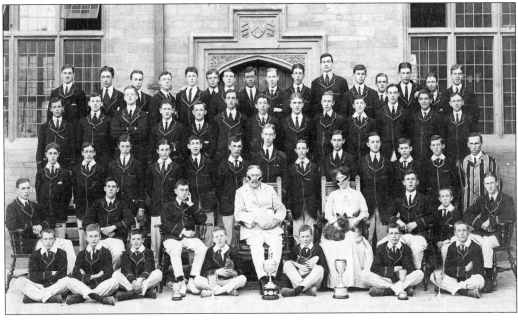

School House 1914, graffiti added!

"Shall we speak to Beans?" wondered Lewis.
"No, he might stop us. I vote we write to the War Office and see what happens."
"All right! Oh, Maynard, wouldn't it be ripping!"

A few weeks later, Lewis found himself being interviewed by Lord Hugh Cecil, a staff captain with the Royal Flying Corps:

"So you were at Oundle?" he said.
"Yes, sir."
"Under the great Sanderson?"
"Er – yes, sir." (Old Beans the great Sanderson! Well I'm blowed!)

Although apparently unaware of the headmaster's fame, Lewis' interview went well until Lord Cecil noticed that the boy was over six feet tall and thought he might be too big for the aircraft! However, after some pleading from Lewis, he was accepted. The boy who would become Oundle's most famous airman just scraped in and probably had Oundle School and Beans to thank for it!

Llewellyn Jones' retirement 1915

While the war caused some boys and staff to leave, *anno domini* meant the retirement at Easter 1915 of one of the School's great masters – the legend that was Llewellyn Jones. He was appointed to the staff a full 10 years before Sanderson's arrival and served the School for 33 years. He was a brilliant sportsman, first and foremost as an oarsman. He was a rowing blue and helped keep Jesus College at the head of the river throughout his four years at Cambridge. He was also in the great Jesus' crews that triumphed at Henley, winning the Ladies Plate in 1878 and the Grand Challenge Cup a year later. But rowing was not all. He twice ran for Cambridge against Oxford in the three mile race and was an excellent rugby forward though too light for the Cambridge pack.

Dryden House with Llewellyn Jones in 1910.

In addition, he was a first-rate classical scholar and his teaching of the Fifth Form was legendary. He could be stern towards shirkers and slackers "like some divine nemesis" but was considerate and sympathetic towards "the genuine duffer". And then there was Dryden House. He was Housemaster there for a full twenty years during which time Dryden, though one of the smaller houses in terms of numbers, carried off most of the sporting prizes.

Perhaps his greatest achievement was to establish Oundle as a rowing school with a national reputation. He was the founder of the School Boat Club in 1886. From a membership of just 30, the number of school oarsmen reached over 200 and a boat house was built and new boats acquired. It was a brilliant and selfless career of devoted service to the School which left the author of this testimonial to wonder, "When again his like?" As it turned out, there was not long to wait. Llewellyn Jones himself reappeared in Oundle just two years later, as wartime expansion in school numbers meant that he was recalled to take over a new boarding house called Bramston!

Impact on sport

To glance through any copy of the Laxtonian at this time is to realize immediately how important sport was to Oundelians. Often half of each issue is taken up with sports reports of one sort or another. As well as the exploits of the XV or the XI or the Crew, there are also detailed reports of the all-important competitions between houses often at junior as well as senior level. In cricket, this meant not only full score-cards for each and every house match but also match reports and batting and bowling averages for the Cricket XI. Here is a flavour of a report on a first round house match played during the war:

Llewellyn Jones and the School Crew of 1910. Robert Bragg would be killed in 1915.

1910. Beat Oundle 2nd Crew by one length. Were beaten by Bedd Grammar by ¾ length.

Elliott & Fry.   55, Baker Street. w.

Lt. R. Jones Esq,   E.S.P.K. James Esq.
(Capt.) W.W. Benyon (str)   F.H. Hutchinson. (2)
R.C. Bragg (bow)   H.T. Bostock. (3)

New House won the toss and played from the Pavilion. The play was even, till Little ran up to the New House twenty-five. New House pressed School House back, but Motley cleared. Wakefield then received the ball and ran through but was brought down by Motley. New House continued to press and found touch close to the line. Vigeon scored from the line-out...

The amount of detail here is astonishing and is testament to the importance of games and house spirit at Oundle. As at other public schools, the house system meant that a large number of boys actually played regularly in competitive matches. With most houses [apart from School House] comprising 40 or so boys, two house rugby teams would use up 70 percent or so of the inmates. And if a boy was hopeless at rugger, he might shine at cricket or fives or hockey or rowing or even shooting.

John Binder, the local grocer, noted in the spring of 1915 that attitudes to sport were changing because of the war: "Horse racing goes on but it is very much condemned by a large section – I think I may say by the large majority of the people. Probably there will be very little cricket this year, and football receives very little public attention." At Oundle School, by contrast, enthusiasm for sport remained the same as ever but the war took its toll. While most games went on as usual, with the weather, ground conditions and illness as the normal problems to be overcome, the war did have a negative impact on school fixtures. In the Michaelmas Term of 1914, the XV's usual matches against a number of Cambridge college sides were all cancelled. In all there were just three matches for the team that season, two of them scratch fixtures against an R.A.Little (OO) XV and

The School Boat House on the Nene 1905.

a team of officers of the Welsh Artillery brought down to Oundle by another OO. Neither proved much of a match for the XV. The war also had a disconcerting habit of taking away senior boys mid-term. Ithel Owen of School House, who was rugby captain as the war began, played only one match and then went off to Sandhurst. Similarly the School Rowing Crew in 1915 found that three of its four members had taken up commissions and that all regattas were cancelled. In the summer, the cricketers reported that the average age of the 1915 team was a year younger than usual.

Breakfast with Beans

For Cecil Lewis the end of the Summer Term 1915 meant leaving Oundle but before he did so, being a School House boy, he had to undergo the traditional leavers' breakfast with the Headmaster: "And Beans! Musn't forget I'll have to say goodbye to Beans – and Mrs. Beans too! Gives me the shakes. What do you SAY to them anyway? Probably glad to see the back of you! Looking forward to breakfast, all the same. They say you get kidneys. Kidneys and bacon! Spiffing!" And the breakfast was a success, though young Cecil was clearly in awe of his Headmaster:

> Never saw him close to, like that. He was always up on the platform or at the desk waving his arms about, taking off his mortarboard and putting it on again not quite straight…Now he was eating toast. Crunching it. Funny to hear Old Beans eating toast! And he really seemed to like it. 'Jolly good kidneys? What?' He made the announcement rather like God might.

And for Lewis that thought triggered a tricky moment in a religious studies lesson some years before. He remembered Sanderson's sharp appraising eyes:

> He might really look at you, really answer you, like he did me, when I asked him in Religion: 'What is God like?' He snorted then. Looked at me quite a long time, then over the whole

Albert Nightingale and W. G. Grace Snr. in 1908.

class. Not a sound. I felt a fool. 'Think you're clever, asking big questions, eh?' He fixed me with a thoughtful eye...'God is not like anything. He is everything. In the thunder. In the dewdrop. In you and me. Spend your life finding out.' A long pause. 'Understand?' 'Yes, sir. Thank you sir.' quite a number of chaps answered.

With breakfast over and farewells said, Cecil Lewis glanced back from the pavement outside School House for a last glimpse of 'the Old Man': "He stood above us, always in his robes, his arms always flying about him like black wings, heavy, rotund, benevolent, smiling behind his glasses, feeling a sort of care for us...seeing us off into life."

Speech Day 1915

The first wartime Speech Day was curtailed compared to its predecessors. John Binder described it as "a very tame affair compared to what it generally is." Gone was the Commemoration Service on Saturday morning; the Grocers and governors made no appearance and Mrs Sanderson's garden party was "very much missed". Nonetheless, the usual Commemoration booklet was produced giving a digest of the School's activities during the year. These reports show that in some ways the war had yet to have a serious impact on school life. Workshops did not begin serious manufacture for the War Office until the summer term of 1915 and agricultural experiments continued in the same vein as usual. Only later would more school grounds be turned over to growing potatoes and other vegetables and boys sent out to help with the harvests. As if to emphasise the degree of continuity with pre-war days, the examination results in 1915 were, as usual, encouraging. Nine scholarships had been won at Oxford and Cambridge and one at Manchester.

Casualties reported

At the end of the first year of war, it was probably the growing list of casualties that had the greatest impact on boys and masters alike. For Sanderson, it would be particularly hard as all except three of the Oundelians who would be killed in the war were boys during his headmastership. As Headmaster and of course, Housemaster of School House, Sanderson would pride himself on knowing every boy in the School. He would often stand on the steps of School House in the mornings checking that the boys were on time for first lesson and enjoyed upbraiding miscreants by name.

The official reports of Oundle casualties in the war started in the December 1914 edition of the Laxtonian. Seven deaths were reported together with brief biographies of six of them, the pages framed by black edging. This issue also reported that four boys had been wounded and one was a prisoner of war. This set the tone for the future. By the March 1915 issue, eight more deaths were reported and a further nine wounded. Interestingly, the magazine was at pains to point out that only one of the wounded was seriously hurt. After all, Captain Tryon "was nearly fully recovered and back at Oundle," and Secretan's wound "was of a trivial nature and he writes very cheerily of encounters with generals galore." Meanwhile, though Harry Turner had received "several wounds near Neuve Chapelle" he had also come through "unscathed" after "exciting experiences near Givenchy." The war, even for the Oundle wounded was one of excitement and dering-do!

School Crew 1906. Frederick Trenchard, seated centre, would be killed in May 1915.

By July 1915 and the end of the school year, the tone was more sombre. A further 12 deaths were reported with Captain Paine, OO and former Housemaster of Crosby, reported missing [in fact he had been killed], 15 more wounded and two more prisoners of war. That made 28 reported deaths during the school year. Deaths of old boys were also reported annually in the School's Commemoration booklets, produced for Speech Day. In the 1915 issue, only 20 Oundelian deaths are reported under the heading 'Roll of Honour.' There was also a list of old boys winning awards, including three Military Crosses and for Lieutenant Colonel Charles Griffith, once of Laxton House back in the 1880s, a Companionship of the Order of St. Michael and St. George.

The actual number of those killed by the beginning of the next school year was actually 42 and as the school year 1914-15 came to an end, Oundelians still at school were aware that the war would not be over soon and that they would be called upon to play their part.

4

Year 2 Away: Before the Somme – September 1915 to June 1916

He would not wait so long. A boy, he spent
His boy's dear life for England. Be content:
No honour of age had been more excellent.

By the start of the new school year in September 1915, 42 Oundelians had already been killed on active service. The war, which some thought would be over by Xmas 1914, had three more Xmases to run. The coming school year (Year 2) would see a further 67 perish for king and empire, and by the end of it, there would still be no end in sight.

The end of Gallipoli

The great and terrible Gallipoli Campaign was no respecter of school years. The last casualty of the summer holidays of 1915 had been Major Noel Money, who was buried in Malta but the doomed campaign would grind on throughout the autumn until an evacuation of all British forces was ordered in January 1916. It is a further sad indictment of this misguided invasion of Turkey by Allied forces that the evacuation was its only success. Before that happened, six more Oundelians would be swallowed up.

Lieutenant Thomas Cook was killed in Gallipoli going to the aid of a British patrol attacked by Turkish forces. Living in Rugby, he naturally came up to Oundle and Laxton House at the age of 15, in September 1902, leaving three years later. After Oundle, he worked first in electrical engineering on the Hastings tramways but later became a partner in the firm of Welch and Horner, drug importers in London. Whist in Hastings, he joined a territorial force attached to the Royal Sussex Regiment and so was called up as early as September 1914. By February 1915, he was in France but returned to England in April to take up a commission in the Essex Regiment. In September 1915, he was sent to Gallipoli with a draft of the 6th Lincolns.

He was killed on 2 October 1915 on Green Knoll, attempting to defend a British patrol which had come

Thomas Cook, Laxton House 1902-05.

under attack from the Turks. The officer in charge of the British patrol was young and inexperienced and Cook volunteered to help out. His Commanding Officer wrote: "He immediately struck me as a very capable and efficient officer, and I appointed him as my adjutant." Like so many others who fell in Gallipoli, Thomas Cook has no known grave and so is commemorated on the Helles Memorial, a great stone obelisk, more than 30 metres high, which was unveiled in 1924. It bears the names of some 21,000 missing men. Thomas Cook was 28 years old at the time of his death and left behind a widow, Lily.

Two days later and not far away, an Oundelian of a less conventional type, **John Henry Wilcock Rhodes** was also killed. He was the third son of Wilcock and Elizabeth Rhodes from Leeds. He came to Dryden House in May 1894, leaving school just three years later. In sport, he was seen as a useful bowler, albeit in the fourth game, while in rugby third game he was criticised in the school magazine for being too interested in the social side of the game!

In 1901 he went out to the Empire, to Australia and became a farmer in the Melbourne area. John Rhodes seems to have been a fairly colourful character. In August 1904, as a farm labourer in New Zealand, he was acquitted of a charge of arson against the property of a local blacksmith and when he joined the Australian Imperial Army in February 1915, he admitted a conviction for drunkenness. He sailed from Melbourne on 10 May 1915 on the *Ulysses* and was sent to Gallipoli. He died of wounds there, aged 34 and is remembered on the Lone Pine Memorial, along with nearly 6,000 other Australians and New Zealanders who have no known grave.

Two weeks later, **Douglas Howard Wilson Greenway**, also once of Laxton House, became another victim of the Dardanelles disaster. A Birmingham boy, he was in Oundle for just one year leaving in July 1907, aged 15. By August 1914, he was Secretary to Gaskell and Chambers Ltd., manufacturers in Birmingham. This company had taken over the Greenway's family firm in 1902. As soon as war broke out, Douglas joined the Royal Warwickshire Regiment but in February 1915, he gained a commission as a second lieutenant in the 13th Worcestershire Regiment and went out to Gallipoli in September. He was killed on 17 October 1915 when bringing in wounded men. The regimental history records his death in the following way:

On hearing the fate of the covering party, 2nd Lieutenant D A W Greenway immediately went out with two men and in two journeys succeeded in bringing in the NCO and one man of the covering party, although it was necessary to crawl under three separate wire entanglements in order to reach the wounded men. He made a third journey and had just reached the last wounded man when he was shot through the heart and thigh, death ensuing instantaneously....It was now too late to fetch in 2nd Lieutenant Greenway.

An officer who witnessed the scene later commented: "For a piece of unselfish gallantry, it will be a long time before Greenway's deed is surpassed." A stone plaque in Azmak Cemetery near Suvla Bay records that Douglas Greenway, aged 24, was probably buried there after his death. The plaque bears the inscription:

Douglas Howard Wilson Greenway, Laxton House 1906-07.

Their Glory Shall Not Be Blotted Out.

Five days after Greenway's death, the School's Bandmaster died of sickness in Alexandria. **Regimental Sergeant-Major Charles Clayson** was for many years bandmaster of the OTC and instructor in wind instruments. He left for the Dardanelles with the Northamptonshire Regiment and died of some unidentified illness in hospital in Alexandria on 22 October 1915. The school magazine recorded that Clayson was "the most painstaking and enthusiastic instructor, and thanks to him we were furnished with no less than three bands – brass, fifes, and bugles with drums – greatly to the benefit of our marching and the envy of other schools."

RSM Charles Clayson leading the School Drum and Bugle Band past the Cloisters in 1906.

RSM Charles Clayson, School Bandmaster.

Twelve days later died **Joseph Hugh Turner Brocklebank**. Unlike Charles Clayson, the School Bandmaster, he did not even reach Gallipoli. He perished on the troopship HMS *Mercian* in the Mediterranean. The ship was heading for Gallipoli with 500 troopers of the Lincolnshire Yeomanry aboard. Not far from Gibraltar, on the afternoon of 3 November 1915, the *Mercian* was apparently shelled by a German U-boat [U-38] which had run out of torpedoes. The troop-ship, in fact a converted cargo ship, had no guns but it survived when the U-boat suddenly dived and disappeared. However, 23 men including Joseph Brocklebank were killed in the attack. The *Laxtonian* wrongly claimed that Brocklebank had drowned, assuming that this must have been his fate, since he died at sea. In fact he and the other victims were taken to North Africa and buried in the Algerian port of Oran.

He was the only son of a farmer, another Joseph Brocklebank, and lived in the Lincolnshire village of Carlton-Le-Moorland, not far from Newark. He was born there on 3 March 1891 and came up to Grafton House in May 1906, leaving a year later at the age of 16. In the Fourth Form he won a workshops prize. At the outbreak of war, he joined the Lincolnshire Yeomanry and in October 1915, they set sail for the Middle East. Ironically, his name is inscribed on the Helles Memorial in Gallipoli, even though he never fought there. He was 24 years old.

Even younger, at 23, was **Hugh James Pearson Hopkinson**. He was born in Devon and came to Sidney House in 1906, leaving three years later. He was keen on games and played for the Cricket XI in his last year. He once recorded figures of 7 for 7 in a house match against Dryden! After leaving school, he was articled to his father, who was Chief Engineer in building the Hull Joint Dock, which was completed in 1914. While there, Hugh Hopkinson played for the Hull and East Riding Football Team and in 1909, the Laxtonian reported that he was "often to be seen with a very black face driving locos on the Hull and Barnsley main line."

At the outbreak of war, he joined the Royal Engineers and in 1915 was sent out to Gallipoli. On the night of 5 November, he was superintending the laying of wire entanglements in front of the trenches and was shot while bandaging a wounded man. He died on the way to the dressing station. He is now buried in Hill 10 Cemetery south-west of Azmak, close to where he fell.

By December 1915, the British had decided to abandon the Gallipoli peninsula. All the hopes of an easy knock-out blow against the Turks and the occupation of Constantinople had evaporated under the glare of the Turkish sun, leaving thousands of dead and wounded to pay the price. Perhaps 60,000 Allied troops from France, Australia, New Zealand, India and Newfoundland, as well as Britain were killed or died of disease and twice as many were wounded.

The decision to abandon the ill-fated campaign meant a massive evacuation of the remaining troops without alerting the Turks to what was happening. Ironically this evacu-

Joseph Hugh Turner Brocklebank, Grafton House 1906-07.

Hugh James Pearson Hopkinson, Sidney House 1906-09.

ation was the most successful part of the whole sorry saga. William Angus, once of School House and now a captain in the Medical Corps, found that he was tasked with helping out with the master plan: "From 14 December [1915] we got very busy not so much dealing with the sick as preparing for the last phase: preparing on the one hand for the unlikely event of ourselves receiving orders to clear out; and on the other hand for holding on with say 500 wounded under a Turkish guard." Things went awry just before Xmas when one of the stores depots caught fire! "Kerosene, jam and bully beef had caught fire about 300 yards from my dug-out. The fire was enormous, and the smoke drifted right over our trenches." The fire of course alerted the Turks and led to shelling which jeopardised the evacuation: "The Turks were evidently worried for they began a bombardment. And now, for the first time, they put some shells in such positions that, if they had kept up a steady fire, the evacuation would have been impossible." Despite this, all was well and William Angus witnessed the successful evacuation of some 21,000 men: "We never heard an unusual sound...

and there, between me and the moonlit sea was a constant stream, single file, as silent as possible – straight onto the pier and out to a motor lighter." A few days later, Angus himself and his men were evacuated to Mudros, on the Greek island of Lemnos, in an operation which went so smoothly that he described it in his diary as "a great anti-climax."

Despite the success of the evacuation from Gallipoli, British soldiers were still dying of wounds received there. Such was Oundelian **John Broadwood Atkinson**, who died of wounds in Alexandria, Egypt on Xmas Eve 1915. He was a Grafton boy from Portadown in Ireland, born in Summer Island House in the village of Loughgall on 1 October 1894 but he lost his mother when he was only 2 years old. He arrived in Oundle in 1909 and left at the end of the Lent Term in 1913. He was a keen member of the OTC, being Section Commander for his House. He also sang bass in the Chapel Choir and took singing lessons. He was a member of the army class and in his last year, 1913, a prefect in Mr Norbury's Grafton.

At the outbreak of war, he joined the Royal Irish Fusiliers and was sent with them to

John Broadwood Atkinson, Grafton House 1909-13.

Gallipoli. He was wounded in the landing at Suvla Bay on 6 August 1915 and was moved to Alexandria in Egypt. There, enteric fever took hold and he died that Christmas Eve 1915, aged just 21. He was buried in the Chatby Military and War Memorial Cemetery in Alexandria. Although wounded back in August, he was the last Oundelian to die as a result of the ill-conceived and totally disastrous Gallipoli campaign.

Loos, September and October 1915

In the autumn of 1915, another name entered the consciousness of Oundelians, that of the mining village of Loos in Northern France. This small, non-descript, even ugly village was the setting for a major battle on the Western Front unleashed by British commanders John French and Douglas Haig. Once again, Loos, like Gallipoli, became associated with military incompetence and huge casualty lists. While the long months of the Gallipoli Campaign cost 14 Oundle lives, Loos saw the deaths of 12 old boys in just 18 days. Five of these were killed on the same day, Wednesday 13

October 1915, which would equal the Oundle losses on Saturday 1 July 1916, the first day of the Somme. They would be the two worst days of the entire war for the Oundle Schools.

The Battle of Loos, where Rudyerd Kipling's only son, Jack was killed, has been over-shadowed by greater and more famous battles yet to come but it deserves to be better known. In all its particulars, the battle demonstrated clearly that great frontal assaults by infantry across no man's land had no chance of success against a German army which had deliberately dug in to defend the territory taken in the West, so that it could focus its energies on the Russian hordes in the East. A year into the war, the Germans had strengthened and deepened their defences, including deep dug-outs and concrete and steel fortifications bristling with machine guns. And in the rear there was a mass of heavy artillery. The slaughter of British troops that then unfolded at Loos would happen again and on a much greater scale at Arras, the Somme and Passchendaele. The British aptitude for heroic failure was set.

Two Oundelians were killed in the first attack on 25 September 1915. **Douglas William Armitage** was the youngest of four brothers who all achieved great things at Oundle. His brother Charles, classical scholar at Pembroke College, Cambridge, described as a man of "wide literary sympathies and conversational powers" died of pneumonia in 1913, aged 25. The remaining three Armitage brothers were all killed in the war. One can scarcely imagine the impact on the boys' parents as all four of their sons, all such accomplished and remarkable young men, died in the space of six years.

In his last year, Douglas Armitage was Head of School as well as Captain of Rugby and of Fives. Of the 1st XV rugby team, which he captained in 1911, all but one joined up and six would be killed. From Oundle, he went to Pembroke College, Cambridge, like two of his elder brothers, with an exhibition in classics. His Christian faith was clearly important to him. In his second year, he won the College Divinity and Reading prizes and was secretary of the College Mission.

The XV of 1911 captained by Douglas Armitage. Six members of the team were killed in the War.
Eric Yarrow [standing left], Robert Bragg [standing 5th from left], James Dixon [standing 6th from left],
Edward MacBryan [seated 2nd from left], Douglas Armitage [seated centre] and Thomas Warner [seated
4th from left].

At the outbreak of war, he joined the Public Schools Brigade and after six months was gazetted as a second lieutenant in the Royal Sussex Regiment. Early in September 1915, he was sent to France and was appointed reserve machine gun officer. After three weeks of operations on the Front Line, he led his men, over the top, on the first day of the disastrous Battle of Loos. Last seen fighting with his fists on 25 September 1915, he was never heard of again and his body was never recovered. His name is inscribed on the Loos Memorial in France with the names of over 20,000 officers and men lost in the slaughter. Douglas William Armitage was 22 years old at the time of his death.

One year younger than Douglas Armitage and the second Oundle boy killed on the first day of the battle was **Russell Simmons**. Born in London in February 1895, he came up to Oundle – Dryden House – in September 1909. In the summer of 1912, he posed for the photograph of the Dryden House platoon. He left Oundle a year later, and won a commission in the 3rd Battalion of the Royal Berkshire Regiment but was fatefully transferred to the 2nd Battalion and so sent to Loos. Like Douglas Armitage, he was killed on the first day of the battle whilst taking part in an attack launched from positions near Bois Grenier against strong German fortifications. His battalion suffered heavy losses that day. Russell Simmons, aged 20, was one of eight officers killed and five more officers were wounded. Thirty-two other ranks were killed, 143 reported missing and 216 wounded. In the face of these terrible losses, Russell Simmons' battalion was withdrawn into billets near Fleurbaix the next day. Like Douglas Armitage, Russell Harry Louis Simmons has no known grave.

The great attack on the first day of the battle cost the British 8,500 men killed, the worst day of the war so far. It was a classic case of what Winston Churchill later called, "fighting machine gun bullets with the breasts of gallant men." The British troops were advancing against heavily fortified German positions including the fearsome

Douglas William Armitage, Laxton House 1906-12.

Russell Harry Louis Simmons, Dryden House 1909-13.

Hohenzollern Redoubt, one of the strongest points in the German line. The British use of chlorine gas had failed to bring any serious advantage, indeed some 2,500 British troops had to be withdrawn from the attack when the wind changed direction. Although the village of Loos was taken, the Germans quickly moved in reinforcements so that when the British attacked again the next day, they were ready. At 11 in the morning, on 26 September, this second British attack was launched in broad daylight and without a preliminary artillery bombardment. Once again the men were mown down by machine gun bullets. The diary of one German regiment facing the advancing troops recorded a massacre:

> Ten columns of extended line could clearly be distinguished, each one estimated at more than a thousand men, and offering such a target as had not been seen before, or even thought possible. Never had machine-gunners such straightforward work to do…The men stood on the fire-steps, some even on the parapets, and fired triumphantly into the mass of men advancing across the open grass-land…the effect was devastating and they could be seen falling literally in hundreds.

In this second attack, Haig made his first use of Kitchener's Army, the volunteers who had flocked to the colours in the autumn of 1914. Amongst the attackers were battalions from the Northamptonshire Regiment with their compliment of Laxton School boys. Here was **Joseph Baxter** from Kettering in action for the first time. He spent four years at Laxton School, leaving in 1911. At the outbreak of war, he joined his local regiment where he was a lance-sergeant. He was killed as the troops advanced against impossible odds. His body was never recovered and his name is inscribed on the Loos Memorial. His name is also recorded with some 800 others on the Kettering War Memorial and on a stone plaque inside the Kettering Church Institute. He was 20 years old at the time of his death.

Also in the Northamptonshire Regiment at Loos was Baxter's school friend and exact contemporary, **Ezra Howard Carter**. The son of Ezra and Fanny Carter, who lived in Lilford, a few miles from Oundle, he left Laxton School in April 1909 at the age of 15 and became an apprentice, probably working on Lord Lilford's estate alongside his father. He joined the Northants. Regiment, like Joseph Baxter, in the autumn of 1914 and was killed a year later on 27 September 1915, the day after his school friend. Like Joseph Baxter, Ezra Carter, aged 21, has no known grave and is commemorated on the Loos Memorial. He is also remembered on the Achurch War Memorial, close to Lilford, alongside nine other local men, from these two tiny villages, killed in the war.

Just 4 days after Ezra Carter's death, a third Laxton School boy was killed in action. **William Edwin Hartley** lived in Alwalton, near Peterborough and left school in July 1905 at the age of 17. From there he went to London University and by 1911, still in London, he was a clerk with a firm of solicitors called Michael Abrahams and Co. He joined up in August 1914 with the 28th Battalion of the County of London Regiment also known as the Artists' Rifles and he served in France for a whole year, from October 1914 until his death in October 1915. In August 1915, he was gazetted as a second lieutenant in the Cheshire Regiment and he was killed, aged

William Hartley, Laxton School 1899-1905.

27, near the Hohenzollern Redoubt on the seventh day of the slaughter at Loos. He too has no known grave and, like his fellows from Laxton School, is commemorated on the Loos Memorial. His name is also inscribed on the Peterborough War Memorial.

Lawrence Collier Hatch and **Colin Holt Hooper** were exact contemporaries at Oundle and died one day apart at Loos. Lawrence Hatch was the second son of a doctor from Wimbledon. He was born in Johannesburg in November 1893 and came to School House in January 1907, staying until July 1911. After Oundle, he went up to Pembroke College, Cambridge and, at the outbreak of the war, obtained a commission in the Durham Light Infantry and was sent to France in September 1915, holding the rank of lieutenant. He was killed just a week after his arrival on 27 September 1915 on the third day of the battle, aged just 21.

The regimental history of the Durham Light Infantry commented on the advance made on the day he died:

Lawrence Collier Hatch, School House 1907-11.

> It was intended to launch another attack, but before 2pm came a spontaneous advance, in which the survivors of the Durham battalions joined forces with the 64th Brigade. Heavily punished in the flank by shrapnel and machine-gun bullets, and unsupported by the British gunners who had not been warned of the attempt, the infantry had no chance of success.

Lawrence Hatch's elder brother Philip, also a School House boy would be killed a year later, leading his men into action.

Lawrence's exact contemporary at Oundle, **Colin Holt Hooper** entered Dryden House in September 1907, aged 14. After leaving Oundle in 1911, he worked for Messrs. R. G. Shaw and Co. and was to have gone out to Calcutta in October 1914 to further his career. Instead, he joined up as soon as the conflict began and gained a commission with the 20th London Regiment. By March 1915, he was in France. He was severely wounded at the Battle of Loos on 25 September 1915 when leading his men into action. He was part of the same advance which saw the deaths of Douglas Armitage and Russell Simmons. When first hit, he remained with his men but he was then hit a second time by an explosive bullet and was found exhausted in a shell-hole where he was helping two other wounded men. He died of his wounds on 28th September aged 22 and was buried at Le Tréport Military Cemetery northeast of Dieppe. He was posthumously promoted to lieutenant in recognition of his work in the Loos

Colin Holt Hooper, Dryden House 1907-11.

The Dryden Seven in 1910. Standing from left to right: John Hartley, Colin Hooper, Langley Attwood, Guy Bostock, James Ricketts, Clive Burrell and Eric Chalker. All were killed in the War.

sector before the battle and was personally complimented by the Brigadier. The Sergeant of Colin Hooper's platoon wrote to his grieving parents in the currency of the times: "His one thought was always for his men; he could never do enough for us. You must always feel proud of him, he was so brave and fearless, always ready and eager for any dangerous and difficult task."

There is a further sad twist to this particular death. Five years earlier, Colin Hooper and some of his friends in Dryden had posed for a photograph inside the House, which was then made into a printed postcard, so that each boy could have a copy. It would be a keepsake to remind them of their friends and their times in Dryden in the years to come. There are ten boys in the picture, seven are standing and three, in front, are sitting down. Colin Hooper is one of the seven Dryden boys standing up. All seven would be killed in the war.

Even though it had now claimed seven Oundelians, the Battle of Loos was far from finished with OOs. Despite such heavy losses and the failure in the earlier attacks on the German positions, Douglas Haig decided to continue the battle, believing, as he always did, that one more assault might bring a significant breakthrough. On Wednesday 13 October 1915, the attack on the German lines was renewed. This time the advance was again directed at the Hohenzollern Redoubt, the strongest point in the German line. The result was inevitable. There were over 3,600 British casualties that day and the Hohenzollern Redoubt remained in German hands. Oundelians Donald Ewen, Charles Gray, Clive Harvey, Herbert Scorer, and Harold Walton were all killed. They achieved nothing except their own destruction.

Like so many of his generation, a sense of duty inspired **Donald Ewen** to join the Territorials as a reservist. So, in 1913 he became a member of the 14th Battalion of the London Scottish and volunteered for foreign service as soon as war broke out. Within weeks he was in France. He was involved in the First Battle of Ypres in November 1914, where his battalion discovered that their rifles and the magazines issued with them, were incompatible. They had to load each bullet singly, seriously reducing their weight of fire.

By early 1915, Ewen's increasing deafness, probably brought on by shell fire, caused him to be made a stretcher bearer for his company and his disability also prevented him from obtaining a commission. A notable scientist, he then asked to return to his laboratory to take charge of optical glass research, an area of work of increasing importance to the British war effort. A telegram was sent by the War Office, ordering his immediate recall to London, but it arrived the day after his death. At the time of his demise, aged 28, he was helping to bring in a wounded man, close to the German lines.

Donald Ewen was born in Edgbaston in 1887, and entered Sidney House at the age of 14 in 1901. At school, he was prominent on the football field and on the river. Leaving Oundle in 1905, he went up to Birmingham University and studied metallurgy. He gained a B.Sc. degree in 1909 and won the prestigious Wiggins and Bowen Research Studentship. Later he was awarded an M.Sc. and in 1911, he joined the metallurgy department of the National Physical Laboratory in Teddington, Middlesex, where he did valuable research work. Donald Ewen's academic prowess and potential were confirmed when he exhibited specimens illustrating the behaviour of metals at high temperatures at the Royal Society in London.

Donald Ewen, Sidney House 1901-05.

Robert Clive Harvey, always known as Clive, was nine years younger than Donald Ewen, meeting his doom at the age of just 19. He was the third son of Colonel Harvey of Rothley, near Leicester and was born in January 1896. He came to the Berrystead in January 1908 and then moved to Crosby House, which he left in July 1912. He then went to Neuchâtel in Switzerland to study French and gained a diploma there. In 1914, he decided to become a missionary but these plans were thwarted by the outbreak of hostilities. In September of that year, aged 18, he obtained a commission in the Leicestershire Regiment and was sent out to France. A year later, he was promoted to lieutenant and was Brigade Intelligence Officer, at the time of his death.

Robert Clive Harvey, Berrystead and Crosby House 1908-12.

On 13 October 1915, the 1st to 4th Battalions of the Leicestershire Regiment lost 20 officers and 453 men, many of them in the first few minutes of the attack. "I cannot think of any occasion when he failed me," Clive Harvey's Commanding Officer wrote. "He had an absolutely imperturbable coolness under trying conditions, a considerable gift of leadership, and was always thoughtful for his men's welfare. Officers such as he will always be followed." Clive Harvey has no known grave and his name is inscribed on the Loos Memorial, alongside 7 other fellow Oundelians.

Captain Charles Shortland Gray, aged 23, was three years ahead of Clive Harvey in Crosby House. He and his men of the Lincolnshire Regiment, advanced on the Hohenzollern Redoubt without artillery cover, only to find that the German wire was uncut and they were mown down by German artillery and machine-gun fire. His body was picked up a fortnight after the battle, lying at the head of his men. He was buried on the battlefield but now has no known grave and is therefore commemorated on the Loos Memorial. His Colonel wrote of him: "He fell in the charge, at the head of his men. He was a gallant fellow, loved by everyone."

Charles Gray was a Stamford boy, with a younger brother and sister, the son of an iron founder and JP, also called Charles Gray. He came up to New House in May 1906 and transferred to Crosby the next year, leaving in 1909. His brother John Parnwell Gray, also a Crosby boy, would be killed in action in September 1918.

Charles Shortland Gray, New House and Crosby House 1906-09.

"I have lost in Herbert a great personal friend, while the battalion has lost a brave, loyal and devoted officer, respected and liked by everyone." So wrote the Commanding Officer of another Oundle captain in the Lincolnshire Regiment in that fateful advance of 13 October 1915. This was **Herbert Selwyn Scorer**, the eldest son of Mr and Mrs John Norton Scorer of Spilsby in Lincolnshire, where another former resident, John Thimbleby OO, had recently been buried after being killed in a motorcycle accident in St. Albans.

Herbert Scorer was born in Thorney, near Peterborough on 5 December 1885 and attended Barton School in Wisbech until the age of 16. His name is commemorated on a plaque in Wisbech Church, along with 41 other old boys of Barton School who were killed in the fighting. He came up to Laxton at the age of 16 in 1901, where he rowed and played rugby for the House. In 1904, he joined the Volunteers (the 5th Lincolnshire Regiment), took a commission two years later and reached the rank of captain in 1910. He was a good all-round sportsman and was well known in hunting circles. Like the other four Oundelians killed in this futile attack during the

Herbert Selwyn Scorer, Laxton House 1901-03.

Battle of Loos, Herbert Scorer has no known grave and is commemorated on the Loos Memorial. Aged 29, he was the oldest of the Oundelians who fell at Loos.

The fifth fatality of 13 October 1915 near Loos was **Captain Harold Henry Walton**. Like Herbert Scorer, he was a Laxton House boy. He was the second son of Mr and Mrs Edmund Walton of the Manor House, Chilwell, near Nottingham. And Chilwell itself would acquire a tragic reputation in the war. It was the site of National Shell Filling Factory No.6 and on 1 July 1918, an explosion there killed 134 people and injured more than 250 others. It remains the worst death toll from a single explosion in British history.

Harold Walton came up to Oundle in September 1908, five years after Herbert Scorer had left, joining his brother Arthur, where their Housemaster was John King. Harold was a promising and enthusiastic member of the OTC and became a good shot. After leaving Oundle, he was articled to a firm of auctioneers in Nottingham called Walker, Walton and Hanson, where his father was a partner. Before the war, like so many others, he joined a territorial force attached to the

Harold Henry Walton, Laxton House 1908-12.

Notts. and Derby Regiment, always known as the Sherwood Foresters. He was promoted in June 1915 and gazetted to a temporary captaincy shortly before his death.

He was awarded the Military Cross for his actions on the night of 30 July 1915 near Ypres. The London Gazette reported the award on 2 October: "He was heavily bombarded with trench mortars and rifle grenades, several of his men having been killed and buried but by his gallant conduct, he kept his men in hand and held on to his position." Eleven days after the official report of his Military Cross, Harold Walton's war came to an end. Aged 20, he led a doomed bombing party attacking the Hohenzollern Redoubt at Loos. A stone plaque commemorating his sacrifice was erected by his grieving father in Beeston parish church.

Captain Vickers wins a Victoria Cross

The next day at Loos, 14 October 1915, Captain Geoffrey Vickers, also with the Sherwood Foresters, was sent forward to relieve the men who had been fighting with Harold Walton. Though help would come too late for Walton, what happened next won Vickers a Victoria Cross. It was the first of three VCs won by Oundelians during the war. Captain Charles Geoffrey Vickers was ordered forward with a party of 50 men from the Sherwood Foresters to try to re-take part of the Hohenzollern Redoubt. Amidst intense fighting, they advanced at 5:30 a.m. to the furthest forward of the British barricades at the north-west end of the redoubt. With most of his men killed and wounded, Captain Vickers continued to hold the first barricade and then ordered his remaining men to build a second barricade, 30 yards to the rear, effectively cutting him off from support. Attacked from the front and the flank, he held his position, alone, for several hours before being severely wounded when the barricade was blown in. In that time, however, his men had constructed the second barricade which they continued to hold. It was the day after his 21st birthday and his undoubted heroism won him Britain's highest award for gallantry in the field. But it could not win the Hohenzollern Redoubt for the British.

Geoffrey Vickers received his VC from George V at Buckingham Palace in January 1916, whilst still recovering from his wounds and later in the war, he would appear as Gallaher Cigarette Card No.99 in their *Great War Victoria Cross Heroes* series. In the summer of 1918, he was again wounded, was awarded the Belgian Croix de Guerre and was still serving as the war ended.

He was born in 1894 and was a very talented boy. In 1910, aged just 16, he helped Sidney to win the rugby cup, playing alongside the mighty Gulliland twins. He was a forward in the XV of 1912 and played (not very successfully) in the house fives competition. In his last year, he helped Sidney's senior cricket team to reach the final, where they were beaten by School House. In the Sidney team that day, alongside the future Victoria Cross winner, were Duncan Gotch, Gervase Spendlove, Reggy Secretan, Edward MacBryan and Edward Vaughan. None of this Sidney quintet would survive the war.

Geoffrey Vickers was a good classical scholar at Oundle, going on to win an exhibition to Merton College, Oxford in 1913. After leaving Oundle, he spent four months

Charles Geoffrey Vickers, Sidney House 1908-12.

in Germany (January-April 1913) in order to learn the language and played hockey for Bonn! At Oxford his classical studies were interrupted by the war. He joined the university OTC and received his commission in the Sherwood Foresters, going to France in February 1915.

The disasters at Loos led to the sacking of Sir John French as Commander in Chief of British forces in France. He was replaced on 1 January 1916 by the man who had been his second-in-command and was, in many ways, equally responsible for the carnage at Loos – Douglas Haig.

Elsewhere on the Front

But while Oundelians suffered and died at Loos, further north, John Russell was finding trench life apparently quite congenial. He noted that "In the south, there was quite a big attack [Loos], which is still going on fairly successfully," a comment which is consistent with British propaganda and his own apparently optimistic approach to British warfare. His diary entries from August and September 1915 remind us that in many parts of the Front Line there was often relatively little fighting. Aged just 19, here is a boy with a real sense of humour, untarnished by the more awful sights and sounds of the trench warfare close by:

> We have a little stream that runs through our trenches. Saw some little fish which may be trout. A trout stream would be a good advertisement for a trench. After 6pm the rats always begin to come out...I got my sights on a little path they always seem to cross and soon saw a rat's head appear. I got him clean through the nose...This is certainly a most desirable trench, private fishing and shooting within a second's walk from HQ.

Two days later, life was even less hectic: "had lunch, dozed, tea, and finished censoring letters." Then he had time for picking fruit: "Met Capt. Wannell coming down the side of a hedge with Sgt. Riles picking blackberries. We set to work ourselves and found them really luscious." But by early September, there is a hint that the war is not their favourite occupation. Reporting on lunch with Doggy, Giles and Ferguson, he says that "we all determined that we would not mind if the war was over tomorrow." Nonetheless they also agreed that the war "was infinitely better than training at Bovington." Three days later, young Russell met up with another Oundelian: "Forgot to say I met Marsden [Cyril Marsden, School House 1899-1907] of the Manchesters, an old School House boy who knew most of the people who were seniors in my day. Spent an hour talking about Oundle, and decided we would rather be back there than in the trenches."

And of course, there was always time for a spot of footer. On 16 September 1915, John Russell reported on the sporting side of life behind the lines: "Blew the good old Footer 'pill' up and punted about a bit. After supper I went to see D Company officers and fixed up a Rugger match with Doggy for 9.30 next morning." There followed a Rugger match against B Company and a Soccer match with A Company. Russell's C Company lost both games but it all sounded rather like impromptu House matches at Oundle! His next letter home reinforces the importance of sport in the trenches. He tells his mother to "Keep happy" and to send "sports clothes, rugger ball, boxing gloves, some decent mouth organs and 1d. [penny] whistles." What with the Adjutant's lecture on the importance of 'keeping cheerful', life in his sector of the trenches was not so bad after all. Even the wounded, it seemed, were happy: "After lunch off tinned lobster and potted meat, I walked along to see Simpson, who has re-joined after a pleasant fortnight in hospital by the sea." And at cards, Russell played for money but all the winnings were to be paid "the day we enter Berlin." Even so, the relaxed atmosphere was sometimes punctuated by sudden death: "At 5pm I was woken by Sgt. Green, who told me the awful news that Walker had been killed looking over the parapet. It knocked us all over pretty much."

Meanwhile not far away, Reggy Secretan's main worry in early November 1915, was when he would get a new car. By the 18th of the month, it had arrived and he reported that he usually went out about 6.30pm with car and dispatch rider, "do the rounds and get back any time between mid-night and 3am." Now based in the village of Aire, he was billeted in an old French military bake-house which he and his friends had made comfortable enough: "We have a large room upstairs where we sleep. We all have beds and a large stove, and plenty of blankets. We have made cupboards out of old packing cases, so you can see that it is a second home to us." In addition to these homely comforts, "there is a BEF Canteen not far from here where everything is cheap. We have awfully good meals."

After Loos – December 1915 to June 1916

On the Western Front

Elsewhere on the Western Front, others enjoyed a rather different fate. Standing on the left in the famous postcard taken in Dryden House in 1910 was **John Hartley**. He was born in Halifax, Yorkshire in 1893, the only son of a lieutenant colonel. After private school in Hunstanton, he came up to Dryden in 1908 for the Sixth Form staying until 1910. With his keen interest in science, no doubt nurtured by his Oundle experience, he then worked in the manufacture of boilers back in Halifax. He joined the Halifax Territorials before the war, where his father was the commander. At the outbreak of war, in August 1914, he joined the 4th Battalion of the Duke of Wellington's (West Riding) Regiment and was sent to France on 17 June 1915. He was killed, aged 22, by gas poisoning at Boezinge, near Ypres on 19 December that year.

Also standing in that Dryden photograph of 1910 was **Guy Edwin Bostock**, who, coincidentally, would be the next Oundelian to perish. The second of three brothers who served in the war, his brothers were both twice wounded but survived. Guy Bostock was not so fortunate. He left Dryden in July 1913 after a glittering school career. He won a maths prize in first year and a drawing prize in his second. He helped Dryden to triumph in house rugby in 1911 playing in the front row. As an oarsman, he was described as having lots of potential. "He has a good swing and works well but is very clumsy," opined the Laxtonian magazine, with its usual no-nonsense approach. He became Head of House, Captain of Boating and won a scholarship to Emmanuel College, Cambridge. There he rowed in the University Trial VIIIs.

John Armitage Hartley, Dryden House 1908-10.

His Cambridge career, so full of promise, lasted just one year and he gained a commission in the Royal Munster Fusiliers as a lieutenant in September 1914, being promoted to captain in October 1915. He was killed at Loos on January 30 1916, aged 22, having been in France just 6 weeks and was buried at Mazingarbe. His Commanding Officer wrote: "We deplore the loss of a gallant soldier, a good friend, and a very honourable gentleman."

And while the Battle of Loos, was long over, that region of the Front claimed yet another Oundelian in the spring of 1916. Very little is known about **Paul Bond** once of Laxton House. He was at Oundle for just over a year from May 1887 until July 1888 and was a Somerset boy. He was born on 6 May 1871 and was killed at 44 years of age, making him the one of the oldest of Old Oundelians to be killed in the conflict. He was a private in the 24th Battalion of the Royal Fusiliers and was killed in Northern France, not far from Loos, on 30 April 1916. He lies buried in the Tranchée de Mecknes Cemetery near the village of Aix-Noulette. The cemetery was named after the home town of French Moroccan troops who first occupied trenches there in 1914 – a reminder of the global reach of the conflict.

Guy Edwin Bostock, Dryden House 1909-13.

It was also in the spring of 1916 that the region of the Somme claimed its first Oundelian. This area of Northern France had been occupied by French forces at the start of the war but had now been selected by the French and British commanders as the setting for the most massive allied offensive of the war. All through the spring of 1916, British soldiers were arriving in their thousands to prepare for 'the Big Push'. The schoolmaster, **Cecil Hoyle Broadbent** an old School House boy was amongst them. He came from Rochdale and arrived at Oundle in 1895. He became a school prefect in his last year and was a member of the XV and the XI. He was elected to a senior scholarship at Oundle in 1898 and confirmed his ability by winning six prizes on Speech Day 1900. Amongst these were a share of the Taylor Exhibition and the Headmaster's prizes for Greek and Latin prose. Naturally enough, he won a major scholarship to Trinity College, Cambridge.

In his first year there, he was reported as "running over inoffensive old ladies and otherwise amusing himself!" Nonetheless, he clearly applied himself to

Cecil Hoyle Broadbent, School House 1895-1900.

his studies, winning college prizes and obtaining a first in the classical tripos in 1903. One of the very few Old Oundelians to opt for a career in teaching, Cecil Broadbent was appointed to the staff of Bradford Grammar School in 1906 after a three year stint at Christ's Brecon. In November 1915, he obtained a commission in the School's new OTC and nine months later took a commission with the Yorkshire Light Infantry. He was sent to France and by February 1916 was in charge of the Brigade Bombing School in Albert, behind the lines. He wrote to his friends at Bradford

saying that he felt "somewhat safer" there. In this he deceived himself. Aged 34, he was accidentally killed when a bomb exploded prematurely while he was acting as instructor on 1 March 1916.

His Commanding Officer, Major Moorhouse wrote to his grieving widowed mother in these terms: "He was a most capable officer and had endeared himself to everyone. No loss yet sustained by the battalion – and we have had many – will be as difficult to repair."

Cecil Lewis arrives on the Somme

It was also in the spring of 1916, that another School House boy, Cecil Lewis also arrived on the Somme. Last seen a year ago, eating a last breakfast with Beans, he was now a fully trained pilot. Though he would survive the war, his account of an airman's experiences over the lines, in the build up to the great Somme Offensive, reminds us of the huge psychological impact of the war on young airmen. Friends

Cecil Arthur Lewis, School House 1912-15.

Cecil Lewis'
school report,
Lent 1914.

Oundle School.

SCIENCE AND ENGINEERING SIDE.

Name _Lewis C A_   Age _16_   Average age of Form _17.3_

REPORT FOR THE LENT TERM, 1914.

Form _Sc VI A₂_   No. in Form _21_

Form Work :	Order in Form.			
	Term.	Exam-ination.	Final Order.	
Divinity				
Mechanics ...	12	10=	13	Has worked satisfactorily + made some progress.
Physics	16	2	5	
Chemistry ...	7	10	9	A good term's work.
English	4	8	4	Very good - a keen and intelligent worker.
History				
Geography ...				
Drawing	1	3	2.	Excellent work: drawn very neatly.
Workshops ...				Good.
Final Form Order ...	7	3	5	

Class :	Order in Class.			
	Class & No in Class.	Term.	Exam-ination.	Final Order.
Mathematics ...	Sc II₁ 35/3	10	8	8	Moderate. Might do better.
French ...	Fr 7c 60	1	6	4	Has done good work & made good progress.
German				
Music				

Prize or other distinction

Conduct in School   Good

Boarding-house Report   Good

A good report —   Except in Mathematics.

J. W. Sanderson Headmaster.

Next term begins on **FRIDAY, the 1st day of MAY, 1914.** Boarders are to be at their Houses by 8 p.m. on the evening of that day. All boys must present themselves punctually at the time named, unless written permission to be absent has been obtained previously from the Headmaster.

and mess-mates would go out on patrol and not return. Lewis felt that it was only a matter of time until his turn came.

Cecil Lewis' first main job in the Somme sector was aerial reconnaissance of the German second-line trenches, in preparation for the great offensive to come. As he explained, however, his plane – the BE 2c – "was completely unsuited for active service." As it was a bi-plane, the field of view for both pilot and observer, especially the observer, was hopelessly restricted by the position of the wings relative to the position of the two occupants. The observer found it hard to observe. This meant that the camera to take the all-important pictures of the German lines, had to be strapped to the side of the fuselage and operated by the pilot! And while taking the pictures, the pilot had also to dodge 'Archie' (anti-aircraft fire) and machine-guns on the ground, and German Fokkers in the air. And when an attack was on, or even when there was no attack on, there was also the small matter of dodging shells both German and British.

In the midst of his first reconnaissance mission, Lewis came under fire from 'Archie'. He survived that but still had two more photographs to take. Preparing to take the last exposure, there was another problem when he was suddenly attacked by a German Fokker. So began Cecil Lewis' first dog-fight with the odds apparently stacked against the two British lads in their bi-plane – their gun jammed and the windscreen in front of Lewis' face was hit by a bullet. Somehow pilot and observer survived to fight another day.

Ypres 1916

While preparations began apace in the Somme area, the more familiar name of Ypres continued to claim more victims. The first Oundelian to be killed there in 1916 was **Edward Reginald Spofforth**. Like the school master Cecil Broadbent and the airman Cecil Lewis, he was also from School House. He joined the 5th Yorkshire Regiment and arrived in France in April 1915. Within a week he was fighting in the Second Battle of Ypres but then came down with scarlet fever and was invalided home for a month, stationed at the regimental depot in Scarborough. He returned to the Front Line in January 1916 and was mortally wounded, aged 25, by a trench mortar shell on 2 March 1916, dying in an hour. His Commanding Officer wrote to his grieving widowed mother: "Your boy was such a keen soldier that we shall find the gap he leaves in the regiment difficult to fill. The gap he leaves in our hearts will be impossible to fill."

Two years younger than Edward Spofforth, **Douglas William McMichael** was the next Oundelian to perish near Ypres. He was described by his Commanding Officer thus: "He was one of the best officers I have come across – always cool, confident and self-

Edward Reginald Spofforth, School House 1906-08.

reliant, and absolutely devoid of fear. I had intended to give him command of the next vacant company. He was a great favourite with all ranks, and leaves a gap which cannot be filled."

An Oundle boy from birth, Douglas McMichael was the only one of the fallen to be counted as being a pupil at both Laxton and Oundle Schools. His name appears on the Laxton School memorial plaque in the Laxton Long Room and also on the marble tablets in the Oundle School Chapel. Actually he was a Laxton School boy throughout his school career but in the Sixth Form, because of his academic prowess, he was allowed to attend lessons at Oundle School.

In 1912, he won a scholarship in natural sciences to Clare College, Cambridge where he rowed for his college in 1913 and 1914 but left at the outbreak of war to join the Public Schools Battalion. Later he was gazetted second lieutenant in the Bedfordshire Regiment. He survived the Battle of Loos in the autumn of 1915, where his battalion had their first taste of action, despite the fact that they had marched fifty miles in the previous four days to get there. He was killed by shell-fire near Ypres in April 1916 when his regiment were on the receiving end of a day long barrage from the

Germans. Promoted to the rank of lieutenant shortly before his death, Douglas McMichael was laid to rest in Essex Farm Cemetery north of Ypres where fellow Oundelian, Eric Yarrow, killed in May 1915, was also buried. On his gravestone are inscribed the words, "we grudge not our life if it give larger life unto them that live." Douglas McMichael was just 23 years old at the time of his death.

Four days after McMichael's death, and just 30 miles to the west, another Oundelian, Reggy Secretan, was still enjoying life behind the lines: "The weather is still glorious and we are bathing every day in the river. I am in the workshops here [just like Oundle] and am having a good time and jolly good experience, as we are always working on our lorries." Three days later, he told his mother about his favourite meal:

Douglas William McMichael, Laxton School 1902-12.

> Sergt. Walker and I are settled in the back room of our pet café here writing letters, whilst *madame* is cooking us a couple of pork chops, onions, apple sauce and fried chips, a splendid dish! We often come in here for a little supper, the people are so nice to us, the only drawback is that we have to embrace 'mother' on both cheeks before we go, a terrible proceeding, we always dread it.

Less fortunate than Reggy Secretan was **John Christopher Hebblethwaite** a Yorkshire boy, who was killed in June 1916 near Ypres. He came up to Grafton House in May 1911 and was a reasonable sportsman, representing Grafton in rugby, rowing and shooting. Leaving school in July 1914, aged 18, his war started with him helping to find horses for the army but as soon as he was able, he enlisted in the Yorkshire Hussars, and in October 1914 obtained a commission in the Royal Field Artillery. After nearly a year's training, he was sent to Flanders and the Ypres salient.

On 22 June 1916, he was killed by a chance shell which also mortally wounded another officer. "In all his work," wrote his Commanding Officer, "he was in every way a first class subaltern. Besides which, we all liked him so very much for himself." On his headstone, his father, echoing no doubt the feelings of many another parent, inscribed some words from a poem by John Drinkwater, printed in

John Christopher Hebblethwaite, Grafton House 1911-14.

the Laxtonian in December 1916 – *"A boy, he spent his boy's dear life for England."* Aged 20, John Hebblethwaite was buried in the military cemetery at Vlamertinghe, three miles west of Wipers.

Neuve Chapelle again

Like Ypres, the village of Neuve Chapelle in northern France continued to be the scene of Oundle deaths in the spring of 1916. Second Lieutenant **John Young Alexander Line** was born in 1895 and came to Laxton House in January 1910. He played cricket for the XI in the summer of 1914 and won an exhibition in history to Downing College, Cambridge, where his father had also been an undergraduate. He played rugby and rowed for his college but towards the end of his first term, he joined up, taking a commission with his local North Staffordshire Regiment. He arrived in France in July 1915 and died on 13 March 1916, of wounds received the previous day. He was hit by a sniper, near the old battle site of Neuve Chapelle, where 12 Oundelians had been killed the previous year. His last action was to supervise a 'work party' which was draining a trench. He was the first of thirty-five undergraduates from Downing College to be killed in the war and was just 20 years old.

John Young Alexander Line, Laxton House 1910-14.

John Line was an only child and his grieving parents erected a memorial window in the church in Stone, where John's father had been the vicar and where his son was born. In the top left of the window are the arms and motto of Oundle School, a tribute to the debt his parents felt they owed to Sanderson, his staff and the boys of their son's *alma mater*.

Also falling at Neuve Chapelle was **Alexander Basil Crawford**, who was 23 when the war broke out. His Battalion Commander wrote that he was "a most able Company Commander, a most gallant man, full of dash and pluck, and would have risen high in the Army." His Divisional Commander was similarly unstinting in his praise: "Your boy was doing splendidly and was, if anything, too brave. He is a great loss to his Regiment…I wish we had more like him."

Originally, Alex Crawford had joined the 5th Lincolns but early in 1915, he won a

Alexander Basil Crawford, Laxton House 1903-08.

commission in the Sherwood Foresters, later transferring to the 17th West Yorkshire Battalion and promoted captain. He was killed in action near Neuve Chapelle in France on 10 May 1916 and was buried in the village of Richebourg L'Avoue. He was 24 years old at the time of his death.

Alex Crawford was at Laxton House from 1903-1908 and was an excellent sportsman. He was a school prefect and Captain of the XV in his last year, though the team did not enjoy a successful season under his stewardship: "Crawford…has been a most painstaking captain…but hardly fulfilled the promise of last year. He deserves all sympathy for the unavoidable disasters [injuries] which befell his team." Crawford was an equally good cricketer, playing for the XI for three seasons, useful with bat and ball. The Laxtonian conceded that he was "A batsman possessed of fine hitting powers" but as usual added a caveat: "He must learn, however, to play himself in more carefully when he first goes into bat." Chosen as Captain of the XI for the 1909 season, he left Oundle before he could take up this position. He then studied law and qualified as a solicitor in 1914 and took charge of a legal practice in Boston, Lincolnshire. His career was ready for take-off but, as with so many others, it had to be put on hold when the war came.

And still Neuve Chapelle had two more Oundelians to claim. **Captain Leonard Sheldon Kench**, once of Dryden House, died on 29 June 1916. Six days earlier, he had been seriously wounded by a hand-grenade whilst out in front of the trenches, leading a working party. A native of Warwick, he joined the Territorials before the war and took a commission in the Royal Warwickshire Regiment, being promoted captain soon after the war started. He reached France early in 1916.

At Oundle, he was in Dryden House from 1902 until 1906. He was keen on the OTC and a good shot, being a leading member of one of the first Oundle shooting teams to be sent to Bisley. There, he and his chum and fellow Drydonian, Hugh Dawson were the best shots for Oundle. Leonard Kench married in 1912 and was 27 years old at the time of his death.

Leonard Sheldon Kench, Dryden House 1902-06.

The very next day, in the same sector of the Front, **George Fenchelle**, a New House boy was also killed. George was the second son of Dr. Fenchelle of Piazza di Spagna in Rome. He was born there, close to the house where the poet Keats had died, and came up to Oundle and New House in 1908, aged 13. For reasons unknown, (and possibly hard to comprehend) he left just two years later and went off to Gresham's. In his last year, he won a prize for French and was on the losing side in the junior house cricket final, where New House were beaten by Grafton. Also in the New House team that day were the future Head of School, Frederick Milholland, together with Justin Willis, James Riley, Audley Lee and Clarence Lyon-Hall. All would perish in the war. Six members of that particular house XI lost their lives in the conflict. The victorious Grafton team that day won the match by a comfortable eight wickets and they did slightly better in the war, losing only five of their number.

George Fenchelle spent his sixth-form years at Gresham's in Norfolk where he was a school prefect, actor and Captain of the XV in 1913. Before the war, he travelled to St. Petersburg to acquire 'work experience' in a business house there. He gained a commission in the Royal Sussex Regiment in November 1914 and died of wounds as a prisoner of war on 30 June 1916 not far from Neuve Chapelle. A fellow soldier later recalled that Lieutenant Fenchelle was leading an advance at 3:30a.m.: "We reached the German front-line trenches and then I saw the lieutenant hit, and fall. I didn't see him again." As he died a PoW, the German government later contacted the War Office to say that they had his effects. All that was actually sent back to Britain however was his identity disc. He was later reburied in the British cemetery of Cabaret Rouge near the village of Souchez.

Geoffrey Donaldson at Neuve Chapelle

Amidst these tragic events at 'New Chapel', Geoffrey Donaldson, like George Fenchelle, a New House boy, was just getting used to life in the trenches in the same theatre of war. Last seen trying not to embarrass an officer who had forgotten to adjust his sights at the shooting range, young Geoffrey by late May 1916 had been sent to France with the Royal Warwickshire Regiment. Before they left, they were seen off by the King and Geoffrey noted the great event in his diary: "We were 'dressed' at 11.15 and at

George John Fenchelle, New House 1908-10.

11.45 the cavalcade appeared in the distance and the Royal Standard fluttered out at the saluting base. The King was attended by Lord French and Sir Henry Selake. The whole show was over by one." As the men unburdened themselves of their heavy packs, one was heard to remark, "If the King and the b...Kaiser had to carry what we have to, the war'd have been over long ago."

Geoffrey and his men sailed on the *Aquitaine*, just back from Gallipoli where it had been a hospital ship and landed at Le Havre on 23 May 1916. The rank and file were not allowed out of camp but officers like Geoffrey were granted a few hours to explore the town. He noted later that the docks were very dusty, that there were German prisoners working there and that there were "an extraordinary number of women in mourning." Two days later, he was in agreeable billets in a French village, not far from the Belgian border:

> The country was extraordinarily flat, in places intersected with dykes, with straight rows of trees and picturesque villages and little towns. Every square yard reminded me much of the Fens...The picturesque country women (there are few men) are most pleasant and very much like having the men billeted on them, unlike many parts of the line. Adjoining our room is a delightful large paved kitchen in which I am sitting and which is our company mess-room. The farmyard is fully stocked, including some delightful little French children and puppies. We can obtain plenty of fresh eggs, milk and butter and the mess sergeant will supplement our rations by stores drawn from the neighbouring town. So, altogether, we don't care how long we stay here...

Once again the senior ranks were a cause of amusement: "The Colonel is most amusing talking French, as it is really pure unadulterated English with just a few French words thrust in at random." Later, Geoffrey visited a French town just 10 miles from the Front where, "everything goes on as usual. Some houses destroyed by shell-fire may be seen here and there but the town has not been bombarded for a long time as the Germans have been pushed back." Even when he moved up to

Brigade Headquarters, rather closer to the Front, the war still seemed a long way off: "as a matter of fact this head-quarters and the villages we are now in have never been shelled. It is, I was told by the billeting officer who met me, a very curious thing but there is a sort of mutual understanding between the Bosche and ourselves, that if we do not shell his billeting areas, he will not shell ours." And Geoffrey's new accommodation was pretty good as well: "Bethel's and my billet are at a chateau, now occupied by a caretaker. It is a large house with a small but pleasant garden." He also noted that for the locals and the soldiers, the war at this distance was a pleasant spectacle: "The inhabitants are sitting out of doors watching the firing line which at night, in spite of the intervening trees, presents a wonderful spectacle."

His first impression of front line trenches in this sector was also not too unfavourable: "After dinner, we were shown the fire-trench. I must admit I was more curious than frightened." After describing the various types of shell in operation, he concluded, "it is really wonderful how very few casualties there are." No doubt this made good reading for his mother, but he concludes in the same letter that this rather quiet state of affairs might mean that the war would go on indefinitely: "What impressed me most about the whole thing, was the hopelessness of it all. I feel convinced that fighting will never end the war." But his tone remained optimistic on the whole. At one point he even thought his mother might like to experience life in the front line trenches:

> I rather wish you could spend an hour or two here, as I think it would reassure you as to the danger we run. Of course it is not a picnic, but really I am quite easy about it all and am rapidly becoming accustomed to all the noises. As a matter of fact, the noise is not as terrific as I expected, not even last night when the Huns attempted a bombing raid on our trenches, accompanied by artillery fire.

One of the worst things about life in the trenches was not the Hun but what he calls, "the Brass Hats outside the trenches, who are an intolerable nuisance." "The General fusses round every day instead of trusting people to do the work in their own way. Of course it is quite right that the General should not live in the trenches…but it is the nagging at us when we come out [of the trenches] which gets on our nerves." "After all," he concluded: "Who is it who has to dodge the whiz-bangs night and day?"

Geoffrey wrote to his mother most days and his letters reveal how easy it was for soldiers to keep in touch with their loved ones. The arrival of the post was keenly looked forward to and Geoffrey received numerous letters and parcels from home. He got his Aunt Mary to send him *The Illustrated London News* every week and on 30 May 1916 was able to report the safe arrival of some pyjamas as he hated "sleeping in my shirt." He asks for some new breeches as his old ones are giving way after this spell in the trenches: "I would like them to be riding breeches with patches at the side of the knees, not too baggy. I should order them at Pratt's." A few days later, he reports that he needs "another pair of Fox's spiral puttees, as mine are getting very dirty."

There are also constant requests for food: "Now that we are doing regular spells in the trenches, we will be very glad of cakes and chocolate biscuits. I think tinned cream of some kind would be very acceptable and a bottle of those semi-transparent acid drops." One important reference in one of his letters is to a recent copy of the Laxtonian. It is clear that many of the young public schoolboys received copies of their school magazines in the trenches. On the 18 June 1916, Geoffrey thanked his mother for sending a copy of the Laxtonian but confesses that he had already seen a copy: "I had already seen Kench's copy of the Laxtonian." Leonard Kench who left Dryden the year Geoffrey came up to New House was also in the Royal Warwickshire Regiment and was badly wounded just 5 days after this letter was written. Geoffrey heard that he "would pull through all right" but this report was over-optimistic. Leonard Kench, as we have seen, died of his injuries a few days later.

Amidst life in the trenches, Geoffrey, a biologist by training, also had plenty of opportunity to observe the local wildlife, especially after a period of rain:

> The effect of rain is to bring out the smells which otherwise are not very noticeable. After rain too, innumerable frogs and toads crawl about like one of the plagues of Egypt. There are even more rats in these trenches than at our last residence. They are not much in evidence during the day-time but at night the place swarms with them…We share our dug-out with several mice. To complete the natural history of the trenches, the water in which you have your daily wash is drawn from a ditch and contains a pleasing medley of snails and goat larvae. More pleasing are the larks which sing gaily over no man's land at dawn.

Other Theatres of War

Two in Africa

Far away from Neuve Chapelle, the spring of 1916, saw yet more Oundle deaths. Aged 35, **Major Geoffrey Spencer Bull** was one of the older old boys to die in the conflict. He was born in Rawal Pindi in India in 1880 and came to Laxton House at the age of just nine, staying for six years. In his later years at school, he developed a fine baritone voice, described as "one of the best we have heard" in the Laxtonian magazine. He was also a keen debater and played a few games for the Cricket XI. Although seen as "a fair fielder", the Laxtonian thundered that "he was absolutely useless as a bat." Despite this deficiency at the wicket, Geoffrey Bull became Head of School and was a member of the XV for several seasons, described as the best all-round forward of the team in his last year.

Geoffrey Spencer Bull, Laxton House 1891-98.

After leaving Oundle he went to Woolwich – he passed 12th in the entrance exams – and was gazetted to the Royal Garrison Artillery and sent back to India. From 1908-13, he served on India's lawless and troubled North-West Frontier, seeing active service for most of that time. In 1913 he came home on a year's leave spending part of the time in Turkey.

When war broke out in 1914, he was attached to the 6th East Lancashire Regiment and sent to France. There, now attached to the 58th Vaughan Rifles, he won the Military Cross for "his gallant defence of a trench". The regimental history recorded: "Captain G. S. Bull was sent from Battalion Headquarters to replace the wounded Captain Willis. He at once barricaded the trench and held the enemy in check with bombs and rifle fire until the counter-attack took place some three hours later." In May 1915, he was seriously wounded in the right arm and recuperated back in England, where he married. Fully recovered, he was sent to Egypt, to help guard the Suez Canal from the Turks and it was there that he died on 25 March 1916.

There are no details in the School's Memorial Book about the circumstances surrounding his death but one book on army officers during the war claimed that his death was 'self-inflicted'. Possibly this might mean an accident of some kind but more likely it hints at suicide. Unusually Geoffrey Bull has his own memorial plaque in the School Chapel which says that he died "in a further heroic effort to serve his country." Was this an attempt to cover up the truth about his death? The plaque's final words are, "Who dies, if England lives?"

William Reginald Matthews also died in Africa one month after Geoffrey Bull but at the other end of the continent. Very little is known about him except that he came to Sidney House in January 1895 and left after just two terms. His younger brother came up at the same time and left at the end of the next year. The boys were born in Ealing and their home address was in Maide Vale in West London. The School Memorial Book merely records that he was a second lieutenant in the South African Railways and Harbours Rifles and that his death in April 1916, at the age of 37, was the result of an accident. His brother, George Barton Matthews did some coxing while at Oundle, served in the army in the war and rose to the rank of major in the Royal Engineers.

Two at Sea

On 31 May 1916, deep into the Summer Term at Oundle and other schools, there occurred the greatest naval battle of the war. The British and German navies had been forced into inactivity after the first few months of the war as the German High Seas Fleet, conscious of its inferiority to Britain's Grand Fleet was kept in port. Chafing under this enforced inaction, both sides came up with a similar plan to lure the enemy into a position where some great naval encounter might take place. Both sides decided to use cruiser squadrons as bait. The Germans hoping that they could defeat a British squadron with the surprise appearance of their own fleet; while the British attempted to use a cruiser squadron to lure the Germans into facing the might of Jellicoe's Grand Fleet. Both plans came to fruition on 31 May 1916, off the coast of Jutland in the North Sea.

John Binder's diary entry for 3 June reflected the common view that the encounter was a defeat for Britain: "We have a blow full in the face this morning. A great naval battle … has been fought off the coast of Jutland, and we, to say the least of it, have met with a great repulse." The day clearly did not go well for the British, it was not the second Trafalgar that most had expected. The Germans clearly won the battle in terms of boats sunk and men killed. The British lost 14 ships including the *Queen Mary*, the (wrongly named) *Invincible* and the *Indefatigable*, a total of nearly 120,000 tons of shipping, while German losses were only half that amount. It was the same story in the loss of men; over 6,000 British sailors perished but only 2,500 of their German counterparts.

Two Oundelians were lost at Jutland. **Lieutenant Percy Strickland** was serving on HMS *Dublin*, a light cruiser, commissioned in 1913 and propelled by 12 Yarrow boilers. In the night action, following the main battle, the *Dublin* helped to sink a German destroyer, firing over 100 shells. She in turn was hit by at least 13 shells and Percy Strickland was hit by a fragment of shrapnel from one of these shells which passed through the ship's chart house and he died almost immediately. He was very unlucky. He was

Percy Strickland, Sidney House 1900-05.

one of only three sailors, out of a total crew of 475, killed that night on the *Dublin*. The ship survived the battle and Percy Strickland was buried in the graveyard of Old Kinloss Abbey, near Forres in Scotland. Forres was the home town of his wife Gwendoline Brodie-Innes. They had married in December 1913.

Born in London in 1890, Percy Strickland spent his early years in South Africa. He came up to Oundle from Capetown, in September 1900, leaving five years later. He was the youngest of three brothers who all came up to Sidney. His brothers also served in the war, the eldest in the Malay States Rifles, the other in the Medical Corps and both survived. Percy trained aboard HMS *Britannia* and his naval career certainly looked promising when he was appointed to serve on Admiral Jellicoe's yacht *Sappho*. However, the appointment was cancelled when war broke out and Percy Strickland then served on the *Aquarius* and was sent to Lemnos to help out with the Gallipoli campaign of 1915. Returning from there in March 1916, he joined the *Dublin* just three months before Jutland. He was 25 years old at the time of his death.

Also killed at Jutland was **Wilfred Robert Ulyatt**, a Laxton School boy for just two calendar years, coming up in January 1908 and leaving in December 1909. He was born in Warmington in October 1895 and by 1911, he was an apprentice draper in Stamford. He was seriously wounded in action at Jutland serving as a bombardier aboard HMS *Lion*, Admiral Beatty's flagship. At 3:45 p.m. the *Lion* first came under fire from German cruisers and was hit by 12 enemy shells during the battle. One shell hit the gun house in the 'Q' turret starting a serious fire. But for the swift flooding of the magazine, the ship would have exploded and been lost. Wilfred Ulyatt was one of nearly 100 men on board to be killed, dying of his wounds the day after the battle, aged 20. He was buried at sea.

Eleven days after the battle, John Binder's tone and perhaps the national reaction to Jutland had changed: "One thing I can affirm without fear of contradiction and that is, as time passes, it is quite certain that ours was the victory in the North Sea... [The Germans] were driven back without ceremony to the shelter of their mine fields and ports and have sustained such damage that it is doubtful if they will ever come out to risk another battle, we hope they will."

Two in the Air

Nearly three weeks after Jutland, on 18 June 1916, the first two Oundelian airmen died, in very different places and under very different circumstances. **Lieutenant Stewart Gordon Ridley** attended a prep school in Harrogate and came up to Grafton House in May 1910. He played a few times for the XV in his last year, including the last peacetime match in November 1913 against the old boys. He left in April 1914 and was preparing for a business career when the war came. In September 1914, he and his older brother Thomas enlisted in the 4th Yorkshire Regiment but by July 1915 Stewart Ridley

Stewart Gordon Ridley, Grafton House 1910-14.

had transferred to the Royal Flying Corps. Acting as an observer, he went to France in August 1915, returning to England in December to take his pilot's certificate. He died on 18 June 1916, in the Libyan Desert.

What was this Oundle boy doing in the Libyan Desert? Britain's war of course involved the defence of her Empire and in the Middle East, she was at war with the Ottoman Turks, a war which started so badly with the Gallipoli Campaign of 1915. In the autumn of that year, the Ottomans, hoping to put pressure on the British in Egypt, made an alliance with the Senussi people of Libya and Egypt. The so-called Grand Senussi signed an agreement with the Turks to launch *jihad* against the British with an attack on their forces in Egypt. By March 1916, the Senussi incursions on the coast of Egypt had been repelled but there was still some trouble in the interior and the use of aircraft for reconnaissance was vital in spotting Senussi camps and movements. So the British were sending out RFC patrols and armoured cars across the African desert until peace was officially made in February 1917.

No doubt Stewart Ridley's last mission was one of many made to gather vital intelligence on Senussi movements. Unfortunately, he and another pilot got lost in the desert and since Ridley's machine was damaged, they were forced to land. The other pilot flew back to HQ to bring help but this left Ridley and his mechanic in a dangerous position and help arrived too late. The Oundle School Memorial Book reported that in order to give the mechanic a chance of surviving, with their water supply running out, Stewart Ridley shot himself.

The Laxtonian later printed a poem, written in Stewart Ridley's honour by a contemporary poet with a national reputation. With tragic irony, the poet's name was John Drinkwater and his poem appeared in his 1916 collection called *Olton Pools*:

Riddles – RFC

He was a boy of April beauty: one
Who had not tried the world: who while the sun
Flamed yet upon the Eastern sky, was done.
Time would have brought him in her patient ways –
So his young beauty spoke – to prosperous days,
To fullness of authority and praise.
He would not wait so long. A boy, he spent
His boy's dear life for England. Be content:
No honour of age had been more excellent.

It was one of Drinkwater's most affecting poems, a moving tribute to the selfless heroism of Stewart Ridley who took his own life at the age of 19. It remains a fitting epitaph on a whole generation of young men "who had not tried the world", swallowed up by the Great War.

Even younger than Stewart Ridley was **Second Lieutenant John Raymond Boscawen Savage**. He was just 17, when he met his death on the very same day. And his death was equally heroic, if in a more orthodox way. He was shot down after a dog-fight, over the lines, with the German air ace Max Immelmann. Savage was seriously wounded in the attack and his machine crash-landed behind German lines. He survived long enough to die as a prisoner of war in a German hospital at Sallaumines near Lens. His death at the hands of the most successful German fighter at that time, was immediately avenged however, when his squadron mate, Second Lieutenant George McCubbin swooped down on Immelmann and shot him out of the sky. It was a great victory for the British as Immelmann was credited with 16 victories, more than any other pilot on either side. Unwilling to acknowledge that Immelmann had been out-fought, the German authorities claimed that engine failure, not enemy shooting, was responsible for his death!

The destruction of the cemetery where John Savage was buried, meant that his body was later re-interred in the military cemetery at Bully-Grenay near Béthune. The citation on the special memorial cross erected over his grave concludes: "Their Glory shall not be blotted out." His Commanding Officer wrote: "Your son was a very gallant boy and I wish with all my heart that he was back with us." He was the second Oundelian [Arthur Gurney Coombs was the first] to be killed by a German opponent who held the *Pour Le Mérite*, Germany's highest military decoration.

The son of a lieutenant colonel, John Savage came up to Oundle and New House from Winton House, Winchester at the age of 14 in September 1912. He left school in December 1914, at 16 and passed into the RMA at Woolwich the next year. He then decided to join the Royal Flying Corps, receiving his pilot's certificate in October 1915 and his 'wings' the following February. Within weeks, he was in France and four months later he was dead. Six weeks shy of his 18th birthday, he was the youngest of Oundle's sons to be killed in the conflict.

John Raymond Boscawen Savage, New House 1912-14.

Oundle's Civilian Loss

During the second year of the war, the School suffered its second civilian loss of the conflict. **Marcel Francis Conran Smith** and his wife lost their lives through the sinking of the SS *Persia* in December 1915. He was born in Trichinopoly in Southern India in September 1876 and was one of that small group of boys who arrived at Oundle at the same time as Sanderson in September 1892. He joined School House at the age of 16 and left two years later. After Oundle, he entered the telegraph service of the Indian Government.

He was returning to India on the liner SS *Persia*, when she was sunk by a German U-boat, U-38, commanded by Max Valentiner off Crete. The passengers were having lunch five days after Xmas, when the U-boat struck without warning. The ship sank in just 10 minutes killing 343 of the 519 people on board. The attack took place as Germany declared unrestricted submarine warfare but the German commander broke the Germans' own rules of engagement as she was, like the *Lusitania* (sunk in May 1915), a passenger vessel. The liner was thought to be carrying gold and jewels belonging to an Indian Maharaja, who escaped drowning as he left the ship at Marseilles. Marcel Smith, the second Oundelian civilian to be killed in the war, was 39 years old at the time of his death.

The sinking of passenger ships like the *Persia* and the *Lusitania*, the first use of poison gas and the infamous shooting of British nurse Edith Cavell in October 1915, all helped to reinforce the notion of the Beastly Hun. Oundle boys, at the Front and at school, always knew that they were fighting for justice and civilization against a depraved and wicked enemy.

5

Year 2 Home: Oundle School 1915-16

> Salt of the Earth, were such as he,
> Whose like no other age has bred,
> What futures we had looked to see!
> But "killed in action", they are dead.

Talks on the War and the Zeppelin threat

In the autumn of 1915, as the war ground on into its second year, Oundelians back at school were given insights into the realities of the conflict. On 12 October 1915 a certain Mr Coleman, (not an OO) who had spent 10 months on the Western Front, beginning with the retreat from Mons, gave the school a powerful and dramatic account of his experiences and the lecture was apparently illustrated with excellent slides. Perhaps even more exciting for the boys, was the visit of Captain Vickers OO, who had recently won the Victoria Cross. He was presented with a silver flask on behalf of the School. In February 1916, Miss Bacon lectured on "Aeroplanes and their History". She started with hot air balloons and traced their development through to what she described as "the most perfect lighter-than-air machine – the Zeppelin."

That same month, John Binder, the local grocer, reported Zeppelins passing close to Oundle after a raid in the Midlands in which 67 civilians had been killed. A short poem about the terrifying raids duly appeared in the Laxtonian:

> Thus on a cloudy night
> Ere preparation's found me,
> The Germans bring the fright
> Of Zeppelins around me.

But the most controversial talk about the war came in November 1915 when Arthur Pollen lectured the School on the deficiencies of the British navy. His views were so controversial that Admiral Jellicoe, in charge of Britain's Grand Fleet, wrote to all naval officers that they were not to have anything to do with him as his comments about the navy "tended to undermine morale and encouraged the Germans." Before the war, Pollen had long worked on trying to improve the accuracy of the navy's guns but this implied criticism of the power of the navy led to hostility from those in charge of the 'Senior Service'. In fact, as the Battle of Jutland was to show, six months later, he was clearly right. The boys at Oundle were not taken in however and Pollen's talk inspired a satirical poem, *To AHP* from one of those present:

> O prophet bold, of land and water fame,
> Subject of satire e'en in Punch's page,
> I wield my pen in honour of your name,
> The leading naval writer of the age.

Still, you can tell us all about the game
The nets we use to catch the submarine;
The admiral on the Iron Duke by name,*
You know, and Balfour you have sometimes seen.

Such are your virtues, but you have one vice
To mar the pleasant total of the list,
One trait which is not now considered nice,
You are a most confounded optimist.

*Admiral Jellicoe

OTC

By September 1915, the Oundle OTC had reached record numbers. Although so many senior boys had left, there were 90 more recruits enrolled at the start of term bringing numbers up to a record 342, some 97 percent of those who could join. Drills were held "practically every day", while the whole corps paraded twice a week. There had been regular practice "with pick and shovel" which had been put to good use in widening the miniature shooting range. There was now a well-drilled signalling squad, with most members of the corps introduced to the semaphore alphabet. More advanced signallers "had a good idea of how to send a service message and some proficiency in Morse Code." Adjusting to the realities of trench warfare, a selected squad "attempted to dig a

School Crew 1912. Guy Bostock, killed in January 1916, is standing on the left.

Oundle School OTC outside the Great Hall, 1915.

firing trench by night." The boys were surprisingly good at marking out and digging in silence and the progress made in an hour's digging was deemed "fairly satisfactory." On the 7 December 1915, a day was spent "on a regimental tour of Ashton Wold, with the aim of posting a battalion on outposts on a defensive position."

By the autumn of 1915, the government was clearly concerned about the state of school OTCs and the War Office began a series of inspections to check that schools were doing their bit to produce the new army officers, so badly needed. In November 1915, the War Office came to Oundle and the inspector was won over by the keenness of Oundle soldiers: "This is an exceptionally good corps, surprisingly smart and precise in all movements. Officers and Non-commissioned Officers very well instructed and smart and capable, all ranks evince the greatest keenness."

With the New Year (1916), the corps reported that their military activities, like the rest of outdoor life "has been considerably hindered by plague and weather." Nonetheless, they had constructed a respectable bayonet fighting course, in spite of the damage done to their trenches "by snow and thaw." However, as regards parades and field-work, things had come to "almost a standstill." Nonetheless, a note of optimism was struck because of developments indoors where boys were now learning about "the theory of range-finders and the trajectory of projectiles."

Yet, by the start of the Summer Term, perhaps because of the disruptions earlier in the year, the Laxtonian described the school corps as a "more or less disorderly rabble." But by the time of Inspection Day in June, the young soldiers from Oundle were complimented by the Inspecting Officer, Colonel W. F. Fawcett of the Northamptonshire Regiment: "The corps is well commanded… and the contingent showed every appearance of having been very carefully trained and well-disciplined." Of course the corps and its training was now a more serious matter than ever before, as so many of the senior boys, on leaving school, would be joining the real army and fighting a real war. For the first time, in November 1915, the Laxtonian produced a list of those who had left the OTC the previous summer, asterisking 27 of the 47 leavers (57 percent) as "having obtained or applied for a permanent or temporary commission in His Majesty's forces." Whilst the boys came through well enough by the end of the school year, the staff in charge of the OTC also attended courses over the Easter holidays to improve their skills and leadership. Five members of the school staff attended courses on Drill and Topography; Physical Training and Bayonet Fighting; and Musketry.

Another appeal

And the appeals to help the troops went on. In the Laxtonian produced at the end of the Summer Term of 1916, as we have seen, there appeared a letter from the British Red Cross and Order of St. John War Library asking boys to send in used books, 'novelettes', games and magazines. It provided the boys with a powerful reminder not only of the suffering of the wounded but also the global reach of the war:

Dear Reader,
Imagine yourself lying in a stifling tent, covered with flies by day and mosquitoes by night – think of the long hot hours, the weariness, the pain – think of the patience, courage and heroism of our sailors and soldiers who endure it all. We have supplied the Naval and Military sick and wounded since August 1914…Kind reader, pause for a moment and think of the suffering men.

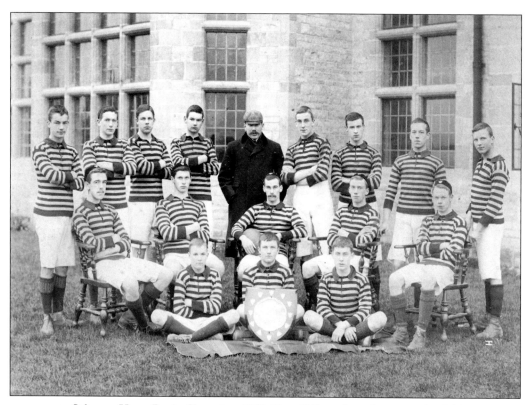

Sidney as House Rugby Champions 1902. Donald Ewen (seated on ground right)
was killed in October 1915 at Loos.

Debating and Singing

As was to be expected, many of the debates held at Oundle in the second year of the conflict, still concerned the war across the seas. In October 1915, the debaters examined the matter of wartime propaganda especially the way in which the conflict was being reported. Though the motion that "the caprice and interests of certain periodicals should not be allowed to lead public opinion" was easily lost, Allan Cole of Grafton was highly critical of Lord Northcliffe, the owner of *The Times* and *The Daily Mail*. He apparently "inveighed against the Northcliffe abuse of the privilege of moulding public opinion. He objected to the blatant criticism of individuals…since those individuals were the captains of the good ship 'British Empire'." Christopher Edwards of School House likewise saw through the propaganda of the British press. He "deplored the way in which victories were blazed and defeats were smothered."

In February 1916, a well-attended debate took place on the motion that "The Forces of Great Britain, both Industrial and Military, should be controlled by fighting men alone." Speaking against the motion, Philip Silk suggested that such a scheme would be a direct road to ruin: "The chaos would be horrible to think of, just as if all butchers became doctors, or schoolmasters human beings!" After the Gallipoli disaster, Winston Churchill was clearly a divisive figure at school. In the same debate, Humphrey Ashwin blamed him (alongside the trades unions) for "all our failures", while Charles Villiers, speaking on the other side, thought that "Mr. Churchill ought to be an ideal man for the crisis, combining both the statesman and the soldier – with a bit of sailor thrown in."

Workshops

The second year of war saw a big increase in the production of desperately needed war materials by the workshops of Oundle School. As a testament to the new importance of the 'shops', the Laxtonian of December 1915, published as a frontispiece a picture of Oundle's munitions workers outside the new science building. There are well over 150 boys and staff in the picture, looking quietly satisfied with their efforts. At the same time, the school magazine noted a new word in the lexicography of Oundle slang. The word 'munished' began to appear in the second year of the conflict. One writer claimed that Oundle boys had "boated, run…drilled, munished and worked with varying degrees of vigour." From the start of the new school year, there was a new emphasis on boys working in the shops in their own time. Previously, forms had gone into workshops for a whole day, thus curtailing their school work. Under the new arrangements, boys were expected to give up one hour of their free time on 'non-halves' and two hours on 'halves'.

And there was much more equipment for the boys to use. Over the summer holidays 1915, "the Engine Laboratory was converted into a filing room", so that there was more space in the workshops for new machinery. Early on in the Michaelmas Term 1915, two new lathes arrived from America. Sanderson had taken the initiative in securing "two new Fairbanks 8.5 inch double geared lathes, fitted with screw cutting, sliding and surfacing arrangements." Apparently these machines had a feature new to the 'shops' namely "an automatic knock-out for the traverse." A fortnight later a third new lathe arrived, this time a Colchester 7.5 inch. There was a moment of drama when the machine rolled over whilst being moved into position but fortunately "nobody received more than a few scratches in its overthrow" and the machine itself was also unhurt. Then there was a new sawing machine, grinding wheels and a gas blast furnace as well. The boys and staff also built a 6hp motor which now drove the main overhead shaft in the workshops.

All was industry and "busyness" in the shops, with output rising considerably compared to the first year of the war. There were three workshop's sessions per day, six days a week – mornings (after morning prayers); 2:00 p.m. until 4:00 p.m.; and 4:45 p.m. until 6:45 p.m. And the drive for increasing production also meant that by the Lent Term of 1916, Laxton School boys were brought in one morning a week "with very satisfactory results." The School, by now, had contracts with the Munitions Board, Brotherhoods of Peterborough and with the Woolwich Arsenal. A team from the latter, inspected the shops in December 1915, "with a view to sending us some urgent work." This work turned out to be the production of important spare parts and accessories for machines at the Arsenal.

For one Laxtonian 'special correspondent' the sight of the workshops at full throttle that year was truly inspiring:

> As I passed into the Munition Shop, I seemed to be entering another world…Passing through the glass doors which divide the power-house from the workshop, my ear-drums were nearly split by the terrific rattle of machinery. Some twenty or thirty boys, so intent upon their tasks that not one looked up when we entered, bent over their work, evidently aglow with patriotic ardour…It was a fine sight and one which filled me with even more complete confidence in the ultimate victory of the Allied cause…and my advice, to those who are feeling downhearted about this war, is to go and see what I have seen.

Sanderson and his staff always claimed that the workshops developed an improved *esprit de corps* amongst the boys and relieved some of the tension existing amongst the older boys, as the time for enlisting approached. Workshops also meant co-operation amongst the boys and a methodical and thoughtful approach to problems. Sanderson explained that "each task was carefully mapped out beforehand in the form of a flow diagram, and the individual worker was thus able to see the way in which his piece of casting, turning or filing fitted into the whole pattern." At the same time, exposing boys to life on the shop-floor would undoubtedly improve industrial relations in the future, when they came to take up responsible positions in the nation's industries.

Meanwhile a new line of war work also sprang up during the year. The 'classical side' and junior forms on the 'engineering side', teamed up in wood workshops to make screens for the Northampton Military Hospital at Duston. Sixty frames with four folds were made and the cloth to cover them was donated by a Hull industrialist, after a visit to Oundle, "as a token of his appreciation of the work done by the young boys." In the Summer Term of 1916, with the frames done, the junior boys moved on to bedrests for the same hospital.

For Sanderson it was vital to have the workshops working at full tilt to avoid them being taken over by the government's Munitions Board. In November 1915, he wrote to the governors making this point clear: "The shops and the men are used to the fullest extent in work for the war. If this had not been done, we could hardly have kept the men and machinery in the school at a time when demand for machinery and skilled labour is so great." While the Munitions Board decided not to commandeer the Oundle workshops, as early as the summer of 1915, they had proposed that a representative Council of Munitioneers should sit "to meet and discuss more efficient organization of the Shops." Sanderson, who always thought that workers should have a say in the organization and working arrangements of industry, agreed to its formation but made sure that he was the chairman! In the same way the School workshops again proved their worth to the nation with another summer holiday 'munitions camp' in 1916.

And what did the boys produce? In November 1915, Sanderson wrote to the governors explaining that the boys "have already machined over 700 castings mainly for torpedo boats, aircraft and mines…and…about 150 boys have been engaged in this." Tools produced for the Woolwich Arsenal included draw punches, clamp screws and punch holders all made from bar steel. As production rose, boys also made spare parts and accessories for machines. At the same time, the operating of the workshops in wartime revealed Sanderson's acumen as a businessman. He ensured that the government paid for the work done, effectively charging for the work hours done by the boys (of which there were many) as well as the wages of the 'skilled men' taking the lead in the shops. The

Workshops production and Workers, Cloisters 1916. This was probably taken during the 'munitions camp' in the summer holidays.

contract drawn up between the School and the Woolwich Arsenal meant that in July 1916, the School received nearly £300 from this source for the School's labour alone, being made up of £212 for the wages of the 'skilled men'; £52 for 6,258 lathe hours at twopence per hour and a further £26 (10 percent of the total) to offset depreciation on the machines. Two similar contracts were drawn up with the Munitions Board and Brotherhoods of Peterborough, meaning that the School made healthy profits in order to invest in new machinery.

In addition, boys and teachers also undertook other commercial work in the smithy and in the workshops during the war as they had done in peace time. They shoed horses, repaired agricultural machinery and carried out other "needful work" for the local community. Once again, the School profited from this work, which neatly fulfilled Sanderson's vision of a school's role in the community.

As early as the Lent Term of 1915, a school tribunal had been set up to consider applications for exemption from routine schoolwork, in order to maximize workshops' production. Early in 1916, one senior school prefect was granted exemption on weekdays from what he called "the indolent pursuits of the classroom!" The tribunal also heard more frivolous appeals against the normal demands of school work. Two brothers claimed to have "conscientious objection to schoolwork" and a School House prefect appealed on behalf of his 'fag' aged 13. He claimed that the boy in question was overburdened with workshops and also that "his own work in training the young was of national importance." Not surprisingly, his application was turned down.

Female Staff

Miss Browning joined the staff, apparently on a part-time basis, in 1912, before the war began. As the war dragged on, more male teachers left to do their bit and, like many public schools, Oundle looked to female staff to replace them. Mr Olley, one of the music masters joined the Artists' Rifles in the spring of 1916 and was replaced by Miss Edge, one of three ladies to join the staff in the school year 1915-16. She was an interesting appointment, in that she taught Russian as well as music. Of English parentage but brought up in Moscow where her father was an engineer, she and her mother and sister were visiting relatives in England when the war broke out, preventing them from returning home. Other ladies appointed to the staff in this, the second year of war, were Mrs Elliott, wife of the school doctor, who was on active service, appointed to teach history and Miss Hattersley, a classicist, who arrived in September 1915.

At the end of the school year came Miss Naylor to teach French. Appointed directly by telegram from Sanderson, she didn't even know where Oundle was and when she arrived to take up her position, she failed recognize the Headmaster: "There at the top of the steps stood a burly man wearing a floppy panama hat." Fresh from graduating from Newnham College in Cambridge, she mistook this figure for the equivalent of a college porter and said, "Please can you tell me where I could find the Headmaster?" Sanderson looked at her and, with a twinkle said, "I am the Headmaster – come into my study." Duly appointed, she soon realized that the war, though far away, was very close to Oundle and its boys: "The War of course was the background to one's life. You could never forget it, seeing school leavers going into the Services and then, quite soon afterwards, hearing that they had been killed or were missing or wounded."

Miss White, Mrs Barlow and Miss Koch also appear in the wartime school lists and by the end of the conflict, there were seven ladies on the staff. It was clear that female staff were a necessity during wartime and all seem to have thrived. Miss Hattersley was still teaching in 1923 and Miss Naylor never looked back. She later wrote, "Could anyone, do you think, have had a happier start to a teaching career and more generous help on all sides, in spite of the tragic background, than I had in Oundle between 1916 and 1919." She, at least, found the crusty bachelors on the teaching staff of Oundle uniformly delightful. 'Tally' Hale, who took over from Llewellyn Jones in Dryden, she thought was "dignified and courteous' while Sammy Squire had "a remarkably high standard in work, games and gracious behaviour." The only man she found "rather fierce looking" (as did the boys) was John King in New House. Winifred Edge not only enjoyed her teaching but also found love. She would go on to marry Mr Cole, the second Housemaster of Bramston and was still teaching at Oundle 10 years after the end of the war. By the time she 'retired' in 1928 there were still two ladies on the teaching staff.

Games

School and house games, in the main, proceeded as usual but there was no doubting that the war had a weakening effect on the top teams. For the rugby team in the Michaelmas Term, there was a new fixture against a Sandhurst XV but the main problem that term was not caused by the war but by the weather. The hardness of the ground in September and October meant that there was no rugby for the first five weeks of the term. Instead all those not engaged in boating on the river, took up hockey or 'soccer' but after two weeks these activities were also abandoned "owing to numerous casualties." Instead senior and junior 'Runs' were organized around the nearby villages. Inevitably, some juniors found such sport rather hard going and on one occasion, a number "found themselves unable to proceed from Cotterstock at more than walking pace." This was clearly unacceptable to the authorities and the junior malingerers, "who found themselves unable to run, were drawn up in column of fours and marched round Fotheringhay".

The next week, the boys were engaged in paper chases or 'hares and hounds' across the local terrain. Once again not everything went to plan as the Laxtonian sports correspondent noted: "The Juniors got hold of the idea that they were going to Biggin and to Biggin the majority of them went, though the hares made towards Glapthorn." The senior run also created difficulties because a number of the hounds followed "an obviously false track which lost us quarter of an hour." Good-natured assistance was however rendered by onlookers to help them back on the right track but

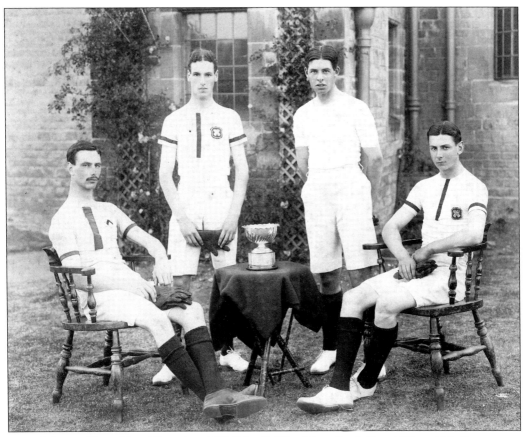

Sidney as House Fives Champions 1911. John Gulliland (standing left) and Edward MacBryan (seated right) would both be killed in July 1916.

they ended up in the village of Warmington, floundering "through streams and drains and back gardens" in a vain attempt to capture the hares. What the residents of those Warmington gardens made of it, is not clear but we do know that such paper chases did sometimes lead to friction with the local gamekeepers. On one occasion, the Biggin gamekeeper ended up in the lake as he tried to prevent boys crossing his land. Some weeks later, his Lilford counterpart, the wily Arthur Malster faced a similar problem as he saw Oundle School hares racing across Lord Lilford's fields. Unable to stop the hares, he quickly called together other estate workers and successfully blocked the pursuing hounds from crossing his Lordship's land!

In the Lent Term of 1916, games, especially rowing and rugby, were again undermined, not by the war effort but by the usual problems of illness and bad weather, especially serious snowfall and floods. The cricketers, in the summer, by contrast were doubly hit by the war. The main coach and groundsman Fred Holland, who had won the county championship three times with Surrey in the 1890s, was now threatened with conscription. His contribution to school cricket was seen as vital: "We have, as usual, much to thank Holland for, both in the coaching line and also in his untiring energy in keeping the playing fields in order, despite the great shortage of labour; if the war continues, the School will suffer a very great loss, when he has to join the Army."

At the same time, the strength of the school team was undermined by the premature departure of senior players (bigger fellows) to join the fighting:

"The School as a whole has not, as might be expected, been up to the standard of other years but it is not through want of keenness or coaching. The chief reason is, of course, that so many of the bigger fellows have had to leave, who might otherwise have stayed on, and matches, as is natural and right in this time of war, have been few."

And some of the matches that they did have were also partly inspired by the war. In the summer of 1916, there was a new fixture against Duston Hospital, Northants. (for which, of course, the boys had built wooden partitions), which was played "to provide entertainment for the wounded soldiers at the hospital."

Our Debt

The shadow of war inspired a number of poems in the pages of the Laxtonian in the second year of the war. One of the most moving appeared anonymously in the summer

Fred Holland of Surrey and Oundle.

of 1916, under the simple title *Our Debt*. It focuses on what was owed to the men who had sacrificed themselves in the cause of "right and duty", while reminding those still at school that they must be prepared to follow in their footsteps, "when duty's claims rise."

Our Debt

The fields of France are sodden red,
Or ploughed with shot and shell;
For every yard some hero bled,
Some soldier there his life-blood shed,
And for his country fell.

The cause, the right, tis this that calls,
And all they gladly give:
No fear of death nor wound appals,
The soldier recks not if he falls,
So be his country live.

A debt we owe to those whose life
Has thus been freely given;
Who did not fear to face the strife,
Where wounds and awful death were rife,
And there have nobly striven.

A debt we owe: they point the way
To whole self-sacrifice.
Let us prepare that debt to pay,
And make us ready for our day,
When duty's claims will rise.

So then let us, who sheltered here
May live, still bear in mind
The names of those who free from fear
Gave life and all that men hold dear,
A nobler crown to find.

Let us live, that we may keep
The path which they have trod
Of right and duty; do not weep
For such as they, who safely sleep
Near to a loving God.

Laxton House XI as Cricket Champions in 1908. Alexander Crawford (killed in May 1916) is seated second left.

Speech Day 1916

The second Speech Day of the war was marked, like the first, with two days of limited celebration on the week-end of 8th and 9th of July, one week into the Battle of the Somme. The weather was fine on both days but the 1st XI cricket match against the Leys was seriously upstaged by the arrival of an old boy in his aeroplane. Young Beanlands, who had left School House in 1914, had moved from the infantry to the Royal Flying Corps late in 1915. Not surprisingly, his arrival on Speech Day, "evoked much enthusiasm by his loops and dives before he finally landed on the football fields." John Coleman Binder, the local grocer, heard the news of Beanlands' exciting appearance in Oundle as well: "To-day has been Speech Day at the School here and much excitement was caused amongst the boys and visitors by the unexpected visit of one of the 'Old Boys' on (sic) an aeroplane. [He] gave a good exhibition of flying before coming down on the School Cricket Field. He circled the Church Spire, 'looped the loop' etc. etc."

Between 5:00 p.m. and 7:00 p.m. that day, the usual experiments were shown with a change necessitated "by the lighting regulations." The evening saw the usual concert in the Great Hall: "Choir, orchestra and soloists were heard with attention by a very crowded audience; and the applause was at once discriminating and appreciative." The choice of pieces was very similar to peace time concerts, though Elgar's *Britons, Alert* and Pointer's *Men of England* perhaps struck a particularly patriotic note in the circumstances. The concert concluded with F. H. Cowen's *The Heroes*, the school song and the National Anthem. On the Sunday morning there was the usual Commemoration Service held in chapel and an evening service in the Great Hall. Here Sanderson

OUNDLE SCHOOL CRICKET PAVILION

School Cricket Pavilion built in 1895.

read the Roll of Honour and two appropriate arias were sung from Handel's *Messiah* – *For behold, darkness shall cover the earth* and *The people that walked in darkness*.

As the School year drew to its close in the summer of 1916, the most direct impact of the war still came in the shape of the Roll of Honour, and the Laxtonian magazines that year were filled with the names, not only of the fallen but also the wounded, the prisoners of war and the winners of medals. The July issue included the names and brief histories of 27 old boys killed, now covering three and a half pages. In addition there were the names of 16 wounded, surely a serious underestimate, and one old boy missing. In fact one reported death was erroneous. Harold Hutchinson Lilly was reported "killed in France, July 1916." In fact he was a prisoner of war, surviving this conflict and going on to fight in the Second World War. The Commemoration booklet for Speech Day 1916, listed all the boys killed so far. In fact the School was unaware of the true scale of the deaths. The booklet listed 61 deaths but the true figure for Oundle School by Speech Day 1916 was 86.

The total number of Oundelians killed in the second school year of the conflict was 67, 25 more than the number killed in the previous school year. Year Two would be the worst year for Oundle fatalities but only just – 65 would be killed in Year Four. By the start of the Michaelmas Term 1916, the total war dead amounted to 109 boys. It was as though nearly three of Oundle's seven senior boarding houses had been wiped out. And, as the boys might have reflected later, it was not yet half-time.

6

Year 2 Away: Mainly the Somme – July to September 1916

> It is too hard to hear. This terrible sacrifice of all our best boys, and of all the best in the nation. It is too sad for words to think that your keen, capable, enthusiastic son, with all his capabilities for the future should be thus sacrificed.

The Somme: The Plan of Campaign and its flaws

And then came the Somme. A campaign and a name which would become dreadfully familiar to Oundelians old and new. For the British army, the Somme campaign was a turning point. Before the battle, there was real hope that this great offensive would finally break the stalemate on the Western Front and hasten the end of the war. By the end of the battle, such hopes were dashed and it seemed as though the war might go on for ever. For the men's morale, therefore, the Somme also marked a turning point. In the weeks before the battle, there was a buoyant optimism amongst many that, after two years of unprecedented stalemate and disappointment, they would finally defeat the Germans. After the battle, with the disasters of the first day, followed by the long, unendurable struggle very slowly eastwards, they were not so certain. The legacy of the Somme, for those who fought in later campaigns on the Western Front, was the knowledge that there was no real prospect of dislodging a resilient enemy from their strongholds. Indeed the events of the next two years seemed to show that the Germans might win.

The plan for the Somme campaign was essentially quite simple. The British and French, for the first time, would launch a huge joint attack astride the River Somme. The scale of the operation was enormous, with the British forces now numbering over half a million but it was based on an unduly optimistic and essentially unrealistic view of the situation. Although the attack was greater in scale than anything yet seen, it still relied on the same failed tactics seen in the previous year. A colossal bombardment of the German lines would be followed by a daylight assault by massed ranks of infantry. Misplaced optimism, fuelled by a desperation to achieve success on the Western Front meant that any doubts as to the chances of success and any worries about the terrible losses were swept aside.

The first day of the battle, Saturday 1 July 1916, would prove to be the worst day ever in British military history by some distance. On that day, the British suffered nearly 60,000 casualties with almost 20,000 killed. Though some ground was gained, in most areas of the battlefield, the British assault was thrown back almost with ease. Why was the first day, which was meant to be a triumphant procession though the German lines, such a disaster? Strategically, one major problem was the massive German attack on Verdun which began in February 1916. Determined to defend Verdun to the last man, this battle would eventually cost the French some 300,000 casualties. This meant that French numbers on the Somme had to be seriously reduced and so the attacking forces did not have the huge superiority in numbers needed to overcome well dug-in defenders.

Also Haig and his generals, despite clear evidence from previous battles, did not listen to warnings about the limited impact of the British artillery barrage on the German front line trenches in the week before the assault began. The British had captured some German trenches in the area before the battle and found that they could be 30 feet deep with concrete reinforcement. At the same time, there were a number of strong points along the proposed line of attack, similar to the Hohenzollern Redoubt at Loos, which British forces would be unable to take and a series of well-fortified villages whose names would become grimly familiar. Furthermore, reports that the German wire had not been destroyed by the British artillery bombardment were ignored. The British infantry, often advancing uphill, were also weighed down heavily with all sorts of equipment and so could not move quickly across no man's land even if they wanted to. Most British Tommies carried at least 66 pounds weight of equipment with them and many rather more than that because they had to change the orientation of the German trenches they captured.

In addition to this, over half of Haig's troops on the first day of the battle were the men of Kitchener's Army, the volunteers of 1914 and 1915, for whom the Somme would be their first taste of action. Here were many of the 'Pals Battalions', friends going side by side to war, to show the Bosche 'what for'. However optimistic and courageous they were, they had no experience of trench warfare. Haig himself acknowledged the need for these new troops to undergo further training in the actualities of warfare on the Western Front, when he repeatedly said that his preferred date to launch the attack on the Somme would be the middle of August, not the end of June. The British High Command also chose to ignore military intelligence reports which claimed, rightly, that the Germans had something like 65 battalions in reserve on the Western Front and so the British superiority in numbers, once the battle started, would last at most five days. Given that success in trench warfare demanded that the attacking force should be six or seven times greater than the defending force, a great breakthrough on the Somme was never a realistic possibility. As always with British military planning, particularly when Douglas Haig was in charge, it was too easy for the fervent desire for victory to cloud out the realities of trench warfare.

The key reason for failure, ultimately, was therefore Haig's misplaced optimism in his strategy, seriously misplaced because, after nearly two years of trench warfare, the same plan of attack had already gone disastrously wrong especially at Neuve Chapelle and Loos the previous year. After Loos, General Rawlinson, who was the operational commander of most of the troops on the Somme commented that "the success of an operation depends largely upon keeping down the fire of hostile artillery," yet on the Somme he directed less than 180 British guns to counter-battery firing, whilst 1200 guns wasted much of their effort firing at German wire and front line trenches. When the men went 'over the top' they would face artillery shells as well as machine-guns. And even though the preliminary artillery barrage was the greatest yet seen, the length of German front to be attacked (over 14 miles of it) meant that there were fewer British guns per yard than in earlier British assaults.

Cecil Lewis prepares for battle

The scale of the 'Big Push', meant that it was preceded by months of preparations as men and munitions and all the other things needed to sustain a great campaign made their way to the front lines. At the same time, there was intense training behind the lines to perfect the manoeuvres and communications needed to ensure success in the field. Cecil Lewis, now a fully qualified pilot, practised a new exercise called Contact Patrol. This meant using the flying men such as Lewis to tell those behind the lines in brigade and battalion headquarters, how the battle was going and how the troops on the ground were progressing. Lewis reported on all sorts of ingenious ways in which the PBI (poor bloody infantry) as he calls them, were to send messages back to HQ via the RFC. There were three main strands to this. During an attack the soldiers were to set off red flares at pre-arranged times, to indicate their position. The pilots then noted down their co-ordinates on a slip of paper which was then placed in a lead weighted bag, which was then dropped on a semi-circular white ground sheet at battalion HQ. Also, the troops, whilst attacking, were to lay out an ingenious black and white venetian blind on the ground. It opened white and closed black and allowed the operator to send messages in Morse code to the planes above. Thirdly, the planes themselves had a Klaxon horn which could also transmit Morse code messages and could be used to remind the infantry to set off their flares!

As so often, however, theory and practice did not match up. The complex Contact Patrol idea proved unworkable on the day. It was one of many examples when the commanders might have seen the weaknesses in their new scheme if they had only asked the PBI what they thought of it. One of the reasons for German success in defending themselves so resolutely on the Somme and elsewhere was that the German commanders expected to be told of deficiencies and problems by their troops and indeed wanted to hear ideas for improvements from the men on the ground. The lack of two-way communication in the British Army certainly contributed to the stunning scale of losses which it endured.

The last few days

Cecil Lewis noted later the growing sense of excitement and confidence in the last week or so before the 'Big Push'. He also explained the vital job done by the airmen to 'range' the British guns on their targets. Just before Zero Hour, Lewis and his colleagues were visited by the RFC's General Officer Commanding, 'Boom' Trenchard, who gave an encouraging talk to the men. He spoke of their all important contribution to the success of the preliminary bombardment. His enthusiasm and his words left the men in high spirits. Cecil Lewis for one, was convinced that victory was at hand and that the British would soon be sweeping into Berlin.

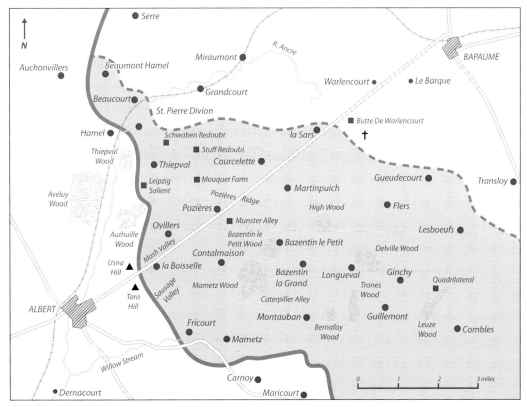

Map of the Somme battlefield 1916.

Saturday 1 July 1916

But such hopes were to be cruelly dashed the next day. The 20,000 deaths on 1 July 1916 included five Oundelians. **Harold Brearley Coates** was the only son of Henry Coates of Johannesburg in South Africa and grandson of Thomas Coates of Harrogate in Yorkshire. Born in Barnsley, he came up to his father's old house, Dryden, in 1909 and left in December 1914. In the L6, he won a geography prize and at the end of Michaelmas Term 1913, he helped Dryden win the senior house rugby competition, beating School House 13-0 in the final. His last term at Oundle coincided with the outbreak of war. Although he won a place at Caius College, Cambridge to study medicine, he did not go up. Instead, he obtained a commission in the Yorkshire Regiment, direct from the Oundle OTC and was commissioned as second lieutenant on Boxing Day 1914. By July 1915, he was in France. On 1 July 1916, he was positioned opposite the village of Fricourt. He was not in the first assault that day but at 2:30 p.m. he and his fellows in the 7th Yorkshire Regiment, rose from the trenches to press the attack on this strongly fortified village. As one private in his battalion later recalled: "We mounted the parapet; some of us got out, some of us didn't but we were under a murderous attack of machine-gun fire. We were falling like ninepins." The casualties of the 7th Yorks. were amongst the worst of the day and amongst them was 20 year old Harold Coates, who led his men into action. He was killed gallantly in no man's land and now lies buried in the Dantzig Alley British Cemetery near Mametz, close to where he fell.

That same day, 22 year old **Captain James Dixon** of the Royal Warwickshire Regiment attacked towards the village of Serre in the northern sector of the Somme battlefield. His colleagues in the 1st and 8th Warwickshire Battalions had attacked at zero hour – 7:30 a.m. – and made some headway before being pinned down. As the 6th Warwicks. and Captain Dixon advanced in support, they sustained heavy casualties and were forced to retreat. James Dixon was badly wounded in the original assault and had to be left behind as his men retired in the face of a German counter-attack. One of his fellow officers later wrote of him: "He showed the greatest bravery, and, after being wounded, carried on for

Harold Brearley Coates, Dryden House 1909-14.

James Evelyn Bevan Dixon, Laxton House 1907-13.

some time before receiving the wound which proved fatal. He was one of the officers I placed the greatest reliance on in getting men out of a tight corner." Dixon's Major wrote simply that "He had a great moral effect on the men, who always saw him absolutely composed."

James Evelyn Bevan Dixon had left Oundle just three years before his death. He was born in Edgbaston in Birmingham and came up to Laxton House in 1907. He was Head of House and played full back for the XV in 1911 and 1912. He was described as an excellent kicker and a man who "was very hard to bring down." In 1913, he went up to Trinity College, Cambridge and returned to Oundle to play for the OOs in the last rugby match before the war. He received a commission with the Royal Warwickshire Regiment in October 1914 and went with them to France in March 1915. He was promoted lieutenant a year later and captain just a few days before his death. He now lies buried in Serre Road Cemetery No.2.

Colin Harold Godwin, Crosby House
1909-11.

Colin Godwin once of Crosby House and also aged 22, fell in the same attack on Serre. Although he was a native of Derbyshire, he was a second lieutenant in the Sheffield City Battalion because he was studying medicine at Sheffield University when the war broke out. His battalion was one of the so-called Pals Battalions raised from volunteers at the start of the war. Godwin's men attacked at zero hour and, like so many others, they failed to even reach the German Front Line. Despite further fighting later in the battle, the village of Serre remained uncaptured. Colin Godwin's body was never recovered and his name is recorded on the Thiepval Memorial on the Somme with the names of some 72,000 other 'unknown soldiers' who have no known grave.

Colin was at Crosby House for just two years from 1909-1911 and played in the Cricket XI in 1910 and 1911. He was described as "a good steady bowler with a fine action" but needed, apparently, to bring more variation into his bowling. In 1910, he took five wickets against both Trinity Hall and Selwyn College, Cambridge. The next year, he was joint top bowler with a haul of 25 wickets during the season. He died four weeks before his 23rd birthday.

The fourth Oundelian to perish that fateful day was **Edward Crozier MacBryan**. He was born in Box in Wiltshire, home of the famous railway tunnel built by Brunel. He spent four years in Sidney House, coming up in May 1908. There were few sports in which he did not excel being a naturally talented games player. He played for the ill-fated XV of 1911, six of whom would perish on the battlefield and died on the same day and in the same battle as his team-mate James Dixon. He was an attacking

Edward Crozier MacBryan, Sidney House
1908-12.

three-quarter who "scored most of the best tries of the year." But whilst strong in attack, he was less sure-footed in defence. The school magazine claimed that he was "rather slow in getting back to defend" and that he "rarely tackles a man."

He also played for the Cricket XI for three years and was captain in 1912. Described as possessing "a nice natural style as a batsman," he was also a really good fast bowler and fielder and he led the team "with excellent judgement." He also captained the Hockey team and just missed out on a place in the fives team and so played for the Masters instead! His ability at fives helped Sidney to win the Senior House Fives Cup in 1911 and there is a fine picture of him and the team displaying the trophy outside the House. And there was still more! He was an excellent athlete, a speedy sprinter and winner of the high jump. In 1912, not surprisingly, he won the Lady Lyveden Challenge Cup as the best athlete on Sports Day.

And he was a notable scholar. On leaving Oundle, he went up to Jesus College, Cambridge, playing cricket for their 1st XI and also for Wiltshire. His brother Jack obviously shared his proficiency at the 'beautiful game'. A prisoner of war for much of the conflict, he would be Wisden Cricketer of the year in 1925. During his Cambridge days, Edward MacBryan also seems to have found time to help out back at Oundle. Sanderson, in writing a testimonial for him said: "he has been a member of staff of Oundle School and has been very useful to me in all kinds of ways."

In August 1914, after two years at Cambridge, Edward MacBryan gained a commission in the Somerset Light Infantry. He was severely wounded by a shell in May 1915 and it was a year before he was well enough to return to the Front. Like all wounded men, he had to write to the War Office for a wound gratuity. His letter reminds us of the suffering of so many men who were wounded: "I was wounded at Ypres on 2nd May (1915) by a piece of shell in the thigh. I was taken to No.7 Stationary Hospital, Boulogne where I underwent an operation. On May 10th I was removed to Highclere Castle Military Hospital, (Downton Abbey!) where I remained until July 2nd."

By July 1st 1916, Edward MacBryan had only just returned to the front line. He and the 1st Battalion of the Somerset Light Infantry attacked the German lines north of Beaumont Hamel. They witnessed the blowing of the Hawthorn Redoubt Mine at 7:20 a.m. and then went over the top. Staff Captain Geoffrey Prideaux of the Somersets later recalled the day's events: "At 7.20 a.m. the Hawthorn Redoubt south of Beaumont Hamel, was blown up by a gigantic mine, the biggest fired during the war…I watched the event from Vallade trench and consider it quite the finest sight I have ever seen." The diary of Lance-Corporal Cook, also of the Somersets, recalled the subsequent fighting in which Edward MacBryan lost his life:

> It is a lovely morning and the birds are singing…The bombardment is now terrific, the German lines are one cloud of smoke, that it seems impossible for anyone to live in such a hell…We were able to stand on the parapet to get a better view. There is not a sign of life in front and no response from the German Artillery…Our men were timed to advance 10 minutes after the Rifle Brigade, but so eager were they to get on, that they left soon after…and consequently were caught in the open by those guns…I led the platoon into the German first line, and after a breather went into the German second line, here I lost control owing to the men rushing from one shell hole to another in their advance. The ground is littered with our dead…

Edward MacBryan was last seen wounded but still leading his men through the third line of German trenches. At first there was hope that he might still be alive. Five days after the attack, Second Lieutenant Codner wrote to his parents in these terms: "I sincerely hope there is a chance of him still being alive and a prisoner of war, as sergeants and men are very poor judges of wounds. Several have reported that certain officers were killed; when afterwards I have seen them myself walk in not even badly wounded." However, the sergeant in question on this occasion, Harry Hunt, was not mistaken. He wrote to Edward MacBryan's parents ten days later, in rather less optimistic tones, confirming their worst fears:

I saw your son before he died and made him as comfortable as possible, I am glad to tell you he suffered very little and was really plucky….I have in my possession two silk handkerchiefs which I used to bathe his forehead and I will forward these to you at the first opportunity… I feel greatly for you. Your son faced the music like a man.

His Commanding Officer was also impressed: "He was a splendid soldier and his company was simply devoted to him: his death has been a terrible blow." Aged 22, Edward MacBryan has no known grave and is commemorated on the Thiepval Memorial, Lutyen's towering archway, which now dominates the Somme battlefield, close to where he died.

Also up near Thiepval on the first day of the battle was **John Crockett Stimpson**, at 19, the youngest of the boys who died that day. He was seriously wounded on that first day of the battle and almost certainly died the same day. He had joined the West Yorkshire Regiment, as soon as he was old enough, in August 1915 from the Leeds University OTC. He went out to France with them in May 1916 and was killed less than two months later. On the opening day, his battalion, known as the Leeds Rifles, had to advance across a swamp on a duckboard causeway to reach their jumping off positions near the village of Thiepval. They made their attack in support of the Ulster division at four in the afternoon but they came under machine-gun attack from Thiepval Fort. Their advance petered out and John Stimpson died of his wounds.

John Crockett Stimpson, School House 1911-13.

He was a native of Northampton, coming up to School House in 1911, staying for just two years. In 1912 he won two prizes on Speech Day indicating some academic prowess. That year, he also helped School House to win the junior fives competition. Three of the four members of that team would be killed in the war. In the wake of his death, his father Alfred contributed £5 to the building of the School's Memorial Chapel. Now he can be seen on the great poster called *The Missing of the Somme*, his face staring out at the observer. Two other Oundelians killed on the Somme later in July, John Russell and Chalmers Carmichael also feature on that iconic poster of lost promise and slaughter.

Meanwhile, up in the air on that first day, Cecil Lewis was patrolling. He had been up before dawn and was over the lines before the troops advanced across no man's land. Just before Zero Hour, he witnessed another of the great explosions of the war. He was warned beforehand to avoid the village of La Boisselle because two huge mines were to be blown just before the advance. Some weeks before the attack, he had taken the officer in charge of the British 'tunnellers' up over the spot and he had heard tales of the miners digging down there in the darkness. Now on this first day of July 1916, the time had come for detonation:

At Boisselle, the earth heaved and flashed, a tremendous and magnificent column rose up into the sky. There was an ear-splitting roar, drowning all the guns, flinging the machine sideways in the repercussing air. The earthy column rose higher and higher to almost four thousand feet.

After the excitement of those moments, the rest of the day was a huge anti-climax for Lewis and his doubts about the new Contact Patrols to monitor the progress of British troops across the battlefield, proved well-founded.

The Somme continues, July 1916

Despite the calamities of the first day, the decision was taken to continue the battle, Haig always believing that one more push might prove decisive. There were then a series of overlapping struggles in various sectors of the fourteen mile front which continued until mid-November. On the third day of the battle, Cecil Lewis and his friend Pip decided to drop a bomb on the battlefield, to leave their mark on the fighting. Their target was a possible German supply dump near Pozières. It wasn't really their job to drop bombs and, after throwing this one over the side and seeing it explode, they never dropped another. Perhaps it didn't seem worth the effort.

Four days later, **Clarence Espent Lyon-Hall** was killed in action. He was from the Caribbean, being born in Haiti and moving to Jamaica before coming up to New House in 1909. He was later a member of the XV and left in April of 1914. He held a commission in the South Wales Borderers and won the Military Cross in June 1916 for bravery at Le Plantinon and Festubert. He fell on the night of 7 July 1916, whilst leading a bombing party in an attack on La Boisselle, where Cecil Lewis had seen the two great mines go off. His Commanding Officer wrote: "Your son had established a reputation for the most intrepid bravery and daring, and was beloved by both officers and men." Initially buried on the battlefield, his body was later reburied in Bécourt Cemetery near Albert.

"Russell had that extraordinary power of winning affection and loyalty from all ranks, which makes his loss an irreparable one to the regiment, as well as the personal sorrow to me and his many friends." So wrote one of **John William Binfield Russell**'s fellow officers in the wake of his death on the Somme. A year earlier, he had been enjoying life with his own trout stream and rats shooting gallery, together with fruit gathering and lots of sport.

A Cornish lad, he came to the Berrystead

Clarence Espent Lyon-Hall, New House 1909-14.

at the age of 12, before moving to School House. He was a keen rugby player and captained the 2nd XV. He also helped School House to win the house cricket competition in the summer of 1914. Highly gifted academically, John Russell won the Senior Classical Scholarship at University College, Oxford. He left Oundle in December 1914 but instead of going to Oxford, he gained a commission in the Duke of Wellington's West Riding Regiment, early in 1915.

He served in France for a year before his death on 7 July 1916. He fell as he led his company in an attack on a German trench south of Mametz Wood. A brother officer wrote in these terms:

" none ever did a year's more arduous and gallant work with such devotion to duty and joy of life…and none have left a happier and more inspiring memory to those who are left behind and have to go on…" John Russell was just 19 years old at the time of his death and has no known grave.

The next deaths came a week later on 14 July and initiated a sad sequence which would see 12 Oundelians perish in just eight days, 10 of them on the Somme. **George William Mountney** was a Laxton School boy (1904-09) from Stoke Doyle, near Oundle. He served in the 6th Battalion of the Northamptonshire Regiment as a lance-corporal and was killed at the age of 25, on 14 July 1916. The official regimental history reported the action of that day as follows:

John William Binfield Russell, Berrystead and School House 1908-14.

> On the 14th July 1916, the 6th Northamptonshire Regiment assaulted the German held Trônes Wood that lay between Montauban and Guillemont on the right flank of the British advance… Advancing at 4am across 1,000 yards of open shell-cratered ground whilst the Germans laid down an artillery bombardment and in the face of heavy machine gun fire, the battalion reached the south-western edge of Trônes Wood with heavy losses including many of the officers.

George Mountney was a stretcher-bearer whose late father had been the butler at Southwick Hall, near Oundle. He was killed by a shell as he tended to a wounded colleague. The chaplain of the 6th Northants. wrote to his mother in Stoke Doyle: "He was always in the thick of the very thick of the battle, when he fell doing his duty, looking after a wounded man." He also reported that George

George William Mountney, Laxton School 1904-09.

"was an earnest Christian" and consoled his mother with these words: "We must always remember, even in our sorrow, that life is not measured by its length but by how it was spent. We have parted for a little while from one whom we could ill spare as a soldier and a friend." George William Mountney, who grew up in the tranquil setting of a stately home in a quiet Northamptonshire village, was killed amidst the carnage and chaos of warfare at the age of 25.

That same day another Oundelian of the same age perished. **Kenneth Champion Jones** and his men were attacking near the village of Beaumont Hamel, when he was reported "missing, believed killed". It was presumed that he was cut off somewhere in the German lines as his body was never found. He was born in Sydenham in Kent in May 1891 and came to School House in May 1904. He played for the Hockey XI as a forward. He stayed until 1909, at which point he became an articled clerk to a firm of chartered accountants. He was about to take his final examination, when the war broke out and he joined the Artists' Rifles and went to France. In June 1915, he obtained a commission in the 1st East Lancashire Regiment.

The next day the Somme claimed an Oundle lad from South Africa. **Chalmers Carmichael** was born in Maritzburg in Natal, in 1886. He was in Sidney House from 1901 until 1904, played as a forward in the XV in his last term and won the 100 yards sprint on Sports Day. He returned to Natal after Oundle, planning to find a profession in the law like his late father. However, the lure of the outdoors life drew him into ostrich farming instead. At the outbreak of war, he joined Botha's Natal Horse and did scout work in the South African campaign against German South-West Africa (now Namibia) which saw the Germans expelled from the country in 1915. At the end of that year, he returned to England with the South African Contingent. By March 1916, he was in Egypt but transferred to France in May, as part of the preparations for the Battle of the Somme. He was clearly a useful soldier. His Sergeant-Major wrote of his courage in carrying out one particularly hazardous mission:

Kenneth Champion Jones, School House 1904-09.

> I picked him to go to the rear to bring up a relief. To do this, he had to make his way through the wood under terrific shell-fire and guide the relieving troops back in the dark. He carried out his duty without a hitch; the slightest mistake on his part might have meant disaster for those under his care.

Chalmers Carmichael, Sidney House 1901-04.

Chalmers Carmichael was part of the attack on Delville Wood, known to the soldiers there as 'Devil's Wood' because of its murderous reputation. The South African boys had been moved up to the village of Montauban the day before and went into action to clear the wood on 15 July 1916. They nearly succeeded in this task but the Germans counter-attacked with gas shells. The fighting went on for five days and nights without pause and the South Africans suffered 2,400 casualties. Second Lieutenant Chalmers Carmichael was killed on the first day of the attack, aged 29 and his body was never found. Victor Brindley, another South African, once of Dryden was involved in the same attack and the regimental diary explained what happened:

The task of the South African Brigade was to capture Longueval and clear Delville Wood and hold it against counter-attacks. The Brigade had a strength of 121 officers and 3,032 Other Ranks and went into action on the morning of 15 July. After Delville Wood had almost been taken by the Allies, the Germans counter-attacked with asphyxiating gas shells, forcing the attackers to fall back a few days later. Owing to the height of the trees it was not possible to use close artillery support. In clearing the village, the South Africans had to face withering fire of great intensity, but they were able to hold on to the village. By 6am on the 17th July all the wood south of Princes Street had been captured. That evening, Longueval burst into flames and the whole wood was enveloped in smoke.

Unlike Chalmers Carmichael, Victor Brindley somehow survived the fighting but was killed two years later, back on the Somme, as a pilot in the Royal Air Force.

Captain Herbert Kersey Turner was another of Sanderson's boys as he was in School House from 1905 to 1908. In 1907, he was cox of the School House IV which won the Challenge Fours. Rowing at 3 in the same boat was Sanderson's son Roy, who would be killed in 1918. Herbert Turner played the part of Mustardseed, one of the fairies in *A Midsummer Night's Dream*. After leaving Oundle, he spent some months in France, and then had three years in the engineering shops at St.Peter's and Grey Friars Works back in his home town of Ipswich. Later he visited mills in other parts of the country to gain experience. In 1911, he joined the Suffolk Territorials and his was one of the first battalions to be sent to France in November 1914. He saw action the following month at Givenchy. Wounded at Neuve Chapelle in March 1915, he returned to England to recover and accepted a post with the East Anglian Munitions Committee. In June 1916, he returned to his regiment and was killed in action on 15 July 1916, when his battalion attacked High Wood. Aged 24 at the time of his death, he lies buried in Flatiron Copse Cemetery, near the village of Mametz, close to where he fell.

Herbert Kersey Turner, School House 1905-08.

Edward Wilmot Vaughan, a Welshman by birth, died the same day. He was serving with the Royal Field Artillery and was in action near Montauban on the Somme. Family tragedy was never far away for Edward Vaughan. He lost his father, who worked in the Indian Civil Service, when he was just 10 years old and his mother when he was 18. He came up to Sidney House in 1910, staying for three years. He won maths and French prizes in July 1912 and played occasionally for the Cricket XI. He had real potential but unfortunately "nerves got the better of him." As a junior, he helped Sidney win the house cup amassing over 300 runs in the campaign. As a senior, he was not so successful. In five innings for the XI, he scored only 17 runs. In 1913, he left school and accompanied his mother to Canada, where he became a cadet in the Ontario Military College. With his mother's death in 1915, he returned to

Wales to live with his uncle and guardian. He then joined the Royal Field Artillery and travelled with them to France.

A fellow officer wrote of him: "I am very sorry to lose him…He was very keen and was learning his job fast, and for a lad just out for the first time, he was wonderfully fearless." Edward Vaughan was another of those 19 year olds who were swallowed up by war.

Five years older and dying two days later was **Captain William John MacCombie** once of Grafton House, killed on the Somme on 17 July 1916. He was killed in the village of Longueval, having advanced with heavy fighting through Bernafay Wood. His courage was recognised in a dispatch from General Sir Douglas Haig.

William MacCombie was a local boy, living in the Manor House in Rothwell, not far from Oundle. At school, he was an excellent games player and represented Oundle in the top teams in fives, rugby and cricket. Leaving Oundle in 1910, he went up to Caius College, Cambridge to study medicine. There he got his blue for rugby and was also an excellent golfer. "He was a splendid soldier," wrote his Commanding Officer, "and his company were simply devoted to him." Another officer wrote: "Never for a single moment did he think more of his own safety than that of his men, nor would he ever ask them to do an act he would not do first himself."

Eric Chalker, next to fall on the Somme, was another one of the 'Dryden Seven', in the postcard of 1910. He took up residence in Dryden in September 1909 and was prominent on the river and on the football field, playing several times for the XV and for the House. A notable boxer, he won the Public Schools' Middleweight Championship in 1912 at Aldershot.

From Oundle he went to Edinburgh University to study forestry and had almost completed his course when war was declared. He immediately gained a commission with the 67th Battery of the Royal Field Artillery and went to the front near Ypres in December 1914. He was mentioned in dispatches in April 1915 and wounded in May, later returning to the front. He served in the battles at St. Eloi, Hooge and Loos before coming to the Somme. It was there that he was killed on 19 July 1916 near Caterpillar Wood aged 23. He was buried near the quarries north of Montauban, close to where he fell. Later fighting in the area meant that his body was lost and so he is commemorated, with so many of his fellows, on the Thiepval Memorial.

Edward Wilmot Vaughan, Sidney House 1910-13.

William John MacCombie, Grafton House 1906-10.

Another Dryden lad, though of earlier vintage, was **Sidney Burrell**. He died of wounds on 20 July 1916. When war broke out, he joined the Public Schools' Battalion before receiving a commission in the Middlesex Regiment. For much of his time he acted as Intelligence Officer for his battalion. His Brigade Commander later wrote of his abilities in glowing terms: "I made him my Intelligence Officer, an appointment he filled entirely to my satisfaction. He was very keen and always worked hard, in whatever capacity he was employed."

He was the second son of the family and had six brothers, five of whom also came up to Dryden. He was born in London and was at Oundle from 1897 until 1900. In 1898, he coxed the School Crew and was in the Cricket XI in his last year. After leaving school, he proved a very able hockey player, joining the Blackheath club and going on to play for Kent and for London in the Southern Counties Trial in 1909. He worked for his father's company – Messrs. Burrell and Co. – and spent some years in the Canary Islands before returning to England as a director.

Eric Chalker, Dryden House 1909-12.

His death on the Somme was not part of a heroic but doomed advance across no man's land but rather more prosaic. He was inspecting the front line with Brigadier General Carleton and Lieutenant Calder on the night of 19 July, when they came under shellfire. Carleton survived but was sacked and sent home soon afterwards. Lieutenant Calder was killed outright, while Sidney Burrell was badly wounded having had one arm blown off. He was taken to the nearest casualty clearing station but died of his injuries the same night. "I must tell you of his gallant behaviour throughout the most trying days of this campaign," wrote his Commanding Officer. "He was continually moving about among the men, organizing and obtaining information under heavy shell and rifle fire." Sidney Burrell was 32 years old at the time of his death. His brother Percy had already been killed at Gallipoli the year before and a third of the Burrell brothers, Clive, one of the 'Dryden Seven', would survive the fighting but die of pneumonia just days after the Armistice that ended the war. Sidney Burrell was buried where he died at Heilly Station Cemetery near Méricourt – L'Abbé.

Sidney Burrell, Dryden House 1897-1900.

"Leslie's cheerfulness under all discomfort and danger was worth a company of infantry." So wrote another Commanding Officer, this time describing Old Oundelian **Arthur Leslie Platts**. He was killed on the Somme on the same day as Sidney Burrell, while going to the assistance of a wounded man. One of seven children, he lost his father at an early age and came up to Laxton House in September 1904 and stayed for six years. Another of Oundle's scholars, he was another Caius man and took his Cambridge degree in 1913. A year later, just weeks after the outbreak of war, he received a commission in the Suffolk Regiment. He was promoted to lieutenant in June 1915 and captain a year later. From January to October 1915, he was on or near the front line in the Ypres salient, after which he was at home for a time working in the munitions department.

With the coming of spring 1916 and with the expectation of great battles ahead, he re-joined his regiment and returned to France in May. Soon he was on the Somme, where he died during the Battle of Delville Wood, the same area where Chalmers Carmichael had died. His body was never recovered so his name adorns the Thiepval Monument, alongside 15 other Oundle names. He was killed a week after his 25th birthday. A fellow officer, writing to his widowed mother, proclaimed that Lesie Platts was "one of the best fellows who ever lived. I always knew that whatever job had to be done at the front, I could rely on your boy to do it, and do it well – no matter how nasty the job might be."

Arthur Leslie Platts, Laxton House 1904-10.

The next day, **Alfred Vernon Oliver-Jones**, once of Crosby House, fell whilst doing his duty on the Somme. He came to the School in September 1906 at the age of 14 and left in 1910 and went on to study engineering. He won a commission in the Royal Field Artillery in October 1914 and came to the Western Front the next February. Seriously wounded at Neuve Chapelle in July 1915, he was evacuated back to England. Amongst the injuries suffered was the loss of a number of fingers on his left hand. Such injuries might have meant the end of his war. But though he could no longer serve with the artillery, he applied for training as an observer in the Royal Flying Corps, which he joined in March 1916, commencing his training with flights at Netheravon in Wiltshire. He was then posted back to France to serve in No.21 Squadron, Royal Flying Corps.

Alfred Vernon Oliver-Jones, Crosby House 1906-10.

Prior to his death, Alfred had flown in his squadron's R.E. 7s on bombing and reconnaissance sorties, which had included surviving a number of forced landings and crashes after reconnaissance flights over Lille and Cambrai in June and July 1916. In all he had completed at least two dozen operational sorties, latterly with Captain Jack Cooper as his pilot. An old Harrovian, Jack Cooper was an experienced pilot with an RFC commission dating from January 1915. The two officers were flying in an R.E.7, on a bombing mission behind enemy lines, when their aircraft was shot down by enemy anti-aircraft fire near the village of Beaulencourt, south of Bapaume. Six R.E.7s of the squadron had taken part in the raid on Epéhy, during which fourteen 112-pound bombs were dropped. Two burst in the station and others on the line north of it and in the town. Alfred Oliver-Jones' body was never found and so his name is inscribed on the Flying Services Memorial in Arras. There is also a plaque in his honour in St. Mark's Church in Broadwater Down near Tunbridge Wells in Kent. His mother and brother also placed a stained glass window in the church of Charles, King and Martyr in the town. Alfred Oliver-Jones was 24 years old at the time of his death.

Robert Francis Cooper Ballard, Dryden House 1911-13.

Four years younger was the next Oundelian to fall on the Somme. **Robert Francis Cooper Ballard** was born in1896 in Surbiton, Surrey. His father was a bank clerk with Coutts & Co and prosperous enough so that Robert was dispatched to be privately educated at Oundle. He came up to Dryden House in January 1911, staying for three calendar years. Playing in the three-quarters, he helped Dryden win the house rugby in December 1913. That same month, in the debating chamber (otherwise known as the art room), he moved that "the present system of government by party has become corrupted and is detrimental to the country."

In August 1914, he joined the Artists' Rifles and reached France in October of the same year and then obtained a commission in the Bedfordshire Regiment. He was killed in action on the Somme on 30 July, one of the 192 casualties sustained by the Bedfordshire Regiment when their brigade assaulted the area around Maltz Horn Farm. The battalion diary records that they moved into position for the attack at 3:30 a.m. waiting for Zero Hour. They then attacked Maltz Horn Farm and Trench and captured it. The attack was a brilliant success with 70 or 80 Germans being killed in the trench and one prisoner taken. The Bedfords then retired to their original positions and at 5:45 a.m. launched another attack to the south of Trônes Wood. This attack was severely hampered by dense fog and in the end, the Bedfords captured only a little ground. The next day, Major General Shea congratulated the surviving Bedfords, telling them that not only had they pushed the Germans back but that they had prevented a German counter-attack in the area with the fresh troops they had brought up. But Robert Ballard was not there to hear this praise and this young soldier's body was never found. Writing of him, his Platoon Commander wrote: "He did exceedingly good work when we were in action on July 11 and 12, and I sent in his name for a recommendation for an award of some sort." His Commanding Officer was similarly impressed: "He was loved by all, officers and men. A better young officer never stepped."

The Somme grinds on, August to September 1916

And so the fighting ground on as battles near Pozières and Delville Wood continued and fresh encounters at Guillemont, Ginchy and Flers-Courcelette were unleashed. One of the victims at Pozières on the Albert/Bapaume road was **Lieutenant Clifden James Crockett**, once of Sidney House, who was 22 years old when he was killed. He came from Dallington near Northampton and was the son of Sir James and Lady Crockett. Leaving school in 1911, after only two years, he joined the local Northamptonshire Regiment in 1914 and went with them to the Dardanelles, landing at Suvla Bay in August 1915. After nine days he was wounded and invalided home. His CSM at Gallipoli wrote of him: "He showed us all enough to enable us to look on him as a good leader, and the boys would follow him anywhere."

He then joined the reserve battalion of his regiment, before being attached to the Royal Warwickshire Regiment. Sent to France in July 1916, he was killed in action on 8 August 1916, during the Battle of Pozières Ridge which had started on 23 July and lasted until early September. His Colonel wrote: "He is the most difficult to replace of all the officers we have lost. He was employed as Intelligence Officer, and was in charge of the Battalion snipers. He went out time and time again to obtain information, and it always possessed the priceless quality of being reliable." After leaving school in 1911, Clifden Crockett went to Germany for a time and on his return, joined the family firm of Crockett and Jones, manufacturers of boots and shoes in Northampton. He is buried in the British Cemetery of Pozières on the Somme close to where he fell.

Clifden James Crockett, Sidney House 1909-11.

Some time that August, Cecil Lewis saw for himself the scale of the German defences on the Somme, appreciating the reasons for British failure. Exploring the ruins of the village of Fricourt, now safely in British hands, he saw dugouts up to fifty feet deep with entrances out of sight of the British. There was even a fully equipped field hospital which had proved quite safe from the British bombardment, with room for hundreds of men to shelter from the enemy guns.

A few miles east of Fricourt, **Second Lieutenant Henry Stephen Spurling**, an Essex boy, born 20 years to the day before the start of the Somme battle was killed in an attack on the village of Guillemont. He attended St. George's School, Windsor and came up to Grafton in 1910, leaving two years later at the age of 16. After Oundle, he worked for the South-eastern and Chatham Railway. His attempts to enlist were at first

Henry Stephen Spurling, Grafton House 1910-12.

thwarted on medical grounds but he eventually received a commission in the East Surreys in May 1915. He took a course at the Army Grenade School and was made Battalion Bombing Officer.

He was wounded by a shell at Messines Ridge, near Ypres, an injury from which he never fully recovered. Nonetheless, he returned to action in June 1916 at Messines and Ploegsteert Wood and his battalion was then moved south to the Somme. He was leading his bombers in an attack on the village of Guillemont on 16 August when he was hit by machine-gun fire. He never regained consciousness and passed away five days later. He was just 20 years old at the time of his death and his heroism is revealed by the fact that he could easily have avoided joining up because of his unspecified medical problems. He is the only Oundelian buried at La Neuville British Cemetery near Corbie on the Somme. From April 1916, this was the site of No.21 Casualty Clearing Station where Henry Spurling died.

"His men worshipped him and all the officers loved him as a brother." This was one description, by a fellow officer, of **Captain Arthur Godfrey-Payton** OO. He was from Warwick, so it was no surprise that he joined the Royal Warwickshire Regiment which was so heavily engaged during the Battle of the Somme. His Brigade Major would later describe him as an admirable company commander: "cool, conscientious and efficient." Arthur resided in Sidney House for three years, arriving in 1904. After Oundle, he went to train as a land agent in his father's office. By 1911, he had qualified for a fellowship of the Surveyors Institute, and received a permanent appointment in the Land Valuation Offices. He joined the Territorial Battalion of the Royal Warwicks in December 1911 and was gazetted as second lieutenant. By October 1914, he had reached the rank of captain and was sent to France early in 1915.

He was seriously wounded in action near Thiepval on the Somme on 26 August and died three days later, aged 27 and lies buried at Puchevillers British Cemetery. His Commanding Officer wrote: "His loss to the regiment is a great one from a professional point of view, and his kindly, generous-hearted disposition endeared him closely to one and all."

Meanwhile, that same August of 1916, the irrepressible Reggy Secretan was facing the possibility of a court-martial. When he returned home to take up his commission with the Hertfordshire Regiment (his home county) he told his mother that he was lucky to get away, "as he had a court-martial hanging over him!" It seems that he was riding around on his motorbike one night and was stopped by an irate colonel "who d…d him sky high because he had his lights on and that he must have been warned at a certain point to put them out." Young Reggy denied this and when told by his Captain that if he admitted his mistake, he would be let off

Arthur Godfrey-Payton, Sidney House 1904-06.

with a slight punishment, he refused, saying that "he preferred a court-martial." Luckily for him, perhaps because he was taking up a front-line commission, no more was heard of the matter.

For **Lieutenant James Trevor Riley**, known as Trevor rather than James, the prospects were not so bright. Having been wounded twice in the autumn of 1915, he was killed on the Somme, at the head of his men on 3 September 1916. He was a Yorkshire boy, born in Halifax in 1894. Coming to Oundle from Hunstanton, he had a three year stay in New House leaving in 1911. He then went into business with his father as a wool-stapler. He was a prominent member of the Halifax Golf Club, a powerful swimmer and played for the Huddersfield Old Boys Football Club. He joined the Territorials in 1912 and went to France in April 1915 with the West Riding Regiment.

James Trevor Riley, New House 1908-11.

His Commanding Officer wrote: "He set a fine example of cheery courage in all circumstances, and the battalion has lost a much loved and respected officer. He was always one of the coolest men in action I ever saw." A fellow officer said merely: "Trevor was always so cheerful, and was simply worshipped by his men." His name appears on the Thiepval Memorial next to that of fellow Oundelian John Russell, killed on the first day of battle, who was also in the Duke of Wellington's West Riding Regiment. Trevor Riley was 22 years old at the time of his death.

Just two years older and from further north than Riley's Yorkshire, was **Captain William John Henry Brown** of North Shields. He was in Dryden from 1906-1909 and went 'home' to Durham University to study medicine. However, the sudden death of his father in 1912 at the age of 52, meant that his studies had to be abandoned and he then set off for the Straits Settlements. These were four separate small territories and ports in Malaya, including Singapore, which had become a Crown Colony in 1867. William Brown, like many another Oundelian in the Empire, hurried home on the outbreak of war and received a commission within weeks.

William John Henry Brown, Dryden House 1906-09.

He went to France in January 1915 and was badly wounded in March. During a slow recovery, he worked as a musketry officer in Felixstowe and went back to France in the spring of 1916. He was wounded slightly in July and, like Henry Spurling, was killed in action near the village of Guillemont, on 4 September. "We all regarded him as a most excellent officer," wrote his Colonel and the chaplain noted: "We all respected him; he had a gentle dignity of his own." William Brown's death has a further tragic twist. His brother, Edwin, who was not an Oundelian, was killed on the same day near Delville Wood, probably in the same attack.

William Brown was 24 years old at the time of his death. Rather older was **Geoffrey Atkinson Gaze** of Whittlesea in Cambridgeshire. He was born in Norwich as early as 1881 and came up to Laxton House at the age of 15. His piano playing in school concerts was described at first as "hampered by nervousness" but in later years the Laxtonian thought that his performance displayed "good taste". He became a school prefect and won a place at St. John's College, Cambridge, where he rowed in the college's third boat and served in the University Rifle Corps. He then lived in London and was keenly interested in social work. He joined the Lady Margaret Mission in Walworth, which had links to his old college, and later worked with the Church Lads' Brigade on Waterloo Road.

Geoffrey Atkinson Gaze, Laxton House 1896-1900.

For many years, he was an officer in a territorial battalion and at the time of his death, held the rank of captain in the Civil Service Rifles. He arrived at the Front in March 1915 and served continuously thereafter. He was killed near the village of Longueval on 15 September 1916 aged 35 and was buried in Caterpillar Valley Cemetery nearby. He was leading his men into action and was hit twice but refused to leave. He was then stuck a third time and was killed instantly.

Three days later, **Christopher Stowell Gell**, a Crosby boy, also died on the Somme, in yet another attack on the village of Serre in the northern sector of the battlefield. Rather younger than Geoffrey Gaze, he was one of those Oundelians who went directly from school to war. His father was a Church of England clergyman, vicar of Pontefract in Yorkshire and Christopher was educated at a school in Buxton before coming up to Crosby in 1911. At school, he did some house rowing, won a Junior French prize

Christopher Stowell Gell, Crosby House 1911-15.

and a form prize. In April 1915, he entered Sandhurst as a prize cadet. Passing out the following August, he was another Oundelian who gained a commission in the West Yorkshire Regiment.

He was sent out to the Somme on 25 July 1916 and was killed three weeks later, aged only 19, in an advance against a German stronghold called the Heidenkopf Redoubt, near the village of Serre. The British called it 'the Quadrilateral' and on 18 September 1916, Christopher Gell and his West Yorkshire colleagues made their advance. As soon as he went over the parapet that morning, he was hit in the shoulder but continued to advance. He was then shot through the temple and died instantly. A fellow officer later wrote that Gell's conduct "just before his death, after his arm had been badly messed up was a most splendid example and incitement to his platoon." Though Christopher Gell was killed, the advance succeeded and the Quadrilateral was finally captured. His body was buried near Combles but lost in later fighting. An officer wrote: "Your son was regarded as one of our best young officers."

And there is a further twist to the sad death of Christopher Gell. Hidden away in a copy of the School's Memorial Book, lies an unpublished and forgotten poem written about him by his Housemaster, George Tryon. He himself was serving in Salonika at the time and would be killed just four days before the Armistice in 1918. Entitled simply *A Schoolmaster's Thoughts on reading 'Personal Notes' in the Times*, it is a sombre reflection by a schoolmaster on the brevity of his pupils' lives. But alongside the grief at the lost promise, there remains a hope that Christopher Gell and his Housemaster will meet again:

Another gone! The well-known name,
And then, the all too brief career,
His home, his School, athletics fame,
"In action, – in his nineteenth year".

Salt of the Earth, were such as he,
Whose like no other age has bred,
What futures we had looked to see!
But "killed in action", they are dead.

Was it in vain we wrought, and they,
Character strong and time to build,
Fit their part in the world to play
Through life's long years, had God so willed?

T'was not in vain; they've played their part,
Example set of highest worth:
Their country took from them new heart,
It saw the Sons of God on Earth.

Their lives were long enough to leave
A trail of blessing in their wake,
And so we have no right to grieve
Nor count them lost – 'tis but a break –

For humbly we may dare to think
Each death but means one friend the more
Who when 'tis ours to cross the brink
Will greet us on the further shore.
G.A.T. Salonika, Nov. 29 1916

And then another battle started on the Somme and one that involved tanks for the first time. Also there and falling at the head of his men was Oundelian **Edward Leicester Stuart Astwood**. He arrived at Oundle a year before Christopher Gell and died two days after him. He was a native of the West Indies being born in St. Andrew, Jamaica in 1893. He spent some time at Jamaica College, before coming up to Dryden in 1910, at the age of 17. He stayed for just one year and returned home to work for three years in the engineering branch of the Jamaica Government Railway. On the outbreak of war, he got a commission in the Royal Fusiliers and was appointed musketry instructor.

He went out to France in May 1916 and took part in the great offensive of 15 September known as the Battle of Flers-Courcelette. Near this unassuming village, not far from Bapaume, an attack was made by 11 British Divisions supported by tanks for the first time. Although much ground was

Edward Leicester Stuart Astwood, Dryden House 1910-11.

gained, the attack did not result in a breakthrough. Of the 49 tanks available only 21 made it into action on the first day, so their impact was limited. Cecil Lewis, as so often, was flying overhead when the tanks made their first appearance. He was impressed as men and tanks "waltzed" through Flers. In particular, he noticed a small white terrier, a mascot he supposed, which followed one of the tanks all the way and survived the onslaught.

Edward Astwood was not so fortunate. He was wounded on the first day of the battle of Flers-Courcelette and died five days later. He was being evacuated to London but died in Rouen and was buried at the Military Cemetery of St. Sever in the city. His Colonel wrote that he "was greatly loved by us all." Another officer noted that "He was a great favourite amongst us, and was extremely popular with his men, who would have followed him anywhere."

The day after Edward Astwood was mortally wounded, Cecil Lewis survived a very close brush with death. Having seen off an enemy plane with a burst from the Lewis gun (what else!), his plane was hit by enemy fire from the ground. Several bullets came up through the floor of his cockpit, knocking the stick out of his hands and sending the plane into a nose-dive. A third bullet pierced the oil tank and the propeller but somehow missed the engine, thus saving Lewis' life.

Beyond the Somme

But it was not just on the Somme where Oundelians continued their fight against the enemy. **John Hutchinson Gulliland** was back near Ypres when he was killed on 18 July 1916. A Cambridge man, having taken his degree from Caius College just before the war started, he had once been a Sidney boy. By the summer of 1916, his military career was on the up and he had been promoted temporary major in the Essex Regiment, still aged just 23. On 18 July, near Ypres, even though he was now attached to the Brigade Staff, rather than on the front line, he died of wounds.

Like a number of other Oundelians, he was born in India, in Calcutta in his case, the elder of twin sons born in December 1892. He was another classic Oundle success story. He was a talented games player, taking his place in the XV and the XI in his last year, then off to Cambridge to read medicine. In the Oundle XV of 1910, John and his twin brother Colin both played for the team and were usually in the thick of the action. John was in the forwards, described as, "a very good but tight player and an excellent place kick. Makes good openings and backs up well." Not surprisingly, the Gulliland twins helped Sidney to romp to victory in the senior rugby, beating School House 33-0 in the final. John Gulliland was also victorious in the house fives, alongside the legendary sportsman Edward MacBryan, who died seventeen days before his friend.

Naturally enough, John Gulliland returned to Oundle to play in the old boys' rugby and hockey teams and attended at least two OO dinners. At Cambridge, he suffered 'an unfortunate accident' but quite what type of accident is not specified. This meant that he had to give up rugby and instead concentrated on golf as well as his anatomical studies. The School's Cambridge correspondent noted with cheerful relish that young Gulliland "divides his time between golf and medicine. It is said that his dissection in the one far excels his 'slicing' in the other!"

A member of the university OTC, he joined the Public Schools' Corps on the outbreak of war and was then gazetted to the 11th Battalion of the Essex Regiment. In March 1915, he was promoted to the rank of captain and was then wounded at the Battle of Loos in October. Re-joining his regiment in the spring of 1916, he found himself stationed near the embattled town of Ypres, where he was killed on 18 July 1916.

John Hutchinson Gulliland, Sidney House 1906-11.

He was just 23 years old, the average age for Oundelians killed in the war and was buried in the Lijssenthoek Military Cemetery at Poperinge. An officer wrote of him: "The men worshipped him, and his officers too. It was not only that he always marched instead of riding...and that he was always cheerful; perhaps it was, most of all, that nothing could make him lose his temper." His twin brother, Colin, served with the Indian army and survived the war.

Also not on the Somme that summer was **Geoffrey Donaldson**. He was now stationed further north, near the remains of Neuve Chapelle. As late as the 13 July 1916, he was still having a pretty quiet time of it in and out of the trenches but he noted ominously that though the focus of the fighting was now on the Somme, "Our part here, is important of course, as our job is to keep the Bosch annoyed and prevent him from moving reinforcements south." Six days later, the British decided to 'annoy the Bosch' by launching an attack across no man's land and Geoffrey's company was one of those chosen to go 'over the top'. For the officers involved it was immediately clear that the attack was not expected to be successful. Donaldson wrote his last but one letter to his mother on 18 July 1916. He always adopted the policy of telling his mother "nearly everything" so he did not hide the risks involved in the forthcoming attack:

> What it came to, was that there was urgent need of drastic measures on this front to hold back Hun reinforcements for the South and to do this some troops had to be well, more or less sacrificed. That is war, of course and all in a day's work. And my company was to be one of the 15 or 16 companies that were to do the trick.

Given the sacrificial nature of the advance (operation certain death?), only three officers were allocated to each company. For most of the day on 16 July, Geoffrey Donaldson prepared for the attack, during which time one of his fellow officers in C Company lost his nerve and had to be removed to the rear. The attack was due to start at 4:00 a.m. on the next day but at the last minute, it was postponed until 8:00 a.m. and then to 11:00 a.m. and then postponed indefinitely six hours later. The strain was too much for the other officer assigned to C Company, who also suffered a nervous collapse. In his last letter home, Geoffrey explained to his mother that officers who suffered mental collapse were taken to the rear but not so the rank and file: "It just depends on the way you are made, some are unconcerned, others must collapse if there is a prolonged strain. Some of the men of course had it too, but I allowed none of these to go back. An officer is a different thing, because on him depends so largely the nerves of the men."

Geoffrey Boles Donaldson, New House 1907-12.

Then C Company was moved to the rear and Geoffrey Donaldson, thinking that the attack had been cancelled wrote to his widowed mother, the next day, expressing his relief: "After a good night's rest and wash, an excellent breakfast...we are as right as rain. I don't think anything will affect my nerves now, so don't worry about me, dear, because I shall pull through all right. I expect we shall have some rest for a few days now."

Sadly, this was his last letter home. His optimism for the immediate future was misplaced. Suddenly, C Company was recalled to the line and the attack was mounted for real at 6:00 p.m. on 19 July. Donaldson's Company was one of the most successful on the day, reaching the German second line. However, failure elsewhere meant that a general withdrawal was ordered two hours later. Geoffrey's battalion suffered nearly 60 percent casualties in this ill-fated attack. He himself, aged 22, was killed by a grenade at the head of his men. His name is recorded on the Ploegsteert Memorial south of Ypres, which commemorates over 11,000 servicemen of the Great War who have no known grave. Amongst the names are those of fellow Oundelians, Russell Simmons and Basil Coates, both killed in September 1915.

Geoffrey's mother Florence received many letters of condolence, all testifying to Geoffrey's great qualities. A proud son of Oundle, he was intelligent, gifted, tolerant and civilized and endured the terrible conditions at the Front with courage and fortitude. A dedicated naturalist, who from an early age had gloried in and wondered at nature in all its forms, he was, in truth, an unlikely soldier. But when the call came, he, like so many of his fellows, seems not to have given the matter a second thought or later cast a backward glance.

Sanderson's tribute was typical of the letters that came from Oundle:

It is too hard to hear. This terrible sacrifice of all our best boys, and of all the best in the nation. It is too sad for words to think that your keen, capable, enthusiastic son, with all his capabilities for the future should be thus sacrificed. How well I remember him, such a fine boy he was, so keen, so good.

Sanderson's long-term friend and colleague, Henry Hale, who had been Geoffrey's Housemaster, wrote with equal compassion:

> We are so deeply grieved to hear of your unspeakable loss in which we have so full a share. Though Geoffrey's years were so few [he was 22 at the time of his death] they were a continuous record of brilliant success, and it is no surprise to us that his service as a soldier was as honourable as his school and university career. You will be very proud of him in the coming years, but the loss is none the less crushing, and in this you have our deepest sympathy, the sympathy of all those who knew him and rejoiced in him at Oundle.

His science master also felt the need to write about his feelings on hearing the news and revealed how Geoffrey had kept in touch since leaving school: "I felt Geoffrey's fall very greatly. I loved him more than I had understood. His brilliant promise had been a source of pride and pleasure to me. His constant letters had endeared him still more to me. I looked forward to the end of the war and to a renewal of friendship. There is no real consolation."

Hugh Courtney Davis, New House 1911-15.

No doubt similar letters of grief and condolence, now lost, were written to the parents of the airman **Second Lieutenant Hugh Courtney Davis**, another New House lad like Geoffrey Donaldson, who also came to grief. He gained his commission in the Royal Berkshire Regiment in the spring of 1915 but in March 1916, he joined the Royal Flying Corps and received his wings in July of that year. He went to the Front, north of the Somme, on 1 August 1916 and met with a fatal accident just four days later. He was returning to his aerodrome from patrol duty when his plane crash-landed and he was killed. He was just 19 years of age. He is buried in the communal cemetery in the village of Aire, nine miles south-east of St. Omer. A year later, he would be joined there by another Oundle airman, John Crosbie of Dryden.

Hugh Davis was born in London but his father, who had worked in Calcutta, died when he was young. He held a scholarship at Oundle and gained distinction in football, cricket and hockey. Playing for the XV at full-back, the Laxtonian correspondent reported: "He plays a hard game but is slow off the mark and is not certain to find touch." In December 1914, he helped New House to win the rugby trophy, defeating School House in the final. Alan Pink who played alongside him for New House and indeed for the XV would also join the RFC and would also be killed.

Like Hugh Davis, **Second Lieutenant Howard Church Burbidge** did not die on the Somme. He is one of those Oundelians about whom we know very little. There is no picture to be found and because, unusually, he was only at Oundle between the ages of 10 and 12, he gets no mention in the Laxtonian magazines. He was born and raised in Brough in East Yorkshire and was in Sidney House. In the spring of 1910, he was working in Hull in the mills of Messrs. Hurtley, not far from home. During the war, he held a commission in the East Yorkshire Regiment and served in Egypt during 1915. He died of wounds received in action on 13 September 1916, aged 26, near Béthune as fighting continued beyond the Somme battlefield.

A few weeks before Howard Burbidge's death, Arthur Elliott, who had been the school doctor, revisited Loos. Arthur was an OO, a Day Boy, who went on to gain an exhibition in natural sciences at Emmanuel College, Cambridge. Now a captain in the Royal Army Medical Corps, he was north of the Somme back in Loos, scene of such terrible fighting the previous autumn. His diary entry for 25 August 1916 tells of the journey up to the new front line: "Went into trenches between Loos and Hohenzollern Redoubt. Marched across a very dreary flat plain with great slag heaps from mines on its edges, then entering a very long communication trench which led up through the village of Loos to the salient." It was an accurate picture of the desolate and blasted wasteland that the war had created across vast tracts of countryside and a reminder of the privations of trench warfare, where men lived, and so often died, in holes in the ground.

By the start of the third school year of the war, the Somme campaign still had two months to run. The generals no longer talked about breakthrough but of attrition, the need to wear down the enemy and to capture territory with a strategy of 'bite and hold'. It was a dreadfully slow and dreadfully costly process and in the winter of 1916-17, the Germans built a vast new defensive line which they called the *Siegfriedstellung* after Wagner's operatic hero and which we call the Hindenburg Line. The war on the Western Front would not be ending any time soon.

7

Year 3 Away: The Somme, Arras and beyond – September 1916 to July 1917

Dulce et decorum est pro patria mori

And so, as Oundelians gathered again at the start of the Michaelmas Term 1916 (22 September), the war continued on the Western Front and elsewhere but now, all but the most optimistic soldier or schoolboy, could see that attrition not break-through was the new watchword. The only way to beat the Germans, it seemed, was to grind them down on as many fronts as possible, so that eventually they would give in. Fighting continued on the Somme into the New Year and in the spring of 1917, there was a new great offensive at Arras. America's declaration of war on the Axis Powers in April 1917 seemed to boost Allied hopes for 1918, when the American army would arrive in France but it actually made Haig more determined to end the war in 1917, before the Americans could rob him of victory. So in the summer of 1917, at the end of the Oundle school year, Haig would revert to his pet project, a huge campaign in Flanders outside the city of Ypres – they called it Passchendaele.

The Somme, Autumn 1916

The Battle of the Somme was no respecter of school terms and so, as the new school year started the battle continued to rage. In October, the so-called Battle of Transloy Ridges began and two more Oundelians lost their lives. **Philip Randall Hatch**, whose younger brother was killed in the Battle of Loos in 1915, came up to School House in 1906 and left in 1910 to take up a place at Christ's College, Cambridge, where he took a diploma in agriculture. Apparently, Philip Hatch was of an unassuming disposition, absolutely trustworthy and conscientious and very loyal to all his friends. He took his part in college life and rowed in the third college boat in 1912. He became a keen student of agriculture, (no doubt his love of the subject started at Oundle) and those who knew him best felt that he had found his bent and predicted for him a successful future.

He was studying in Denmark in August 1914 and immediately returned home to join the army. He gained a commission in the 6th Battalion of the East Kent Regiment, known as 'the Buffs' in December of that year and was sent out to France in October 1915.

Philip Randall Hatch, School House 1906-10.

By the time of his death on the Somme, on 7 October 1916, he was acting captain and like so many of his fellow Oundelians, fell whilst leading his men into action. The attack that day was the start of the Battle of Transloy Ridges. The village of Le Sars was captured but the atrocious weather and the strength of the German defences meant that casualties were high and little more was achieved. Philip Hatch was 24 years old at the time of his death and is commemorated on the Thiepval Memorial. His Commanding Officer wrote to his grieving parents: "During the course of this miserable war, I have met many excellent officers, but I think I have never met a more charming boy than your son. He died leading his men in action – a very gallant boy. Your son was an officer whose death all ranks deplore and his loss is very keenly felt by the battalion."

Also killed at Le Transloy and remembered at Thiepval but four years younger than Philip Hatch was **Francis Gifford Perkins**, a Laxton boy, born in 1896 in Astwood Bank in Worcestershire. He came to Laxton School at the age of 14, when the family lived in Ramsey, out in the Fens and left school, not quite 17 years old, in 1913. He enlisted in Bishop's Stortford in Hertfordshire, served as a private in the 26th Battalion of the Royal Fusiliers and was killed on the Somme on 10 October 1916, aged just 20.

By contrast, **Major Charles Edward Andrews**, aged 45, was the oldest Oundelian to die in the conflict. He was born in Gibraltar in August 1871, though his family hailed from Leeds in Yorkshire. He came up to the old Laxton House (at the end of West Street) in 1887, staying for three calendar years and playing for the XV in his last year. A professional soldier before 1914, he followed his father and gained a commission in the Highland Light Infantry. Seven years later, he joined the West African Frontier Force and saw service there.

He re-joined the Highland Light Infantry in 1899 and served with them during the Second Boer War in South Africa, being present at the actions of the Modder River and Magersfontein. In the latter encounter, ironically, he and the British got their first taste of the losses suffered when advancing against an enemy in trenches. For services rendered in the Boer War, Andrews received the Queen's Medal with two clasps. During the fighting there, he had a lucky escape when a bullet hit his belt buckle and glanced away rather than passing right through him. Promoted major in 1908, he re-joined his original battalion in India and was present at the Coronation Durbar for George V at Dehli in 1911, receiving the Durbar Medal. He was one of the four officers, all afterwards killed in action, who received the new Colours from His Majesty the King.

He left the army in December 1913 at the age of 42 but re-joined at the outbreak of the war as second in command of a Service Battalion of the Highland Light Infantry and went to the Front with them in May 1915. He served continuously from that date and was mentioned in dispatches in January 1916.

He was killed in action on 25 October 1916, in the so-called Battle of the Ancre in the last stages of the official Somme battle. The regimental diary recorded the appalling conditions in which the men fought and died:

By October the battlefield had dissolved into a vast sea of mud and slime, in which the tanks could not

Charles Edward Andrews, Laxton House
1887-89.

in any case do very much. It was quite as much as the infantry could do to wallow through it and more than one unfortunate soldier, weighed down by his arms and equipment, was swallowed up in its noisome mess. It even swallowed up some of the mules bringing up the supplies.

[The]Glasgow Highlanders were in the trenches south-east of Lesboeufs, up to their knees in the mud and cold, wet and exhausted, with many of them suffering from 'trench feet'. In spite of these conditions, the battalion was ordered to attack, in order to secure a low ridge in front of Le Transloy. Upon receiving orders to attack, Captain Whitson protested in writing. It was in fact impossible to put off the attack, for it had been planned in conjunction with the French, who were attacking on the right on somewhat higher and less waterlogged ground.

Therefore after the usual bombardment, the Glasgow Highlanders left their trenches at 3 in the afternoon. The business of going 'over the top' in these conditions was not easy. There only being a few sets of trench ladders, steps had to be cut in the parapet, but mud and water poured down them and as the men climbed up them they crumbled away. They had to haul one another up and flounder through the mud towards the enemy line. It being impossible to keep up with the 'creeping barrage' the attack petered out against the enemy fire and the battalion had to take what cover it could in the flooded shell holes and remain there until dark."

Charles Edward Andrews left behind a widow and a daughter. He lies buried in Peak Wood Cemetery, near the village of Fricourt.

Arthur Ernest Wynn, once of Grafton House, also came to grief in the autumn of 1916. Born in Eastbourne but raised in Harrogate in Yorkshire, he arrived in Oundle at the age of 14 in 1910 and left seven terms later. He won a prize for French in his last year and had the satisfaction of playing a part in the humiliation of Crosby House in the first round of the senior rugger matches, in the autumn of 1912. Grafton, even without their captain, Eric Yarrow, won that encounter by 96-0. Alas, Grafton's success was short-lived as they were beaten 24-4 in the second round by New House.

When war broke out, Arthur Wynn was an engineering student at Leeds University. He first enlisted as a private in the Motor Transport Service but in December 1915, he gained a commission with the Royal Flying Corps. On 1 November 1916, his machine was shot down behind German lines near Bapaume on the Somme. He was 20 years old

Arthur Ernest Wynn, Grafton House 1910-12.

and his body was never recovered. He is commemorated on the Arras Flying Memorial, designed like the Thiepval Memorial by Sir Edwin Lutyens, and recording the names of nearly 1,000 British airmen killed on the Western Front, who have no known grave.

William Michell Clarke, a Grafton boy like Arthur Wynn, was the next to die on the Somme and officially, the last Oundelian soldier to be killed there in the 1916 battles. He came from Bristol and was named after his grandfather, another William Michell Clarke, who had been a surgeon. The younger William's father, John Michell Clarke was an even more eminent doctor in Bristol becoming vice-chancellor of Bristol University in 1911. John Clarke, a Caius College man, was in charge of one of the big military hospitals in Bristol during the war and apparently worked himself to death in 1918 at the age of 58, having achieved the rank of lieutenant colonel.

Although he himself had been a pupil at Clifton College, John Clarke sent his second son William to Oundle. He was in Grafton from January 1911 to the summer of 1915. On leaving, he immediately joined the South Midlands Royal Engineers. He reached France in September of 1916 and was killed on the Somme just two months later. With winter approaching and no breakthrough possible, the British commanders were still keen to impress the French and the politicians and public back home with some sort of victory on the Somme, so young Clarke and his comrades were sent 'over the top'. William Clarke was buried at Martinpuich British Cemetery, south-west of Bapaume, close to where he fell. He was 19 years old at the time of his death.

William Michell Clarke, Grafton House 1911-15.

And still the Battle of the Somme had one more Oundle victim to claim. **Henry Berners Begg**, usually known as Bernie, lived in Watford. He and his two younger brothers all came up to School House and his younger brother, Rivers Begg would also be killed in the conflict. Henry arrived in Oundle in September 1907 and stayed for nearly six years. After school, he went to Calcutta to join the family firm of Begg, Dunlop and Co. which had a range of trading interests including tea and jute. He joined the Calcutta Light Horse at the start of the war but in July 1916, he came back to England to join the RFC. He gained his wings in October and was sent to France to join the 24th Squadron stationed in the Somme sector.

On 23 November 1916, he was reported missing during a scouting expedition in the neighbourhood of Achiet-le-Grand, a few miles west of Bapaume and was later presumed to have been killed on that day. He took off at about 10:00 a.m. from Bertangles airfield near Bapaume, flying a de Havilland 2 scout plane. He and the other members of his squadron

Henry Berners Begg, School House 1907-13.

encountered the infamous 'flying circus' led by the greatest German air ace of the war, Manfred von Richthofen – the Red Baron. Begg was shot down, near Morval, south of Bapaume around eleven in the morning by Dieter Collin, for whom this was his first 'kill'. Later that same day, Major Hawker, who commanded Begg's squadron was also shot down by von Richthofen himself.

The shooting down of Henry Begg on 23 November was not the first time that he had been in trouble in the air. In October 1916, he wrote an exciting letter to his parents, saying that his engine had suddenly packed up: "My machine was going beautifully and I had just had a good fight with a Hun machine and had dived from 10,000 to 4,000 feet when bang went my engine and I was helpless. I managed to glide back until I was a mile and a half behind our lines." Eventually, he contacted his aerodrome by telephone and his plane was taken to pieces and transported back to base to be repaired. In the midst of this adventure, in an unfamiliar part of the British line, he met up with a Staff Captain Raymond who had taught classics at Oundle since 1912.

After Henry Begg's death, his Flight Commander wrote: "I was very sorry to lose Begg from my flight, for he had plenty of pluck and would have become a good hun-strafer." He was 22 years old at the time of his death. Like Arthur Wynn of Grafton, killed three weeks before, his body was never found and so he is also commemorated on the Arras Flying Memorial.

Henry Begg was the last Oundelian to be killed during the 1916 Battle of the Somme, which claimed the lives of 32 sons of Oundle during its four and a half month duration. The battle officially lasted 141 days until November, when bad weather supposedly put an end to the carnage. In fact, Haig continued to launch lesser attacks and raids in the Somme area, long afterwards. With what he called his 'winter sports,' fighting on the Somme continued until the next February, when his forces would be ready for the Battle of Arras, further north. As a result of the 'Big Push' on the Somme, the British and French gained a few square miles of territory at the cost of some 600,000 casualties.

By this time, Cecil Lewis, the School House airman, was on his way home with eye problems. He had refused to wear goggles, as he found that they fogged up too easily and late in 1916, he was sent away from the Somme to recover. Here, in a rather comfortable French château, he experienced first-hand the conditions in which the top-brass lived. Curiously, it was only now, after eight months over the battlefield that he realised the extent to which the war had taken its toll. As soon as he was able to relax he felt distinctly shaky.

Beyond the Somme

Although the Somme claimed so many victims in 1916, **Robert Mann**'s death near Ypres was a reminder that nowhere on the Western Front was safe. Robert Leonard Mann was born in Finchley, London in 1897. He came up to New House for the four years immediately prior to 1914 and went to train as an accountant, articled to the firm of Morrish Grant and Co. in London. On reaching his 18th birthday in July 1915, he enlisted with the Artists' Rifles and was then gazetted to the Royal Welsh Fusiliers in November of that year. He came to France in July 1916 but not to the Somme. He was killed in action near Ypres on 9 October 1916 and is buried in Essex Farm Cemetery in Boesinghe, alongside fellow Oundelians, Douglas McMichael and Eric Yarrow. It was in this cemetery that the Canadian poet John McCrae penned his

Robert Leonard Mann, New House 1910-14.

most famous lines, *In Flanders Fields*. Robert Leonard Mann was yet another of those 19 year olds who died for their country.

Spring 1917

Meanwhile, the plan for the spring of 1917 was to launch a big attack north of the Somme, in the Arras sector of the Front. Before that could happen, the daily hazards of trench warfare continued to take their toll on Oundle boys.

Norman Charles Achille Negretti was killed on 30 January 1917, near Ypres, the first Oundelian victim in another terrible year of losses. "I shall miss him tremendously," wrote his Commanding Officer, "and so will all ranks, officers and men. He was a favourite of everybody, and, in addition, an excellent officer, always cheerful, painstaking and competent." Despite his exotic name, he was born in Hampstead, London on 14 July 1897, the youngest of five children including two older brothers. His paternal grandfather was an Italian merchant who, in 1850, founded Negretti and Zambra, opticians and scientific instrument makers. During the war, the company produced instruments for the Ministry of Munitions, including gun-sights and ranging equipment.

Norman Negretti came up to Laxton House for 10 terms, leaving in December 1914. He won a workshops prize in the Fourth Form but his appearances in the Laxtonian are

Norman Charles Achille Negretti, Laxton House 1911-14.

meagre. We know that he sang in the altos in the School Choral Society and that he was confirmed by the Bishop of Peterborough. With his hopes of studying modern languages on the Continent dashed by the outbreak of war, he first became a tutor in Maidenhead and then enlisted in the Inns of Court OTC. He trained at Berkhamstead and in May 1916 was gazetted to the Middlesex Regiment and went with them to France in September of that year. He was killed on 30 January 1917, near Ypres, aged just 19.

Further south, in the Somme area, was **Henry Collister Mulock**. Always known as 'Bunny' at school, he was a Lancastrian who attended New House for just one year, leaving school in 1908, six years before Norman Negretti. In 1914, he joined the South Staffordshire Regiment but then transferred to the Royal Flying Corps where he was put in charge of all the photographic work of his squadron. He was a notably brave young man and this was reflected in the praise heaped on him by other officers after his death. His Commanding Officer, Major Walsen wrote that "He died as he lived, a brave man and a gallant officer: always prepared to do his job without thinking of himself." Another officer, Captain Keith Murray was even more effusive: "He was about the bravest and most popular man in the squadron and was tremendously keen on his branch of the work – he took the finest series of aerial photographs of our Corps' front I have ever seen, often under considerable interference from enemy scouts."

While photographing a forest several miles behind enemy lines, on 15 February 1917, his plane came under attack from three German aircraft. Flight Lieutenant 'Bunny' Mulock battled against them in vain. His observer was shot ten times and killed instantly, while 'Bunny' himself was apparently shot through the spine and paralysed. His plane fell behind British lines and was discovered by members of his own squadron. He was 25 years old at the time of his death and was buried in Grove Town Cemetery in Meaulte near Albert on the Somme. On his headstone his family put the following inscription:

> Simple Service
> Simply Given
> To His Own Kind
> In Their Common Need

His name is also inscribed on the Royal Masonic School's war memorial in Rickmansworth in Hertfortdshire. He attended the school for 5 years before coming to Oundle.

Three days after Henry Mulock's death, again on the Somme, **Christopher Benson** also fell in action, in a more conventional way. The third son of Reginald Benson, a solicitor in Sheffield, Christopher was born in 1894 and came up to Grafton House in September 1908, staying for five years. He was an exact contemporary of Eric Yarrow and the two of them formed half of Grafton's prefects in the school year 1912-13. Benson, like Yarrow also went up to Cambridge. He won a classical exhibition to Clare College, Cambridge and would have taken up residence in October 1914 but for the outbreak of hostilities.

He joined up immediately and came out to France in November 1915, where he served as a private in the Royal Fusiliers. He was one of nearly 80 men from his battalion killed or wounded in an attack on Miraumont

Henry Collister Mulock, New House
1907-08.

on 17 February 1917. This attack on the Somme was part of the British decision to keep the Germans occupied, while they prepared to hit the Germans hard further north at Arras. The Miraumont attack started badly when, in the midst of a snow storm, the British front line there was shelled by the Germans just before the men went over the top. It was said that the Germans got wind of the assault from a British deserter or prisoner of war. Although the Germans were later pushed back, the attack of 17 February, where Christopher Benson was mortally wounded, was a failure. He died of his wounds the next day, aged 22, in a casualty clearing station. He was buried in Varennes Military Cemetery on the Somme not far from the town of Albert

At Oundle, Benson was a classical scholar and won the English Essay Prize in his last year. In February 1913, he gave a paper at the Classical Society entitled *'The Life and Social Position of the ancient Greek Woman'*, which was well received by the audience. He was a useful all-round sportsman and athlete. He, alongside Arthur Wynn, scored a number of points in that record-breaking rugby match, in the autumn of 1912, where Grafton trounced Crosby 96-0! In the next term, he was a very creditable second in the Cotterstock Run and was also runner-up in the half-mile race where the winner was his fellow Graftonian, Stewart Ridley who would later die so tragically in the Libyan Desert. Christopher Benson also played a few matches for the XI in the summer of 1913, without being a regular in the team and in the debating chamber, he defended cricket against tennis. In a debate about the relative merits of the two sports, he claimed that cricket instilled "sublime moral truths to which the tennis player could not hope to aspire." He also trod the boards in a rather limited fashion. He appeared in *The Taming of the Shrew* but only as Adam, one of 10 servants of the lead character Petrucchio.

That February of 1917, when Christopher Benson was killed, also saw Lieutenant Reggy Secretan settling down to life in the trenches, where the main problem was the intense cold. Once again he was in the Ypres sector but now a little closer to the action: "That night [4 February] we spent in reserve about a mile behind the trenches in awfully nice trenches along the banks of a canal [Yser] which is frozen over, so we spent the next day in glorious slidings on the ice, and getting ready for the trenches. I was awfully cold that night, twenty degrees of frost outside!" The other problem, when he reached the front line trenches outside Ypres, was, ironically, the lack of water for washing:

Christopher Benson, Grafton House 1908-13.

> I can't write much, there is an awful din on, we are strafing the Bosche a bit…We can get no water to wash in, only enough to make tea in, none of us have had a wash for four days, it will be six shortly! The frost is just as hard as ever, no signs of it breaking, we all hope not, as I am sure the old trenches would all fall in. It is so awfully cold at night.

A few days later, they were back in reserve trenches for what Secretan called "a sports rest ie. a lot of football, running etc. which will be very nice, much better than drill." No sooner did they get there than young Reggy realised that his servant had left his cap back in the front-line trenches. It took him all day to retrieve it but he noted that the exercise was worthwhile because, as he told his mother: "I met a school friend in my old dug-out."

At the end of the month, Secretan's platoon was suddenly inspected by the General of the Corps:

> It was awful, as the unfortunate men had to polish up their equipment and make it look like new, and they only had short notice. I was in charge of No.5 Platoon which only came out of isolation last night on account of a case of diphtheria. Of course, they all had long hair, so at 10.30 last night I was to be seen rooting out the hairdresser for the men to have their hair cut. After a bit, they took it as a huge joke, with the result that they all had it cropped close! [Imagine] my horror on seeing them the next morning, they all looked quite bald! Anyhow, the General noticed the lack of hair in the platoon and inquired if they had had any skin disease on their heads! Immediate collapse of me and the Platoon Sergeant.

Two weeks later Reggy Secretan recorded another incident which demonstrates the amazing resilience of the men under such appalling conditions. His platoon had moved into some pretty wet and insanitary trenches where "the floor is three or four inches under water" and his servant brought back the wrong rations and instead of coal for the primus, he had brought some bricks by mistake:

> So here am I having had nothing to eat since breakfast at 7.30am, and no prospect of any 'til tomorrow's breakfast, wet through in a leaky dug-out, and yet one doesn't feel a bit fed up, as there are thousands of other fellows just as bad as me, and perhaps a good deal worse. The men are splendid, they have to sleep on duck boards, with water almost up to them in some places, and I can hear them from here laughing and joking – it's grand – you should have heard them laughing at my servant when they heard about the bricks, but he is a good fellow. Well good-night mother. Your loving Son.

A few weeks later the mood was still positive and hearty, even after being in action against the Germans: "It was rather funny, but when the Bosche raided our Company, my platoon and I happened to be on duty!! It was grand!!!…They never reached us as we were all ready for them, it was splendid, I'm so glad I was in the thick of it".

But while Reggy Secretan was revelling in the fighting and lived to fight another day, other Oundelians, not far away, were not so lucky. On 6 March 1917, **Gerald Maurice Gosset Bibby** was killed. Like Henry Mulock, he was a flyer. The only son of the Rev. and Mrs Bibby, he was born in Kimbolton, where his father was Headmaster of Kimbolton Grammar School, and came up to Crosby in 1911. He sang in the School Choral Society, played in the junior house fives team and was confirmed by the Bishop of Peterborough. He left just four months before the outbreak of the war, joined the Royal Flying Corps as an observer and served during the Battle of the Somme. He then returned to England to train as a pilot. He returned to France in February 1917 and was killed in action near

Vimy Ridge, north of the Somme battlefield, just a few weeks later, aged 19. He was apparently shot down by the 'Red Baron', Manfred von Richthofen, Germany's greatest airman of the war. Young Bibby was to be his 24th victim. He was buried in Barlin Communal Cemetery Extension and his grieving parents chose the following inscription:

> Blessed are the pure in heart, for they shall see God.

Not far from Barlin at this time was the Laxton School boy, **Jesse Eugene Wallis**. He hailed from Alwalton near Peterborogh and arrived at Laxton Grammar School in September 1908 at the age of 11, leaving six years later on the eve of war. He won a school prize on Laxton's Speech Day in 1910 and after leaving school, he became a student teacher at Fletton Secondary School in Peterborough, before moving down to London to study at the Chelsea Teacher Training College. But hopes of a schoolmaster's career had to be put on hold. In January 1916, days after his 19th birthday, he enlisted

Gerald Maurice Gosset Bibby, Crosby House 1911-14.

as a private in the London Scottish Regiment. He was killed in France aged 20, on 28 March 1917. He was probably one of 15 men from the London Scottish Regiment killed by German shell-fire that day, as his company moved forward from the village of Agny, near Arras, towards the new Hindenburg Line, which the Germans had 'retreated' to a few weeks earlier.

After their losses at the Somme and Verdun in 1916, the Germans had built a new 90 mile long defensive position which enabled them to shorten their line considerably. However, they were determined not to allow the British and French an easy advance. The German policy was called 'flexible defence'. They allowed individual enemy units to advance and then, whilst they were isolated and vulnerable, hit them with shell fire or launched fierce counter-attacks. Such was the fate of Oundle's Jesse Wallace.

Second Lieutenant Edward Favill George Hopkins, like Jesse Wallace, left Oundle in the summer of 1914 and in the early spring of 1917, was operating about 10 miles east of his fellow Oundelian. He was a Cambridge boy and came up to Dryden in 1912 at the age of 14. In his last year, he helped Dryden win the Junior House Rugby Cup and represented the School in U16 rugby. The day war was declared, he began work as secretary to the Remount Officer in Cambridge. This official and his staff had the crucial task of purchasing and training horses for the army. Edward's choice of career was not surprising as his father had always worked with horses and was a Livery Stables Keeper in the town.

In September 1915, Edward Hopkins obtained a commission in the Royal Field Artillery and went out to France at the start of 1916. Early on the morning of 30 March 1917, he and another man went out to reconnoitre the village of Hendicourt, north-east of Bapaume. As with Jesse Wallis at Agny, the enemy allowed them to enter the village but then counter-attacked. In the ensuing fight Edward Hopkins, aged 19, was killed. "We were greatly grieved at his loss," wrote a fellow officer, "because he was a good soldier, utterly fearless and beloved by his men."

Jesse Eugene Wallis, Laxton School 1908-14.

Edward George Favill Hopkins, Dryden House 1912-14.

On the front line, a few miles further south and three days later, former Sidney House boy, **Captain Sydney Truman Durose** was also killed in very similar circumstances. Like both Hopkins and Wallis, he fell whilst leading his men, this time in a night attack, on yet another French front-line village. Once again the British attack was launched as the Germans retreated towards the Hindenburg Line. In their haste to advance, however, Sydney Durose's Sherwood Foresters attacked the village of Le Verguier at night before the German wire had been cut and this resulted in the British troops being repulsed with serious losses. Durose and four of his men were killed by machine-gun fire.

When war broke out, he had joined the Nottingham University OTC and then gained a commission in the Sherwood Foresters. He was educated at West House in Edgbaston before coming up to Sidney House at the age of 14, leaving three years later in 1910. Apart from playing a few games for the 2nd Cricket XI, he left relatively little mark on Oundle in terms of academic and sporting achievements. After school, he joined the family firm of chartered accountants and was articled to his

Sydney Truman Durose, Sidney House 1907-10.

father. He was preparing for his final examinations set by the Institute of Chartered Accountants, when he joined up. He departed for France in July 1915 and was involved in the fighting at Loos and Hooge. Invalided home at the end of the year, he was in England for some months before being posted to Ireland, to help quell the Easter Rising in Dublin in April 1916. He stayed there until January 1917 when he returned to France with his regiment and was in the line near St. Quentin. His father, like so many grieving parents contributed towards the building of the new Memorial Chapel to commemorate his son and all the other sons from Oundle who fell in the conflict.

Oundelians in the Battle of Arras, April-May 1917

The Battle of Arras in the spring of 1917 saw the British make significant advances on the first two days, including the capture of Vimy Ridge by the Canadians. This success was based on improved tactics including the use of a creeping barrage and more accurate and more intensive shell-fire, which allowed troops to make initial advances across no man's land without facing such serious machine-gun and shell fire as they had at the Somme. Reggy Secretan noted in a letter to his mother: "Isn't the advance splendid! We all long to be in it but don't think we ever shall. At present we are making a railway for our advance, but I am going up for a week in charge of a party for a Tunnelling Company, a good job, miles underground and quite safe." However, the German tactic of 'elastic defence' with well-organised counter-attacks meant that Secretan's optimism was not justified. The British could not achieve a strategic breakthrough and anyway, the Germans were able to retreat to the Hindenburg Line, which would continue to defy British assaults. At Arras a little ground was gained but the war of attrition continued. Although less well known than the Somme and Passchendaele, the Battle of Arras actually saw the highest average daily death toll amongst British troops of any battle on the Western Front. There were some 160,000 British casualties (killed and wounded) in just five weeks of fighting.

The first Oundelian to be killed in the battle was Graftonian **Lieutenant John Dickinson** from Sunderland. He won a workshops prize in the third form and appeared as a bourgeois young lady called Isabelle in Racine's play *Les Plaideurs*. He was also on the losing side when Grafton were beaten in the final of the junior house fives competition. After Oundle, he took a BSc in Mechanical Engineering at Durham University. Like his younger brother Stanley, also a Grafton boy, John Dickinson was in the Royal Field Artillery. During his army career, his valour was noted when he was mentioned in dispatches and awarded the Military Cross. He was killed on 8 April 1917, when his unit was part of the preliminary artillery bombardment before the successful attack on Vimy Ridge, by Canadian troops. His Commanding Officer wrote: "His men adored him and would do any mortal thing for him". Another officer observed that John Dickinson, "knew and understood his men as few officers do. He helped them in his quiet way out of their little troubles and by his brave example many times won their confidence and respect."

Arriving at Oundle a year after John Dickinson and dying just one day later, **Kenneth John Wharton Mowbray** was in Dryden House from 1910-14. His father was the vicar at Castle Hedingham in Essex and then at Spalding in Lincolnshire. At Oundle, Kenneth played for the 2nd XV and was part of the victorious Dryden senior rugby team of 1913, which defeated School House in the final. However in the house cricket final of 1913, matters did not go so well. Mowbray and Dryden were defeated by an innings and 175 runs!

After training at Sandhurst, he joined the Suffolk Regiment as a second lieutenant and found that his battalion was commanded by Lieutenant Colonel Stubbs whom he had

John Dickinson, Grafton House 1906-09.

Kenneth John Wharton Mowbray, Dryden House 1910-14.

served under at Sandhurst. He was wounded in August 1916 and was killed on 9 April 1917, the first day of the Battle of Arras, leading his men in an attack. Stubbs wrote later:

> He was under me at Sandhurst, and I was glad to get him as an officer. His loss is a great one to us, and the consolation must be that his company achieved a great performance.

Three days later, the new offensive gathered up **Captain George Hamilton Williamson**. He was not an Old Oundelian but one of the four members of the teaching staff killed in the war. He was born in Manchester in 1890 and educated in Buxton and on the Isle of Man. He went up to Edinburgh University and took a degree in classics before going on to Emmanuel College, Cambridge. He was appointed to the staff at Oundle by Sanderson in 1913 and served as Assistant housemaster in School House. A keen rugby player, in his first term he coached the 1st XV backs while Mr Kitching, another new member of staff, took the forwards. Their team, captained by Bostock of Dryden won six of its ten matches. In the next term, Williamson was responsible for introducing a Colts (U16) XV for the first time at Oundle. For a school that prided itself on the quality of its rugby, this innovation was heartily welcomed by the boys.

George Williamson was also a good hockey player and in February 1914, he played in an invitation XI against the School, his team winning the match 6-2. He also played

George Hamilton Williamson, Classics Master 1913-14.

cricket against the boys in the Masters' XI which managed to scrape a draw against a superior 1st XI. He joined the School's OTC, undertook the training needed to become an officer and joined the local territorial force. But his promising career as a schoolmaster had to be put on hold. He joined Kitchener's Army at the end of Michaelmas Term 1914 alongside another colleague Maurice Miskin, who would also be killed in the fighting. George Williamson joined the King's Royal Rifle Corps and in 1915, he was posted to the Ypres salient experiencing the terrors of 'hellfire corner' and was wounded at Hooge, where the British had detonated a huge mine to dislodge the Germans. A little later, the Germans launched a surprise night attack against British trenches using their new *flammenwerfer* (flamethrower) which launched a jet of liquid fire to a distance of 15 yards. Initially driven out, the British re-took their positions the next day but suffered heavy casualties. George Williamson was wounded in the fighting and invalided back to England.

The next year, he saw action in the Battle of Delville Wood on the Somme where his exploits in capturing part of a German trench were recognised by the award of the Military Cross. He was again wounded and invalided home a second time but returned to the front in February 1917, promoted to the rank of captain. He died of wounds on 12 April 1917, during the Battle of the Scarpe, which was one of the many localised battles in the Arras campaign. Two days earlier, he had led two companies into action. The next day, in a further advance, amidst heavy snow showers, he was hit by gunfire and died the next evening aged 27. His Commanding Officer wrote: "Undoubtedly one of the best of my splendid soldiers that the war produced and the many successes of the Battalion were down to him." But this battle had another tragic twist for George Williamson's family back home. His younger brother Kenneth, fighting in the same battalion, died of wounds just one week later, aged 19.

In the three days after George Williamson's death two more Laxton schoolboys perished. Though in different year groups, they both left Laxton School in 1914. **John Appleby Robson** from Tansor was at school from 1912-14, leaving at the age of 15. His parents owned Tansor Wold Farm and kept horses, so it was no surprise that John joined the Northamptonshire Yeomanry, which was a territorial cavalry unit. He was seriously wounded as the British took the village of Monchy-le-Preux on 11 April 1917. One eyewitness account portrays the horror of the attack on the village: "We got to Monchy and what a sight met our eyes. Men and horses lying everywhere in the place. Blood was running like rain in the gutters." John Robson was wounded in this attack, in what was probably the last cavalry attack of the war and died two days later. He was buried at Duisans Military Cemetery, near Etrun where over 3,000 British soldiers are buried, the vast majority from the Battle of Arras. He was just 18 years old at the time of his death.

Two years older was his fellow Laxtonian, **Hugh Victor Turnill** who died two days later, not at the Front but at home in Warmington, near Oundle. He was born in Ashton in 1896 and baptised there the next year. He arrived at Laxton School in September 1909, aged 13 and stayed for 5 years, leaving at the end of the Michaelmas Term in 1914. He then joined the Honourable Artillery Company and was serving with them as a private on the Ancre in November 1916 when he was wounded. He died from his wounds five months later on 15 April 1917, aged 20.

Two days after Hugh Turnill's death, Reggy Secretan also came close to getting home:

> At last we got going again and then I had a bit of ill luck. A piece of shell flew past me and embedded itself in my sleeve. If only it had been half an inch further back, I would have caught it in my hand, and ten to one be in Blighty by now. I am fed up about it, only half an inch.

About the same time, Cecil Lewis reappeared in France. Late in 1916, just before his 19th birthday, he was sent to London Colney to join No.56 Squadron. This was to be the crack squadron of the RFC and Lewis longevity, reputation and experience clearly

Hugh Victor Turnill, Laxton School 1909-14.

recommended him to the authorities. He was especially excited as the squadron was equipped with the best fighter plane yet developed – the SE (Scout Experimental) 5. It was a bi-plane built by the Royal Aircraft Factory, had a top speed on the level of 120 miles per hour and was fitted with not one but two guns. It had a Lewis gun (!) clamped to the top wing which could be easily manoeuvred on a quadrant mounting for re-loading or for firing straight up. Then perhaps even more useful, there was a Vickers machine-gun which could fire through the propeller by means of a synchronised gearing system. For Cecil Lewis, this new plane opened up the prospect of a more exciting war. There was no more ranging of guns and contact patrols as on the Somme, now he would be engaged in offensive patrols, the dog fights always associated with this particular group of 'magnificent men'. Now, his first priority was to shoot down enemy pilots.

However, there was little sign of coming success for the new plane on Lewis' first offensive patrol over the skies of Northern France. His Vickers gun refused to fire and the Lewis gun fired two shots before it too jammed. Even when he managed to reload the Lewis gun, Cecil couldn't push it back up the sliding quadrant as it had become twisted, so the only way he could shoot was straight up! Although he got safely back to base, it was a rather inauspicious start to his career in No.56 Squadron.

While Lewis survived, a few days later, the Battle of Arras, going on below him, claimed its next two Oundle victims, both from Laxton House. **Second Lieutenant Bernard Valentine Colchester** was killed in action 24 April 1917. Born in Royston, Hertfordshire, his family emigrated to Canada when he was a child, so he initially enlisted as Private 77929 in the 16th Canadian Infantry and served in France. Subsequently serving with the 6th Bedfords, he survived the Somme battles of 1916 as well as two assaults during the Arras battle in April 1917. On 24 April, however, Bernard's luck ran out. He was killed alongside many of his colleagues when his battalion attacked towards the wide open Greenland Hill. They were badly mauled by a nest of machine guns firing from the infamous chemical works to the south. Bernard's brother, Edward (not an Oundelian), had been killed by a shell on board HMS *Irresistible* at Gallipoli in 1915, just before she was torpedoed and another brother, Geoffrey, was severely wounded and won the Military Cross in the Royal Engineers in 1916. Bernard came up to Laxton House in 1903 staying for just two years. His older brother Geoffrey was a great athlete, winning the Lyveden Challenge Cup on Sports Day 1904. Bernard was a useful bowler but left school at 15, before his promise had been fulfilled. He was 27 years old at the time of his death.

Five years younger was his fellow Laxton House boy, **Oliver Francis Rands**. Young Oliver Rands appears infrequently in the Laxtonian magazines of his day, except for a rugby house match which saw Laxton beaten 71-0 by New House! He also went out in the first heat of the junior fours rowing competition. More positively, he did win a form prize at the end of his second year. He left Oundle in 1913 and went to the Royal School of Mines in Kensington, which, in 1907, had been incorporated into Imperial College. He completed only two terms before joining the University and Public Schools' Battalion of the Royal Fusiliers. Unusually for Oundelians, he did not apply for a commission but enlisted as a private.

He went out to France with the 8th Battalion of the Royal Fusiliers and was killed in the fighting at Monchy-le-Preux, where fellow Oundelian John Robson had been killed three weeks earlier in that fateful cavalry charge. Oliver Rands probably died on 3 May 1917 but we cannot be sure and his body was never recovered. His name is inscribed on the Arras Memorial alongside some 35,000 other British servicemen, most of whom were killed in the Battle of Arras of 1917.

On the same day, 3 May 1917, and not far away, 28 year old **Stanley Oswyn George** was also killed. His body too would never be recovered. He attended Laxton School for less than two years, leaving in July 1909 apparently aged 21! Helped no doubt by

Oliver Francis Rands, Laxton House 1909-13.

being several years older than his fellow pupils, he swept the board at Athletics Day 1908. The Laxton School Journal reported events as follows: "The races were all full of interest although there was rather a lack of excitement owing to the numerous successes of George. He gave a splendid all-round display and won all the open events – with the exception of the Mile – and broke the school record for the Long Jump." In his last term at school, he again put on a great display on Sports Day. Once again, he carried off "premier honours" in most of the open events. The one disappointment for him and Laxton School was his failure to improve on his own long jump record of the previous year!

Stanley George was also a useful all-rounder in cricket and helped Laxton School win six of their ten matches in the summer of 1908. In addition, he was a very promising footballer. In the 11 matches played by the School in the academic year 1908-09, Stanley George, also the captain, scored 25 goals, half of all the goals scored by a very successful team. He came from Raunds, not far from Oundle and went on to play centre-forward for Raunds Town. After school, he qualified as a schoolmaster, teaching at a school in Kent. He was married and enlisted with the Bedfordshire Regiment.

About the same time, in the same battle, another Laxton School boy was more fortunate. Walter Holdsworth left school five years after Stanley George and in the spring of 1917, was involved in the push towards the Hindenburg Line. His battalion attempted to recapture the village of Bullecourt:

> The village had been taken and re-taken no less than six times, when we were detailed to try our luck…Rockets of all descriptions went up, and, as soon as Fritz had ascertained what was in progress, those significant red lights which were signals for artillery support, made their appearance. Still we advanced and very soon, with an ominous wail and a deafening crash, the first shell came. After that we were fairly soaked in the barrage, and it was not long before the machine-guns and rifles added their noise to the terrific din.

Despite this, Holdsworth and his colleagues gained their first objective but having reached the Hindenburg Line, where he described the tunnelling and dugouts as "truly remarkable," the battalion was forced back to their starting positions by the Germans' fierce and sustained counter-attack:

> Employing huge reserves and masses of artillery, the Huns attacked again and again and finally succeeded in bombing us out of our positions. Then, crawling on our stomachs across 'No-Man's Land,' followed by intense fire from machine-guns and rifles, we made our way back…and one could only congratulate one's self on emerging alive from that very trying ordeal.

He emerged actually with a serious wound to the knee and was sent to Birmingham Hospital. Despite the lack of success of the attack and his own misfortune, he later wrote to the school magazine to encourage others to join up: "To all those who will be leaving the school to join H.M. Forces, I wish the best of luck. I can assure them that active service conditions are not half so bad as one might think, and also that Fritz is rapidly becoming very demoralised."

Also in the spring of 1917, Cecil Lewis mourned the loss of one of Britain' greatest air aces, Albert Ball. Described by von Richthofen himself as "by far the best English flying man," he was in Lewis' squadron and crashed in unknown circumstances on 7 May 1917, being subsequently awarded the VC. Lewis was the last man to see him alive. The next day a sing-song was held in a barn near the aircraft sheds. Cecil Lewis sang Robert Louis Stevenson's *Requiem*:

Under the wide and starry sky,
Dig the grave and let me lie.
Glad did I live and gladly die,
And I laid me down with a will.

These be the words you 'grave for me:
Here he lies where he longed to be;
Home is the sailor, home from the sea,
And the hunter home from the hill.

The next two victims of the Arras campaign were killed at Vimy. **Henry Hayr Cox** was a Leicester boy, being born in the city in August 1896. He was to be the third Laxton House boy to die in the battle in just three weeks. He was Head of House, Section Commander in the OTC and a member of the Shooting VIII. Leaving Oundle in 1914, he gained a commission in the Wessex Royal Field Artillery and was soon in France. In the spring of 1916, he fought at the Hohenzollern Redoubt, near Loos which had proved such a deadly obstacle to Oundelians in 1915. Moved to the Somme, he was wounded there in November of 1916. He then took part in further fighting near Vimy Ridge and was killed there on 16 May 1917. His Colonel wrote: "I personally feel his loss very much, having known him [for] well over a year. He was an extraordinary, cheery, bright young lad, full of push and go." Cox's Major commented: "Although he was so young, he was a very useful and competent officer. In a recent attack he acted as forward Observing Officer for the brigade – which he did most successfully." Henry Cox, aged 20, was buried in Chocques Military Cemetery, not far from Béthune.

Less than three weeks later, again not far from Vimy, **Lieutenant Clayton Howard de Vine** was killed. The youngest son of the late Captain John de Vine, who had served with the Army Service Corps, Clayton was born in Surrey but lived mainly in Sevenoaks in Kent. Perhaps hoping that his son would follow him into the army, his father sent him first to Wellington College in Berkshire. At the age of 16 however, he left Wellington and came up to Dryden. He was a good all-round sportsman, playing for both the XV and the XI and was also prominent on the river.

He intervened at least once in a school debate about the relative merits of cats and dogs. Young Clayton pronounced himself against dogs "because one of them had run off that morning with much meat intended for the Dryden dinner."

Seven years after leaving Oundle, like Bernard Colchester, he sailed to Canada where he became a farmer, perhaps inspired by studying agriculture at Oundle. He married out there and enlisted in the Canadian Infantry, (Alberta Regiment) in Calgary in 1915 and returned to England in the autumn of that year. By August 1916, he was in France and fought on the Somme, at Messines, and Vimy Ridge, being twice mentioned in dispatches. He was killed in action leading his men in an attack on enemy trenches on Trinity Sunday, 3 June 1917 at Avion north of Vimy. The village was eventually captured by the Canadians at the end of the month. Clayton de Vine has no known grave and is commemorated on the Vimy Memorial which records the names of over 60,000 Canadians who died on the Western Front. He was 32 years old at the time of his death.

Clayton Howard de Vine, Dryden House 1900-02.

Exactly one month later, Laxton School matched Laxton House with a third victim of the fighting near Arras. **Edward Hunt** became a gunner with the Royal Field Artillery in August 1916 and came to France in May 1917, aged 23. Just five weeks later, on 3 July 1917, he died of wounds at Achiet-le Grand, south of Arras. The village had been captured in March 1917 before the Battle of Arras itself but would be lost again when the Germans launched their Spring Offensive in 1918. Edward Hunt was an architect, the son of Henry Hunt and his wife who lived at the Old House in Caldecott, Rutland. His parents ran a farm and trained racehorses. Edward was born in April 1894, and came up to Laxton School in September 1908, staying for two years. He was a forceful and talented captain of the soccer team. In the match against King's School, Peterborough, according to the school magazine, he "led by voice and by example" to

Edward Hunt, Laxton School 1908-10.

turn a two-all draw at half-time into a resounding 7-2 victory by the final whistle. He was also one of the two patrol leaders in the recently formed school scout troop. The other patrol leader was his friend Joseph Baxter, who had been killed in September 1915. Edward Hunt was buried at Achiet's communal cemetery extension, close to where he fell.

The Western Front beyond Arras

Of course, beyond the Arras sector, fighting continued elsewhere on the Western Front in the spring of 1917. Two more Oundelians were killed on the Somme and two more close to Ypres. **Captain Colin Turner Young** was a Londoner from Highbury Park. In the years leading up to 1914, he obtained a law degree at London University and qualified as a solicitor. He also joined the Inns of Court OTC in 1908 and this may explain why he volunteered on 4 August 1914 – the day war was declared. By September, he had obtained a commission in the West Riding Regiment and went out to France in December 1914 as Bombing Officer. He was severely wounded at Hill 60 outside Ypres in April 1915 during the Second Battle of Ypres, when he spent some 10 hours exposed to enemy fire. In 1916 he was promoted to the rank of captain and appointed Bombing Instruction Officer.

He then volunteered again for the Front, and returned to France with the 17th Welsh Regiment in July 1916, fighting on the Somme. Back on the Somme the next year, he was killed,

Colin Turner Young, Dryden House 1903-07.

east of the town of Albert which remained a major British base town behind the lines. Just as in the Arras sector, the British were attempting to advance as the Germans retreated towards the Hindenburg Line. Typically, he was leading an attack when he was killed at the front of his men, aged 26, on 24 April 1917.

Buried nearby in the same cemetery (Fins New British) lies **Hugh Charles Greenhalgh** a close contemporary of Colin Young, who also died at the age of 26. He was in Grafton House from 1904 to 1906, leaving Oundle at the age of 17. He was a Shropshire lad, born 11 years before the death of Queen Victoria and was on the losing side in a rather one-sided cricket final against Dryden in his last summer at school. After Oundle, he seems to have returned to Shropshire as there is a report in the Laxtonian of him playing cricket for Church Stretton Cricket Club. Within days of the outbreak of war, he joined the Public Schools Battalion of the Middlesex Regiment and qualified as musketry sergeant. He went to France in July 1916 and was killed on the night of 5 May 1917, while leading his platoon into action, near the village of Fins which saw fierce fighting in April and May of 1917. The village was taken by the British in April 1917 as the Germans withdrew to the Hindenburg Line but the German strategy, as always, was to counter-attack the British advance as often as possible which they did.

Further north, near the Ypres salient, two more Oundelians made the ultimate sacrifice. **Philip Edmund Sharples** enlisted in the Sheffield City Battalion, one of the famous Pals Battalions which suffered heavy casualties on the first day of the Somme. He was given a commission and proceeded to France. He was killed in action near Ypres on 7 June 1917. He was 21 years old at the time of his death and lies buried in the Railway Dugouts Burial Ground, south-east of the city. Philip Sharples was an only son from Blackburn and came up to the Berrystead in 1909, moving later to Laxton House, which he left in December 1912, at the age of 16.

Further north and hoping to be part of a daring offensive operation against a Belgian port, **George Nelson Kington**, once of Laxton

Hugh Charles Greenhalgh, Grafton House 1904-06.

Philip Edmund Sharples, Berrystead and Laxton House 1909-12.

School, was also killed in the early summer of 1917. He was born in May 1897 in Bulwick, not far from Oundle and was brought up on Manor Farm in Deenethorpe. He came to Laxton School for just five terms, winning a prize on Speech Day 1909 and coming 3rd in the U14 100 yards dash.

During the war, like so many other Laxton School boys, he joined the Northamptonshire Regiment and in the summer of 1917 his battalion was sent to Nieuport on the Belgian coast, between Dunkirk and Ostend, to prepare for Allied landings on German held territory along the Belgian coast. However a German pre-emptive strike against British forces on the River Yser in July, meant that the Allied attack, codenamed 'Operation Hush', never took place. George Kington of Deenethorpe was killed on 10 July 1917, the worst day of the fighting near Nieuport, with 260 British soldiers being killed or mortally wounded by the German *Marine-Korps Flandern*.

However, this was not how the fighting was reported. Back in Oundle, John Binder the grocer and occasional special constable wrote proudly of the actions of the Northants. Regiment on that fateful Tuesday. "All Northamptonshire today," he claimed, "is glorying in the splendid behaviour of the Northants. Regiment at the affair of the Belgian coast…They one and all fought like heroes and the deeds of some of them read like romances. A considerable number of them were cut off by the breaking of bridges across the Yser…When last seen, the officers were standing back to back calmly using their revolvers. The whole country is intensely proud of them." Perhaps this kind of reporting helped George Kington's widowed mother come to terms with her loss. Her son was another of the Oundle 20 year olds killed in the war and another boy whose body was never found.

Captain Dr Frank Rhodes Armitage also died in Belgium in July 1917. He was the eldest of the four Armitage boys who all came up to Laxton House, three of whom perished in the conflict.

He was born in Edinburgh in 1883 where his father was a doctor. He came to Laxton in 1896 and stayed for six years, enjoying a splendid school career. He was Head of House and a school prefect and was an excellent all round sportsman. He was a member of the XV and well as the XI. In cricket, he headed the bowling averages for 1901 and knocked off 58 against Queens' College, Cambridge. That same year, he took 5 wickets for 16 runs against the Masters' XI, a particularly satisfying haul no doubt, and in 1902, he went on the Oundle Rovers' (OOs') tour and scored a creditable 95 against Burghley Park. But this was not the end of his sporting prowess. He was also an excellent golfer. He held the course record at the South Staffordshire course at Tettenhall, when he went round with a score of 66. He was also a member of the Wolverhampton Cricket Club. Academically, he was similarly in the front rank. In his last year at school, he won the Langerman Prize for classics and a maths prize. He won a scholarship in classics to Pembroke College, Cambridge but decided to switch to medicine.

In 1906 he was working as a medical assistant in the London Hospital in Whitechapel and later succeeded to his father's practice.

Frank Rhodes Armitage, Laxton House 1896-02.

When war broke out, he joined the Royal Army Medical Corps and was awarded a DSO early in 1917. He was killed on 30 July 1917, near Ypres, while attached to the Royal Field Artillery. He was in a dug-out with Captain Hickman and hit by a shell. Described by a local newspaper, *The Express and Star* as "one of the bravest and best", he had been in the line for nearly two years and "had many miraculous escapes from death". On one occasion he was inches away from a shell which crashed into a dug-out, but escaped without injury. He also saved the life of a Lieutenant Finnis. He married Frances Snape in 1913 and had a daughter Prudence two years later. Frank Rhodes Armitage was one of the older Oundle victims of the war at 34 and was buried in Brandhoek New Military Cemetery just west of Ypres. Two of his younger brothers, also perished because of the conflict. Douglas, as we have already seen, was killed at 22 in October 1915 and another brother James would die in 1919 aged 30, his health fatally undermined by his wartime experiences.

The Macedonian Front

The First World War, of course, was not all about the Western Front. Austria's attack on Serbia in 1914 and the subsequent entry of Bulgaria (September 1915) and Romania (August 1916) into the war – Bulgaria on the German/Austrian side, Romania for the Allies – meant that the Balkans became another holocaust of war. Serbia, at the centre of so much fighting would lose over one million of its citizens in the conflict – 27 percent of its population and some 60 percent of its adult men. Attacked on all sides, with large areas occupied by its enemies, over a quarter of Serbia's mobilized soldiers perished, the highest percentage of any of the combatants. France and Germany lost around 15-16 percent of their soldiers and Britain 11 percent.

Faced with a deteriorating situation in the Balkans, France and Britain felt duty-bound to send troops to help the Serbs. Most of the British troops landed in Salonika (modern Thessaloniki) in Macedonia and looked to advance into neighbouring Serbia. By 1917, our allies, the Serbs were very much on the retreat and the British 'tommies' now faced Austrian and Bulgarian troops in a war which was apparently being lost and in conditions which were every bit as bad as those on the Western Front.

Amongst the British troops sent to Salonika was nineteen year old Oundelian **Richard Nynian Irwin**. He came from Gloucestershire and arrived at Sidney House in 1911. He played for the newly instituted U16 rugby team but left Oundle in 1914, at the age of 16, and took a commission in the Gloucestershire Regiment. After training in England and a brief spell in France, in November 1915 he was transferred to Salonika. By early 1917, his battalion was facing Austrian troops on the Greece/Macedonia border. At 2:30 a.m. on the morning of 6 March 1917, Lieutenant Irwin was in a raiding party which cut through the enemy wire, only to find an enemy force of about 300 men advancing from Krstali. As there was a danger of being surrounded, Captain Ashmead gave the order to withdraw. With supporting fire from the artillery, most of the party made it back to the British lines but Richard Irwin and four of his men were killed. One of his superior officers noted: "He was so capable and manly, so industrious and intelligent, and always thinking of his men first of all, that all of them, I know, loved him – as I did myself." Another officer wrote to Richard's older brother John, also a Sidney boy, who was wounded in the war but survived: "From what I have heard, your brother behaved in a most gallant manner after he had been wounded the first time. It was only through him insisting on being the last to go through the wire on the way back that he was killed."

While Richard Irwin was fighting against Austrians, young **Norman Prynne**, who had left Dryden House only in July 1915, found himself facing the Bulgars. On 24 April 1917, the decision was taken that the 10th Battalion of the Devonshire Regiment, including young Norman Prynne, would attempt to dislodge the Bulgarians from a ridge they held called *Petit Couronne*. Previous attempts since February had failed and this attack would be no different. One eyewitness wrote: "There was no elation in the air, rather a sullen determination." As the column of men climbed the hill in a night attack, the Bulgarians switched on their searchlights: "Promptly the barrage descended with most disastrous results. In that confined space, with the men pent in between precipitous rocks, the bursting effect of the high explosives was multiplied many times, bullets and fragments of bombs and shells ricocheting off the hard rock instead of burying themselves in the ground. Casualties were terrible." When the survivors were later gathered in, just over 200 answered their names out of 650 who had started the attack. Amongst the names unanswered that day was Norman Prynne's.

He was the fifth son of his parents' marriage and born in Ealing. His father was a successful architect and the family lived in comfortable circumstances in Kensington, with at least three servants, including a governess for the children. Norman, the youngest, was born in 1897 and came to Oundle at the age of 16, the year before war broke out. He left school in 1915 having won a place at Selwyn College, Cambridge. There he joined the University OTC and in January 1916, he received a commission in the 3rd Devon Regiment and sailed for Salonika in November 1916. His Commanding Officer wrote: "During the time he had been with us, he had shown himself to be possessed of very fine qualities and a high sense of duty. He is a great loss to all in his battalion, by whom he was much liked and respected." Aged just 19, his body was never found and he is commemorated on the Dorian Memorial in Macedonia, which records the names of more than 2,000 British soldiers who died there and whose bodies were never recovered.

John Myles Dunwoody, once of Laxton House was also heavily involved in the Salonika Campaign but did not die there. The only son of Dr and Mrs Dunwoody of Newark, he was born in October 1896 in county Monaghan in Ireland and had an older and a younger sister. After Oundle (he left Laxton in 1913), he went to learn

Norman Fellowes Prynne, Dryden House 1913-15.

John Miles Dunwoody, Laxton House 1911-13.

about the manufacture of linen and worked with Richardson and Owen in Belfast. He enlisted in September 1914 and in May 1915 he was gazetted into the Royal Dublin Fusiliers. In September of that year, he was on his way to the Dardanelles when his battalion was diverted to Salonika. Reaching the front line, rather earlier than his fellow Oundelians, he endured the retreat of Allied forces from Serbia in the autumn of 1915, in the face of Bulgarian advances and by December 1915, all the British troops had been driven back to Greece.

Having survived that arduous and inglorious retreat, John Dunwoody was granted leave back in England. Aged 20, he was returning from that leave when his ship, the SS *Transylvania* was sunk on 4 May 1917. This passenger ship, built in 1914 was converted into a troop transport ship at the start of the war. With nearly 3,000 men on board, the ship was apparently on its way to Alexandria in Egypt when it was torpedoed by a German U-boat (U-63) off Italy, in the Gulf of Genoa, just south of Savona. After the ship was hit, its escort vessel the Japanese destroyer *Matsu* came alongside to try to save the men. 20 minutes later, the U-63 fired a second torpedo at the *Matsu*, which took evasive action. Instead the torpedo hit the *Transylvania* and she sank quite quickly. Eyewitnesses reported that as the ship sank beneath them, the men "stood to attention." The *Matsu* helped to rescue nearly 2,500 men but some 413 others were lost that day including John Dunwoody and his body was never found. His name is inscribed on a memorial in Savona erected later.

His Company Commander wrote: "He died as he lived out here. During the nine months he was in my company, he proved himself one of the pluckiest young officers I have ever had the honour to command." His Commanding Officer was equally fulsome in his praise: "He was the Battalion Scout Officer; and as such was always running risks. Let me assure you that he was always ready to do so, and with a cheeriness that was a great asset to his men."

Gaza and Mesopotamia

Desperate for a victory to report in 1917, after the failure of the Salonika Campaign and the continuing stalemate on the Western Front, the British government looked to redirect their attack onto the Ottoman Empire, an attack which had gone so badly wrong at Gallipoli in 1915. So in late March 1917, the Egyptian Expeditionary Force attacked the Turks, across the Suez Canal at Gaza. The ensuing battle was hard fought but resulted in the British being repulsed, suffering some 4,000 casualties. They decided to try again three weeks later but in the meantime, Turkish defences had been strengthened and the number of Turkish troops increased. The Second Battle of Gaza began on 17 April 1917 and lasted just three days. On the first two days, the British took Turkish outposts and consolidated their positions, ready for the assault on the town itself on the third day.

Attacking the city from the east that third day was the 4th Battalion of the Northamptonshire Regiment but like other battalions, it was held up some 400 yards short of the Turkish trenches because British artillery had proved insufficient in power and range to silence their Ottoman counterparts. Amongst the gallant Northamptonshire lads that day was **Stanley John Marlow**. He lived at Preston Deanery Hall in Northampton, where his father was a boot manufacturer. Stanley, who was the only son of the marriage (he had three younger sisters) attended Bilton Grange prep school before coming to New House in January 1910. He was a keen member of the OTC passing two happy school camps on Salisbury Plain before leaving school in 1912. In May 1914 he joined the Northamptonshire Territorials and was promoted to lieutenant just a month after the war broke out.

He saw action in Gallipoli and was then moved to Egypt in August 1915. From there he served in Palestine and was killed on the third day of the Second Battle of Gaza, 19 April 1917. At the time of the attack, he was second-in-command of his company and with characteristic courage was right in front of his men, cheering them on by his gallant example when he was killed instantly. He was buried in Gaza Military Cemetery. His Commanding Officer reflected: "He justified every responsibility placed upon him and he met his death with the cheerful courage that characterized his whole life." To honour their son, Stanley's parents erected a rood screen, choir stalls and an altar rail in their local church of St. James in Northampton. The dedicatory plaque ends with the Roman poet Horace's words, made famous after the war by Wilfred Owen: "Dulce et decorum est pro patria mori"

At the end of that third day of the Second Battle of Gaza, where Stanley Marlow fell, the British forces had once again failed to take the city and had suffered some 6,500 casualties compared to under 2,000 for the Turks. Only with the coming of General Allenby, (ironically sacked by Haig for sustaining too many losses in the Battle of Arras), and the decision to deploy many more men and resources to the area, did the British eventually gain the victory that young Marlow (he was 21) had fought for. Not only did the EEF (Egyptian Expeditionary Force) take Gaza in November 1917 but they then swept north, helped by 'Lawrence of Arabia' and Arab forces, to take Jerusalem in December of that year. Allenby, sacked from the Western Front earlier that year,

Stanley John Marlow, New House 1910-12.

now triumphed where even Richard the Lionheart had failed and the British at last had something to celebrate. This was just as well, as by that time, on the Western Front, Passchendaele had, rather predictably, proved a very costly failure.

At the same time as the Battle for Gaza, British troops were also engaging Ottoman troops further east in Mesopotamia – modern day Iraq. After the disastrous loss of Kut in April 1916, where some 13,000 British troops had surrendered to the Turks, the British re-doubled their efforts to capture territory and to drive the Ottomans back. One Oundelian who was nearby in Basra but in hospital when Kut fell to the Turks was Leslie Murray, who had left Dryden in 1913. From his hospital bed, he recorded the fall of the city and described his role as a pilot in trying to keep British troops supplied during the siege:

> It was in the afternoon that I got news of the fall of Kut, which was rather depressing, although most of us were fairly certain that we could not hold on much longer...We expected Kut to surrender any time as we knew we could not feed them from the air much longer. Neither the machines nor the pilots could stand it.

In February 1917 however, Kut was recaptured and in March, Baghdad also fell into British hands. However, the British could not afford to rest there. The Ottoman threat to Baghdad was still real and so the British commander, General Maude ordered the Samarrah Offensive.

Amongst the troops in that advance was **Lieutenant Alan Edward Scarth**, who was killed on the second day of the Battle of Istabulat. He was born in India in 1896, where his father ran a tea estate in Assam. He was sent to England in the care of his uncle Rev. C. H. Crossley of Willingham Rectory in Cambridgeshire. Alan Scarth was in Crosby for just two years from 1911 until 1913, leaving just before his 18th birthday. He then returned to India to work on the tea plantation but in February 1915 he joined the Indian Army Reserve of Officers and spent some time training with the 1st Yorkshire Regiment stationed at Rawal Pindi. He was then attached to the Corps of Guides at Marden on the North-West Frontier.

In October 1916, he was sent out to Mesopotamia and was in charge of the Gurkha Company of the Corps of Guides, attached to the 53rd Sikhs. With them, he took part in the successful advance on Baghdad in March 1917 but was killed a few weeks later. Alan Scarth was hit on 22 April 1917, the second day of the Battle of Istabulat where the 53rd Sikhs suffered heavy casualties. He died of his wounds in the first-aid station. The regimental diary records the action near Samarrah as British troops took on the Ottomans that day:

Alan Edward Scarth, Crosby House
1911-13.

> At 16.50, two companies under the command of Captain A. E. Scarth and Lt. G. N. Mackintosh were sent to reinforce the 56th Rifles on the left flank by the railway. At 17.40, the left flank met with heavy enfilade fire from across the railway lines with heavy losses. Captain Scarth was wounded and died of wounds. The attack was successful, Samarrah was taken.

Accordingly, his company were congratulated on their success. One officer wrote to Alan's parents in India : "Alan's Company of Gurkhas did splendidly, in fact brilliantly – no less than three generals have congratulated our C.O. on this company…and this success was no doubt due to your son's example and leadership as he was a fine officer." Despite the success and fine words, conditions in the Mesopotamia campaigns were appalling. Extreme heat and cold, allied to arid desert conditions and virulent diseases with limited medical supplies, together with the broader problems of supply meant that, in many ways, British troops suffered even more here than they did in France and Belgium. Some 15,000 British troops were killed in the region during the war but nearly 13,000 more died of disease. In these conditions, Alan Scarth, once of Crosby House, Oundle, played his part in stabilizing the British position in the Middle East.

5 pilots lost in July 1917

The final group of five fatalities from the summer of 1917 were the airmen. By an extraordinary twist of fate, Oundle lost five 'fliers' in just 18 days in July that year, three of them, in the space of 10 days, from the same boarding house – the one run by Frederick William Sanderson. **Donald Wyand Ramsay** was from Newcastle and came up to School House in September 1911. He became Head of School in his last term, played for the XV for three seasons, becoming captain and was described as "a sturdy Full Back and an excellent tackler." He played the cornet in the school orchestra and did his bit for the war effort whilst still at school as he worked for two weeks in the workshops in his summer holidays in 1915. A very good all-round sportsman he had helped School House to win the Fives in 1915 and the Cricket in 1914 and 1915.

After Oundle, he joined the Royal Naval Air Service and, after training in England, went out to France. He was reported missing on 7 July 1917 and his death was afterwards presumed to have occurred on that day. He was just 20 years old at the time of his death and lies buried in Bousbeques Communal Cemetery, north of Lille, close to the Belgian border.

Described by his Commanding Officer as "one of the bravest and best pilots in the squadron," **Alexander Perceval Matheson** was the fourth Oundelian pilot to be killed in 1917. Born in Brighton in 1895, he came up to Dryden House from St Ronan's prep school in Worthing just before his 15th birthday. He won two workshops prizes and was involved in a memorable house rugby final in December 1912, which Dryden eventually won 16-0 after a replay, with Matheson scoring one of the tries. He stayed just three years and then, like several other Oundelians went to seek his fortune in Canada. Here he started but was unable to complete a four year course at the Ontario Agricultural College.

Donald Wyand Ramsay, School House 1911-15.

In 1915, he gained a commission in the Army Service Corps having joined up a week after arriving back in England. In November of that year, he transferred to the 55th Squadron of the Royal Flying Corps, arriving in France as a trained pilot in 1916. He was then almost continually in action over the Western Front until his death on 13 July 1917. He was shot down over German held territory in a dog-fight near Oudenaarde in Belgium and died prob-ably as a prisoner of war. At the time of his death, he had risen to the rank of Acting Flight Commander. He was buried by the Germans along with six other victims of the Great War in Oudenaarde Communal

Alexander Perceval Matheson, Dryden House 1910-12.

Cemetery. For his grieving parents, Alexander's death was the final hammer blow. Their other sons, Roderick and Ian, who were not Oundelians, had been killed just months before. Roderick in September 1916 and Ian in May 1917. At 22 years of age, Alexander was the longest lived of their sons.

Sub-Lieutenant Frank Bray was killed just two days after Alex Matheson, on 15 July 1917, aged only 18. Like his fellow School House resident, Donald Ramsay, (one year his senior), he enlisted in the Royal Naval Air Service. He trained as a pilot and received a commission. He went out to France and was killed just seven months after leaving school. He was out patrolling with several other machines when they were engaged by a German squadron. Reports claimed that Bray's machine was shot down in flames behind enemy lines. His Squadron Commander reflected on a popular and courageous officer: "His loss is deeply mourned by everybody in the squadron, with whom he was very popular. I know that I have lost a very good and extremely gallant officer." His body was never found.

Frank Bray was born in Leeds in 1898 and came to School House in 1912, leaving in December 1916. He was a house prefect and played in the 2nd XV. He, like Donald Ramsay helped with war work in the workshops during the summer holidays in 1915.

Very much a contemporary of Donald Ramsay in School House, **Rivers Gordon Begg** was the younger brother of Henry Begg killed on the Somme in November 1916 and was the third School House airman to be killed in July 1917. Like his brother, he was born in Calcutta and came up to School House in 1910, staying for five years. He was a keen gymnast at school and was a member of the School VI in 1914 and 1915. Leaving Oundle in the summer of 1915 and inspired by his older brother and possibly Cecil Lewis, who was also a School House boy, he determined to train as a pilot. He joined the Beatty School of Flying at Hendon and was later accepted by the Royal Naval Air Service, like fellow School House boys, Frank Bray and Donald Ramsay. Unlike them, his death was not as a result of a heroic aerial dog-fight.

In March of 1917, he joined the Adriatic Squadron and was stationed in southern Italy. Italy had joined the war on the Allied side in May 1915 and it was natural for the British to have air squadrons stationed in the south of the country to support the Royal Navy and Merchant Navy in their control of the Mediterranean sea-lanes, especially with British troops fighting across the Eastern Mediterranean in Macedonia, Gallipoli and Egypt. On 17 July 1917, while returning from a routine service flight, Begg's propeller broke off, striking a control wire and rendering the

Frank Bray, School House 1912-16.

Rivers Gordon Begg, School House 1910-15.

machine unmanageable. It fell into the sea and both Rivers Begg and his observer were drowned before they could be extricated from the wreckage. "He was universally popular," wrote his Commanding Officer, "his keenness and independence and confidence in himself endeared him to everyone". He is buried in Otranto, south of Brindisi in southern Italy. His parents had now lost their two older boys in just 8 months, leaving their final son, also a pilot, still serving. Luckily he survived the conflict. Rivers Gordon Begg was just 20 years old at the time of his death and School House, though it didn't know it yet, had now lost its third pilot in just 10 days.

Two weeks later, back in Oundle, John Coleman Binder heard about the loss of yet another young Oundle airman, though typically, he and others hoped that 'missing' might mean prisoner. He reported that the air war was now being pursued with renewed vigour: "The air fighting is also being waged with great vigour, 61 German machines were destroyed yesterday and Saturday. We lost 16. Amongst the missing pilots is a young fellow named Curtis whose father is a seed merchant here. Possibly he may be a prisoner." **Henry Neville Curtis** was born in 1899 and spent 5 years at Laxton School, leaving at Christmas in 1914, aged 15. He was born and raised in Oundle itself, where his father, William Curtis was a prosperous 'cake seed' merchant supplying local farmers. He lived at 22 West Street, near the Ship Inn, where the name Curtis can still be seen above the window. His grandfather ran a local brewery.

Young Henry was gazetted to the Royal Flying Corps on 25 May 1917, aged 18 and sent to France. The RFC's Sopwith Strutters were inferior to the German Albatross and consequently, casualty rates on the British side were high. When Henry Curtis arrived, the new Sopwith Camels were being deployed, which were meant to even things up a little. Two months to the day after his arrival in France, Henry Curtis and his observer W. S. Wickham set off on a reconnaissance mission behind enemy lines. They did not return and were classified as missing. In September of that year the RFC found a notice posted in a German newspaper of British planes which had fallen into German hands the previous July. This reported that Curtis and Wickham had been discovered dead in their plane. Henry Neville Curtis had been on active service for only 53 days and was just 18 at the time of his death. Unknown to him, just a few days before his death, he was mentioned by Sanderson on Laxton School Speech Day, as one of the many Laxton boys who had gained commissions. The Laxton School Journal also recorded that Henry had paid a couple of visits to the School in the Summer Term 1917 while on leave from France. They were to be his last visits home.

An Oundelian 'pilot' who didn't make it to the Front

Actually there was a sixth 'pilot' fatality in the spring and summer of 1917 for Oundle School and another boy of 18. Sadly, this lad did not make it as far as the Front, he never saw active service and he did not even have time to qualify as a pilot. Nonetheless, his death was, of course, just as much of a blow to his family and the school community. **Walter Maynard Hoyle** was a South-African by birth. He was the only son of the late Johnson Hoyle, who had been a successful solicitor in Johannesburg. He was born in 1898 and spent some time at St. John's College in Johannesburg before coming to Oundle at the age of 17. He was in Laxton House for just one year before going on to Sandhurst. In April 1917, he won a commission with the Norfolk Regiment and was later attached to the RFC. Tragically, he fell ill with pneumonia the same day that his move to the RFC came through and died just 11 days later, on 11 May 1917 at the Cottage Hospital in Weybridge, Surrey. He was still five days short of his 19th birthday when he died. His ashes were scattered at the Golders Green Cemetery in London and later, his name was inscribed on a memorial made of Portland stone designed to commemorate all the servicemen and women who were cremated there.

At Oundle, the Summer Term of 1917 ended on 31 July. Since the start of the calendar year, the Oundle Schools had suffered 34 more deaths amongst their 'old boys', the irony being that none of them were old at all, most, as we have seen, were 20 or younger. In total that made 41 fatalities since the start of the school year. If the staff and boys thought that the worst was over, they were to be cruelly deceived. As the boys left school for home, a new British campaign was starting. 31 July 1917 was the first day of the battle which would become known as Passchendaele. In due course it too would claim its fair share of Oundle boys.

8

Year 3 Home: Oundle School 1916-17

Was it in vain we wrought, and they,
Character strong and time to build,
Fit their part in the world to play
Through life's long years, had God so willed?

The third school year of the conflict then had seen no let-up in the death and destruction caused by war but rather an intensification of both. By the end of the year, victory in the field seemed as far away as ever. The failure of the Battles of the Somme and of Arras to breech the German lines, pointed to a long and awful struggle ahead on the Western Front and towards the end of the third school year of war, the British would launch another huge offensive which would be equally doomed to failure.

Challenges and responses

Back in Oundle, the School carried on as best it might and in truth the normal rhythms and routines of school life were maintained. But the top end of the School was now rather smaller than it had been with Sixth Formers setting off to train for war as soon as they were old enough. Speaking on Laxton School Speech Day in July 1917, Sanderson noted this change in the age profile of the boys: "We are working [in] both the schools of Oundle in time of war, under vastly changed conditions – changed in many ways, especially so because the boys are much younger, all the senior boys being claimed for service. In the Oundle School we are more than a year younger." Despite this change however, Sanderson also noted the way in which the boys had risen to the challenges posed by the conflict:

> Many of the forebodings that we had when the war began have not been realised. In schools, we found that the boys rose to the height of their opportunities, to their privileges, and to their responsibilities. It is the same in the Laxton School as it is in the Oundle School, and it is quite extraordinary to see the zeal of all these young boys who found themselves at the head of the school quite a year younger than they would have been in ordinary times.

And for the senior boys, the continuation of the war meant that they were waiting their turn. Since March 1916, when Asquith's liberal government had brought in the first of five 'conscription' acts, all boys over the age of 18 were obliged to join the army and the age would be lowered to 17 in April 1918, in reaction to the German's successful Spring Offensive on the Western Front. For Oundle boys, knowing, by this stage, quite a lot about the horrors of trench warfare and the scale of the casualties, it must have been an anxious time as their 18th birthdays approached. They faced the very real possibility of being killed or maimed in the conflict.

Oundle School Library before the War.

The first Laxtonian of the school year 1916-17, included three contrasting poems influenced by the war. The first poem, which was given pride of place in the introductory editorial section, was John Drinkwater's poem in honour of Second Lieutenant Stewart Ridley who had died in such tragic circumstances in the Libyan Desert, the previous June. Then came a poem by R.C.E. entitled *'Lines on returning to Oundle after 35 years'*. Scanning the school registers, the most likely author is Richard Cromwell Edwards who came up to School House in 1881, 35 years before 1916. The early verses are nostalgic and wistful, focusing on time that has passed:

> In Oundle once again I stand,
> As wanderers return
> To greet the past with heart and hand,
> And memories that burn.
>
> Here are the well-remembered scenes
> I knew so long ago,
> And Ghosts of many "might-have-beens"
> Glide softly to and fro.

Then he spots the soaring church spire and the poem takes a more serious turn as the war, never far from his thoughts one suspects, resurfaces in his consciousness:

> The old grey church with pious aim
> Lifts high its stately spire,
> In beauty worthy of its fame
> As any in the shire.

And famous too, the dauntless pair
Who climbed its dizzy height;
Better that men should do and dare
To scale the infinite.

May "God Grant Grace" is still our payer
For all her many sons,
The men who on Life's Highway fare
And for those other ones

Who answered to their country's call,
And fight in freedom's name,
Their Mother glories in them all,
And Oundle shares their fame.

Zeppelin Raids

The third poem in the December 1916 issue of the Laxtonian concerned a raid by German Zeppelins in the Oundle area in October 1916. Since the start of the war, there had been serious concerns about the impact of air raids by German airships on the civilian population. In June 1915, John Coleman Binder, our local grocer reported in his diary "another Zeppelin raid" over the East Coast. A few months later, he noted that "Mr and Mrs Ashworth of Oundle School have just returned from London. They had been there for a short holiday but had been so terrified by the bombs from the Zeppelins that they came home at once." By February 1916, the raiding had come rather closer to home: "The Zeppelins came during the night about 2 o'clock this morning. So war has been very close to us today....The police, who were about, tell me that it was very low down and quite over the town." There were then confused reports about the number of airships and the damage done in the area. A few weeks later, John Binder was roused from his bed by the police. He was a 'special constable' and was called upon with eight others of that rank to check that all lights in Oundle were out as, "Zeppelins were in the neighbourhood." In fact they only came as far as Wansford so no bombs were dropped on Oundle.

By September 1916, Zeppelin raids somewhere over England seemed to be a daily occurrence. No doubt many of the boys were disappointed that no bombs had so far been dropped over Oundle! In the night of 1 October 1916 however, their dreams nearly came true. An air raid that night apparently dropped bombs over Corby, only 11 miles from Oundle. "The flash of these was quite visible here and their explosion caused the houses to shake," explained John Binder. Later an unexploded German bomb was destroyed near Kirby Hall. Back in the boarding houses, or at least in Major Nightingale's Sidney House, boys were excited at the prospect of a raid:

While drowsing in our chairs one night,
(Please note the time was after prep.)
Our faculties became more bright
Because of rumours of a Zepp.

So up we rushed in haste to bed,
And put the lights out in a hurry.
We looked for Zeppelins, instead
No noises came to make us worry.

The XV of 1916-17. The Captain, Seisyth Lloyd (Lx), plus Frank Booth (G) (back row fourth right) George
Renton (G), (front row right), and Arthur Stace (C) (back row second left) would all be killed in the War.

But this was just the quiet before the storm and some while later, they were woken from their slum-
bers and escorted to the basement:

> But later we were roused from sleep
> By bangs and flashes in the sky,
> Which caused us from our beds to leap,
> And look around with startled eye.
>
> The Major came along, ah woe!
> Full well we realised what his face meant,
> i.e. that we had to go
> And seek a haven in the basement.
>
> So most unwillingly we sought,
> The cellars inches deep in dust.
> No matter what we said or thought,
> We had to swallow our disgust.
>
> And in the rush some little lad
> Was so unlucky as to spoil a
> Delightful evening; for he had
> Sat violently on a boiler.

And many others did the same,
And some said "dash!" and some said "blow!"
And other words I may not name,
Because the boilers burnt them so…

And when once more we all emerged,
Covered with dust and very "fed,"
And up the stairs our footsteps urged
To seek again the welcome bed,

We found that we'd have been as free
From harm, if we had not descended
To regions haunted by the flea;
And thus a pleasant Zepp raid ended.

Whether this heading for the basement happened very often is unlikely but it was a salutary reminder that the war was not confined to lands across the seas.

At the same time, the debaters also caught a touch of 'Zepp fever'. In November 1916, the motion before the House was that "Cellars are not the best place of refuge in a Zeppelin attack." Mr Bright assured the House that the breadth of England was more desirable than a restricted space, besides, he would be able to see it coming. Mr Field thought that the ground floor was best as "he could see the fun and not be gassed!" Mr Denison of Sidney (killed in April 1918) believed that "our life being our own, why not take it easily and stay in bed". After the vote, the motion was carried and the House opted to go into the open whenever German airships threatened.

OTC

The Laxtonian also records that seeking shelter during a Zeppelin raid was not the only time that Oundelians lost sleep because of the war. In a poem entitled *Night Operations*, it seems that 'the Major', who ran the OTC as well as Sidney House, had other ways of cutting down the boys' time in bed:

Say who are these shadows that pass through the night?
Celestial forms or infernal?
Can it be they are chattering skeletons white
Or Goblins unknown and nocturnal?

Perhaps they are warriors going to war,
Regretting their distant relations –
But no; 'tis the great Major Nightingale's corps
Departing for night operations.

They walk up a hill till they get to the top,
(An excellent method of drilling,)
They run for about fifty yards, then they stop,
The which is exceedingly thrilling.

They experience next with sensations of awe
The joys of preparing for action;

They dismiss and depart to their houses once more
With a feeling of great satisfaction.

And the light-hearted tone towards extra drilling practice would be maintained throughout the year. A poem from the July 1917 issue of the Laxtonian paints a slightly dispiriting picture of boys from the OTC practising for the Corps Cup:

Early every other morning,
Cold and mist and weather scorning,
In a martial fashion yawning,
And with shuffling of our feet,
On the roadway's sloping border,
We arrange ourselves in order,
Whilst some cynical applauder
Stands and grins across the street.

But reports on the activities of the OTC during this school year, reinforce the notion of an increased martial spirit at Oundle. In December 1916, came reports that the OTC had just enjoyed, "the most vigorous term in the course of its existence." "In addition to the two weekly parades, there have been classes three days in the week and a lecture on Thursday afternoons. Most cadets over the age of 17 have been attending these classes." Furthermore, the work of the OTC was now being directed increasingly by the War Office itself: "Precise drill and open fighting are the two subjects on which the War Office require us to lay especial stress, while not discouraging a certain amount of practice in trench warfare."

Meanwhile boys and staff who were officers in the OTC received extra training: "Half of our officers have recently attended Chelsea, and we should be quite proficient in the new drill by the summer term. Seven officers have passed through the Hythe School of Musketry." Leading the

Oundle School OTC in 1912.

way in terms of extra training, naturally enough, was the energetic Major Nightingale, who spent three weeks with the 2nd Artists' Rifles Cadet Unit. Further evidence of increased training in the Michaelmas Term came in the form of a Field Day near Seaton on 7 November. This was the first of its kind for two years, where Oundle joined forces with other schools. Apparently the weather was "vile" but "all ranks stuck to their work under trying circumstances". The boys were engaged in "wood fighting and a night advance".

In the Lent Term of 1917, the OTC was pleased, at last, to take delivery of "new rifles to replace the dummy rifles." The NCO class did lots of good work in parades and lectures and the results of the examination in practical work for Army candidates was very encouraging. They were examined by Major Hume of the Sherwood Foresters, sent down to Oundle by the War Office, who also conducted a snap inspection, expressing "a high opinion of the work of the corps."

The full annual inspection took place on 27 June 1917. Brigadier-General Colomb, Commander of the 18th Training Reserve Brigade noted that the NCOs were clearly profiting from their extra parades but thought that the corps as a whole "was not quite at its best on the day." While drill was good, "attack was too hurried and fire control requires more attention." In manoeuvres, Oundle needed "more practice in changing objectives and in switching fire off and on to several different objectives." In particular, "more instruction is required in outpost duties and duties of commanders of picquets." In fact, "some useful work was done in Outposts and Advance Guards," earlier in the term on the Field Day held at Morehay Lawn, near Apethorpe but clearly not enough to satisfy the army high command! Unfortunately, the OTC camp organized for the start of the summer holidays 1917 was cancelled, as other schools from the Midlands dropped out.

One particularly sad death reported by the school OTC was the passing of Captain George Williamson, teacher of classics and coach of the XV, who was killed during the Easter Holidays on 12 April 1917. The Laxtonian gloomily noted that he was one of three young masters who joined up in the first few months of the war – all of whom were now dead.

School Cloisters in 1905.

Talks on the War

And the War Office did not confine its efforts to inspecting and examining Oundle's young soldiers. They also organized visiting lecturers to encourage recruitment in schools. In November 1916, they sent in Captain Harold Hemming of the RFC to give a talk at Oundle. Happily, he was an OO who had left New House in 1911 and now he returned to talk to the boys about the work of the RFC at the Front. The Headmaster was in the chair to introduce him and Captain Hemming began his lecture with slides of aeroplanes used for teaching and in combat. He talked about the mounting of guns on the 'planes and how they fired through the propeller. He explained the vital role of the airmen in reconnaissance and in photographing enemy positions, looking out especially for gun emplacements, engineering stores and even horse-exercising grounds! Apparently a fall of snow was really helpful in this work. It meant that every available plane was scrambled because trenches and gun emplacements show up very clearly covered in a blanket of white. Planes were also crucial, of course, in directing battery fire and some were now able to report back to the gunners by wireless. Major Nightingale returned a suitable vote of thanks and no doubt many of the boys present gave consideration to joining the RFC in the months to come. Captain Hemming was stationed at a training school in Oxford and finished his lecture "by sketching the training of anyone desirous of obtaining a commission in the RFC." He also "offered his assistance to anyone who entered the corps." The lecture was clearly something of a recruiting drive.

But not all talks delivered to the boys that year were about the war. Captain Seton Carr's lecture in October 1916 was entitled "Wild animals I have known". Apparently, the captain, a well-known hunter of African wildlife, was attacked as much by people as by animals. Many objected to what they saw as his "indiscriminate slaughter of wild animals". Seton Carr retorted that he only killed two of each species and then only to provide food for his men. His favourite anecdote concerned the time he tied up a goat to entice a lion into range. The same lion appeared and retreated three times, each time being shot at by the gallant captain. When all was quiet, he came out of hiding to see what had happened. The goat was unharmed but behind a tree nearby, he found not one but three lions!

Agriculture

Hopes of reviving the annual corps camp during the summer holidays of 1917 were dashed as one by one other schools from the Midlands region cried off. And for Oundelians, the camp proved to be a non-starter "because of the demands of agriculture." With the resumption of unrestricted submarine warfare by the Germans and the consequent threat to the nation's food supplies, 1917 would prove to be a year when increased agricultural production trumped most other considerations. Despite shortages elsewhere, food supplies in Oundle seem to have been maintained in the winter of 1916-17. Mr Binder, local grocer, writing in January 1917 claimed "there is really no lack of anything here." Though there was enough food, the downside, of course, was an increase in prices. He thought that the cost of food had gone up by some 90 percent since the start of the war but the only food in short supply was sugar. By March 1917, potatoes were scarce and in some towns and villages "quite unobtainable."

But Oundle School was ready to meet the potato challenge. In February 1917, two talks on the importance of agriculture were given by Christopher Turner and in April the Laxtonian proclaimed that Oundle was widening the scope of its agricultural endeavours: "In answer to the appeals of the Board of Agriculture, the Headmaster has decided to break up the lawns around Sidney and Grafton, (about 9 acres) for the purpose of planting potatoes." The digging was all done by hand and, being incomplete by the end of term, it seems that some boys stayed on in the holidays to finish the work. Much of the 'trenching' was done by forms on the classical side, who also helped "with the hoeing and 'moulding up' of the plants." Of course, for the boys, this new focus on growing potatoes was a great subject for lampooning. A poem entitled *the Potato-Diggers* duly appeared in the Laxtonian:

> Come and brandish Pick and Shovel, come the sharpened Fork to wield;
> For your country needs your help to dig Potatoes on the Field.
> The labour may prove difficult, but each must take his share
> And do all he can to cultivate the valued *Pomme de Terre*.
> If asked to give our Spare Time up, such patriots are we,
> To help our King and Country we most willingly agree;
> But if they want our School Time, well, I think we must confess,
> We give it up, if possible, with yet more readiness.

Finding a rhyme for potatoes is not easy but one Oundelian found a classical solution:

> Let the nations know our prowess in the field:
> How with will as stern as Cato's, we shall woo the coy potatoes.

And the potato mania was of course discussed in the debating chamber. Ivo Bright of School House proposed the motion "that everyone should go home at the end of term and not stay behind to dig potatoes." And he won by a small majority!

At the same time the School responded to a request from the Board of Agriculture, to grow crops of leguminous herbs to improve the fertility of derelict land. Boys would be sent out to collect seeds and experiments concerning the best time and depth for sowing the seeds would be carried out. As well as potatoes and leguminous herbs, Oundle now kept pigs "in some numbers" for school consumption. By the summer of 1917, ten had been killed and the School had "two breeding sows with litters and eight half-sized porkers." In the calendar year 1917, the School literally 'brought home the bacon' producing a ton of home grown bacon and ham to ensure that Oundelians remained well fed in the most difficult year of the war so far for finding food. Meanwhile another striking addition to the experimental gardens already established was the development of an outdoor vivarium to house snakes and lizards. This had nothing to do with the war but everything to do with Oundle's widening curriculum.

All told, by the end of the school year 1916-17, some 15 acres of land were now being cultivated. Nine acres for potatoes, two for peas, two for swede and the last two for a variety of other vegetables. As in workshops, so in agriculture, important war work was being undertaken by the boys. By the summer of 1917 each form was giving up at least one day of the term and often more, to work on the school farm. By 1917, Sanderson concluded, in a letter to the governors that,

> The teaching of agriculture is steadily taking root [!] in the school and growing [!] in value and importance. We have many boys who have natural aptitudes for the work and amongst them boys of the land-owning class. I suppose the best work a school could do would be to give such boys a scientific interest in agriculture as a branch of applied science.

True to his word, Sanderson introduced a Farm Class for boys destined for work on the land.

Debating

We have already seen how the war impacted on the Debating Society with motions about air raid precautions and potato cultivation. And the trend continued with a motion about Romania's entry into the war on the Allied side (August 1916) and one about the importance to the nation of "games in public schools". In the latter, the links to the current conflict were evident. Arthur Stace (killed May 1919) reminded the House that the Battle of Waterloo was won on the playing-fields of Eton and inveighed against "the unsporting spirit of the Germans." Even the opposition main speaker linked his arguments to the war effort. Clement Hindley argued that as "no keenness was shown in junior games, members of these games might be handed over to farmers for work on the land." John Denison, supporting the motion and incensed by the opposition claim that "cricket was useless" declared that cricket was in fact vital to Britain's war effort. "The Germans", he averred, "were unable to throw bombs as far as the British." He alleged that this was because the Germans "encouraged gymnastics rather than cricket."

Later in the year there was an extended debate about 'War Economy', with calls for theatres and picture-palaces to be closed down. Even the French Society got in on the act with a motion (which was lost) declaring that war contributed to the well-being of humanity. Other debates during the year followed more traditional lines with motions wondering if examinations were "a fair test of a term's industry", whether "further research in hypnotism was desirable", or whether "Ladies Fashions were cruel to the animal world."

Sport

But there were complaints about potatoes from the footballers: "Football [rugby] this term [Lent 1917] has been rather unsatisfactory, since our time has been otherwise employed in a new form of labour, namely, agriculture." In other ways too, the war impacted on the quality of football. In December 1916, the Laxtonian commented on "the extreme youth of the school at present" which served as an excuse for a poor set of results. Nonetheless, although the number of seniors available to play was in decline, more boys played in school matches. In the Michaelmas of 1916, the School managed two fixtures for the 2nd XV and even one, against the Leys for a 3rd XV. More boys were clearly playing senior rugby matches. Such was not the case for boating. In the same term, the rowers complained that "there was very little boating this term". Apparently, there were three causes of this unfortunate situation and two were clearly linked to the conflict across the water: "munition work took away many of the old members, and recruit drills many of the new". Cricketers too had cause to rue the impact of hostilities on their favourite sport. Though the summer season 1917 was deemed a success, the captain noted that senior boys "have paid more attention to military work this season than during the two previous years of the war." More directly perhaps, the war undermined the efforts of the cricketers when Fred Holland, the grounds man and cricket coach left to join up with the Army Service Corps. He had won the county championship three times with Surrey and came to Oundle sometime after 1908, when he retired from county cricket. Although he went off to war in 1917, he actually returned to coach Oundle cricket again in the summer of 1918!

A cold snap at the start of 1917, allowed Oundelians, or at least the senior boys, to enjoy a change from the normal sporting diet, with some ice skating: "A sharp spell of frost enabled the School to enjoy some skating. This was allowed by the Headmaster on certain specified fields. One day a party of the bigger fellows went to Biggin to clear the snow off the lake, but the ice was not considered safe enough for the whole school to venture upon it."

School fixtures throughout the year took on a more militaristic tone in terms of the opposition that Oundle encountered. Footballers played the Machine Gun Corps, the Cranwell Naval

Whole School in 1903.

Air Station and the King's Own Yorkshire Light Infantry. This last team was organized by OO Captain Guy Roberts, ex-New House and Grafton and the match was played on 20 November 1916. On the first anniversary of this match, which the Light Infantry boys won, Guy Roberts himself was seriously wounded leading his men in an attack on the French city of Cambrai. He died two days later. For the cricketers as well, the fixture list was dominated by the military. As well as hosting Major Gotley's XI and Lieutenant Winter's XI, there was also a match against the Motor Machine Gun Corps!

Music

The School Choral and Orchestral Societies also had cause to complain about the impact of the conflict on their activities. In the Michaelmas of 1916 there was a serious shortage, "a very small number" of basses and the singers "were weak in all parts." At the same time, the orchestra recorded that it had "made its sacrifice for the War." Instead of the spacious hall in the new Science Block, it had been relegated to a cramped class-room "which is well filled with players and more than filled with sound." Despite these difficulties, music was still an important part of school life. Organ and violin recitals were given on Sunday evenings in the Great Hall, the Speech Day concert went well and the tradition of house concerts on the last night of the Summer Term continued. In the third school year of the conflict, some 120 boys, a good 25 percent of the school, were learning a musical instrument, most the piano.

Workshops

Relatively little is heard of workshops activity during this school year but probably because it was continuing in the usual way, with 40 boys working there at any one time and any extra boys being sent to the carpenters' shop, which was now housed in the old gymnasium in the Cloisters, opposite the workshops. We have already seen that workshops interfered with boating and we can see that 'the shops' took up many hours of some boys lives. The Commemoration booklet for this year claimed that each boy might be called upon to give eight or nine hours per week to workshops production. In the Michaelmas Term of 1916 the Laxtonian editor noted that "the forms on the engineering side have their leisure hours filled up by workshops, much to their enjoyment. What an enviable time the classicist has!" By the summer, there was one significant change in the way the boys worked. Now each form went into the 'shops' for a whole week (this continued into the 1980s) and was then free the rest of the term. During their week, however, boys worked for some 55 hours.

In this year, they produced "brass finishing in connection with torpedo gear" as well as tools for the Woolwich Arsenal and gauges and shoes for horses and mules for the Munitions Board. One boy recalled being quite unaware of what he was making: "It took me a long time to find out what the object was I was working on, but it turned out to be part of a submarine – and I only hope that my contributions weren't responsible for any naval disasters in the First World War!" The same writer, a boy in Sidney House 1913-17, was also nearly expelled because of his late arrival one day at the 'shops':

> One day, the times of the shifts were altered…and we, thoughtless louts that we were, had not noticed the fact. As a result, we turned up at the shops half an hour late – by which time a keen supervisor had reported our absence to the great man himself. Sanderson flew into a rage. We had scarcely settled down to our portions of submarine when a peremptory message reached

Sanderson and Workshops production 1917.

us saying that the headmaster wished to see us in the Great Hall immediately. We hastened along there and found 'Beans' already up on the stage and more or less purple with suppressed fury. Very briefly, he informed us that we had betrayed the school, the war effort and society in general and that he would not have such boys any longer in his school.

The boys were given just one hour to pack their bags and to return to the Great Hall to receive their journey money. Luckily, when they returned they found the Head in more emollient mood: "He had, he confessed, been thinking it over and he had decided that he had been a little bit too hard on us. In short, he would not, after all, sack us." So workshops' production carried on in its usual fashion after all.

Due to some urgent 'rush' orders, boys once again stayed on in the workshops in the summer holidays of 1917. 30 volunteers worked for a month, two groups of 15 boys working two weeks each. But as well as the hard work during the days, the volunteers, who slept in the School Sanatorium, also played hard. They bathed, boated, danced and played tennis. A boating picnic went off to Lilford Hall and, at the end of the first fortnight, there was even a concert and a dance in the Great Hall organised by Mrs Hale wife of the Dryden Housemaster.

Wartime experiments

Making clear that, even in wartime, educational advances were still being made at Oundle, the Commemoration booklet of 1917 contains an article written by Sanderson on the School's new cinematograph. The article was also sent to the Cinema Commission, indicating the national potential of this splendid new machine. "There is no doubt," he wrote "that in most cases of motion, or change in [over] time, the cinematograph is a fuller revealer than the unassisted eye. In one way it acts as a camera – it sees deeper and in one direction; in another it can magnify and bring nearer the object under consideration." Sanderson was confident that the new instrument had a promising future "in opening out new worlds, and the better understanding of old ones." He explained how the machine was being used by the boys to study motion, properties of materials under stress, the behaviour of birds and animals and the growth of plants. In addition, it was hoped in the future to create films to illustrate scientific developments as well as the lives of great scientists such as Faraday and Darwin. In the end Sanderson believed that "the persistent use of the cinema is needed to change the thought from 'the static' to 'the dynamic'."

And beyond the cinematograph came experiments commissioned by the Royal Flying Corps using unmanned pilot balloons to measure the velocity and direction of the wind at different heights. Once again Oundelians were doing their bit for the war effort. The experiments were undertaken by senior boys between March and May 1917 when two balloons, filled with hydrogen, were sent up every day between 7 and 8 in the morning some rising as high as 13,000 feet. Readings were taking by means of a theodolite and some complicated mathematical formulae were used to work out the wind velocity at a variety of altitudes.

Losses in the war – deaths real and imagined

Meanwhile the Laxtonian magazines for the school year 1916-17 continued to catalogue the horrors of the war with lists of those killed, wounded, missing, prisoners of war as well as those decorated by their country for valour. Forty deaths, with brief citations, were reported during the year but one death was taken away. In the December issue 1916, the Laxtonian reported that Harold Lilly, pronounced dead in the last issue, was in fact alive and a prisoner in German hands. More worrying, and revealing the confusion engendered by war, was the misreporting of the death of Arthur Franklin Baker (Grafton 1904-06). Serving with the Duke of Cornwall's Light Infantry

Sidney as House Fives Champions 1917. John Denison (standing left) and John Emtage (seated left) would both be killed the next year.

and recently attached to the Royal Flying Corps, the Laxtonian reported that he was killed on 11 April 1917. But in fact Oundle's Arthur Baker was actually alive and well and manufacturing boots, presumably for the army, in the family firm in Wolverhampton. The Arthur Baker who was killed was in fact Arthur Forbes Baker, quite another man but with the same initials as the Oundle lad. The same kind of mistake was even made later in the Oundle School Memorial Book of 1920, where the citation for Captain Gilbert Kennedy actually gives details of the death and career of Captain Gilbert Stuart Kennedy who was not an Oundelian. Oundle did have a Captain Gilbert Kennedy and he in fact outlived the war but only just. He died in December 1918, a victim of the influenza pandemic which swept across Europe in the wake of the conflict.

As well as deaths in the war, real or imagined, there were also deaths amongst the boys still at Oundle. Between 28 December 1916 and 17 March 1917, three schoolboys died. The causes of their deaths are not clear, given only as "fatal illness". Alexander Tait of Grafton was 16, Crosby's William Howarth and David Cohen of New House were both 15 years old. Rather older was the ex-School House boy William Fuller who was killed "in a motor accident" in Eastbourne aged 45.

No fewer than 60 boys were listed that year as wounded but unlike previous years no details of their injuries were given. In the March issue two years before, readers were told that Lieutenant Humphrey Bostock (whose brother Guy was killed in January 1916 at Loos) had had his right arm amputated and there must have been many more who were severely wounded and maimed but whose injuries were not recorded by the Laxtonian. And there was the growing number of Oundelians who found themselves prisoners of war and living in pretty awful conditions until the end of the war brought release. In this school year, Bryan Millard, John Plews, George Elliott, Herbert Dickson and Leslie Holman were reported as prisoners in German hands while Paul Edmonds' war ended in captivity at the hands of the Turks. And then there were the many who were merely described as missing. Where bodies were destroyed or never recovered, families had to endure the uncertainty of their loved ones as 'missing'. In this school year, eight Oundelians were officially recorded in this category but there were probably many more. While the Laxtonian kept old boys and parents up to date with the most recent information concerning those serving in the war, the Commemoration booklets produced for Speech Days recorded all the losses since the start of the war. In the 1917 issue of this worthy publication, no fewer than 119 deaths are recorded over five pages – a sobering list indeed.

Memorial Chapel and memorial scholarships

And it was in the summer of 1917, on the Sunday of the Speech Day week-end, (1st July), that the idea of building a new Memorial Chapel at Oundle was formally mooted and then endorsed by further meetings of parents and old boys later in the month. They agreed to pay for the chancel of the new chapel, while the Grocers, who had been planning to build a new chapel before the war started, would fund the rest. At the same time, parents, old boys, Grocers and staff were unanimous in demanding that a fund be set up to educate the sons of the fallen at their old school free of charge. At the meeting of parents in the Great Hall on 1 July 1917, Sanderson assured them "that no son of an old boy would lack, for want of means, education at his father's old school." The School also committed itself to printing a memorial book "containing the records and photographs of Old Boys who have fallen in the war". A notice to this effect appeared in the Laxtonian of July 1917, in the hope that "parents will assist in making the record as complete as possible." Meanwhile, the School received donations in honour of individuals amongst the fallen. Mrs Rathbone presented a set of books on British Birds and Fishes, in honour of her nephew, James Dixon killed on the first day of the Somme.

Better news of Old Oundelians

But amidst the death and destruction of war, there was also the glory of promotions, awards and decorations. In this academic year, six old boys won the DSO, 31 boys and one master won the MC, while John Shettle was awarded the *Croix de Chevalier* of the Legion of Honour and Richard Westcott received the Serbian Gold Medal.

The Lent Term issue of the Laxtonian also contained more cheery news of old boys at the Front. This was a letter from two exact contemporaries in Sidney House, Colin Gulliland and Clement Little. By the chance encounters of war, they had met up again in the War Hospital in Bombay. Gulliland, younger brother of John Gulliland killed in July 1916 near Ypres, had been invalided out of Mesopotamia with shell shock and Little, who was serving in the Indian Army, had gone down with "a bad attack of enteric". Apparently, the dormitory of the Bombay Hospital reminded them of school and so they decided to write a letter to the Laxtonian detailing the other Oundelians they had met in their travels. Both had come out to India towards the end of 1914 and in December 1915 they even organized a School Dinner in Calcutta where five other OOs appeared. By all accounts the party, though small, was very cheery and "the toast to the old school was drunk with great gusto." Of those present that evening only one, the pilot Henry Berners Begg, who was born in Calcutta, would die in the war. He was killed in November 1916, the same month that Gulliland and Little wrote their joint letter to their *alma mater*.

Meanwhile the Summer Term of 1917, saw two more old boys, contemporaries in Sidney House, paying (literally) flying visits to their old school. Arthur Wills, managed to crash through a brick wall on landing and escaped with only slight injuries. A week later, William Emtage appeared in the skies above Oundle. He landed safely enough in the long grass behind the cricket fields. Getting out of the plane he remarked, "I hear Wills crashed here last week." However, his own good form and good luck did not last. Taking off the next day from the same long grass, his plane struggled to gain height and he crashed into another wall, just down the road. Luckily, his machine did not catch fire and he only sustained a broken ankle. After two crashes in one week, the Headmaster banned further visits to Oundle by air.

Laxton School, Summer 1917

There is only limited material on the fortunes of Laxton Grammar School during the war. While they may not have helped out with agriculture like their counterparts at Oundle School, they did join in with munitions production early in 1916 and they seem to have led the same slightly schizophrenic existence as their close twin, in terms of prospering and growing during the war, while also lamenting the deaths and injuries of old boys. Laxton Grammar School may have produced 13 school magazines during the war but only two survive, those of July 1917 and July 1918, so they provide only a limited snapshot of the School in the last two years of the conflict.

Unlike the Laxtonian, these Laxton School Journals start with the impact of the war on old boys and masters. In the summer of 1917, former teacher Henry Reynolds (who would be appointed to the Oundle School staff after the war) is mentioned first. He had taught at Laxton only for a year or so before the war began and his military career proved successful. He gained a commission in the Lancashire Fusiliers, won the Military Cross in 1917, (at which the Laxton boys were awarded a half-holiday), added a bar to this award late in 1917, was promoted captain and survived. After his successes, the latest deaths are recorded – Jesse Wallis, Hugh Turnill, John Robson and Henry Stranger. Wallis had been killed in March, Turnill and Robson had died within two days of each other in April of 1917 but Stranger had been lost back in August 1915. In total, Laxton School would lose 30 boys, nearly 12 percent of the total killed in the two schools, which, as Laxton School formed roughly 11-12 percent of the Schools' population during the war, was very much the same 'strike rate' as their larger twin.

The full list of the names of the Laxton School fallen so far was also recorded in the magazine in the report on the School's Speech Day of 1917. The magazine printed the address by Sanderson, which included the reading out of the Roll of Honour, which then stood at ten names. He noted that this was the first occasion he had read out the Laxton School names – something he did once a term in Oundle School. Sanderson also took the trouble to mention and comment on the names of boys currently serving, often to the accompaniment of cheering from the boys. On Speech Day 1917, he knew of 120 Old Laxtonians doing their bit. John Anderson who gained a scholarship to Clare College, Cambridge was currently in the Machine Gun Corps. Victor Siddons, well known in Oundle, was in the RFC, going first to France and then to Palestine. Sanderson affirmed that he was currently, "in Mecca, flying over the desert and learning Arabic." Other boys in action for their country were well known as sons of local shopkeepers. Amps and Cotton boys came in this category but which particular brother in these two cases is not clear. Was he referring to Harold John Amps (L.S. 1901-06) or William Percy Amps (L.S.1902-10?). In the case of Cotton, he should certainly have said Cottons. Albert Hector Cotton, always known as Hector, had certainly joined up early in the war and got married on leave in 1916. His older brother Charles Frederick, always known as Fred, also did his bit. He

Marriage of Hector Cotton once of Laxton School, in 1916. (Jacqueline Cheetham, Oundle)

had gone to Australia after leaving Laxton in 1904 and then returned to join up. Like his brother, Fred Cotton also survived the war. The Cotton name was still well-known in Laxton School in 1917, as the youngest brother Philip George, (always known as Phil rather than George!) had left just two years before.

Then there was Kenneth Butlin described by Sanderson as, "a dear, good, clever boy, who is in the Royal Engineers and employed now (as he ought to be employed) in high scientific work." Two brothers Turnill of Warmington were still fighting, though the third brother, Hugh had now died of his wounds. In terms of numbers serving, pride of place perhaps went to the Streathers brothers – five of them – who were all 'doing their bit'. Frederick in the Royal Engineers in Mesopotamia, George in the Yeomanry in France; John in the 7th Middlesex had been to Gibraltar, Egypt and France; Robert in the 4th Northants. and Cecil, also of the Northants., currently wounded and in hospital in Essex. "A great record I think," opined the Headmaster and indeed an excellent record for their parents as all of them seem to have survived the war. Meanwhile, Sanderson also reported that at least one Laxton boy was now a prisoner of war: "North, who is at any rate safe for the present, though he doesn't like it, is a prisoner employed, I believe, by the Germans making railways to take them to Russia."

And the war theme continued. There were several pages of the journal then dedicated to Old Boys News, recounting tales and achievements of boys currently serving in the war. In 1917 John Aeschliman reported being "in a fairly quiet part of the line" so his experiences "have not been very thrilling." Henry Curtis (who had since been killed) had called in at his old school after an unfortunate accident "with his machine" led to an injury. Likewise, Walter Holdsworth reported that he had been wounded in the knee at Bullecourt but was looking forward to re-joining his unit in the near future. Ex-teacher Henry Reynolds wrote "very cheerfully from rest-camp in France" where he was enjoying a well-earned break after taking part in the Battle of Messines Ridge.

Unlike the Laxtonian magazines of this period, the Laxton Grammar School Journal included letters from boys at the front. Some were still engaged in training. Donald Wadlow, not yet old enough to join up, reported that he had spent two years in Training College doing electrical engineering, with special classes in Military Science, including wireless work. Here he was helping his principal carrying out important research. "It is very interesting but rather ticklish," he noted. J. W. T. Jones had just completed his wireless course and was hoping for a commission in the Royal Naval Air Service. He had just gone through the medical tests, when he wrote in, proclaiming them "without doubt the stiffest tests going."

And then, as with the Laxtonian magazines, there is sport and lots of it. The cricket season is dealt with in the same manner as at Oundle. There are pen portraits of each team member, lots of averages both batting and bowling and reports on all the matches, though, in 1917, there were only four of them, all against King's Peterborough! That summer, there was also a fives tournament between the Top and Lower Dormitories with 22 boys taking part; a boating excursion to Perio Mill in four boats lent by Oundle School; a biking excursion to the remains of Christopher Hatton's Elizabethan mansion at Kirby and a chess tournament won by Woodcock, who collected the prize of a camera donated by Mr Mossman.

Overall, the Laxton journal provides a useful snapshot of life in Laxton Grammar School during the war. On official occasions, such as Speech Day, the war of course was very prominent in everyone's thoughts as the school took stock of the impact of the conflict on old boys. At the same time, the everyday business of the school went on very much as in peace time. Lessons, sports and societies continued as before.

Oundle School Speech Day 1917

Oundle School's Speech Day was held on the same rather abbreviated lines as in previous war years. The weather was fine for both the Saturday and Sunday, which suited the new item on the Speech

Day agenda, namely a cricket match between the Town Houses and the Field Houses on the Saturday afternoon. This ended in good time for parents to view the scientific experiments between 5 and 7 and there was a band to play during the afternoon and early evening, followed by a School Concert in the Great Hall which included the singing of Lady Maud Warrender. Her son Harold had joined School House at the start of the academic year. She was a celebrated singer, daughter of an earl and was a powerful figure not only in the performance of music but also in its promotion. She sang before the royal family on many occasions, was great friends with Elgar (they went cruising together) and is said to have persuaded George V to change his family name to Windsor in order to sound less German. Once at dinner, apparently, she told the King that some people thought that he was pro-German because of his German name and the fact that the Kaiser was his cousin!

On the Sunday morning, the Commemoration Service was held in the Chapel and extra seating had to be brought in to cope with the numbers. In the evening service, Sanderson read the ever lengthening Roll of Honour and the list of distinctions and medals won by Oundelians serving with his Majesty's Armed Forces. Lady Maud Warrender sang again, perhaps in more sombre mood than earlier, with Handel's *Laud we our God* and there was an organ recital to round things off. It must have been

Lady Maud Warrender, 'Oundle mother' who sang in the Speech Day Concert 1917.

a particularly poignant service for all those present because of the date. It was 1 July 1917, exactly one year since the first day of the Battle of the Somme, with all the reminders of lost promise and lost hope which that particular battle carried with it.

While the war touched so many aspects of school life, it clearly did nothing to stop the increasing size of the School. War or no war, or perhaps because there was a war, Oundle was increasingly popular with parents and prospective parents. Did a school with munitions workers, lots of science and agriculture seem more relevant in wartime? Despite the loss of the most senior boys to the widening conflict, actual numbers at Oundle continued to rise. So much so, that in January 1917 and again in the September, new boarding houses were opened. As there was no time to erect purpose-built houses like School House and the Field Houses, Oundle now acquired two substantial town houses and converted them for school use. At the start of the Lent term 1917, Laundimer House in North Street began trading with Mr Ault as Housemaster of 24 boys. In the autumn, Bramston in the Market Place was added as well and Mr Llewellyn Jones came out of retirement in Wales to take charge.

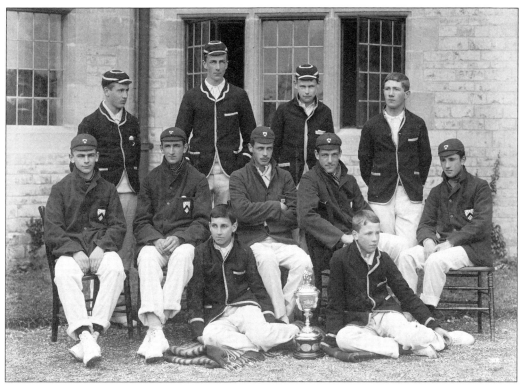

Laxton House Cricket XI 1902, captained by Frank Armitage, who was killed in July 1917.

Laundimer House, Oundle.

Laundimer House which opened as a new boarding house in January 1917.

First Laundimer House Photograph in the Summer of 1917.

Sanderson and the War

In the speech he made at the Laxton School Speech Day in 1917, Sanderson gave some clues about what he thought the results of the war should be. Despite the horror at the carnage and the extraordinary number of deaths, Sanderson believed that the war would be an engine of social progress. He thought it should produce, "what philosophers now call transvaluation of the value of things," and "the opportunity...to set the world free." More generally he explained that the terrible conflict would do away with what he called 'the Age of Capture' and usher in a new spirit of creativeness. The object of this creativeness was to be "radical changes in the welfare of the people." Here schools and education would play a prominent role. "Changes," he explained, "will take place in the organization, buildings and methods of schools...We are abandoning the class-rooms, with the methods they imply, for the larger space of workshops, art-rooms, libraries, theatres, fields and gardens." Here was Sanderson's familiar appeal to spaciousness and within this spaciousness, he thought that masters (and mistresses) should be carrying out important work and that the pupils should be their assistants in that work. Together they would be engaged in "tool sharpening." "Technical education," he proclaimed "is the breath of life – and should be brought within reach of all children."

It was all rather heady stuff but it showed that for all the war's destructiveness, Sanderson believed that it was, in a way, a necessary evil to usher in a better world. Despite all that had happened, Sanderson still believed in human progress. Perhaps it was easier for a man steeped in the terrible scourges and sufferings recounted in the Old Testament, to see the current conflict as a divinely planned great step forward towards a better future, perhaps towards the Promised Land?

But in the summer of 1917, Sanderson had not yet lost his own elder son.

9

Year 3 Away: Mostly Passchendaele – 31 July to 7 September 1917

> To have led your men with a daring adored and reckless,
> To have struck your blow for Freedom, the old straight way:
> To have loved men more than yourself and have died to prove it -
> Ah yes! This is to have lived: was there more to do?

Passchendaele

Just like the Somme campaign, the previous year, the terrible Third Battle of Ypres, known as Passchendaele, was no respecter of school years. It began on the first day of the summer holidays and ended in the early days of November in the next school year, though the last Oundle victim was killed at the end of October. Despite the very mixed results of the Somme in 1916 and of Arras in the spring of 1917, Haig was determined to launch a further major offensive, this time in Flanders. He had always nursed the hope of attacking here as this was territory which the British had always held and which had already been the scene of two great confrontations with the Germans in 1914 and 1915. For many British politicians, appalled by the attrition and ever mounting casualties, the entry of the Americans into the War in the spring of 1917 should have led to a policy of the British remaining on the defensive on the Western Front, waiting for the hundreds of thousands of fresh, well-equipped American troops to arrive the next year. For Haig the opposite was the case. He now wanted a great British offensive in the summer of 1917 to secure a great British victory before the Americans arrived.

Despite the evidence of previous campaigns, which showed how well the Germans had developed and honed their defensive capabilities, Haig blindly convinced himself that the Germans were on their last legs and that a powerful thrust eastwards from Ypres would be a knock-out blow, allowing the British to capture the Belgian ports, neutralise the U-boat menace (at its height in the spring of 1917) and finally push the Germans back to their homeland. After the First Battle of Ypres in 1914, General Sir Horace Smith-Dorrien, commander of the British 2nd Army had proposed that the British should retreat to the outskirts of the city itself, in order to shorten and straighten out the Ypres salient, to make it easier for the British to defend the city. He was sacked for his views, which meant that as the Third Battle of Ypres developed in 1917, the British advance would inevitably just make the salient bigger and harder to defend as the Germans would be able to attack from three sides.

Quite wittingly, Haig in fact created a British Verdun. Despite the appalling weather and appalling losses, he continued the attacks as he had at the Somme until the winter closed in. It is hard now to understand how he could remain optimistic about a final British breakthrough, when everything in the Passchendaele campaign and in the war so far pointed to continued stalemate and failure. It is hard for us to comprehend why he started the offensive and even harder to fathom why it continued for so long. After some 325,000 casualties and possibly 100,000 deaths, the British had merely enlarged the salient around the city. And in the spring of 1918, as the Germans prepared, for the first time, to launch their own great offensive on the Western Front, Haig decided that the ground so painfully gained could not be held and so it was given up. A few weeks after the end of the battle, Haig decided to shorten the salient around Ypres, essentially to the line suggested by General Sir Horace Smith-Dorrien early in 1915.

The first of 19 Oundelians to die in the carnage and mud of Passchendaele was the ever optimistic **Reggy Secretan**. His letters home, so full of hope, enthusiasm and reassurance came to an end on the last day of July 1917, the first day of the battle. The advances made that day came at a high price in terms of casualties including the men of Secretan's 1st Herts. who were driven back by German counter-attacks in the afternoon. The tales of the exploits of Secretan's Hertfordshire boys became legendary but in reality it was another case of heroic yet futile failure. The men were told that their part in the advance was to consist of "merely walking behind a creeping barrage with slung rifles and that no opposition would be met with." It was to be the same tactics as the 1 July the previous year on the Somme. The Daily Mail took up the story:

Reginald Herbert Secretan, Sidney House 1909-14.

> The highest sacrifice in the third battle of Ypres was perhaps paid by the Hertfordshire Regiment. I have heard no more splendid or moving tale of gallant men going out to death and glory since the War began. About 10 o'clock, after St. Julien was captured, the German shelling with 5.9 howitzers grew hotter than many officers had ever seen it…The men reached the approaches to a trench defended by 400 yards of uncut wire, six yards deep, and running along a contour swept by machine guns from left, front and flank. Still they did not stop.

Reggy's mother, Mary pieced together the last moments of her son's life:

> The Herts men were in the centre. They soon got to the hill and killed or captured all the enemy. The Hun aeroplanes were out in numbers and very few of ours. A tank and three machine guns which were to have protected the battalion were all knocked out before getting there; so when the battalion got to the hill, they found the wire uncut.

Suddenly the Herts men were dangerously exposed and attacking a heavily fortified German position:

> Just beyond the Springfield Road, which ran along the commencement of the slope was a big redoubt full of machine-guns, surrounded by pill boxes and wire. It was here that R.H.S. and his platoon stopped for a few minutes, lying down in the shell holes near the road.

No-one could have blamed them for staying there and later retreating in the face of such impossible odds, for they had outrun the troops on either side of them. Such thoughts did not occur to Reggy Secretan and his men:

Then he sprang up, shouting Come on No.8 and waving his arms. His Sergeant and several of his men tell me that a German officer with a bandaged head, and some men, ran out from behind the redoubt. They distinctly saw the officer aim at R.H.S.; he fell forward on his hands and knees, and was killed instantaneously, for he never moved again.

Of the 120 men in Reggy Secretan's company only 18 came out unscathed. But his death was immediately avenged. His Sergeant recorded what happened next:

When that brute of a German officer shot Mr. Secretan, I lost my head completely, and went for him, and what was left of the platoon came with me. We had a rather sharp fight, but the men stood by me and I had the pleasure of shooting that German officer (a Colonel) with my own rifle and when I did it, I knew I was avenging an officer and a gentleman.

And so the tributes for Reginald Herbert Secretan began to pour in. They were gathered together and later published by his grieving mother. They all tell the same story of a gallant, highly respected officer who looked after his men:

Your son was very good to all the men…He led us over the top, and was very happy and he was smiling all the time…He passed away very happy, and about the time he fell it was about eleven in the morning, and all the lads of No.8 Platoon was all sorry to hear about it for they all liked him so much…I shall never forget it.

I was about the last one he spoke to, and I made him laugh just before he was killed, he was laughing and joking all the time.

Dear old 'Sec.' the truest comrade I ever had in this land of glory and sadness.

To think that we shall never meet dear old 'Sec.' again. He was always so jolly and ready for anything that came along, no matter how dangerous the duty. He was just as bright and cheerful as ever when we went over the top.

The night we went up, he was so merry and cheerful with the thought that he was going to kill some more of those baby killers. He always took the shelling like a football match.

He had a glorious death, and died doing his duty for dear old England.

I never saw him out of temper or low spirited, he always had a joke on his lips even under the most depressing circumstances. The night before the fight, we had a long march, and then had to lie in a field until about 5.30. Some slept and some couldn't. I'm sure Mr Secretan did not try to rest, he was always walking around and saying something cheering to a wakeful man. I heard him say, 'Seems as if there's a War on!' and you had to laugh.

Finally three comments from his military superiors:

If ever I'm in a tight place, give me Secretan.

I don't care how much Secretan plays the fool when off duty, he's a damned fine officer.

There was no braver boy in the whole army.

Reggy Secretan's body was never recovered. The Germans retook the place where he died and it was another eleven days until the British recaptured it. His mother concluded her collection of his letters with a quotation from the Rev. Cyril Alington, who was Headmaster of Eton College during the war. When she sent her son the verse, he liked it so much he kept it in his pocket case.

> To have led your men with a daring adored and reckless,
> To have struck your blow for Freedom, the old straight way:
> To have loved men more than yourself and have died to prove it -
> Ah yes! This is to have lived: was there more to do?

At Oundle, Secretan had been a great success story. He was not an academic by any means – his prep school masters had despaired of him. But at Oundle he discovered the workshops and sport. As a boarder, he was apparently quite a handful. His mother confessed that he was "always in the thick of any prank going, he was a terror to his House Master (Major Nightingale)." Once into the Sixth Form however, he became a different lad. He became Head of House and Mr Nightingale was astonished to find what a good House Captain he was. He later confessed that he and his great chum, Gerald Greenfield (also killed at Passchendaele) "vowed to do their best to keep up the tone of the House and encourage keenness in all games." And games were young Reggy's real joy, through thick and thin. One letter home from Sidney gives a flavour of the importance even of house games at Oundle: "Alas! Alack! In the second innings, we only had 88 runs to make, and the whole lot of us collapsed, and we only made 45! I stayed in the whole time but there was no-one to stay in with me. I am fed up with life!"

On the day before his death, he wrote home in his usual manner, still apparently cheerful, in spite of all had lived through in the last three years of his life:

> Being continually under fire is very trying. I am afraid I am getting very hard hearted out here, one has to be, as everyone is so casual about death, but what's the good of making a fuss about it? The whole time out here, we try to instil into the men's minds that death is quite a small matter. Anyhow it's all for one cause, and you can bet we will see it through all right.

Killed the same day as 22 year old Reginald Herbert Secretan but much less well known to history was **Lance-Corporal Thomas Spencer**. He was a Laxton School boy for just three terms and lived in the village of Elton. When war came, he joined the Northants. Regiment and was killed at Passchendaele aged 32. He is buried in Perth Cemetery (China Wall), near the village of Zillebeke, a few miles east of Ypres, close to where he fell.

Five days later, across the border from Ypres, Alan Jerrard, who left Sidney House two years earlier, crash-landed his Spad S7. It was just his second operational patrol in France. Jerrard's Sidney career rated few mentions in the school magazine except to note that he was confirmed in his Christian faith by the Bishop of Peterborough and, in the summer of 1912, he helped Sidney to win the junior cricket title, though his own contribution was limited. There was little clue here of the hero to come.

Jerrard joined up from Birmingham University and won a commission in the South Staffordshire Regiment in January 1917. In August of that year, he transferred to the RFC. After training in Thetford and Norwich, he gained his wings and by July he was stationed at Liettres in the Pas de Calais, south of St. Omer. On his first patrol, he lost contact with the other planes and, running low on fuel, had to land near St. Omer. The second patrol was worse. Once again poor visibility caused him to become detached from his fellows. Descending below cloud cover, he strafed enemy vehicles with his machine-gun before climbing again. Once back in the cloud cover, his engine inexplicably cut out and he had to glide back through the cloud, desperately looking for somewhere to land. Because of the mist, he was unaware of his height above the ground and crash landed onto a railway embankment. Luckily he came down on the Allied side of the lines and British troops were on hand to prise him out of the aircraft. He had sustained serious facial injuries and was evacuated back to England, after undergoing surgery in France. He would not fly again until January 1918 but when he did, he won a Victoria Cross.

Nine days after Alan Jerrard's accident, another Oundelian was killed close by. He was another young man who could easily have avoided joining up on medical grounds but who nonetheless followed the path of honour and duty. **Frederick William Butcher** from London was in Grafton for nearly six years. He was Head of House and was in charge of Grafton when his former Housemaster, Francis Norbury was killed in January 1915. Freddie joined the Inns of Court OTC but failed to gain a commission owing to heart trouble. He enlisted in the London Rifles in December 1916 was then attached to the Royal Irish Rifles and was fighting with them when he was killed, three days shy of his 21st birthday on 9 August 1917. He died at Frezenberg, north-east of Ypres. His body was never recovered and so his name was inscribed on the Menin Gate.

Frederick William Butcher, Grafton House 1909-15.

"He was a good soldier and was spoken of in the highest terms by his comrades," wrote the army chaplain. "He lived a noble life and died a heroic death."

Langley Latton Attwood, like Freddie Butcher, was a Londoner and had a widowed mother. He was killed at Passchendaele three days after Butcher and he was the first of seven Oundelians killed in a week in the mud of Flanders that August of 1917. He was also the fifth member of the 'Dryden Seven' to be killed. He was an only son, and was in Llewellyn Jones' House from 1906-10. When war broke out, he was out in British Columbia and he joined the 47th Battalion Canadian Infantry (Machine Gun Section). Later he transferred to the 1st Canadian Pioneers and arrived in France in April 1916. He fought with the Canadians in all their engagements until early 1917, when he transferred to the Royal Garrison Artillery. He was killed during the Battle of Passchendaele, aged 24, on 12 August 1917 and was buried in the New Military Cemetery in the village of Vlamertinghe outside Ypres. At school he won

Langley Latton Attwood, Dryden House 1906-10,

prizes for gymnastics and although Dryden was just pipped by Grafton in the junior house competition in 1908, they got their revenge a year later. Attwood was also a useful diver coming second in the school competition held in 1909.

Harold Wilfred Asbrey, born in 1896 was two years behind Langley Attwood at school and was killed in action the day after the Dryden boy. A Kettering lad, he attended Laxton School for four years leaving in 1912. At U14 level, he came second in the 100 yards dash and that same year, (1909) he won a speech day prize. He attended Borough Road College in Iselworth, Middlesex from 1915-17, presumably to train as a teacher but it is not known if he achieved any qualification there. He joined the Royal Sussex Regiment in 1917 as a private, so must have been killed within weeks of arriving at the Front. He was buried in Klein-Vierstraat British Cemetery near the city, close to the School House boy, Walter West, who had been killed 15 months earlier, in the Second Battle of Ypres. Harold Asbrey was 20 years old at the time of his death and his parents had the following words inscribed on his gravestone: "His bright spirit still lives in the hearts of those who loved him dearly." He is now commemorated on the Kettering War Memorial and in the Royal Sussex Regiment's Chapel in Chichester Cathedral.

A year younger than Harold Asbrey was **Seisyth Hugh Lloyd**. Born in Wrexham, he was the second son of Colonel G. Lloyd and, despite his seriously Welsh background, lived in Warwickshire by the time he came up to Laxton House in 1912. He stayed until December 1916 and early in the next year, aged 18, he joined the Royal Naval Air Service. He trained in England and crossed to Dunkirk on 29 July 1917 to join the 10th Squadron at Winnerzeele. He went missing just two weeks later, on 14 August, while flying a Sopwith Triplane in a squad of four planes sent out on "offensive patrol." Whilst over the lines near Zillebeeke, south-east of Ypres, he was seen turning westwards and leaving the squad. At the time the squad had run into heavy anti-aircraft fire. Lloyd was never seen again.

At Oundle, he became a school prefect and captain of the XV. The Laxtonian critic claimed that "As captain in the field, he might make his voice heard more loudly at times." Nonetheless, from the detailed match

Seisyth Hugh Lloyd, Laxton House 1912-16.

reports, he was clearly a good kicker and scored a number of important tries. He scored twice in the match against Cranwell in his last term, where atmospheric conditions became a problem: "Unfortunately the latter part of the game was played in rather dim light, so that friend could hardly be distinguished from foe."

He was also a keen debater and was elected secretary of the Debating Society in his last year. With his Wrexham birth, he seems to have seen himself as a spokesman on Welsh affairs and in a school debate about strikes during the war, he castigated one of the main speakers for using the phrase Welsh Miners, saying that "miners in Wales" would be more accurate! On another occasion, he proposed the motion that "the forces of Great Britain, both industrial and military, should be controlled by fighting men alone." In August 1915, according to the Munitions Gazette, he gave up a fortnight of his summer holidays to labour in the workshops.

Two days after Lloyd's death, another Oundle airman, operating just south of Ypres was killed. **Arnold Rennie Baker's** father was a boot manufacturer in Wolverhampton. He sent his son to New House in May 1908. There he played for the Hockey XI and for the 2nd XV. He played rugby and cricket for his House, alongside Frederick Milholland and Geoffrey Donaldson, who also died for their country. When war came, he joined the RFC and went missing presumed killed on 16 August 1917. It seems that he came down behind enemy lines as he was buried at Lincelles Communal Cemetery near Lille which was used by the Germans during the war. The city of Lille was in German hands from October 1914 until October 1918. Arnold Baker was 23 years old at the time of his death. His headstone is inscribed with the words: "He gave all and freely."

Norman Steel, New House 1911-15.

The very same day, also at Passchendaele, another Novarian, three years Arnold Baker's junior, joined the ranks of Oundle fatalities. **Norman Steel** was an only son born in Stroud, Gloucestershire in February 1897. He was in New House from 1911 until 1915 becoming a member of the XV. He was a useful rugger player, speedy and with an eye for tries. In 1914 the Laxtonian said that "He is very good at making openings for the backs. He is very fast and knows when to cut in. He passes well and saves well but his collaring is too high." In 1912, New House lost in the final to Dryden after a replay – the first match being drawn when both sides failed to score! Two years later, New House and Norman Steel triumphed, thrashing Dryden in the semi-final and making light work of School House thereafter.

Leaving at Xmas 1915, Norman Steel joined the Gloucestershire Regiment and went with them to France. Aged 20, he was killed at Passchendaele by a machine-gun bullet while leading his men 'over the top' on 16 August 1917, during the Second Battle of Langemarck. His Commanding Officer wrote: "We are all very sorry, as he was popular with everyone in the Battalion, and always led his platoon with skill and in a fearless manner." Norman Steel's body was never found and his is now one of four Oundle names on the Tyne Cot Memorial to the Missing, alongside some 35,000 other names.

The very next day, Reggy Secretan's great friend in Sidney House, **Gerald Henry Greenfield** was also killed at Passchendaele. He came from Southwell in Nottinghamshire, arriving in Sidney in September 1910 and in the Summer Term of 1914, took over as Head of House when Secretan left. He was a school prefect, played for the XV, described as "an excellent tackler and a good scrummager" and was a sergeant

Gerald Henry Greenfield, Sidney House 1910-15.

in the OTC. Like Secretan, he was more of a doer than a thinker. Taking part in a debate about whether the pen or the sword was the mightier, he came down firmly in favour of the latter.

Leaving in the summer of 1915, at the age of 18, he became a senior sergeant at the Royal Military Academy, Woolwich. In August 1916, he was gazetted to the Royal Field Artillery and went to the Front the next month. On 15 August 1917, aged 20, he was hit by a sniper while acting as Forward Observation Officer near Zillebeke and died two days later in the Canadian Casualty Clearing Station. An officer wrote: "He was always so cheerful and absolutely fearless at all times, and a general favourite, not only in his battery but in the whole brigade. We shall miss him sadly – always." On his gravestone, his widowed mother, Mary put the words "Into Thy Hands O Lord."

His younger brother Charles, also a Sidney boy, joined the Northumberland Fusiliers and became a prisoner of war. In June 1918, he sent his Housemaster, Mr Nightingale a postcard from his place of incarceration, showing himself and several other prisoners performing in a play and not looking too badly off, for being in the hands of the 'beastly Hun'.

The next day fell **Captain Richard Ivan Robson**, a School House boy from Belfast who was fighting with the Royal Irish Rifles in the advance towards Passchendaele. Winner of the Military Cross, he was killed on 18 August, aged 26. At Oundle, he won a workshops prize and played some house rugby, when the team was captained by the Head's younger son, Thomas. More significantly he shot for the School in 1909, when the team enjoyed one of its best seasons winning 15 of the 21 matches. Oundle's success was apparently due to the adoption of the 'Tippin's extension' sight on the rifles. Richard Robson also shot for Oundle at Bisley but the team did not perform at its best.

The next victim of the battle in Flanders, was one of the more highly ranked of Oundelians. **Major Alexander Jewell Stannard** was from Southsea, near Portsmouth, born in August 1891. He was, like so many, an only son.

Richard Ivan Robson, School House 1904-09.

Another Sidney boy (of 1905-08 vintage) and a member of the XV, the review of the rugby season of 1908, described him as "most useful, for a light-weight, always on the ball and playing a capital game." In that same season, he helped Sidney become Cock House in rugby, beating Grafton in the final. He was also keen on the cadet corps and a useful shot, being ranked 10th at the School in his last year. He appeared in a performance of *A Midsummer Night's Dream* but only in the guise of one of the four lords attending Theseus, Duke of Athens. He spent some time at London University and became a regular attender of OO dinners in London and Cambridge.

Doubtless influenced by his OTC experience at school, he entered Sandhurst. After serving a year in the Royal Garrison Artillery Special Reserve of Officers, he joined the regular army in June 1914 and found himself in France in September 1915 with a siege battery. He was killed by a shell on 20 August 1917, while serving with the Australians in the Heavy Artillery Division of the 1st Anzac Corps. One month after his death, he was mentioned in dispatches having served "continuously with the battery" for exactly two years and having "on many occasions displayed great gallantry under shell fire" and being "a fine example to his men." An officer wrote:

"He was an excellent officer in every way: conscientious, painstaking and thorough, and he endeared himself to us all. His men, I am told, deeply feel his loss also. Your son did his duty to the end." Despite his high rank, Alexander Stannard was still only 26 years old at the time of his death.

Beyond Passchendaele

Charles Frederick William Morbey of 7th Battalion Suffolk Regiment overlapped with Alex Stannard in Sidney by just one term. Moreby was the older boy, being born in 1888 in Soham, Cambridgeshire. He was the eldest son of another, rather colourful Charles Morbey, who made his fortune in horse racing. In 1901, he built a very substantial home called Beechurst House in Soham and he also owned Brandon Hall in Suffolk. He was well connected and joined shooting parties with the Royal Family at Sandringham.

The younger Charles Morbey, residing in Sidney House from May 1903 to December 1905 was a pretty good sportsman at house level but was beaten in the junior fives first round by John Thimbleby, who was killed in that unfortunate motor-cycle accident in August 1915. By 1911, young Morbey was a shipping clerk living in Leytonstone and working for Sir William Dunn and Co. of London. He was always interested in association football and was captain and treasurer of Ilford Wanderers. He enlisted on 20 August 1914, gained a commission in October of that year and went out to France in 1915. He was wounded at Loos in October and returned to England to convalesce. Returning to France in July 1916, he was killed by an enemy aircraft on 9 August 1917, after a successful raid on German trenches near Monchy, aged 28. He was buried at Monchy-le-Preux Cemetery near Arras. His Colonel wrote:

> He had led his men in a successful raid on the enemy's trenches, and was returning to our front line carrying a captured machine gun, when he was hit; and he died a few minutes afterwards in our trench. He was a splendid officer, full of courage and devoted to duty. He was very popular with officers and men, and we shall miss him greatly.

Alexander Jewell Stannard, Sidney House 1905-08.

Charles Frederick William Morbey, Sidney House 1903-05.

His Company Sergeant-Major contributed these words: "A better Captain, I shall never have. He was loved by all the men of his Company and I miss him terribly. He was a soldier – one of the best." At his old school in Soham, the following fulsomely patriotic tribute duly appeared:

> His lion-hearted courage and pride of race carried him on to the supreme end; a gallant English gentleman, he died that the England he loved so well might rise triumphant over an unscrupulous foe.

At 28, Charles Moreby was hardly very old but **Geoffrey Sewell**, who was killed near Loos in September 1917 was only 19. Geoffrey Edward Sewell, born in March 1898, was the eldest son of a St. Albans family. He was in Dryden from 1912-1915, was in the Shooting VIII and won a prize for German in 1913. From Oundle, he went to Sandhurst and on passing out joined the Buffs (Royal East Kent Regiment) at Dover. He specialized in grenade warfare and took a physical training course in Aldershot and, on his return to Dover, was appointed Physical Training Officer to his battalion. As soon as he reached the age of 19, in March 1917, he was eager to get to France and moved to the 1st Battalion, crossing the Channel in June of that year. He died of wounds at Loos on 2 September 1917, still aged just 19. His Major wrote: "during the time he was with us, he proved himself to be a most popular, gallant and trustworthy officer."

Geoffrey Edward Sewell, Dryden House 1912-15.

John Colin Crosbie was not in Crosby. He was another Dryden boy. He and Geoffrey Sewell played rugby and cricket for their House together and they died just five days apart. Born in Muswell Hill in 1897, the only son in the family, John Crosbie came up to Dryden in 1911 and left four years later. In his last year, true to the traditions established in Dryden by the Housemaster and one-time mighty oarsman Llewellyn Jones, he stroked the School Crew. Despite a tendency "to hurry his finish," he "kept a very fair length and made a very useful stroke." In his first year, he helped Dryden reach the final of the junior cricket competition, where they lost to a strong Sidney team. At the Dryden House concert that year, he teamed up with Norman Prynne (killed in Macedonia in April 1917) for a sketch entitled '*The Indian and the Scout*'.

John Crosbie initially joined the Royal Garrison Artillery but then transferred to the RFC. He reached the rank of lieutenant but was killed on

John Colin Crosbie, Dryden House 1911-15.

7 September 1917, aged 20. He was buried close to Hugh Davis, once of New House, in Aire Communal Cemetery, near Béthune in France.

As the new school year dawned on 21 September 1917, the third year of war had claimed another 55 Oundelians, making a grisly total of 164 deaths amongst old boys and staff since 1914. And there still seemed to be no end to the suffering in sight. Haig's tactics on the Western Front guaranteed unbelievably high casualty rates which could not really be justified morally or militarily but British politicians, unlike their counterparts in most other countries (friend and foe), refused to sack him, fearing that his dismissal would fatally undermine the British war effort. And so the slaughter continued.

10

Year 4 Away: No End in Sight – September 1917 to April 1918

I wish that I were going to play a game of rugger or have my school days again.

We shall meet him again in Heaven.

The end of Passchendaele

The first of nine Passchendaele victims in the new school year was **Audley Andrew Dowell Lee**. Like Norman Steel and Arnold Baker, both killed there on 16 August, Audley Lee was in New House. He stayed for nearly six years, leaving in the fateful summer of 1914. He went up to Lincoln College, Oxford the following October but by December 1914 he had gained a commission in the Leicestershire Regiment, despite the fact that he was born in Wales. He arrived in France 10 months later and fought throughout the Battle of the Somme in 1916. In January 1917, he was awarded the Military Cross, for his work there, having already been promoted to the rank of captain. On 1 October 1917, Audley Lee was near Polygon Wood leading his men forward to repulse a heavy attack. The British were edging towards the village of Passchendaele, when the Germans counter-attacked through a thick mist. Much of the hardest fighting took place in front of the wood. The Leicestershire's regimental diary records what happened with 'military' precision:

> 5.25 a.m. Enemy put down a heavy barrage on front Company and Polygon Wood and at the same time put up a smoke screen all along Battalion front.

> 5.27 a.m. Enemy attacked through smoke screen. SOS went up. First wave of enemy driven off by A Company by Lewis Gun and Rifle Fire. Captain A. A. D. Lee killed.

Perhaps Lee inspired his men as Lieutenant Colonel Bent did that same day with the cry of "Come on the Tigers." An officer wrote of the 22 year old OO: "We feel his loss more than words can express, for he was beloved by all ranks." His body was never found and his name appears near that of his fellow Novarian, Norman Steel on the Tyne Cot Memorial to the Missing.

Audley Andrew Dowell Lee, New House
1908-14.

The Laxton School Five

Audley Lee died on 1 October, then in the space of just 15 days, five Laxton School boys were killed at Passchendaele – five consecutive Oundle deaths, all from the same 'House'. The fate of 'the Laxton School Five' is a worthy and equally tragic match for 'the Dryden Seven'.

Robert Hoare, at 31, the eldest of 'the Five' was a Nassington boy and left Laxton School in 1904. He taught for a year at his old school "learning the methods of education" as Sanderson put it. He was apparently still able to play for Laxton School at cricket and football at this time and was briefly secretary and treasurer of the Old Laxtonian Club. This excellent grounding allowed him to gain a post as schoolmaster (in charge of geography) at Halesowen Grammar School in the West Midlands. At that time, he had joined the Territorials and was a second lieutenant in the Worcesters in 1912. He was heavily engaged on the Somme in 1916 and was promoted captain. By October 1917, the Worcesters were called to Passchendaele. In the darkness and pouring rain of 9 October, Robert Hoare led his company into action, attacking the German-held village of Poelcapelle. They took prisoners and gained some muddy territory but Hoare perished. He had frequently told his Colonel that if he were to be killed, it would be when leading his men into battle. He lies buried in Poelcapelle Cemetery. On his headstone, his parents inscribed a verse from Isiah:

"Thou wilt keep him in perfect peace".

Robert William Hoare, Laxton School 1899-04.

Next oldest of 'the Five' was **Charles Vipan**, 26 years old when he was killed. He was born in Ailsworth, near Peterborough and left Laxton School at the age of 17 in 1908. He is remembered on the war memorial in his home village of Barnack. Enlisting in Peterborough, he naturally joined the Northamptonshire boys (Peterborough was in Northamptonshire until 1965), before switching to the Royal Berkshire Regiment. He was killed on 17 October 1917, six miles south of Ypres not far from Messines Ridge.

Wilfred Henry Gann was only 22 when he fell. He was a native of Oundle and was at Laxton School for just 18 months, leaving six years before the start of the war, when he was just 13. He was next heard of in Australia, New South Wales. He emigrated there in 1914 and worked as a butcher. He enlisted on 20 January 1916, aged 20 as a private in the 33rd Australian Infantry Battalion. He was 5' 8" tall, weighed 11 stone, of sallow complexion with blue eyes and light brown hair. He sailed back to England for training in July 1916 and arrived in France in November of that year.

In June 1917, he was commended for his bravery at Messines. He was badly wounded in the left thigh on 17 October in an attack on Passchendaele village and died two days later. "I deeply deplore the death of so splendid a man and so excellent a soldier," wrote his Commanding Officer to his parents. "Your late son always distinguished himself in action by his courage, his coolness and his determination. With his willing and cheerful obedience of all orders, his loyalty, his upright and honourable bearing and his devotion to duty, he set us all a splendid example." Wilfred Gann was the last of the 'Laxton School Five' to be killed, dying of wounds on 19 October. He was buried in the Nine Elms Cemetery, west of Poperinghe. His headstone bears the simple inscription, "Faithful unto death".

The next youngest of the group of five was **William Horsford** from Benefield who was three weeks short of his 22nd birthday when he perished, the first of 'the Five' to be killed at Passchendaele. He spent four years at Laxton School, leaving in July 1909, two terms after Wilfred Gann. At school he was the champion high jumper. His farming family, including two brothers and three sisters, were then living in Stoke Doyle. He enlisted in the Lincolnshire Regiment in October 1915 just before his twentieth birthday and travelled to Grimsby for training. He was killed in action on 4 October 1917 in the Battle of Broodseinde, part of a wider offensive towards Passchendaele Ridge. Unlike many of the young victims of the fighting, William Horsford was married. He is remembered on the Tyne Cot Cemetery Memorial to the Missing and is also commemorated in Stoke Doyle church.

Letter on the death Wilfred Henry Gann, Laxton School 1907-08.

Another name on the Memorial to the Missing at Tyne Cot is that of the youngest of the 'Laxton School Five', **John Anderson**, who was still only 19 when the mud of Passchendaele swallowed him up. He was mentioned by name by Sanderson in his address to Laxton School on their Speech Day in 1917. Like Douglas McMichael, four years his senior, he was deemed sufficiently academic to attend lessons at Oundle School in his last two years, and again like McMichael, won a scholarship to Clare College, Cambridge as a result. However, plans to go to Cambridge had to be put on hold and he enlisted instead. He joined the Machine Gun Corps and was killed alongside William Horsford just eighteen months after leaving school, near Ypres, at the place where Douglas McMichael had died eighteen months before.

Two from Sidney

Two of the last three Oundelians killed at Passchendaele were both Sidney boys. **John Eric Stirling Pritchard** was the only son of a chartered accountant from Sutton Coldfield in Warwickshire. He came up to Oundle in September 1910, was a member of the Shooting VIII and left in the summer of 1915. After a few months in his father's accountancy firm, he joined the Inns of Court OTC and was drafted later into the Artillery Cadets' Training School. He won a commission into the Royal Field Artillery in July 1916 and a fortnight later was at the Front. He was hit by a bullet in the abdomen on 26 October 1917 and died from his injuries the next day. His Colonel wrote: "Your son had been with me for over a year, and was an excellent officer, most popular with the men, and always cheerful under the most unpleasant conditions." He was buried in Lijssenthoek Military Cemetery outside Poperinghe, and joined two fellow Sidney boys, Gerald Greenfield and John Gulliland also buried there – a cemetery that is for ever Sidney.

Yet another Sidney boy was **James Outram Morris**, John Pritchard's older 'compatriot'. He died, aged 31, on 30 October 1917 whilst leading his men in an attack, in the latter stages of the Passchendaele campaign. He was the son of a vicar from Thame in Oxfordshire and resided in Sidney from 1902-05. He was a latecomer to Oundle, arriving in the Sixth Form but was made a school prefect in his last year. He was prominent on the football field, playing for the XV in his last two years. He also won the half-mile in an impressive time of two minutes and ten seconds in his last Sports Day. He went up to Emmanuel College, Cambridge but his science studies were apparently much interrupted by illness. Leaving Cambridge in 1910, he became a schoolmaster, firstly at Stone in Staffordshire and then at Rugby. He joined the Artists' Rifles when war broke out but poor eyesight prevented him from obtaining a commission. As an NCO, (he

John Eric Stirling Pritchard, Sidney House 1910-15.

James Outram Morris, Sidney House 1902-05.

was a lance-corporal) he was apparently very popular with both officers and men. His body was never found.

The last victim of the carnage at Passchendaele was **Maurice Frank Foulds** who died on the same day as James Morris. He came from Kettering where the family lived in Regent Street. Attending Laxton School for six years (1909-15), he enlisted in the London Rifles and held the rank of second lieutenant in the London Regiment when he was killed at Passchendaele at the age of 20. His body like so many others, was never recovered.

When Passchendaele was over

Though the committee which drew up the exact dates of each of Britain's battles of the war set 10 November 1917 as the end of Passchendaele, there would be three more 'Wipers' casualties for Oundle before the year was out. **Talbert Stevenson** was a Scotsman from Dundee, where his father ran a dye works. Born in 1895, he was in Crosby House 1910-12. At Oundle, he was a keen OTC man and won a cup for shooting. He also excelled at French, winning a school prize and appearing in two French plays. After Oundle, he spent some time on the Continent and then studied in Manchester. He looked set to join his father's business when the war came.

He received a commission in the Black Watch as early as 2 September 1914 and trained in Dundee and York, before being sent to France in February 1915. He came through Neuve Chapelle and Festubert but was then wounded and was out of action for five months before returning to his battalion in France. He turned down promotion to the rank of brigade major, preferring to stay with his men as captain. He was wounded again on the Somme in November 1916 but re-joined his men in July 1917. He was killed by a sniper on 14 November near Polderhoek outside Ypres and buried at La Clytte. The chaplain wrote: "I have just come from his funeral. I am glad we managed to get your boy's body down from the line. It wasn't an easy task, and it is a proof of his popularity that there was no lack of volunteers to bring his body down. There was a large turnout at the funeral and the body was carried to the grave by four of the oldest officers. Our pipers played *Flowers of the Forest* over the grave. The battalion could not have suffered greater loss."

Talbert's bravery earned him two Military Crosses. The citation for the second one reads: "For conspicuous gallantry and devotion to duty. He got

Talbert Stevenson, Crosby House 1910-12.

his battalion into its assembly position with great skill. On the morning of the attack, he made a very valuable reconnaissance, obtaining urgent information under heavy machine gun and rifle fire. His gallantry and courage were most marked." His Commanding Officer also mourned his loss: "His loss to the battalion is irreparable. Brave to a fault, brimming over with energy and keenness, a prime favourite with officers and men, he also possessed a very old head on young shoulders." Talbert Stevenson was 22 years old at the time of his death.

The final victim in the Ypres Salient that year was also one of the youngest. **Ernest Walter Winton** was a Londoner and one of two of Oundle's fallen who changed their German surnames because of the conflict. In June 1915, a year after leaving Oundle, he and his parents changed their name to Winton, having "formally and absolutely renounced, relinquished and abandoned the use of the said surname of Weintraud." He also seems to have swapped his middle name Hans, for the more English sounding Walter. He came up to Grafton in September 1911 then as Ernest Hans Weintraud and was clearly a boy of much promise. He won a form prize in 1913 and was an excellent violinist. In 1914, the Laxtonian declared that Weintraud, "will be much missed in the musical life of the School." And he was similarly commended for his acting ability in Molière's play *Les Fourberies de Scapin*, where he played the deceitful valet Scapin himself. On leaving school and still only 16, he went to University College, London and then, in October 1915 up to Clare College, Cambridge. There he studied economics and also devoted considerable time to music.

Ernest Walter Winton, Grafton House 1911-14.

After two terms at Cambridge, having reached the age of 18, he went to the Royal Military Academy in Woolwich, and was gazetted to the Royal Garrison Artillery in June 1917. He reached France only in November of 1917 and was killed, near Ypres, within weeks of arrival on 15 December. Almost certainly, he was hit by a shell while taking ammunition up to the front line. Aged 19, it was only his first day in action. He lies buried at Bleuet Farm Cemetery near Ypres and his headstone proudly tells that he was "a gifted, noble and devoted son and brother."

Ernest's elder brother Frank was a talented scientist and cellist, who went on to become Professor of Physiology at Cambridge. The parents endowed the Weintraud prize for Chemistry at Oundle first awarded in July 1913 – to their son Frank!

Although he died in the reserve lines on the Somme, it was really Passchendaele that killed Tom Warner. **Thomas Lovell Warner**, always known as Tom, was an elder son from Leicester, where he was born in January 1894. His father Charles, who died when Tom was just 10, ran a horticultural business and his tulips were renowned across the county. Young Tom came up to New House in January 1908, aged 14 and stayed the full five years. He became Head of House and a school prefect and was prominent in the XV in his last two years. The haunting photograph of this team at the end of the Michaelmas Term 1911, shows him sitting to the right of the Captain, Douglas Armitage. Six of the XV in the picture would be swallowed up in the conflict. Warner played in the backs and was officially described thus in his final year at school: "He has played a vigorous game all through the term. Although individualism has been his stronghold, he has combined much better than last year."

Tom Warner also captained the New House team which famously had to replay the final against Dryden, where New House eventually lost by six points. He also played for the OOs in the last major game in peace-time alongside Eric Yarrow and Roy Sanderson, two of the more notable casualties of the conflict. During the war, he took a rugger ball with him as he was always ready, as he said, for "a little rugger if the opportunity arises." After Oundle, he went up to Caius College, Cambridge for a year, reading theology with the intention of becoming ordained. The Laxtonian's Cambridge correspondent noted that he had taken to wearing "a homburg" and

Thomas Lovell Warner, New House 1908-13.

that "a bishopric in the Hindoo Konks is said to be kept vacant for Warner." In a mock trial held at Oundle, he appeared as a witness called "the Rev. T. L. Warner D.D."

When the war began, he obtained a commission in the Leicestershire Regiment. Sent to France in July 1915, he was twice wounded and three times mentioned in dispatches. He fought in the Battle of Bazentin Ridge on the Somme in July 1916 and the next year, at the age of just 23, he was promoted to major and won the DSO. Later, he served at Polygon Wood at Passchendaele and he could not disguise how this had affected him. In a letter home he called it: "not normal but consolidated hell up here and I shall be glad to go to more human and healthy parts." Similarly, when writing about his DSO, he claimed that he didn't know what it was for but concluded that it would be "a souvenir of umpteen journeys through hell."

And all the time at the front, he remembered his school days at Oundle especially as he wrote regularly to his younger brother Ted, who was in New House throughout the war. In one letter, he wrote that he has "just come safely through a most hellish ten days" but immediately wished his brother well in a forthcoming rugger match. "I wish" he wrote, "that I were going to play a game of rugger or have my school days again." By the end of 1917, Tom Warner was clearly badly affected by the war. In his last letter to Ted, he wrote: "If I come through the war I shall help you be a farmer, as I shall be a broken down old crock." But he asked his brother to send him a copy of the School Roll of Honour, which ironically he would join thirteen days later.

He had just recovered from flu, was weakened by dysentery and by two years in the trenches and did not survive an emergency operation for appendicitis. He died two days after Xmas at Tincourt near Péronne on the Somme and was buried there. His headstone states simply –"He loved others". Had he lived two weeks longer, he would have returned to England for a three month staff course and promotion to Lieutenant Colonel Warner. The tributes to Tom Warner were many. Perhaps the most noteworthy and eloquent was from his servant and batman Private B. Hewitt, who was with him when he died:

He was the bravest of the brave, fearless of danger, cool and resourceful, he combined good leadership with a kindliness and understanding of his fellow men. He was a man that seemed to us to be alone in his beautiful character insomuch as he lived the life of a Christian amidst surroundings that make it a terrible difficulty.

Two months after his death at the age of 23, tragedy struck the Warner family again when Tom's sister Rachel died aged 26.

Beyond Passchendaele

Ian Morehouse Metcalfe was another only son, born in Kent 17 years before the start of war. He was in Crosby from 1910-14 and rated few mentions in the school magazines of his day. He was confirmed by the Bishop of Peterborough and at 6 stone 12, he was the fairly small cox, who guided his boat to victory in the School's scratch fours competition of 1910. Soon after the outbreak of hostilities, he enlisted in the Royal Fusiliers and was sent to Malta in December 1914. He then came back to Sandhurst and from there was gazetted to the Worcestershire Regiment in August 1915 and then to France a year later, when he was just 19. He served for 15 months at the Front, including the great attack on Messines Ridge, south of Ypres in June 1917, which was the prelude to Passchendaele at the end of July. The Battalion's diary takes up another sad and successful story:

Ian Morehouse Metcalfe, Crosby House 1910-14.

> Throughout the whole of the attack the men had shown the greatest eagerness to press forward and there is little doubt that some of them ran straight into our own barrage. Direction was certainly lost at times, and the subsequent disorganisation lasted throughout the attack. The resistance of the enemy had been rendered very half-hearted by the heavy shelling of the preceding days, and for the most part when reached [they] showed little inclination to fight. During the advance the enemy did not systematically barrage any particular line, but fired indiscriminately over the whole battle front. Machine gun fire was also encountered at several points, some of it certainly being indirect fire from guns in rear.

On 1 November 1917, Ian Metcalfe's luck ran out. He was killed leading a patrol and endeavouring to enter enemy trenches. Wounded behind enemy lines, he died as a prisoner of war at Givenchy and was buried by the Germans near Festubert. His burial place was later revealed to the British military via the German Red Cross. Aged 20 at the time of his death, having reached the rank of lieutenant, his Company Commander praised him in the currency of the time: "I shall never be able to replace him: his men absolutely adored him; there was nowhere they would not go with him, so fearless was he."

Cedric Arthur Jackson died not in France but in England. A Yorkshire boy from Dore, on the outskirts of Sheffield, he spent two years in Grafton 1908-10, leaving at the age of 17. At the outbreak of war, he joined the York and Lancaster Regiment as a private. In May 1915, he gained his commission as second lieutenant and acted as Bombing Officer. He served in Egypt and then France, being promoted lieutenant in February 1917. In August that year, he got a transfer to the Royal Flying Corps and was accidentally killed while training in Dover on 5 November 1917, aged 24.

How is the Empire?

And Cedric Jackson was not the only Graftonian to die that day. Thousands of miles away near Basra in Mesopotamia, **Donald Farrow Milne** also made the supreme sacrifice. From Whaley Bridge near Stockport, he was an only son. Like Cedric Jackson, he came to Grafton for the Sixth Form arriving in September 1910, just weeks after Cedric had left the school. When Donald Milne left in 1912, he joined the staff of the Calico Printers' Association in Manchester and in his two years there was making a successful career for himself.

In October 1914, he joined the Manchester Regiment and received a commission in a fortnight. Just before the Somme, he came home on leave, where he was taken ill in London. On recovery, he was sent out to India, arriving in Bombay on 31 July 1917. After five weeks in Bangalore, he was sent to Mesopotamia in September. Here the British position had recovered after the disastrous fall of Kut to the Turks in April 1916. A new commander, Major-General Stanley Maude, was appointed and in February 1917, the British defeated the Turks and took Baghdad and the Berlin-Baghdad Railway the next month. On 5 November 1917, the British decided to attack Turkish forces outside the northern city of Tikrit. Although British losses were heavy, the Turks withdrew and Tikrit was taken the next day.

Cedric Arthur Jackson, Grafton House 1908-10.

Donald Farrow Milne, Grafton House 1910-12.

Donald Milne had been in Mesopotamia just two weeks when he was killed in action, aged 22, in the attack on Tikrit. He was one of some 160 British soldiers killed that day. His Commanding Officer wrote: "Though he had only been with us sixteen days, we liked him from the beginning, and all ranks spoke well of him." His name would be inscribed on the Basra Memorial, along with those of two other Oundelians who also died there – Alan Scarth, killed the previous year and Reggie Plunkett who accidentally drowned in 1918. The memorial carries the names of nearly 42,000 servicemen who died in this largely forgotten corner of the war and have no known grave.

Still out in Mesopotamia but some weeks later, Alan West once of School House was accidentally killed. **Alan Herbert Manwaring West**, from Sussex, born in 1897 was in School House 1911-15, became a school prefect and was a great sportsman. He was in the XV and captained cricket and fives in 1915. He won the Whiffen Prize in the summer of 1915 and was described as "a good captain" (pretty high praise in Laxtonian terms!) of the XI. He was apparently, "A very good all-round cricketer and promises to become first-class. Quick on his feet when batting and hits the ball quite hard." He possessed "a fine action for a fast bowler" and was also "a fine field." School House duly won the senior cricket that year but were pushed all the way by a better than expected Crosby team.

He passed the examination for the Indian Army while still at school and sailed for India in September 1915, aged 18. He had six months training at Wellington College there before gaining a commission with the 36th Sikhs and moving to Delhi. In January 1917, he took a draft to Mesopotamia and was there until his death at Amara on 7 January 1918, at which time he was Regimental Bombing Officer. He was accidentally killed during bombing practice when he attempted to throw clear a bomb which had been accidentally dropped by one of his men. The latter escaped unhurt but Alan West was mortally wounded. His Commanding Officer noted: "I saw enough to realize that the regiment has lost one of its most useful and promising

Alan Herbert Manwaring West, School House 1911-15.

officers. I can confidently say that to each of your son's brother officers the loss was a personal one."

Also out defending the Empire at that time was **Norman Stuart Edmondstone**. He was born in Melbourne, Australia in 1896 and came up to Dryden House in January 1913, at the age of 16. He won a maths prize and helped Dryden win the swimming cup. Leaving school in the summer of 1914, he first joined the navy as an ordinary seaman but then gained a commission in the Queen's Westminster Rifles and went with them to Palestine. He was killed on 7 November 1917, at Kauwukah, east of Gaza being hit by a shrapnel bullet whist waiting with his company for the order to assault the enemy's position. Two previous attempts to take the town of Gaza by frontal assault in 1917 had failed but the new commander, Allenby learnt from his predecessor's mistakes. He moved his GHQ from a first class Cairo Hotel to the Front Line, which helped to boost British morale and he determined to take the town without the massed frontal assaults which had failed twice before. Haig, who had sacked him earlier, might have learnt something from his tactics. Gaza fell in a week and Allenby went on to capture Jerusalem the next month. Norman Edmonstone didn't live to see this success. He was buried at Imara, aged 21 and later moved to Beersheba War Cemetery, near the Negev Desert to rest alongside nearly 1300 other British casualties from the war in Palestine. His headstone bears the following idiosyncratic inscription:

Norman Stuart Edmondstone, Dryden House 1913-14.

> He is quietly calling us from paralysing grief to high endeavour.

His Colonel wrote: "He is a very serious loss to me and to the battalion, as he was an untiring and dependable officer with a very good knowledge of a soldier's duty...He was universally beloved by men and officers, and this I mean literally for he had a very lovable disposition."

Cecil Darley Farran Leech was also killed a long way from home, in his case in India's turbulent North-West Frontier. He is one of a small group of those killed for whom we have no known picture. He was born on St. Cecilia's day in 1892 in Manchester, was a second son and came to Crosby House in 1906, staying for three years. He took up banking after Oundle and at the outbreak of hostilities was in the London branch of the Mercantile Bank of India. He was a keen cricketer and hockey player. As a junior he did show some promise as a bowler, taking 9 for 55 over two innings against Grafton, and 8 for 80 against School House. But by his last year, the only record of him playing in a house cricket match was when he scored just 1 run in two innings and took one wicket for 79 – a match which Crosby's opponents, Sidney won easily. The man he trapped lbw that day though was John Gulliland, another of the war's victims.

He gained a commission in the North Staffordshire Regiment and was sent out to Rawal Pindi in India, where he arrived in August 1915. During the war, the British were aware of the need to maintain garrisons with British troops in many parts of the Empire but especially in India, in the North-West Frontier region. He was accidentally killed on 2 March 1918, his rank at the time being captain. He was originally buried in Attoc New Cemetery but was later re-buried by the Commonwealth War Graves Commission in Karachi (now in Pakistan, then in India) as it was proving impossible to maintain other cemeteries like Attoc scattered across North West India.

The Battle of Cambrai, November to December 1917

Late in 1917, the British aided by 476 tanks, decided to launch a surprise attack towards the German held city of Cambrai. Despite gains in the first ten days, the British did not come close to capturing the city and by the first week of December had been pushed back, close to their starting lines by spirited German counter-attacks. Both sides suffered some 45,000 casualties. **Guy Hepworth**

Roberts, a Yorkshire boy, was one of those killed on the first day of the battle. He was an unusual Oundelian, in that he lived in two boarding houses. He started in New House in 1907 but later transferred to Francis Norbury's Grafton. He won a history prize in the L6 but his academic progress was perhaps overshadowed by his sporting prowess. He played amongst the backs for the XV in his last year but the Laxtonian felt that he did not pass out often enough as he was "too fond of trying to burrow through his opponents." Nonetheless, the same critic acknowledged that he had "helped greatly in the defence and plays a vigorous game." He was clearly a good all-round sportsman as he also captained Grafton in football and cricket and rowed in the house boat. In athletics he was 2nd in the half-mile and 3rd in the quarter-mile in his last Sports Day. He left Oundle in 1911 and was articled to a firm of chartered accountants. Rejected by the Artists' Rifles and the Public School

Guy Hepworth Roberts, New House and Grafton House 1907-11.

Boys Naval Division for defective eyesight, he managed to join the King's Own Yorkshire Light Infantry in October 1914. By July of 1915 he was a lieutenant and appointed to Brigadier General Lassiter's staff. He was then appointed ADC to General Braithwaite but resigned from this post to re-join his regiment. In July 1917 he was promoted captain and given command of a company. He led his men into action in the great attack on Cambrai on 20 November 1917 and died of his injuries two days later, aged 25. His Commanding Officer wrote:

> We all mourn the loss of a cheery, gallant friend and I, in addition, the loss of an excellent company commander, who I cannot replace. Your boy was looking forward with great confidence to the attack, and I saw and spoke to him just before our troops were launched. All his arrangements were in perfect order, and he was as merry and cheerful as ever. The last words he said when we left him was 'We are going to have a great time today.'

His Major said: "Guy died leading his men into an attack which was completely successful and it was his gallant example and leadership which greatly helped us to gain our objective."

Maurice Barber, another son of Yorkshire, was just ten days older than his friend Guy Roberts and was also a Grafton boy. He would be the fourth Graftonian to die in November 1917. Furthermore, he came from the same Yorkshire village as Cedric Jackson, the first Graftonian to perish in that unlucky month. At school, Maurice won a form prize but appears, rather refreshingly, not to have been a sportsman of note! After Oundle, he went to the Continent spending time in Tours and Lausanne to see more of the world and to learn French. Returning to Sheffield, he joined an engineering company and then joined up in September 1914. He did not reach France in a military capacity until January 1917. He was a captain in the York and Lancaster Regiment when he was killed at Cambrai four days after his Grafton friend, Guy Roberts. He too was 25 years old at the time of his death having lived just two weeks longer than his fellow Yorkshire man. However, while Guy Roberts body was found and buried, Maurice Barber's body was not and his name is now among some 7,000 on the Cambrai Memorial to the Missing.

His Commanding Officer noted: "I have lost a friend, but I am glad that I was privileged to know such a gallant, modest gentleman as he was, and I shall never forget him." The chaplain wrote: "Always quiet and somewhat reserved – always working hard and spending himself for the welfare of his battalion...he was what I like to think a typical British gentleman should be."

With Maurice Barber's death in late November 1917, Francis Norbury's Grafton House had lost four of its old boys in just three weeks. Of course, their gallant Housemaster never knew this as he had been killed back in January 1915.

Frank Pass Johnson from Kettering was the next to pay the price for answering his country's call. He spent 4 years at Laxton School, leaving on the eve of war in July 1914. It is thought that he joined the London Regiment at first and then moved to the Tank Corps presumably in 1917 or late 1916, as a gunner. He died of wounds on 5 December 1917, under unknown circumstances. He was just 19 years old and was buried at Rethel French National Cemetery, north-east of Rheims. Burial here means that he was originally buried in German-occupied France

Leslie Eric Rundell also died near Cambrai. He was born on Valentine's Day in Finchley in 1896 and the family lived in Muswell Hill. He lost his father at an early age and came up to School House in May 1910. He was in the extraordinary junior house cricket final in 1910, when School House beat Sidney by and innings and one run! Leslie Rundell took no wickets that day and contributed just seven runs in this victory, the real credit going to Maurice Hatch who hit a splendid 112. Leslie was a decent oarsman and would have been bow in the School Crew in the Summer Term of 1913 but he left at Easter! He enlisted in the London Regiment and won the Military Star twice for gallantry in action. Staff captain to Brigadier General Kennedy, he did not die leading his men into action but was wounded by a fragment of shell while

Maurice Barber, Grafton House 1907-10.

Leslie Eric Rundell, School House 1910-13.

taking tea in a shelter. He was taken to the casualty clearing station where he died at 1:00 a.m. on 11 December 1917. He was buried at Ruyaucourt east of Bapaume on the Somme. An officer wrote: "He certainly was one of the finest men I have met during the two years I have been over here." His Company Sergeant-Major noted: "Believe me when I tell you that he was admired and liked by his men, who always placed great confidence in him as a leader."

Alfred Cecil English was the final victim of Cambrai, for now. He was born in Wisbech in Lincolnshire but brought up in West Kensington. He came to Dryden House from Oakham School in 1900 and left Oundle three years later at the age of 16. Leaving early, he rated few mentions in the Laxtonian magazine, unlike his older brother Arthur, who was a regular sporting hero, playing for the XV and rowing for the School Crew. Alfred joined the Artists' Rifles in 1904 and so booked an early ticket to France in October 1914. Later, he returned to England to take a commission and then re-joined his battalion at the Front. He was killed

Alfred Cecil English, Dryden House 1900-03.

in action, aged 30, in the Cambrai sector, near Marcoing on 30 December 1917. This village was much fought over during the Battle of Cambrai. Captured by the British and then re-taken by the Germans, it produced casualties well into the New Year. Alfred English has no known grave and his name is inscribed with the names of 16 other Oundelians on the Thiepval Memorial. An officer noted all his good qualities: "I was in France with him from October 1914 and knew then, and now since he has been back with us, what a fine character he was and what a fine soldier. He was always working, always cheery, always helping the men, and you could not help loving him." The chaplain commented that "the men always spoke of him with real affection."

Three Flying Men

Frank Booth of Grafton was the first Oundelian to die in 1918 (on 3 January) and the fifth Graftonian to perish since early November, the previous year. He was the eighth son of a family from Crewe in Cheshire but the only one who came to Oundle. He was in the XV, scoring a number of tries and was one of the youngest Oundelian casualties of the war, dying at the age of 18 years and 8 months. He was in Grafton for two years from 1915-17 and went off to join the Naval Air Service. On 3 January 1918, he was shot down, badly wounded behind German lines, north of Arras and died the same evening, officially as a prisoner of war. Buried by the Germans, his

Frank Booth, Grafton House 1915-17.

body was exhumed after the war and re-buried at the Cabaret-Rouge Cemetery in Souchez, along-side Arthur Railton and George Fenchelle. His life after Oundle had lasted barely five months.

Sidney Brothers in the Air

Humphrey Eames Barwell came from Edgbaston and had two older brothers – all three came up to Sidney House. Humphrey arrived in September 1912, aged 14 and left at Xmas 1916. He played for the XI several times, described as "a good mid-on and someone who hits the ball quite hard." He was also a member of the 2nd XV. He helped Sidney win the senior house rugby competition in 1915 but sadly missed the final for some reason. He played soccer for the school as well, alongside middle brother Brian, who would later fly with the Royal Naval Air Service. In his last year, Humphrey became a school prefect. In July 1917, aged 18 he joined the Royal Flying Corps, at the same time as his eldest brother transferred there from the infantry. Humphrey reached France the following November and was killed just three months later on 3 February 1918 near Albert "while flying on active service" on the Somme. His Commanding Officer commented: "I cannot express my grief at losing him. He was a good steady pilot and was a favourite with everyone in the Squadron. He set a splendid example." Humphrey Barwell was 19 years old at the time of his death.

Humphrey Eames Barwell, Sidney House 1912-16.

His bother **Hugh William Eames Barwell**, aged 25, was killed whilst flying just two months later. He went missing on 25 March 1918, four days after the Germans launched their great attack on the Western Front and his body was never found. Hugh Barwell had also been in Sidney House and was the eldest of the three Barwell brothers. His CO said: "I had only the previous day recommended him for a bar to his MC…and if anyone deserved it your son did." He was awarded his first MC and the Croix de Guerre for conspicuous gallantry at Beaumont Hamel on the Somme in November 1916 whilst serving in the infantry.

After Oundle, he had gone to Birmingham University, where he gained a BSc. before the outbreak of war and he played cricket for Warwickshire. He joined up at the start of hostilities and was given a commission in the Royal Warwickshire Regiment, serving on the Western Front for two years and promoted to captain.

At Oundle from 1907-11, he had a splendid career. He was a regular player for the XV alongside Edward MacBryan, John Gulliland, Tom Warner

Hugh William Eames Barwell, Sidney House 1907-11.

and Douglas Armitage. Hugh also played regularly for the XI for two years, teaming up with MacBryan and Gulliland again, in what turned out to be a topsy-turvy season for the Oundle cricketers. Against the Leys, it looked as though Oundle would be beaten, needing 40 more runs when Hugh Barwell came in at 10. But he scored 26 that day and with the help of the last man secured victory.

He was also a useful debater, opposing "with a sound speech" the motion that manners maketh man was now an outdated concept. Clearly proud of his *alma mater*, Barwell declared that "manners in the highest sense of the word did exist at the present time, amongst those who constituted the future greatness of the British Empire, namely the Public School boy." Barwell and his fellows completely believed in the greatness of Great Britain and saw themselves playing a key role in sustaining and enlarging that greatness. Did Hugh Barwell imagine that just three years after his speech, he and his fellows would be called upon to sacrifice their lives for that high ideal?

Infantry on the Western Front, Spring 1918

Head of School 1914

Frederick Raymond Milholland, Head of School on Speech Day 1914, now met his own appointment with fate. He was born on New Year's Day 1896 in Kingston, Jamaica and came across the

waters to Oundle and New House in September 1909. He had great academic prowess, carrying off a raft of prizes – four in 1912, five in 1913 and six in 1914. He was the top school classicist in his last two years but also a member of the XV in his last three years. In 1913 he was described as "improving considerably in the course of the season, he is fast enough and strong enough to make a really good forward." In his last term, New House, led by Milholland triumphed 28-3 against School House in the house final. Frederick Milholland was clearly the obvious choice as School Captain and he held that position for four terms. In his last term, he won an exhibition to Balliol College, Oxford and was elected Rhodes Scholar for Jamaica. But he never took his place at Oxford, instead he went straight into the Yorkshire Regiment as a second lieutenant. In 1916, he was wounded in Mametz Wood on the Somme and in the next year won promotion to the rank of captain. He died in a casualty clearing station, near Béthune in northern France on 27 February 1918. He was out with a runner inspecting a front-line trenchwhen he was hit by a sniper. He died an hour after reaching 'hospital'. He lies buried at Chocques Military Cemetery near Béthune, close to the Laxton House boy, Henry Hayr Cox who was killed at Vimy Ridge the previous year. His headstone carries the admonition: "Lest We Forget".

Frederick Raymond Milholland, New House 1909-14.

On Speech Day, later that year, Frederick's father sailed to England from Jamaica and proposed the vote of thanks to the staff and the Grocers on behalf of his three sons educated at Oundle. The Master of the Grocer's Company in reply remarked on how fond he was of "Captain Milholland" revealing that if he had lived, he would have been made a member of the Grocers' Company.

Nine days after the demise of Milholland, **Guy Stevenson Hewitt** was also killed in France. He went out to France with his regiment in March 1917 and was there for a year, being killed in action on 8 March 1918 at Ribecourt near Cambrai. The chaplain of the regiment recorded that "death was caused by the bursting of a shell and was instantaneous." Hewitt was buried where he fell but the grave was subsequently lost, so he is commemorated on the Arras Memorial to the Missing, which records the names of some 35,000 Allied servicemen, including three Oundelians.

Born in 1898 in Wilmslow, Cheshire, the only son of Edgar and Florence Hewitt, he was brought up in Buxton in Derbyshire, where his father was a solicitor and was in Grafton 1912-15. He seems to have made little impact in terms of the written records of the school, except for being confirmed, on 18 March 1914, by the Bishop of Peterborough, Edward Glyn. He then went to Sandhurst at the age of 18. For some reason he did not take up a commission but joined the Artists' Rifles as a private.

Guy Stevenson Hewitt, Grafton House 1912-15.

The German Spring Offensive, March 1918

On 21 March 1918, the German's launched their great Spring Offensive on the Western Front. With victory against Russia secured on the Eastern Front, via the Treaty of Brest-Litovsk but with American troops arriving in their thousands on the Western Front, Ludendorff had to gamble on a huge and decisive offensive hoping to reach Paris and end the war. In the first day of the so-called Ludendorff Offensive, nearly 20,000 British troops were killed – it was the Somme all over again and it was fought in the same place. In just a few days, the Germans re-took most of the ground won by the British in the dreadful months of the Somme battle in 1916. Needless to say, many Oundelians were caught up in this renewed fighting.

Philip Selwyn Whiston was at Oundle a little earlier than Guy Hewitt, from 1905-08. He was killed on 21 March 1918, aged 27, near Loos and his name is inscribed on the Loos Memorial. He is among that small group of newly discovered Oundle fatalities in the war. The School's Memorial Book lists him as serving but not as a casualty, so his name is not (yet) on the memorial tablets in the Chapel. He was a lieutenant in the 5th Battalion of the Notts. and Derby Regiment, always known as the Sherwood Foresters. He came to Oundle from Winchester House prep school, going first to New House, before moving on to Crosby. References to him in the surviving school records are rather sparse. As a junior he played cricket for Crosby against Dryden in a rather one-sided first-round house match. Dryden scored 121 in their first innings, with Philip Whiston taking 1 for 37 but Crosby responded with just 46 in their two innings, with young Whiston contributing just two runs to the total. As seniors, cricketing fortunes were not much better for the Crosby boys. They were defeated in the first round by an innings and seven runs, with Whiston contributing his standard one run per innings. He did have some success however in the 2nd XI helping in the defeat of the village team from Thurning. In rugby, he was mentioned as a promising three-quarter in one of the lower 'rugby games' and he seems to have helped Crosby to win two but lose three of their games in 'house leagues'. In his last season, he even played occasionally for the XV as emergency cover, in what was a pretty poor season, where "some 31 fellows" played for the team at one time or another. This meant that he played alongside the Headmaster's younger son Tom Sanderson.

Richard Henry Moore, once of Laxton House, died on the same day as Philip Whiston. He came up to Oundle in 1913 and left in July of 1916. He was a good all-round sportsman without being at the front rank, representing his House at rugby, fives and cricket. In his last summer, he played a few games for the XI. He was described as "a fair medium-pace bowler" who "occasionally hits with effect but without much style." His finest hour came in the match against Lord Lilford's XI. Batting at No.9 he made a spirited 28 when the rest of the XI only scored 33 between them. It proved to be a match saving innings as heavy rain intervened with Lord Lilford's team just twenty or so runs short of victory with only one wicket down! In his final term at school, Richard Moore won the Headmaster's Prize for scripture.

Determining upon an army career, he entered the Royal Military Academy, Woolwich at the age of 18 and was given a commission in the Royal Field Artillery in January 1918. The next month he went to France and was fatally wounded on 21 March 1918 after just six weeks at the Front. His men were attacked, close to the town of Bapaume, on the first day of the

Richard Henry Moore, Laxton House 1913-16.

Ludendorff Offensive, which saw the Germans advance rather further and at greater speed than the British had managed throughout the war. Richard Moore's commanding officer wrote: "Though only with us a very short time, he endeared himself to all: he was such a bright, nice boy and I am sure he would have made a gallant and efficient officer". The commander of his brigade wrote:

> The Germans made their big attack on our front early on the morning of the 21st and the whole area around brigade headquarters and my batteries were shelled throughout the day. About mid-day, I sent Lieutenant Moore to deliver a very important message to one of my battery commanders. I heard afterwards that Lieutenant Moore delivered the message and the

map accompanying it all right after gallantly winning through the heavy German shelling…I presume he was wounded by shell fire on his return journey…I can only add that although I had known him only a short time, no-one could help liking him and I had always found him a very gallant and useful officer, who could ill be spared.

Richard Henry Moore was just 19 years old at the time of his death. He is commemorated in a fine oil painting donated to the School.

We shall meet him again in Heaven

Richard Moore's best friend in Laxton House was Avalon Hutchins and both lived in Bournemouth when not at Oundle. Avalon would die the day after his friend, plunging Laxton House into mourning at the end of the Lent term 1918. Though he lived in Bournemouth, **Alfred John Avalon Hutchins**, always known as Avalon, was born in Avalon a newly built resort town on Catalina Island off the Californian coast. He was the elder son of five children and was in Laxton House from January 1912 until December 1915. At school, he sang treble in the choir in his early years, otherwise he only appears in the hallowed pages of the Laxtonian in terms of being confirmed by the Bishop of Peterborough. He played some house cricket, making the junior final in 1913 only for Laxton to be thumped by School House, with pesky Alan West making 128! A year later, Laxton again made the final but Avalon did not play, just as well since this time they got thumped even harder with Ithel Owen, the Captain of Cricket making 271 runs in his two innings.

Alfred John Avalon Hutchins, Laxton House 1912-15.

After school, Avalon went to Sandhurst and passed out in October 1916. Joining the Royal Sussex Regiment, he was in France by December 1916 aged 19. He was severely wounded in the face and left thigh and gas poisoned on either 20 or 21 March 1918 near Boesinghe, north of Ypres and died in a field hospital near Thielt, on 22 March. He was buried at Bergmoolen Military Cemetery and later reburied at Harlebeke New British Cemetery, twenty miles east of Ypres. His headstone reads: "Brave and True, Loving and Beloved by All."

A brother officer wrote to his grieving parents: "Your son had endeared himself to all the officers of the Battalion, and with the men of his platoon, he was very popular. At his work, he was most willing, cheerful and enthusiastic, and in himself he was so unselfish and so lovable, that I cannot help but feel for him the warmest friendship." Avalon Hutchins was the cousin of Fred Trenchard, also killed near Ypres in May 1915. He was 20 years old at the time of his death.

His grieving father Alfred wrote to his son Douglas, who was then in Laxton House, to tell him the news. Interestingly, the family only received the news of Avalon's death, some seven weeks after the event.

My Dearest Douglas,

It is with the greatest grief that I am writing to tell you that this morning we received a notice from the War Office that your dear brother Avalon died on 22nd March. This is sad news for you and your poor mother as well as the rest of us. Please tell Mr Sanderson and Mr Squire about it. My dear boy, this is the Will of your Heavenly Father who has taken him where he will be far happier and we shall, if we obey God's laws and love and worship him, meet him again in Heaven. What memories we have of our dearest Avalon who was kind to us all and of such a lovely disposition that I cannot remember during all his life that he had done anything to displease us – how he loved us all, poor boy. Mother is heartbroken about it.

He signs off in the formal style of the day: "I remain your affectionate father A. Hutchins". Six days later he wrote again to Douglas, trying to strike a more 'normal' note. He tells Douglas that they had "two bad thunderstorms this afternoon with lots of hail" and that "all the soot came down the dining room chimney, such a lot, this afternoon." However thoughts of Avalon are not far away. He tells Douglas that he is now "head of the family of children" so he must be "a good obedient boy and polite and kind to everybody". He tells him that he has been very busy writing letters as "we have had a fearful lot sent [to] us." He hopes that his poor boy has been properly buried in a marked grave – "so that we could find it after the war is over. We could put up a nice cross on his grave." This time the letter is signed "Your loving father".

Wilfrid Redfern died the same day as Avalon Hutchins. He was from East Yorkshire, born in Elloughton in July 1887. He came up to School House, in 1898 aged 10 and left 6 years later. He worked in his father's business in Hull and was a keen cricket and hockey player. He enlisted as early as August 1914 in the Royal Fusiliers and went with them to France. In November 1915,

he gained a commission in the East Yorkshire regiment and was severely wounded, probably on the Somme in July 1916. Promoted to the rank of captain in 1917, he was killed, near Beaulencourt on the Somme by a sniper on 22 March 1918 as he was handing over his company after a day's severe fighting. He was 30 years old and lies buried in Beaulencourt Military Cemetery.

In School House he was part of School House's triumph as Cock House in rugby in 1903 and 1904, in the latter year, playing alongside future captain of the XV, Roy Sanderson. Wilfrid played mainly for the 2nd XI where he was described as batting "in good style but is too anxious to make runs quickly." He also played piccolo in the school orchestra.

Whilst two Oundelians died on 22 March 1918, that same day, Oundle won its second VC of the war. As it happened, it was also the day after the first VC winner, Geoffrey Vickers got married in Hertfordshire. And the second Oundle VC winner would survive the war, just like the first Oundle recipient of the award. 29-year-old Cecil Leonard Knox, who had left Laxton House in 1908,

Wilfrid Redfern, School House 1898-04.

was decorated for heroism in the field. On 21 March 1918, the Germans had begun their Spring Offensive and Knox and other engineers, stationed south-west of St. Quentin, were given orders to blow up bridges across the Somme Canal, to slow the German advance. The next day, at the aptly named village of Tugny-et-Pont, he was entrusted with the task of demolishing some twelve bridges. In the case of one steel girder bridge, however, the time fuse failed to act and as the official citation later recorded:

> Without hesitation, 2nd Lieutenant Knox, ran to the bridge, under heavy rifle and machine gun fire and when the enemy were actually on the bridge, he tore away the time fuse and lit the instantaneous fuse, to do which he had to get under the bridge. This was an act of the highest devotion to duty, entailing the gravest risks, which, as a practical civil engineer, he fully realised.

Amazingly, Knox emerged unscathed. He was decorated in the field and awarded his Victoria Cross by the King at 2nd Army Headquarters on 6 August 1918 near St. Omer. He had already served at Messines Ridge in June 1917 and would go on to play a part in the Battle of Cambrai.

He was the eighth of nine brothers, three of whom came up to Laxton. As well as Cecil, there was his next oldest brother Archibald and the baby of the brothers Cedric. Six of the brothers served in the war and two were killed. At Oundle, Cecil Knox was a good all-round sportsman representing Laxton in cricket (when they won the senior final in1908), rowing, rugby and gymnastics. After the war, he built himself a splendid new house which he named Fyves Court because it had its

Cecil Knox VC, Laxton House 1902-08, decorated in the field August 1918, by King George V.

own fives court and it had its own fives court because he had many happy memories of playing the game during his time at Oundle. Strangely enough, he does not seem to have played fives for his house, let alone the school! After the dash and glory of his exploits in the war, his death at the age of 53 was as a result of a tragic accident. Travelling at only 15mph, his motor-bike skidded coming downhill, for no apparent reason and he was killed.

Jaime Cavel Brown was yet another Laxton House boy who came to grief in the spring of 1918. Despite a Glasgow home address, he was actually born in Spain on 24 August 1896 and this explains his unusual first name – the Spanish form of James. He came up to Laxton in September 1912, leaving in July 1915. He seems to have made little impact at school in terms of sport or work. From Oundle he started training as a lawyer and joined the Inns of Court OTC before gaining a commission. He held the rank of lieutenant in the Argyll and Sutherland Highlanders from March 1917 and a year later, on 24 March 1918, he was reported missing near Pozières on the Somme, as his brigade fell back. At that time the British Fifth Army was being driven back across the Somme battlefields by the great German advance on the Western Front. His body was never found and his name is commemorated on the Pozières Memorial, part of the Pozières British Cemetery, which commemorates 13,000 men who were killed at this time and have no known grave. He was 21 years old at the time of his death.

Jaime Cavel Brown, Laxton House 1912-15.

Sydney Guy Davey was a vicar's son from Horningtoft in Norfolk. He was also killed back on the Somme in the so-called First Battle of Bapaume, where British forces abandoned the town and most of their gains on the Somme in the face of that German Spring Offensive. Born in the summer of 1893, he came up to New House for a four year stay in 1908. He sang solo in school concerts "receiving well-deserved applause" and played for the Hockey XI and the 2nd XI cricket team, on one occasion taking 7 wickets for 38 runs against the village side from Thurning. He also had talent as an actor and linguist. He appeared in *Much Ado about Nothing* and also in a French play where he received "special commendation as regards acting and fluency of speech." In house rugby, he was part of the ill-fated New House team of 1911 where 14 of the 15 players served in the war and eight, including Justin Willis,

Sydney Guy Davey, New House 1908-12.

Tom Warner and Frederick Milholland were killed. Leaving Oundle, he won a place at Clare College, Cambridge and studied history. There, he got his commission in the OTC in 1914 and took his degree in June 1915. He joined the Norfolk Regiment and was attached to the Machine Gun Corps in June 1916. He reached France in December of that year, was promoted to the rank of captain and then major in February 1918. He was reported missing, believed killed in action on 25 April 1918, aged 24, at Ervilliers. His Colonel wrote: "He fought with his company with the greatest gallantry and devotion to duty – their work was of the utmost value to the country. He was beloved by all who met him; he was absolutely unselfish; he was absolutely brave. We have lost a very gallant, Christian gentleman." Sydney Davey's body was never recovered and he is remembered on the Arras Memorial for the Missing. In his local church in Aldborough, Norfolk, his fiancée placed a memorial brass plaque and his name also appears on a stained glass window there.

John Harvey Bainbridge Kayss was another vicar's son and an only son. He became one of the Oundelians buried on home soil, though he lies there as a Canadian soldier. Born in May 1894, in Wigton, Cumbria, he left School House in 1910, at the age of 16, after a two year stay. A good athlete, he helped School House to the athletics trophy in his last year, coming second in the U16 100 yards dash and winning the hurdles competition. In 1912, he emigrated to Canada where he worked for the Bank of Montreal. He joined Princess Patricia's Canadian Light Infantry and served in France for fourteen months where he was awarded the Military Medal, was recommended for the DCM and was mentioned in dispatches. He then returned to England to train for his commission. His Platoon Commander wrote: "In the field, he was perfectly cool and absolutely fearless, loved and respected by both officers and men. He was an example to us all of endurance under trying circumstances and of cheerfulness under all conditions."

John Harvey Bainbridge Kayss, School House 1908-10.

He died at Shorncliffe on the Kent coast on 25 March 1918 as a result of an accident whilst drilling at the Canadian School of Musketry. Apparently, he was involved in fire drill training when he tripped and hit his head on a steel bar, dying of a cerebral haemorrhage almost instantly. He was 23 years old. During the war, Shorncliffe was an important base for the Canadian army and Canadian Army Medical Corps had hospitals there. The citation for his Military Medal makes clear his courage under fire:

> On 26th August 1917, Kayss led a bombing party up the sap, showing the utmost gallantry in holding the enemy off while the working party established a block behind him, killing two Germans with his revolver and putting others out of action with grenades. The success of this operation was largely due to his example which inspired the men with him.

Dying in Kent, he was taken back to his home town of Wigton for burial.

Back on the Somme, **Charles Bertram Dyson** was killed on 26 March near Gommecourt. A Lancastrian by birth, born and brought up near Burnley, where his father was a cotton manufacturer, he came up to Grafton House in 1909 at the age of 14. He was there for five years, leaving at Easter 1914. He played a few times for the XV, without being a regular. He won his school colours twice for gymnastics and as a junior, he was one of Grafton's quartet which won the house competition in 1912.

In December 1914, he gained a commission in the East Lancashire Regiment. He went to France in December 1916 and was later appointed Intelligence Officer. He was killed in action at Gommecourt on the Somme on 26 March 1918. He was with two other officers at the front line and was killed by a shell, before he could take cover. He was 21 years old and was buried at Beaulencourt alongside the

Charles Bertram Dyson, Grafton House 1909-14.

Yorkshireman, Wilfrid Refern of School House, killed four days earlier. On his headstone, his parents paid a simple tribute: "Faithful and True". Charles Dyson's younger brother John, also in Grafton was wounded (gassed) but survived the war.

Michael Beverley was also caught up in the dramatic fighting associated with the German Spring Offensive of 1918. He was also one of the oldest Oundelian to be killed in the war and one of those whose death was not reported to the School. In School House for just five terms from January 1890 until July 1891, he is one of the very few old boys killed, who attended the School before Sanderson's time. Michael was presumably a keen oarsman as in 1890, his father donated money to help with the expenses relating to the School's entry at Bedford Regatta. Michael Beverley went to Australia aged 18, in 1892 and enlisted 11 October 1915 at which time he was a stockman living in James Street, Guildford, Perth. He was a private in the 9th Battalion of Australian Infantry and embarked for Europe on 20 April 1916 on board HMAT SS *Hawkes Bay*. In October 1917, he won the Military Medal:

> During operations at Broodseinde Ridge, east of Ypres on 6th October 1917, Pte. Beverley was conspicuous by his consistent good work and gallantry. On one occasion, when carrying rations to the front line, several of his party were wounded. Though subjected to intense enemy shell fire, this soldier with great coolness assisted in carrying them to the aid post and eventually finished his journey and delivered the rations at their destination.

On 27 March 1918, Michael Beverley's luck ran out and his courage could not save him. He went out on a raid at Spoilbank, south of Ypres. He was attempting to bring in a wounded man when he was hit by a machine-gun bullet in the stomach. An attempt to rescue him failed and he died in no man's land. He was 44 years old at the time of his death and buried in Bedford House Cemetery, near Ypres.

Robert Ainslie Hamilton was the eldest son of Dr R. J. Hamilton, a fellow of the Royal College of Surgeons and Mrs Hamilton of Liverpool where he was born on 13 August 1894. He resided in School House from 1909-12 but his school career rarely made it to the pages of the Laxtonian.

All that can be gleaned is that he won a prize for French and played for a not very successful senior School House rugby team. After Oundle, he gained a commission in the King's Own Light Infantry and went out to France in November 1915. His Commanding Officer explained how he died to his parents: "The enemy had filtered through a weak part of our line, and your son took a platoon out to bomb them back. In this he was successful, but was killed by an enemy machine-gun... he was always cheerful and set a fine example to all ranks." He was killed in the early hours of 28 March 1918, aged 23. His body was never recovered and he is commemorated on the Pozières Memorial on the Somme, close to where he fell.

Two days later, a third Oundelian won the Victoria Cross, which meant two VCs were won for Oundle School in eight days. Alan Jerrard was last seen crash landing and being seriously injured in August 1917. By March 1918, he had been posted to Italy, flying Sopwith Camels against the Austrians – such was the war of many fronts. On 30 March 1918, he and two other pilots were sent out on an 'offensive patrol' over the Austrian lines. The orders came through unexpectedly and Jerrard was roused from his bed, slipping on his flying suit over his pyjamas. The three English pilots first engaged four Austrian Albatross D.IIIs heading for their base at Mansue aerodrome. Jerrard shot one down and attacked another, by which time he was close to the aerodrome. He then attacked Austrian planes stationary on the ground and those attempting to take off. In the midst of this, Jerrard shot down an Albatross which was attacking one of his colleagues. His friends then watched as Jerrard was pursued by one aircraft and crashed west of the aerodrome.

His comrades disengaged and flew safely back to base believing that Jerrard was dead. Their verbal report of the incident was then written up and a month later, on 1 May, Jerrard, by this time a prisoner of war, was awarded the Victoria Cross. The official citation claimed:

Robert Ainslie Hamilton, School House 1909-12.

Alan Jerrard VC, Sidney House 1910-15.

He then attacked an enemy aerodrome from a height of fifty feet from the ground and engaged single-handed some nineteen machines…A large number of machines then attacked him and whilst thus fully occupied, he observed that one of the pilots of his patrol was in difficulties. He went immediately to his assistance regardless of his own personal safety and destroyed a third enemy machine…(He) only retreated, still engaged with five enemy machines, when ordered to do so by his patrol leader…

The story of Jerrard's exploits that day spread like wild-fire, to be picked up by another airman, W. E. Johns who would go on to write the Biggles novels. In Johns' account, written up later, he managed to heighten the drama further and it became an exploit that Biggles himself would have been proud of:

…regardless of the streams of bullets that converged on him from all sides, he succeeded in driving the attackers away from his comrade, shooting one of them down out of control… Fresh enemy machines continued to take off from the aerodrome, but still this very brave pilot was undaunted and he attacked them one after another…Although wounded, he turned repeatedly and attacked, single-handedly the pursuing machines until he was finally over-whelmed by numbers and driven to ground.

Of course, Jerrard himself, as a PoW until the end of the war, had no say in what had 'officially' happened that day. In an interview with his Austrian captors, he did not mention an attack on the aerodrome and neither did the man who shot Jerrard down Oberleutnant Benno Fiala von Fernbrugg. Nonetheless, all reports agreed that Jerrard had displayed outstanding bravery, shot down at least one enemy plane with his own plane hit by at least 150 bullets, some of which pierced the petrol tank and this may have saved his life. When his plane crash-landed it did not catch fire. The exact details of what happened that day will never be known with certainty and Jerrard himself found it hard to remember details. Whatever the exact truth, he was clearly a fearless and skilled airman who almost certainly deserved to receive his Victoria Cross.

At School, in the Berrystead and then Sidney House, Jerrard made only a limited impact on affairs. All that can be gleaned from surviving records, is that he was confirmed by the Bishop of Peterborough and that he played in one house cricket match where he scored no runs and took no wickets. There was no clue here of the heroism to come.

11

Year 4 Home: Oundle School 1917-1918

> T'was not in vain; they've played their part,
> Example set of highest worth:
> Their country took from them new heart,
> It saw the Sons of God on Earth.

The Michaelmas Term of 1917 began on Friday 22 September. Across the Channel, the Battle of Passchendaele raged on and back in Oundle the boys reassembled after the long summer holidays, at the start of the fourth year of war. But they returned to a school which was not only coping with the conflict abroad but which had clearly risen to the challenges which the conflict presented. Were it not for the scale of the losses, Sanderson might have reflected that the war had in some ways been good for Oundle, showing how schools could contribute materially to the well-being of society in times of need, with boys playing a real part in social and material progress. Nothing showed more clearly Oundle's apparent prosperity in the face of the national crisis than the opening of another new boarding house – Bramston – in the autumn of 1917. The great Llewellyn Jones, once Housemaster of Dryden, was persuaded out of retirement to take charge of the new House in the centre of town, with a compliment of 29 boys in its first term. And the growth in numbers is reflected in the number of new boys appearing in all three terms of this particular school year – 66 in September 1917; 42 more in January 1918 and a further 33 at the start of the Summer Term, a total of 141 new entrants. Comparable figures for the school year 1912-13, immediately before the outbreak of hostilities, were 51, 12 and 23 – just 86 new pupils.

OTC

One cause of celebration in the Michaelmas Term 1917 was the setting up of a Cadet Sixth, which was apparently "hailed with joy" by "members of the over eighteen class." This meant that apart from Monday afternoons, none of their spare time was occupied with military duties, instead these were pursued in class time. The Cadet Sixth was for boys on the verge of military age and the work they did was "of such a nature as will prepare them for what they will have to do in Cadet Units and for service in the field." In particular, they studied military history, map reading, physics, mechanics and chemistry, with special reference to the making of TNT and other explosives.

On 6 November 1917, a successful Field Day took place somewhere to the west of Market Harborough. Uppingham, Oakham and the Oratory held a strong position near the village of Glumley, which was then attacked by Rugby and Oundle. Rugby on the left were held up by "stout resistance" but Oundle had better fortune on the right because the defenders "through lack of time or some misunderstanding of orders" left a road on their left practically undefended. As a result Oundle's NCOs "received a special word of commendation." There was also an extra, informal inspection of the cadets that term by Major Walter of the 16th Training Reserve Battalion. Clearly

Bramston House opened for business in September 1917.

Dryden House Platoon 1917.

the War Office needed to assure itself about standards of military training in schools as the war ground on and the Major "expressed entire satisfaction at all he saw."

By the end of the Lent Term that year, reports from the OTC were still very encouraging. Some 40 new recruits had joined since January and a long period of fine weather had improved spirits in the school corps. New recruits and others were now parading four times a week including two parades in front of the CO, Major Nightingale; then there were two NCO classes and a lot of varied work "in school time" from the newly established Cadet VIth. During the Xmas holidays, the Major was attached to an Officer Cadet Battalion and was instructed on "the latest methods of training officers" and these were then introduced at Oundle. The War Office's determination to produce fine soldiers in the future was also reflected in the appointment to the corps of real soldiers. Lieutenant Morris, from the Border Regiment apparently proved himself "of very great value in instructing the NCO class in the various branches of Musketry." The termly inspection, this time by a lieutenant colonel was again favourable and six cadets who had taken army examinations all passed the practical tests for "military efficiency." Lent 1918 also saw, unusually, another Field Day, this time made up of just Oundle and Rugby schools. The fine weather and lack of illness encouraged both schools to arrange a day at Neville Holt with Oundle defending and Rugby attacking. This time it was Oundle who were a little below par because a crucial message went astray. The other disappointment for the boys was that although there was a chief umpire of the day's events, he failed to issue a written report.

The annual inspection report on the OTC was again very satisfactory. In his concluding remarks Colonel Petre commented that the Oundle contingent was "thoroughly efficient and smart…The march past, advance in review order, and salute were all well carried out." In drill however "whistles were not sufficiently used, and there were too many words of command in place of signals." As usual the OTC had to contend with "examinations and epidemics" and this ate into practice time for

Crosby House winning Shooting Team 1917. George Brewster took charge of the House while George Tryon was on active service and became Housemaster on the latter's death.

shooting. Oundle entered an VIII for the National Rifle Association's sniping competition but the team had only five practice shots before the contest in mid-July. With a score of 708 out of 840 and 9th place out of 60 schools competing, the school correspondent felt that Oundle had made a good showing in the circumstances. The final good news at the end of the school year was that after a five year interval, the School was sending 200 cadets to a summer camp at Welbeck. With the desperate fighting continuing on the Western Front that summer of 1918, two more members of staff, who were also officers in the OTC, left to enlist. Lieutenant Kingham joined the Royal Engineers and Lieutenant Woodall the Guards Machine Gun Regiment. They of course did not know that their stint in the army would be only a few months long.

Talks on the war

In late October 1917, Lieutenant John Walker, who had left Crosby in the summer of 1916, returned to Oundle to give a talk on the subject of "Attacks at the Front." Unfortunately there is no detailed report on what he said and it would be very interesting to know how he saw the current fighting at Passchendaele. In March the next year, it was the turn of Lieutenant Aliston (not an OO) to give "a very enjoyable lecture" to the boys on the work of the RFC, illustrated with slides. In the same month, the great actor-manager, Sir Frank Benson gave a talk on "the Spirit of Shakespeare and the War".

Xmas Holidays 1917

One cause for joy in the Michaelmas of 1917 was that Oundle broke up for the Xmas holidays five days earlier than usual! It was the very first item in the Laxtonian published that December. Apparently the government was behind this welcome change from the normal routine:

> The authorities have awakened to the fact that the Schools' going down adds considerably to the traffic already swelled by Christmas holiday-makers. And, joyous thought! They have issued a mandate bidding schools break up on December 14. What schoolboy now will invoke curses on the devoted heads of the Government? If everything goes wrong, schoolboys will always remember that they cut short one term by at least five days.

Another reason for celebration just before Xmas 1917 was the marriage of the Head's elder son, Roy to Margaret Rowell. Roy was currently on leave from the Royal Garrison Artillery, after being wounded in France. It is said by the family however, that his bride did not win his mother's approval and that at the wedding she told her new daughter-in-law, in her usual abrupt manner, "No babies. No Babies." The picture of the wedding party that December day, seems to confirm some latent or perhaps not so latent tension between the important ladies present. Roy is looking isolated, whilst his father, behind him, attempts to raise three cheers but there is a look of hostility between Roy's mother and his young bride! Sadly the marriage would last just four months. Roy would be killed in action in April 1918.

News of casualties

Rather less celebratory in tone, were the continuing reports on deaths and casualties. In this school year 51 old boys were reported killed, 26 wounded, seven missing and eight prisoners of war. The fourth school year of the conflict would in fact see 65 deaths just two short of the 67 in the year 1915-16. In the Commemoration booklet, distributed on Speech Day 1918, the full Roll of Honour of those old boys killed or missing since the start of the war was printed, a sobering 175 names in

Roy Sanderson's marriage to Margaret Rowell, December 1917.

all. As if to offer a little 'balance', after six pages of the dead, there were seven pages of awards won by Oundle's servicemen. Particularly poignant was the one page obituary of the recently married Roy Sanderson published in the summer term Laxtonian of 1918. Killed in action in April 1918, Roy was remembered as one who was "endued with great physical strength and powers of tenacious endurance" which testified to "the actual force of his character and intellect." The writer concluded that much might have been expected of him, "if he had lived his full length of days."

While casualties were perhaps the top priority, the school magazine continued to report with pride on the number of awards gained by OOs. In the school year 1917-18, there was a particularly rich crop – 10 DSOs, 37 MCs and two Bars, and of course two Victoria Crosses in eight days. In addition there were some more esoteric decorations won by Oundelians that year. Six old boys, including the unfortunate Eric Gore-Browne, killed later in Portuguese East Africa, won French awards, while three naval officers won Russian decorations. Cecil Bermingham RN won the Order of St. Stanislas, while the bravery of John Shettle and Harold Foot was recognised by the Order of St. Anne.

Workshops

In the school year 1917-18, workshops' work continued as before with whole forms devoting at least one week of each term to war production. And by this time, that one week usually meant some 55 hours in harness. Despite the squeeze on academic work, the Laxtonian claimed that rising to the challenge of the national emergency actually improved the quality of the boys' school work:

> And with all the takings out of school, away from their regular work at odd, but serviceable times, the regular work of the school does not suffer. In fact, the life [sic] and elasticity of these calls to help do seem to have the effect of invigorating the regular work. Nor is this an unlikely effect. The call to special work of this kind is inspiriting [sic] for the boy and develops alertness, attention and creativeness.

School Cloisters with scrap and field gun, probably taken in 1918.

With the workshops now in full war mode, the Cloisters began to fill, at least temporarily with rusting scrap. Even this was turned to advantage. In 1918 the School produced a postcard of the Cloisters with the accumulated scrap as well as a captured German field gun!

The December 1918 issue of the Laxtonian would see the publication of an extraordinary poem about the school workshops and their by now traditional summer holiday output. Presumably by one of the senior boys, it is brilliant in aping epic Latin poetry with the use of trochaic tetrameters. Proof, if proof were needed, that Oundle, though often seen as an engineering school, continued to produce outstanding classical scholars!

August 1918

Come, my Muse, a lofty paean of a labour Herculean; shew the mythical Augean stunt but
    futile, out of date;
Let your lyre withal be singing of the hammers ever ringing, of the filings wildly flinging, of
    the oil jets still in spate:

Lay the fount of elocution under special contribution; though awhile
your resolution shirked the Future's stern appeal,
Lo, the cartridge-plug and nipple, in creative evolution, call you grimly to usher in with them
    the Age of Steel.

Comes there yet before my mind a cloistered soul within the Grinder, one whose output left
    behind a multitude of other men;
One again, who, never-ending, o'er the Capstan hourly bending, found his functions still
    extending, to the utmost powers of n;

OTC Radio Wireless Signals Section 1918.

The summer holidays of 1918 saw boys return for a month to labour in the workshops. With eight hour working days, running between 6 and 4, they apparently created "a record output." And at week-ends they amused themselves cycling via Apethorpe to Kirby Hall to promenade amongst the ruins and later to row some of the staff to Fotheringhay to take tea.

Meanwhile, the School's reputation in workshops and engineering meant that it was the recipient of a number of loans and gifts in this period. Early in 1918, the School had been lent a 90hp Curtiss aero-engine, which by the summer had been placed in a special building near the armoury. Sir Alfred Yarrow presented the School with a model of a Yarrow water tube boiler, used in his ships, while Mr J. Taylor of Blackburn presented the library with books on Textile Fibres of Commerce; Industrial and Manufacturing Chemistry and a two volume set of Manuals of Dyeing.

Poetry for the fliers

The school year 1917-18, saw the deaths of 10 Oundle airmen and a poem published in the Laxtonian in July of that year reflected the growing awareness of the bravery and short service-lives of these young men. The poem appeared first in the *Church Family Newspaper* and was written by Old Oundelian, Alfred Cotterill Kermode. He was in Grafton from 1911-15 and joined the RNAS in 1916 at the age of 19. He was seriously injured in April 1918, in a flying accident near Dover and spent some six months in hospital. The poem, invoking God's protection for the gallant airmen, was written during his recuperation. After the war he would go on to become Air Vice-Marshall and author of several books on the mechanics of flying.

FOR THOSE IN THE AIR
Lord God, who stretched the heavens above
Creator of the sky,
Who made the eagle and the dove,
All creatures that do fly;
Oh, keep our brethren in the air
Beneath Thine own Almighty care.

When storms roll up from every side,
And dangers seem so near,
Fresh courage then, good Lord, provide,
And drive away their fear:
Thy presence, like a Heavenly shroud,
Protecting them from rain and cloud.

And when they climb to dizzying heights,
Along our sea-coasts roam,
Or through the dark and lonely nights,
Keep watch o'er hearth and home:
Uphold them on Thy loving arm,
And keep them safe from every harm.

If called to fight a ruthless foe
For honour and for right,
Do Thou, O Lord, before them go
And be their guiding light:
By night and day, o'er land and sea,
Oh, give to them the victory.

Agriculture

As the boys returned from their elongated Xmas holidays at the start of 1918, John Binder, the local grocer was concerned about how they would all be fed: "The influx of about 600 people into a small place like this will make most serious demands upon the food supply and there will be much difficulty in finding food for them." "Indeed," he noted gloomily, "I should not be surprised to know that if the war continues that it will compel them to break up the School." In reality, his pessimism seems to have been rather misplaced and failed to take account of the boys continuing efforts to produce their own food. Agriculture remained a high priority for Oundelians in the fourth year of war. The hay crop (some 30 tons of it) in the Michaelmas Term was "good and abundant" and the two largest ricks were sold to the War Department. Potatoes and swedes grew abundantly as well and peas and wheat also appeared on the menu. Meanwhile Oundle School was still bringing home the bacon with "nearly a ton of home grown bacon and ham" produced during the school year. In the Summer Term of 1918, the Laxtonian reported that the boys had spent a lot of time on the land "to meet the needs of the times" and much digging was done "both on the plots and on the fields behind the laundry." In total, the School now farmed some 30 acres of land. And the results impressed the Laxtonian editor: "We may consider ourselves to have been extraordinarily well fed, and until we return home we will not perhaps realise the trouble to which those concerned have been put in order to amass the necessary provisions."

Despite the increased acreage and productivity, the School's governors had tried to put a brake on further expansion. In November 1917, Sanderson proposed that the School should buy more land "belonging to the Glebe" which was currently on offer, in order to create "a miniature Rothamsted" (experimental farm) at Oundle. The governors however, as so often with Sanderson's schemes, demurred and they seem to have been worried that the Head was more concerned about profit than food production! In March 1918, they wrote in these terms: "We have come to the conclusion that an experimental farm at a public school should in fact be an open-air laboratory and that it should be worked on strictly educational lines and not for profit." Not for the first time, however, Sanderson outwitted the Grocers. He took out a lease in his own name on part of the Glebe and took a yearly tenancy on lands belonging to the vicarage. He then had the land ploughed and made a start on his little Rothamsted. In this endeavour, he also got help and advice not only from Rothamsted itself but also from Cambridge University and from "a well-recognized authority" in these matters, Dr Russell "whose two boys are with us." Not for the last time, Sanderson made use of his parents to further his ambitions for the School!

While these developments went ahead in Oundle, despite the governors' objections, Oundelians continued to help out in agricultural matters further afield! On two or three days in the Summer Term, parties were sent over to Apethorpe to hoe beans. The School had links with that particular village as Mr Wrey, land agent to Lord Brassey of Apethorpe, who had been "extremely kind to the school in various ways recently," lectured the boys on scientific agriculture.

Towards the end of term, the boys also helped out in a local emergency. A large number of women workers were expected in the neighbourhood of Wansford and Peterborough to gather flax but there was no accommodation for them. Oundelians leapt into action to meet the crisis: "For four days, the School sent detachments of between forty and sixty to various centres and with their help, the requisite number of tents and marquees were put up." In a satirical poem printed in the Laxtonian, the process was described in this way:

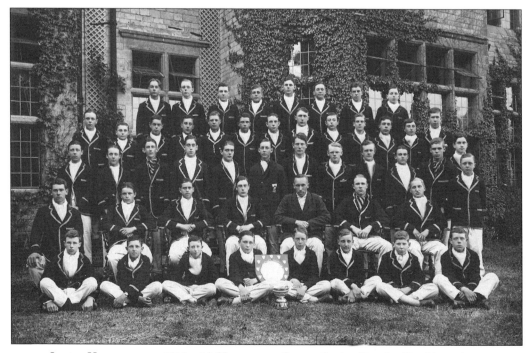

Laxton House, summer 1918, with Housemaster Sammy Squire. Douglas Hutchins, whose brother Avalon was killed earlier that year, is third from left on front row.

Now in these days, strange women came into the land round about for to gather flax, and, Lo,
 there were no houses for them to dwell in.

Therefore for four days were the men of Ound sent out by fifties, on the first day into the ford
 of Wan, and on the other even past the city of Peter.

And there did they set up many tents, both small tents, like unto a bell, in which the women
 might sleep, and large ones, even those called mar-kees, in which they might take their
 food.

As well as the OTC camp at Welbeck, the first since 1913, the summer holidays of 1918 also saw
Oundle boys attending two agricultural camps, sponsored by the War Office, at Edlington and
Keelby, both in Lincolnshire. At Edlington, (near Horncastle) 42 boys from four houses plus four
members of staff (Messrs. Hale, Squire, Spurling and Walker) were in attendance. Reveille was at
7:00 a.m. and groups of boys (usually from the same House) were sent off to different farms to work.
In the first week, work finished at 6 "so as to settle down gradually" but in the second week "with
the harvest to gather," they often worked until dusk. The boys "turned peas" which was "rather
monotonous" but they soon got onto more agreeable pursuits "reaping and stooking, leading and
stacking corn" which was apparently much more enjoyable apart from the thistles! The camp at
Edlington lasted for nearly four weeks and was so sited that they could just see Lincoln Cathedral
some 20 miles away.

The boys slept in fourteen bell tents and had three soldiers to do the cooking. The food was
excellent: "Though the arrangements seemed primitive, the results were simply extraordinary:
everyone was delighted with the fare, and it is no light matter to satisfy manual workers!" Evenings
seem to have been pretty jolly as well: "In the evenings we got plenty of amusement – the attractions of Horncastle were very popular, especially the swimming baths." However, in later weeks,
longer hours of work and the mending of punctures "owing to the execrable nature of some of the
by-roads" meant that most people stayed in camp in the evenings. They had a Mess tent which
could be used after meals for "letter writing, chess and cards." Sundays were always looked forward
to as an opportunity to bike further afield. A number of the boys, described as enthusiasts, "got
out to Lincoln and Skegness, both good twenty-mile spins." The camp was twice visited by a War
Office inspector who "expressed his complete satisfaction" at the work being done. The only disappointment for the boys was that the Headmaster was unavoidably detained and unable to make his
promised visit.

Further north in Keelby Camp, it was a similar story, this time with 44 boys under the direction
of the indefatigable Major Nightingale. The feeling was that they did well despite fearing that they
were the poor relations compared to their Edlington brothers: "Although we were far from living in
the Sybaritic comfort enjoyed by those at Horncastle, nevertheless there are many who will cherish
a pleasant memory of the camp at Keelby." Amongst the pleasant memories were "the appearance of
porridge and tea in the same bowl, the sounds approximating to reveille on a dismal morning, the
bakery, the King's Head and the elusive charms of the [Church] Institute" which provided "reading,
recreation and billiards." The entertainment highlight at the Institute were two concerts given by
NCOs and men of the 4th Manchester Regiment, stationed in nearby Cleethorpes. The Oundelian
reporter did not go into detail about specific work done by the boys but recorded that "occupations
were as diverse as the temperaments of the farmers."

Business as usual

While the war cannot have been far from the thoughts of staff and boys at this time, yet the
normal business of school life continued as before, perhaps with even greater intensity than in
peace-time days. Certainly examination results continued to be very satisfactory, with lots of passes

and distinctions in the Higher Certificate, School Certificate and Lower Certificate papers. In the summer examinations of 1917, Sanderson could report that 215 boys had scored a total of 745 passes. The next year 1918, saw 181 boys take 606 passes. The war of course had led to a diminution of Oxbridge scholarships, as boys had other matters to anticipate after Oundle. Pre-war, there might be a total of six or seven scholarships and exhibitions to Cambridge and occasionally to Oxford in a year. 1914-15 saw a last pre-war flourish of eight, but the next year saw just five and 1916-17 just one. Three were won in the next two years until a recovery to pre-war levels in 1919-20 with six awards.

Music and drama continued to flourish at this time. In December 1917, the senior French sets took on Act 1 of *Cyrano de Bergerac*. With "fifty odd performers" this play was a great success with the pupil troop seemingly bringing out "the bustle of the action and the snap of the complicated Alexandrine verse." Special praise was heaped on the Cyrano himself, played by John Coubrough of School House:

> Of Coubrough in the title role it is difficult to speak without seeming to exaggerate; but it must in ordinary justice be said that members of the audience who had seen the original production of the play in Paris, could hardly believe that such a realisation of the character was possible in a school performance...As a feat of memory alone his performance was quite marvellous: his pronunciation faultless; his readiness, *verve*, and resource never once failed throughout the most exacting French part which has ever been attempted at Oundle.

In the same month as *Cyrano*, there was music as well as drama when the junior school put on an abridged version of *A Midsummer Night's Dream*. Naturally each part was played simultaneously by three boys. The Laxtonian explained Oundle's unusual but worthy approach to drama:

> As has previously been the custom, the parts were allotted in triplicate; which may seem strange to the uninitiated, but, from an educational point of view, has much to recommend it. By the time rehearsals are over, and the trios are more or less (principally more) unified, a regular visitor would forget that plays were ever acted on the 'one man one part' plan.

The Atcherley twins and Gainsford were the three Bottoms and splendidly entertaining they were but it was perhaps the trio of Quinces who had greatest impact. They "rose – or rather sank – to the occasion inimitably, and their efforts and those of the other clowns culminated in a dance before Theseus which brought down the house." The costumes were equally exciting and thanks went to Jane Sanderson as well as Mrs Ault, Mrs Cox, Mrs Hough and Mrs Bray who made and fitted them: "These ladies tasks were far from light. The two copies of Oberon's costume had to be covered with over 120 yards of zigzagged gold paper, which had first to be stuck on muslin, then cut out, and finally sewn on."

The School Choral Society, though unbalanced in favour of trebles, usually mustered some 150 singers, about one-third of the School. The Chapel Choir did even better with over 200 participants. The Orchestral Society reported in the Michaelmas of 1917 that it had "more members than it has ever had previously, the increase being in the number of violins," a fact pleasing in itself but "slightly embarrassing in view of the amount of floor space in Mr Woodall's class-room." While house concerts seem to be less frequent, there were regular organ recitals throughout the year at 6:30 p.m. in the Great Hall and other recitals for solo instruments and voices. In addition, the School Orchestra played in several dramatic productions. In April 1918, orchestra, singers and actors joined forces to present an exciting double bill of *Songs from the Pirates of Penzance* and the second and third acts of Sheridan's satirical play *The Critic*. The Laxtonian's literary critic was overwhelmed by the spectacle:

There are perhaps those whose memory, dating back longer than that of the writer, can recall as inspiriting [sic] an evening at Oundle as that on which were given these two plays. But the performance certainly beat all records for recent years. The combination of Gilbert and Sullivan with Sheridan afforded, we should imagine, an entertainment such as falls to the lot of few schools at the present time.

Though Coubrough, playing the Pirate King was unable to quite repeat the scale of his triumph as Cyrano de Bergerac, the excerpts were "admirably and beautifully done. The police were duly cautious and stolid, the pirates picturesque and truculent, while Mrs Cox turned out a vivacious bevy of Major-General's daughters." This was of course a real compliment considering that all the daughters were boys but once again the Atcherley twins (Richard and David) were in action here, building, no doubt, on the success of their Bottoms the previous December! In *The Critic*, Francis Marshall wowed the audience: "His sense of his own greatness, his conviction, his enthusiasm for the beauties of his tragedy were not acting. They were real." Also picked out for special mention was George Wells, (son of H. G.) last seen in the debating chamber, but now with his "splendidly finished performance of Tilburina – once again as good a rendering as we have ever witnessed."

The orchestral school year culminated as usual in the annual Speech Day concert. Over 900 people packed into the Great Hall in 1918 to listen and the concert was a great success. Starting with works by Corelli, Elgar and Dvorak the strings apparently "played with assurance and were well together…and the whole orchestra played with excellent tone and expression." The chorus, like well-oiled oarsmen, sang two part-songs "with crispness of attack and smartness in release." The trebles of the singing class sang cheerfully, contributing songs in Spanish and French as well as English, all from memory. Frank Bromley and John Graham were commended on their piano solos and Jocelyn Chase though "handicapped by nervousness" was deemed to have "artistic insight and a musicianly manner" in his violin playing. Bernard Robinson was apparently rather more assured on the violin, playing a gavotte "with refinement and good feeling." The whole evening came to a rousing climax with the *Soldiers' Chorus* from *Faust* (appropriate as it was the 100th anniversary of Gounod's birth on the 17 June 1918) and finished in fine style with the school song, *Carmen Undeliense*.

Debating continued to flourish with greater numbers in attendance, though the Laxtonian had to admit that this increase was the result of a little prompting from the Headmaster: "The attendance has much increased this term [Michaelmas 1917] by the presence of senior fellows whom the Headmaster has prevailed upon to come to meetings." The next term several members "made their maiden speeches." Few of the debates that year were directly about the war. The first motion of the year explored the question of how the war was being paid for. The motion was that "Conscription of Wealth is more Equitable than Borrowing at Huge Rates of Interest."

Other topics suggest perhaps that the Head had some influence in determining the motions as they were often on great social questions of the day. In October of 1917, the motion before the House assembled in the art room was that "The Education of the British Working Man is adequate." Meanwhile arguments in favour of the abolition of corporal punishment were soundly defeated. While Mr Villiers (Charles Villiers of School House) suggested that floggings could easily lead to vindictiveness, Mr Little (Robert Little also of School House and Captain of the School) had the answer – administer another flogging!

With greater numbers at the School, all sports seem to have been doing well in this school year, with more boys than ever involved in school and house sports. Rugby continued to flourish and indeed expanded. A 2nd XV and a Colts XV were now a regular part of school games and serving men provided much of the opposition. As well as the usual opponents such as Bedford (ancient and modern), Rugby and the Leys, in the Michaelmas of 1917, there were also matches against the New

Zealand Machine Gun Corps and the Royal Naval Air Station, Cranwell. Other sports carried on in the usual way during the year with much rowing, fives and cricket. The cricketers also benefitted from having special 'war time' opposition in the shape of teams such as No.3 Royal Field Artillery Cadet Officers' School, Weedon, the Machine Gun Corps from Harrowby Camp, Grantham and the Marlborough Royal Air Force. Unfortunately all three of these matches were lost and the XI seems not to have had a vintage season. On Sports Day 1918, Sidney House won by a mile (!) with 757 marks, compared to just 400 for second place Laxton House. Sidney captain, Francis Marshall won the Lady Lyveden Cup, winning the 100 yards in 12.2 seconds and coming second in the hurdles and the quarter-mile.

And then there were the usual round of illnesses suffered at school. The Lent Term of 1918 was surprisingly free of pestilence but in the summer they had not one but a variety of epidemics. In the Laxtonian, there appeared a splendid biblical satire entitled *The Story of the Plagues*:

William Woodeson and his friend Donald Raby (right), both of Grafton House in 1917. Donald Raby would be killed the next year.

Now it came to pass that in the fourth year, when there was war, great pestilence came over the land of Ound.
And many divers plagues were upon the land, so that the men of Ound got them not down to the place of bathing, lest so the plagues should be spread and the knees of more should be weakened.

Some of the boys clearly hoped that they might be sent home as a result of the plagues:

And in those days rose up the children of darkness, even the rumour-mongers, saying, Lo, such and such a one has said it, that if but two more are taken by the plague then shall we depart every man into his own home.
Howbeit most laughed them to scorn, saying, Away, get ye hence, and tell it even unto the marines; as for us, we have been bitten before. Yet some few there were that cherished the rumours for a while in their hearts.

And then each of the 'plagues' is discussed in detail and two are of especial note – German Measles and the Spanish Flu:

Now another of the plagues, it was called the measles of the men of Hu.
And this plague was not sought after, for it was both thought unpatriotic – since in those days there was war with the men of Hu – and also he that was taken with it only escaped from school for fourteen days, even for a fortnight.

And the last plague, it was called span-ishflu, which is, the disease of the Dagoes, and it was worse than all the other plagues rolled together.

And a man would rise up in the morning and see many empty places around him: then he would say, Behold such a one is Con-ked, which signifieth one who has weak knees.

However, the many diseases apparently had their good side as some boys managed to miss their higher or lower certificate exams:

Now the days of the Certificates drew nigh, and they were an abomination unto the men of Ound. For fierce people came down called examiners, who said, Lo, give an account of your scholarship: tell us what knowledge ye have gained this year. And it came to pass that many were found wanting, and there was wailing and gnashing of teeth.

Those however, who missed the exams were apparently joyful:

These therefore, were bucked with life, and said one to another, Lo, we have wangled it a treat: let us gloat. And with these there was joy, but amongst the rest of the men of Ound there was lamentation and sorrow.

Laxton School, Summer 1918

As in the previous year, the Summer 1918 journal of Laxton School starts with news of the war. Mr Reynolds, one time Laxton teacher, now of the Lancashire Fusiliers, has now become Captain Reynolds and has added a bar to his Military Cross. Other young Laxton boys have now joined the forces. Robert Green, Norman Smith and William Turnill all joined the new Royal Air Force; Douglas Skinner was with the Siege Artillery, Edward Hunt, (actually killed the previous year) had joined the Royal Field Artillery and Douglas Barlow was now in one of the Officer Cadet Battalions. The OCBs were created in February 1916, offering a four month course for suitable men, serving in the ranks to gain a commission as an officer.

Sport continued to prosper at Laxton School in 1918. The Cricket XI of 1918 was captained by Seddon and it played rather more matches than the previous year, winning three, losing four and drawing one. This year, for the first time, house matches were played in cricket and football, which was a successful initiative: "The idea of playing house matches has proved itself a good one both in cricket and 'footer,' inasmuch as it produces extra keenness in the sports." Unfortunately, the 1918 summer magazine seems to have gone to press before Speech Day, as there is no report of the events of that day.

Oundle School Speech Day 1918

Speech Day 1918 for Oundle School was notable for being the first since 1914 to be held on the old lines, "attended by the Governing Body, the Master and Wardens of the Worshipful Company of Grocers." The weather was rain free but rather windy. Despite railway restrictions and an outbreak of measles, attendance was very good and with the increased number of boys (and two new boarding houses) since the outbreak of war "the seating capacity of both the Great Hall and the Chapel was taxed to the utmost extent." In his speech, Sanderson read out the scholarships gained by Oundelians since the beginning of the war and the military awards they had won. He spoke feelingly of Frederick Milholland, Head of School in 1914, who had been killed the previous February. His father had travelled across from Jamaica for the occasion and proposed the vote of thanks to the Master of the Grocers' Company.

The XI of 1902. Frank Armitage, killed in 1917 is seated second from left. Victor Adendorff (standing second from right) would score 322 runs for Laxton as they beat Sidney in the 1904 Senior Cricket Final by an innings and 681 runs!

Mr Milholland believed that the war had enhanced Oundle's reputation. Years ago, he said, he got very annoyed when everyone he spoke to mixed up Oundle and Arundel. Now, he said things were different. At the end of his recent voyage from the Caribbean, when he mentioned his destination, his companion told him that Oundle School "was the best science school in the country." He didn't speak of his son Frederick by name but said that he had tried to instill on all three of his sons, three maxims, which he believed Oundle had helped to foster. These were: "to play the game, to do their best and to help the underdog, even if it were necessary to handle him roughly at first!"

The Master of the Grocers' Company, Sir Ernest Pollock KBE KC MP echoed the sentiment about 'playing the game'. He believed that the war was fought "between the principles of Prussian kultur and freedom, and that the rule of the Hun was absolutely intolerable" and that what was needed to win the war was the public school spirit, epitomised in Sir Henry Newboult's fine poem – 'Play up, play up and play the game'. At the same time, he realised that the war had drawn the Empire together in a common cause against barbarism. He also told Frederick Milholland's father that his son would have been made a member of the Grocers' Company if he had lived.

The proceedings in the Great Hall closed with the National Anthem, the school song and "the usual cheers" and the assembled company was then led by the school corps to the new museum, donated by Sir Alfred Yarrow, in memory of his son, Eric, killed in 1915. The OTC formed an open square, everyone sang Jerusalem and the Master formally opened the new building and inspected the troops.

The new Yarrow Museum, 1918.

From 5:00 p.m., on Speech Day the usual exciting range of scientific experiments could be viewed and at 8:30 p.m. there was the usual Speech Day Concert. The previous year Lady Maud Warrender had been the star turn; in 1918 the singer was David Ellis "who sang five songs in all, two in Welsh." The concert, ending with the National Anthem was a great success, the Laxtonian reporter claiming it to be "one of the most successful concerts we have ever had." It was not until the next day, Sunday 23 June that the School remembered the dead. The Headmaster read out the Roll of Honour and David Ellis returned to sing the anthem *'Be thou faithful unto death.'*

Though they did not know it at the time, the Summer Term of 1918 was to be the last full term of the war and, reviewing the year and indeed the previous years of the conflict, two important points are clear. Firstly, the two Oundle Schools, perhaps more than others, rose to the many challenges posed by the conflict. With her pre-war workshops and agricultural experiments, Oundle was well placed to make a serious contribution to the war effort in terms of munitions and food production. At the same time, expansion of the OTC produced boys who were better equipped, than their forebears had been, to take commissions in the armed forces, to do their bit for their country.

Secondly, though the war clearly had a profound impact on the School, in terms of war work, food production, debates, talks, patriotic songs and the ever lengthening Roll of Honour, it was also a case of business as usual. Games at school and house level continued apace and continued to take up at least 40 percent of the space in Laxtonian magazines. Boys continued to act and sing, to play instruments, to have all sorts of academic lessons, to attend Chapel, to win scholarships and to prepare for life beyond the hallowed portals of Oundle, even if that now meant joining the war effort. Overall, with growing numbers and two new boarding houses, Oundelians, during the war, 'played the game' as well as their games. They knew that they were involved in a great national struggle, the like of which previous generations had never seen or faced and they did their bit. Despite the heart-ache of the losses, and they seemed impossibly great, Oundle School rose to the challenge, showing that schools were a vital part of the national community, part of the reason for eventual victory and perhaps part of a brave new world to come.

Cricket XI of 1912 with their coach, Fred Holland. Sundius-Smith, Mason and MacBryan would be killed in the War.

12

Year 4 Away: More Stalemate – April to September 1918

It is hard to think we shall see the boys no more.

With the great German Offensive on the Somme petering out by 4 April 1918, their attack was renewed in the Ypres/Neuve Chapelle sector five days later, in what became known as the Battle of Lys. After driving forward in the first two days of the attack, it seemed as though the Germans might break through to the Channel ports. On 11 April 1918, Haig issued his famous order of the day: "With our backs to the wall and believing in the justice of our cause, each one of us must fight on to the end." However, the German offensive soon stalled because of supply problems and exposed flanks. Although the Germans gained rather more ground in a few days than the British had at Passchendaele in many weeks, the hoped for break-out did not materialize and on 29 April 1918, the German offensive was called off. Justin Willis, the boy who forecast the start of war and "the final Armageddon" so prophetically in 1912, wrote home in April 1918 saying that he thought the German advance would soon be stopped: "Beastly sorry I haven't written before, but we have been most extraordinarily busy lately. This battle has been a funny old show hasn't it? I think we can hold the Bosche alright now though. There has been a lot of very severe fighting, and the Bosche has been slaughtered in thousands." Once again his forecast was right. Personally though, his own condition was deteriorating: "I have got a tremendous great boil on the side of my nose, and have gone about the place with my whole head surrounded with bandages and things. I have also got scabies, which is a bloody disease; you itch all over and cannot sleep. I think I am going mouldy with all these diseases."

April to June 1918 on the Western Front

Although the German Offensive did not lead to a breakthrough, the fighting near Ypres was as intense as ever and a number of Oundelians were caught up in the carnage. **Lieutenant Henry Kenyon Bagshaw**, once of New House was one such. He was another of those vicars' sons. Brought up in Chatteris in Cambridgeshire, he was at school in Hunstanton before arriving in Oundle where he stayed for just five terms, leaving in the summer of 1909. He then took up land agency work. He joined the Public Schools' Corps in September 1914 but then transferred to the Army Service Corps, having failed to get into the infantry because of defective eyesight. He served in France throughout 1915 and 1916 and had four months sick leave when he went down with typhoid

Henry Kenyon Bagshaw, New House 1908-09.

fever in August 1916. In 1917, he was attached to the Duke of Wellington's West Riding Regiment and served at the Front.

In the spring of 1918, Henry Bagshaw fought in his last battle. He was caught up in the desperate fighting of the Lys offensive and was killed in action near Ypres on 13th April. His body was never found and he is now one of the four Oundelians commemorated on the Tyne Cot Memorial. In memory of their only son, his parents erected a pulpit in the church in Chatteris.

John Denison was also caught up in the German attack at the battle of Lys and was killed the same day as Henry Bagshaw. John came from Leeds in Yorkshire, arriving in Sidney House a year before the war began. Fives was his major sport, he was in the School VI and helped Sidney to win the senior trophy in 1917. He was a keen debater too. He contributed in the famous Zeppelin Debate, claiming that "boys lives being their own", they should be allowed to stay in bed during a raid rather than being forced into

John Denison, Sidney House 1913-17.

dusty cellars at their Housemaster's command. He famously argued fiercely that the Germans were unable to throw bombs as far as the British Tommy because they did not play cricket!

Aged 18, he joined the Royal Naval Air Service in September 1917 and after a spell at the Naval College in Greenwich, he did further training at Cranwell and Manston. He arrived in France on 16 March 1918 and was flying over the lines between La Bassée and Armentières, near the Belgian border. He was killed just four weeks after his arrival at the Front. He was shot in the head, while returning from patrol and although he managed somehow to land his machine, he died shortly afterwards. His Commanding Officer noted: "Most of the older fellows have had much more experience of course and consequently it was much more difficult for him to do his work in as efficient a manner as they; but all in B Flight were glad to have John with them, in every attack they made on the advancing enemy." He was buried aged 18, in Pernes British Cemetery, where he is the only Oundelian. As a result of his death, his sister came to work at Oundle School.

Further south, **Captain Ronald Christie** had been killed the day before Bagshaw and Denison, on 12 April. Like his Headmaster, Christie was a Geordie by birth, being born in Tynemouth in January 1896. Later the family moved to West Kensington in London, via Hemel Hempstead in Hertfordshire. He was in School House from 1911-13, where his main skill seems to have been in shooting. He won the Recruits Cup and helped School House to a creditable 3rd place in the house matches.

He left Oundle, as so many did, at the age of 17 and he was serving his apprenticeship as a naval architect with Swan Hunter when the war came. He

Ronald Christie, School House 1911-13.

immediately joined the Army Service Corps and went out to France early in 1915. He then transferred to the regular army and became a captain in the Royal Garrison Artillery. He was awarded the Military Cross for gallantry during the retreat on the Somme in March 1918 and died of wounds on 12 April 1918 in a French Hospital at Vasseny, near Soissons. His Colonel wrote: "I need not tell you how sad we all were to hear of his death. We were all so very fond of him. He was such a really good man at work and play, we shall have to go a long way to meet his equal."

Also killed that April was a young man who had married in the previous December. **Roy Broughton Sanderson**, the Head's elder son was born in Dulwich in 1889, three years before the family came to Oundle. He officially entered School House in 1898, at the age of 9 and left, some 10 years later in July 1908. He was Head of School, Captain of the XV and a prominent swimmer, winning both the Ferrar Challenge Cup and the Royal Humane Society's Medal in that sport. He also rowed for School House but the Laxtonian reviewer, as so often, was not impressed: "Sanderson is still clumsy and apt to disturb those rowing behind him but Roy has greatly improved on last year." Nonetheless, he was part of the winning School House crew in 1906. Academically, he was clearly his father's son. He won prizes for maths and owned a book about ellipses, written in French! He won a scholarship in maths and mechanics to Queens' College, Cambridge where he was later Captain of the College XV.

Roy Broughton Sanderson, School House
1898-1908.

After serving a pupillage with the chief engineer of the London and North Western Railway, he was appointed to the staff of the Royal Naval College, Osborne, Isle of Wight. When war came, he joined the Royal Garrison Artillery as a second lieutenant and went to France. There, he was seriously wounded and invalided home for a year, during which time, as we have seen, he married. Returning to the Front soon afterwards, Roy was promoted to lieutenant and was attached to an artillery battery, equipped with 6" Mk VII howitzers. He was stationed near Kemmel in Belgium, on strategic high ground commanding views of the flat valley of the River Lys. Once there, their first task was to dig deep gun pits. An artillery captain later wrote: "Deep pits must be dug for the guns, and slopes cut into these pits by which the said guns may be hauled in and out. These pits must be floored with an elaborate platform and their sides revetted, to prevent them falling in. Most difficult of all, they must be roofed over with as much earth as such roof beams can be made to bear."

On 9 April 1918, the great German offensive began and Roy's battery was told to turn their guns, which could fire more than 8,000 metres, to try to halt German progress. The next day, the enemy had taken the village of Ploegsteert and Roy's battery had to withdraw "with the enemy in close proximity." By 12 April, the guns had been moved back once more. Amidst the confusion of these exhausting withdrawals, Roy wrote to his wife that rations were very low and he and his men were eating ginger biscuits sent by his mother. During the night of 15/16 April the withdrawal continued as far as Mont Noir and on the morning of the 17th, the battery received heavy shelling and Roy was seriously wounded. He was evacuated some 15 miles to the nearest casualty clearing station but died the same day.

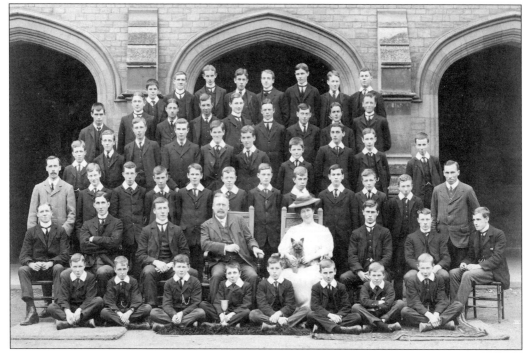

School House 1908 with Roy Sanderson, next to this father, as Head of House.

Roy Sanderson was buried in Haringhe Military cemetery, not far from Ypres. On his headstone his parents wrote:

> God Bless Thee Wheresoe'er In This Wide
> Universe, Thou Art Today.

He was 29 years old at the time of his death. He and Margaret had been married for just four months. It was later claimed that his father intended to appoint him Head of Workshops if he had survived the war.

The next to perish was not directly involved in the fighting at the time of his death. **Wedgwood Vaughan** was in Dryden House from 1896 until 1899, where he was a prominent sportsman. He was a stalwart amongst the forwards in a pretty successful XV and he helped Dryden romp to victory over School House in the inter-house tournament. He was also stroke of the School Crew (a IV in those days) weighing in at 11 stone. The crew was described as rather clumsy and unpolished but with potential. Naturally, Vaughan's rowing style did not win entire approval in the pages of the Laxtonian: "His swing forward was

Wedgwood Vaughan, Dryden House 1896-99.

good and steady but his finish was weak…He will make a capital racing stroke if he has any further chances of rowing."

After Oundle, he went into shipping and in 1908 was back in his home area as manager of the Blyth Shipbuilding Company, north of Newcastle. His war was different to many of his fellows as just before its outbreak, he sustained serious head injuries after a motorcycle accident. An experienced yachtsman, he then obtained a commission to drive his brother-in-law's motor-launch delivering mail in Scotland. But by November 1914, his health broke down again and he underwent an operation to relieve pressure on the brain. Still determined to do his bit, he spent six months after that in France as a Red Cross motor driver and later worked in an aircraft factory. In the spring of 1918, he contracted a severe chill which developed into pneumonia and he died on 25 April 1918 at the age of 36.

Roland William Trubridge, like Wedgwood Vaughan and the Headmaster was from the North-East, born in Newcastle in November 1898. He was a Crosby lad for three years, leaving in Easter 1915. He came first in the U14 150 yards swimming race and won a prize for German, perhaps not surprising for a boy whose name during his school days was Keiffenheim! He was a good flautist, playing a solo by Gounod in the school summer concert in 1914. The reviewer for the Laxtonian averred that: "The flute solo was quite expressive and very nicely played. R. W. Keiffenheim should be encouraged to persevere with this useful instrument." In the same concert, the other Oundelian with a German name, Ernest Weintraud also played an instrumental solo, this time on the violin. When war began the Keiffenheims, like the Weintrauds changed their name in order to sound less German. So Roland Keiffenheim became Roland Trubridge. Thus anglicized, he joined the Royal Flying Corps and gained his wings in September 1916, aged just 17. He was operating on the Western Front, to the north of the Somme when he was wounded on 29 April 1918. He died of his injuries a week later, aged 20 and was buried in Crouy British cemetery not far from Amiens.

Another airman was the next to perish. **John Hollick** was an only son and an Essex boy, born in Ingatestone in 1899 and brought up in Upminster. After a spell at Winchester House in Brackley, he resided in Sidney House from 1913-17. Sporting-wise, he was not in the front rank but he played his part in house rowing and cricket. And he was part of that gallant band of volunteers who toiled in the workshops during the summer holidays of 1915. And he had a pretty good bass voice, giving a stirring rendition of *Funiculi, Funicula* as part of a bass octet.

Leaving school at the time of Passchendaele, he joined the Royal Naval Air Service as Flight Sub-Lieutenant Hollick in November of that year. He arrived in France in January 1918, and did good work continuously until he was reported missing on 18 May 1918. He was last seen in conflict with several German aeroplanes about ten miles over the German lines near Sailly-sur-Lys, not far from Armentières. The presumption is that he was shot down. His body was never recovered and he is remembered on the Arras

Roland William Trubridge, Crosby House 1912-15.

Flying Services Memorial, along with seven other Oundelians. He was killed less than a year after leaving Oundle, aged 19.

Back on the ground and just one year older than young Hollick was **Wilfred Dexter Rees**, a Laxton School boarder, born on the last day of 1897 and staying in Laxton School from 1909 until 1912. He was part of a generation of boys who saw Laxton School flourish and develop in the benign shadow of Oundle School. He was from Kettering and was killed, aged just 20, on 29 May 1918 near Soissons on the Western Front.

At the end of May 1918, with their attacks on the Somme and the Lys petering out, it was in this same area, in the so-called Battle of the Aisne, that the Germans opened up their latest offensive. Wilfred Rees, once of the Royal Fusiliers, was a private in the Machine Gun Corps but his body was never found, so he is remembered on the Soissons

John Hollick, Sidney House 1913-17.

Memorial. This commemorates over 4,000 officers and men killed in this area in 1918, who have no known grave. Ironically, many of the British troops like Wilfred Rees had recently been sent to this normally quiet sector of the front for rest and recuperation after the earlier German onslaughts.

Two days later, **Reginald Hardy Platts** also died; not at the Front, but as a result of an accident in a chemical laboratory in London. He was the elder brother of Leslie Platts killed on the Somme in July 1916. By the time he arrived in Laxton House in 1901, his father had died and his mother was left to bring up her seven children. Rowing alongside the mighty Frederick Trenchard (killed in May 1915 at Ypres), Platt's Laxton crew impressed the School's sports correspondent: "Laxton improved immensely. They were well together and rowed very long. When it is remembered that this is only

their third crew after being unrepresented for several years, they may congratulate themselves on making such a good show." In the end they were beaten in the final by Llewellyn Jones' Dryden in what was clearly a very close race. Reggie Platts was also a school prefect and played for the XV on the wing, running in some useful tries. Playing cricket for the XI, he was described as "a good patient batsman" and put together some useful knocks, including a 61 against the Rev. Brown's XI. Platts was also a member of the Laxton House all-stars of 1904, who crushed Dryden by an innings and 681 runs, having scored 849 in their first innings! Platts contributed just 25 runs to the total, while the South African Victor Adendorff knocked off 322! When Adendorff returned home, Reggie Platts was elected in his place as secretary of the School Science Society.

Reginald Hardy Platts, Laxton House 1901-05.

Leaving Oundle in the summer of 1905, Reggie Platts teamed up with his step-father W. G. Whiffen in his firm which specialized in vegetable alkaloids – drugs used in pharmacology. At the outbreak of war, he joined the Royal Garrison Artillery but in August 1915, returned home, seconded to the Whiffen firm because of his scientific expertise and the war's huge demand for pain killing drugs. He died from shock on 31 May 1918, when he sustained severe burns at work. He was carrying out an experiment in the works' laboratory when, for some unknown reason, the vapours exploded. He was 31 years old and left a widow Irene and three small children.

Two weeks later and back on the Somme, scene of renewed fighting, **Edward Alfred Murtagh Stevens** died for his country. He was the only son of Mr and Mrs E. Stevens of Pakhoi in Southern China, where his father was the Harbour Master. He was a Grafton House boy from 1913 to 1916, leaving just as the Battle of the Somme was beginning. He was a member of the XI for two years and described as "a steady medium paced change bowler who varies his pace well." He also helped Grafton reach the final of the house competition.

This match against Crosby took place over three days and Grafton seemed to be on course for victory with a useful first innings lead but the outcome may have hinged on the fact that Edward Stevens was forced to withdraw on the third day through illness: "At this stage of the proceedings, Grafton had a stroke of very bad luck in losing, owing to illness Stevens, one of their best bowlers and a useful bat." Although disappointed in the cricket, Stevens did help his House to win both the fives and the rugby competitions in his last year. He also won his school colours for fives.

In the war, he held a commission in the East Kent Regiment (the Buffs) and won the Military Cross for "conspicuous gallantry and devotion to duty". The citation for this award read as follows:

> During a hostile attack, he led his platoon with great dash and gallantry, in a counter-attack on a hostile strong-point. On the re-taking of this position, which was of great importance, when his bombing section was nearly surrounded, he personally held the block to cover their retirement. He showed great disregard for personal danger and an unselfish devotion to duty.

On 18 June 1918, however, Edward Stevens was caught up in the renewed fighting in the Somme region, as the Germans continued to advance westwards. He was killed, aged 19, north-west of the town of Albert and was buried in Harponville Communal Cemetery. At the bottom of his headstone, as a tribute to his son's *alma mater*, his father inscribed the words:

God Grant Grace
Oundle School

Edward Alfred Murtagh Stevens, Grafton House 1913-16.

Three days later, Steven's exact contemporary at Oundle, **John Hirst Ainley**, a son of
Yorkshire, met his own appointment with
death, also aged 19. He was a good all-
rounder at sport, playing for Sidney in fives,
rugby and cricket and for the School in colts
rugby. He also played cricket occasionally for
the XI as a medium pace bowler but "adopted
rather a crouching attitude at the wicket." He
was in the Rifle Brigade and was killed in the
fighting following the Battle of Lys on 21
June 1918 while waiting for stretcher bearers
for a wounded colleague. His Major wrote:
"He was long enough with the battalion for
me to realize he was just the type of officer
we want out here – full of keenness and
energy – the kind the men appreciate." The
chaplain wrote in a similar vein: "He put such
splendid keenness and energy into all he did,
and throughout kept a high standard, which,
by his influence and perhaps unknowingly, he
made attractive to many round him." He was
buried, in Le Vertannoy British Cemetery,
near Béthune and on his headstone his
grieving parents wrote: "There is no death but
forgetfulness."

John Hirst Ainley, Sidney House 1913-16.

The start of a pandemic

As if the fighting was not enough, by the
summer of 1918, starting at the end of June,
British troops and civilians were hit by the
deadly influenza pandemic. **Thomas Beech
Barton**, an exact contemporary of Edward
Stevens in Grafton, was probably the first
Oundelian victim of the disease. His first
attempts to enlist in the army failed on
medical grounds but, determined to play his
part, he finally joined up with the King's
Liverpool Regiment and died of pneumonia
on 30 June 1918 whilst training at Park Hall
Camp in Oswestry. He was buried, aged 18
at All Saints Church in Gresford the village
in Wales where he was born. "Until the Day
breaks and the Shadows flee away" is inscribed
on his headstone.

Born near Wrexham and an only son, he
was brought up in Congleton in Cheshire and
was in Grafton, like Edward Stevens from

Thomas Beech Barton, Grafton House 1913-16.

1913 until 1916. He scored 40 runs as Grafton beat Sidney to win the senior house cricket in 1915. In the Oundle tradition, he was one of three boys playing Old Gobbo in *The Merchant of Venice*. More significantly, he was a member of the Manchester School of Music, where he was regarded as one of the most promising violin students.

Edward Dermot Ledlie Gonner, School House 1907-11.

Two days later another Oundelian died of pneumonia brought on by influenza. **Edward Dermot Ledlie Gonner**, known as Dermot, was the only son of Professor Edward Gonner. He was born in Liverpool and resided in School House from 1907 until 1911. Here he enjoyed great success in house sporting competitions. With him in the team, School House was 'Cock House' in gymnastics, athletics (twice) and cricket. He was a member of the XI described as "the hitter of the team who he has made some useful scores and worth his place in the team for his fielding at extra-cover." In the summer of 1911, his best showing was as top scorer with a plucky 35 against Sanderson's old college Christ's, Cambridge when all around him fell rather cheaply. He later played for the Oundle Rovers (OO cricket) team and played for the OO rugby team in 1911, having appeared occasionally for the XV. He was also a useful and keen fives player, representing the School and described as possessing "a strong service and hits hard with both hands but does not use his head as much as he might."

After school, Edward Gonner spent a year studying architecture in Liverpool before being articled to a surveyor and land agent. While there, he played for Birkenhead Rugby Club and represented Cheshire. He enlisted in the Liverpool Scottish in August 1914 but was invalided out of the army in the spring of 1915 when he spent some time in a corn merchant's office and later married Miss Winifred Twigge. Despite being medically unfit and therefore unable to serve in the front line, he got a commission in the Royal Warwickshire Regiment and was engaged in training new recruits. Based at Gosforth in Newcastle, he contracted influenza which was followed by pneumonia and he died on 2 July 1918, aged 25. He was buried in Willaston, Cheshire, where he had lived after his marriage. Tragically, his father, Sir Edward Gonner, Professor of Economics at Liverpool, died just four years later, also of influenza.

The Western Front, August–September 1918

A month after Edward Gonner's death, back on the Somme, **Justin Charles Willis**, the boy who had confidently predicted the coming conflict in 1912, penned what was to be his last letter to his mother. After a bout of illness, he was currently on the mend and in need of further supplies. Though now Major Willis, he still wrote, as he always did, with the language and tone of an excitable schoolboy:

Thanks most awfully for the tomatoes and peas, they were top hole. I am feeling fit, and have had no more boils yet, and I have also succeeded in avoiding this so-called Spanish flu. Could you go to Beresford's in town the next time you happen to be there, and tell them to send me out six small electric lamps (bayonet socket) sixteen candle power, eight volts. So sorry to trouble you. Please give my love to Daddy. Goodbye my dearest Mothie. Much love from Justin.

A few days later, Justin's mother received another letter. It was from Major General Sir Richard P. Lee:

> I cannot tell you how deeply we, the officers of the staff of the 18th Division deplore the loss of your son. He was a great signaller and a most gallant officer with a keen sense of duty. He was mortally wounded on the 6th inst. (August), the day the Germans made a strong counter-attack on our position…The wound was a gunshot wound in the stomach and, to our great grief it ended fatally.

Justin Charles Willis, New House 1909-13.

He died on the operating table. The local chaplain wrote: "It may comfort you to know that I buried him in a quiet little graveyard well away from the front…marked with a cross. May God grant you comfort in your sorrow, and to him eternal rest and peace." The tributes to Justin were many. His uncle wrote to his sister, Justin's mother, in these terms:

> I am glad I read his letters and felt what a dear simple-hearted boy he was. You have (though you cannot count it now) a wonderful treasure in the future of a beloved son who will never grow old or commonplace – who will always be your own, and has bequeathed to you the honour of his unstained, loyal life, and will welcome you – yes he will – on the other side.

Sanderson wrote to Justin's father: "Both Mrs. Sanderson and I can sympathise with you as we lost our eldest son in April. Only, I think, those who experience it can fully know what it all means. The School has lost very heavily. It is hard to think we shall see the boys no more."

Three days after Justin Willis' untimely death, another Oundelian airman gave his life for the cause. **John Edmund Emtage** was the third Sidney boy to die in a five week period in 1918 and had left school just a year before his demise. He was the second son of the Hon. W. T. A. Emtage from London and Vacas in Mauritius and the younger brother of William Emtage who made quite a stir by landing his plane in Oundle in the summer of 1917. John was born in Nottingham, in March 1899 and was in Sidney from 1912 until 1917. He, like most boys, was confirmed by the Bishop of Peterborough during his school career and he helped Sidney win the senior fives title in the Lent Term of 1917. Otherwise, he is one of those boys who left little trace in the official school records. He joined the Air Force and held the rank of lieutenant when he was reported missing on 9 August 1918. His death, at the age of 19, was presumed to have taken place at that time. He has no known grave and is remembered on the Arras Flying Services Memorial, with seven other Oundelians.

Eric George Renton was even younger than John Emtage, only 18 when he met his fate. Like Emtage, he was a flyer and another one who had an all too short career. He would be the second Oundle airman to die in five days. Born in Harrogate, he arrived in Grafton in 1913 and later appeared regularly in the 2nd XV where he was a forward. Though he won his colours, they were not awarded that year (1917) because of a shortage of dye-stuffs. In his penultimate summer term, Grafton lost to Crosby in the senior house cricket final, by just 12 runs with Eric Renton contributing only four in his two innings. This result was revenge for Crosby who had lost the junior final to Grafton and Eric Renton in the previous year. In Renton's last year at the School, Grafton were skittled out by Laxton in the first round!

John Edmund Emtage, Sidney House 1912-17.

Leaving Oundle in the summer of 1917, as Passchendaele was beginning, he joined the RFC and a year later, he was in France. Just days into his career as a pilot, on 14 August 1918, he was patrolling over the German lines, when he was attacked by a number of enemy scouts. His observer dispatched at least one of their foes but they were themselves shot down amid fierce fighting near Rosières, east of Amiens. Eric Renton was killed two weeks before his 19th birthday and lies buried in Heath Cemetery in Harbonniers on the Somme.

The next to be killed was, as chance would have it, also from Harrogate in Yorkshire. This was **John Coates**, the seventh son of Thomas Coates also of Harrogate. He was in Dryden for just two years, leaving in 1906. As a junior, he was a demon bowler taking 5 for 20 and 7 for 10 in a two innings match against Grafton. Later in the competition, he took 11 for 77 against Laxton. After leaving school, he took up banking back in Yorkshire. In the war, he served naturally enough with the Yorkshire Yeomanry and was killed on 15 August 1918

Eric George Renton, Grafton House 1913-17.

as the British and Germans counter-attacked each other after the German advance in April 1918. Aged 29, John Coates was buried in Le Grand Hasard Military Cemetery in Morebecque in northern France. He was married and his wife Margery inscribed on his headstone, "Greater Love hath no man." John's nephew, Harold Brearley Coates had been killed on the first day of the Somme.

Back on the old Somme battlefield, **Edward Norman Andrews** fell near the old British base of Albert a few days later. He left Oundle in December 1916 and went to the Royal Military College at Sandhurst. The next year, he gained a commission as a second lieutenant in the Buffs (East Kent Regiment) but his arrival in France was delayed until July 1918 by a broken arm. He was involved in the British slog back across the Somme battlefields in August of that year and was fatally wounded on 22 August while leading his platoon in an attack near the town of Albert. He died the next day. A brother officer wrote: "He led his platoon with complete disregard of danger, encouraging the men until wounded. His bravery and devotion to duty were an inspiration to his men." Edward Norman Andrews was just 19 years old at the time of his death. His two older brothers also served in the army and survived the war.

He was born in November 1898, in Hampstead, the son of a doctor and the youngest of three brothers. Like them, he came up to School House and stayed for five years from 1911 until 1916, enjoying a distinguished school career. He played some matches for the 2nd XV, sang bass in the School Choral Society, was appointed a school prefect and Captain of Boating.

Also killed on the Somme that summer was **Stanley Harold Slater**. A Barnwell boy, born in Sutton, near Peterborough in July 1899, he was brought up with his parents, William and Elizabeth at 24 Barnwell. He came up to Laxton School just weeks after the start of war in 1914 and left at Easter 1916, aged 16. He was a private in the Royal Fusiliers and was killed on the Somme on 24 August 1918 aged 19. He is buried in Bagneux British Cemetery

John Coates, Dryden House 1904-06.

Edward Norman Andrews, School House 1911-16.

in Gézaincourt. On his headstone, his mother chose the familiar and appropriate words: "In the midst of life, we are in death".

The next day, **Lawrence Arnold Wilkins** once of Laxton House, was also killed on the Somme, as the British finally turned back the great German advance, which had started in the spring of that year. When war broke out, he obtained a commission in the York and Lancaster Regiment and, in August 1915, after eight months training, he was sent out to join the Service Battalion in France. Apart from a six month spell back in England, he served nearly three years in France and by June 1917 had been appointed captain. Re-joining the York and Lancaster Regiment in April 1918, he was killed in action near Ervillers, a village close to Bapaume.

Lawrence Wilkins was a Notttingham boy, the son of a vicar and was born in the city in August 1894. He came up to Laxton House

Lawrence Arnold Wilkins, Laxton House 1908-13.

in September 1908, leaving five years later. In his last year, he won one of the top awards – the Lilford Prize – and for two years running took the prize for French composition. He was also in the School Crew, rowing at 2, even though, weighing just 10 stone 8, he was thought to be too light for that position. The crew went all the way to Durham, where, as guests of the Headmaster of Durham School, they won the Corporation Challenge Cup. In the famous debate about the relative merits of cricket and tennis, Wilkins opined that "tennis was 'slacker' than cricket" and so personally, he preferred tennis! Ironically, in that same debating chamber, he once claimed that "the advance of civilization" had been attended by "a decrease in war." When war came, he was articled to a solicitor in Nottingham. Lawrence Wilkins was killed eight days after his 24th birthday. On his headstone, his widowed mother put the words "In His Steps."

Victor George Brindley, aged 27, was yet another victim of the Somme in 1918. He came from Orange Free State, having been born in Natal in 1891 and spending his early years in Johannesburg. He was the elder of two brothers and came up to Dryden House in 1905 staying for four years. At Oundle he was a keen sportsman and a good runner. He also 'trod the boards' as the harlot, Doll Tearsheet in Shakespeare's *Henry IV*. After Oundle, he returned home and took up farming with his father.

He volunteered in August 1914 and fought first in neighbouring German South-West Africa. A year later, he joined the South African Infantry and stayed with them, even though offered a commission in the Scottish

Victor George Brindley, Dryden House 1905-09.

Horse. He first served in Egypt and then came to the Somme in 1916, seeing action with his compatriot Chalmers Carmichael around Delville Wood, as we have seen. A year after these terrible experiences on the Somme, Victor Brindley then decided to join the RFC. By December 1917, he had gained a commission and began patrol work back on the Somme in July 1918. Returning from a routine patrol in a Sopwith Camel on August 30th, he died of wounds, probably incurred as a result of a dog-fight with a German opponent. A fellow officer wrote of him: "A better man in a tight corner one could not wish to meet." Now he lies buried on the Somme where he saw action in 1916 and 1918 and where he died after serving in the war for three years. His younger brother, Knight Brindley was also in Dryden and served with South Africa's Imperial Light Horse during the war, mainly in East Africa. He died of wounds in December 1922. On his headstone in South Africa, his grieving parents recorded the names of their two lost sons.

Bruce Lionel Siddons, Day Boy 1898-1902.

Two days later and five years older than Victor Brindley, **Bruce Lionel Siddons** was also killed on the Somme. The eldest son of J. M. Siddons of Oundle, who ran a 'cake and seed' business in the town, (like Henry Curtis' father) Bruce lived in a house called Silver Birch on Milton Road. He was a Day Boy at Oundle School from 1898-1902. In 1912, at the age of 26, he went to Australia, in the Sydney area, where he trained as an engineer. Described later as "tall, dark and thin", he came back to England in February 1915 with the second detachment of Australian Imperial Forces, having enlisted in the infantry. He could have taken a commission with an English regiment but decided to stay with the Australians as a sergeant.

He was wounded in Gallipoli in June 1915, when he was hit by a bullet in his left forearm. He was sent to Cairo where the bullet and several fragments were removed and then spent the rest of the year recovering from his injuries. In the summer of 1916, he and his men were sent to Marseilles and made their way to the Somme battlefield. In July 1918, he was back in England on a musketry course but re-joined his unit on the Somme two days before it attacked the small town of Péronne. He was killed on 1 September 1918, in that attack, when a shell burst in front of his face, killing him instantly. His commanding office said that this action covered the brigade with glory but that Siddons could ill be spared because he was one of their best NCOs. He died, aged 32, and was buried in the Péronne Communal Extension Cemetery.

John Parnwell Gray was another local boy. He was a boarder in Crosby but came from Stamford. The brother of Charles Shortland Gray killed at Loos in 1915, he was at Oundle from September 1911 until July 1915. As a rugby player, he was on

John Parnwell Gray, Crosby House 1911-15.

the receiving end of that infamous 96-0 defeat suffered by Crosby in the first round of the house matches in 1912. In house cricket it was scarcely any better as Parnwell's team was routed by School House by an innings and 95 runs! However, he was victorious as cox for Crosby in the Junior IVs.

He became a Gentleman Cadet at the Royal Military Academy in Woolwich, then won a commission in the Royal Field Artillery in January 1918. He served in France from February 1918 until May of that year, when he was seriously wounded. He died at York Hill Military Hospital, Glasgow on 13 September 1918 as a result of illness stemming from the injuries suffered on active service. It seems that these injuries were the result of an accident rather than caused by enemy fire. He was 20 years old at the time of his death and was buried at home in Stamford.

How is the Empire?

John Laughton was six years older than John Gray and died in South Africa after a long illness, in July of 1918. His father, known as 'Pom-Pom', was born on the Isle of Man and was a successful lawyer and QC. John, one of six brothers, was at Oundle (Sidney House) from 1906-09. He was a keen rugby player and played for Natal. At Oundle, he was a member of the XV for two years but in a supporting role, in the first year and described as 'the best of the rest', being a useful reserve forward. In Michaelmas 1909, the term he left, he played regularly at No. 8. With his help, Sidney won the house rugby in both 1908 and 1909, beating first Grafton in a final which was described as "not of a very interesting character," and then romping home against Dryden, the next year, by 33 points to nil. Before the war, he attended agricultural college. He served in the South African Volunteer Force but was invalided out and died, after a long illness, on 19 July 1918. He was 26 years old.

John Laughton, Sidney House 1906-09.

Douglas James Aitchison served in the Middle East, though he died in Hampstead. He enlisted in September 1914, taking a commission in the East Anglian Brigade of the Royal Field Artillery at Christmas. Training in England during 1915, he was sent out to Egypt in January 1916. He was on the Suez Canal for some time, before being sent to the Front in the wake of the First Battle of Gaza in March 1917. He then transferred to the Royal Flying Corps and served through the British advance into Palestine, until his aeroplane crashed, soon after take-off on 30 December 1917, as a result of engine failure. Seriously injured, he was sent back to England to recover. Four months after the crash, he contracted blood poisoning and died on 17 April 1918 in the RFC Central Hospital in Hampstead. His Commanding Officer wrote that he did very good work on the observation machines during the Second Battle of Gaza, the encounter with the Turks in which Stanley Marlow of New House, who was in the year above Douglas Aitchison, died. Young Douglas was just 21 years old at the time of his death and was buried in Beckenham, Kent, his home town. His mother by this time had lost her husband as well as her youngest son.

Douglas was the third son of the family. A Dryden boy from 1911 until the summer of 1913, he played in the final of the house rugby competition of 1912, where Dryden beat Sidney after a replay. Also a good athlete, he won the 100 yards, the quarter-mile and the Ferrar Challenge Cup on Sports Day 1913. In the debating chamber he was sometimes controversial. In a debate where Mrs Sanderson spoke in favour of women being allowed the vote, Douglas Aitchison opposed the motion declaring that if they got the vote "women would work to better the poorer classes and so waste a great deal of money"!

Eaten by a crocodile?

For **Eric Anthony Rollo Gore-Browne**, every inch a colonial soldier, there was to be no known grave and the terrible suspicion that he met his fate in the jaws of a crocodile. He was a Sidney boy, the youngest of four children, born in Ryde on the Isle of Wight, in June 1890. He was brought up in Buckinghamshire, where his father was a vicar. Though he spent only two years at Oundle, he was a school prefect, keen cricketer and a sergeant in the OTC. After Oundle, he determined on a military career, entering Sandhurst and then obtaining a commission in the Dorset Regiment in 1910. After three years in India, he was seconded to the King's African Rifles and sent out to British East Africa, where Oundle's war had begun in earnest in September 1914, with the death of Sam Edmonds.

Eric Gore-Browne was promoted captain in 1915 and was wounded in action at Longido as the British incursions into German East Africa continued. He was evacuated to a hospital in Nairobi but recovered and continued to serve. In 1916 he became a major and was awarded the Croix de Guerre by the French, the next year, for his part in training French troops in Nairobi. Early in 1918 he returned to German East Africa but was then transferred to Portuguese East Africa – modern day Mozambique – where he died, on 3 July 1918. Now acting Lieutenant Colonel Gore-Browne, he was in charge of the fort at Nhamacurra when it was overwhelmed, after a gallant three day defence, by a large German force of Askari warriors:

> Now only the KAR [King's African Rifles] on the right held fast. The cheering Germans raced across sugar and sisal fields, the British troops found themselves all but riveted down by cross-fire. Their commander, Major E. A. Gore-Browne had no choice but to order a

Douglas James Aitchison, Dryden House 1911-13.

Eric Anthony Rollo Gore-Browne, Sidney House 1906-08.

gradual withdrawal towards a wide stream in the hope of fording it and taking up stronger positions on the opposite bank. Suddenly the usually unflappable KAR were infected with the Portuguese panic. Instead of retiring in order, they swarmed into the river and tried to swim to the other side…nearly half the force was shot dead, snapped up by crocodiles or drowned in the boiling current. Among those lost was Gore-Browne, who went under while trying to stem the rout…

Ironically, the German force that day was commanded by Paul von Lettow-Vorbeck, the same German commander whose men had killed Sam Edmonds of Laxton House back in 1914. Eric Gore-Browne was 28 years old at the time of his death and his name is recorded on the Mombasa British Memorial in Kenya. He has recently made a surprise appearance in Nigel McCrery's book, *Final Wicket: Test and First Class Cricketers Killed in the Great War*. He is officially a first-class cricketer on the basis of one appearance for the Europeans against the Parsees during a Bombay Presidency match in August 1912, played at Poona. He scored 12 and 0 and took no wickets. His brother Harold (who did not go to Oundle) had been killed aboard HMS *Invincible* in the Battle of Jutland.

Reginald Frederick Desmond Plunkett also died out in the Empire and, like Eric Gore-Browne, was swallowed up by a mighty river. Born in Cairo in April 1898, he was in School House from 1912-16. He was a useful athlete, playing fives, rugby and cricket for the House. In rugby, he was on the losing side in the final of 1915 but in cricket, in the summer of that year, he was more fortunate. Playing alongside the mighty pairing of West and Sundius-Smith, who both made centuries in the semi-final, Reggie Plunkett helped School House to the title in a nervy finish against Crosby. School House looked well set but in the end, limped home with one wicket to spare. Reggie Plunckett contribution was hardly spectacular; he scored just eight runs and took one catch in this two innings match. In death too, he was not quite the equal to his friends West and Sundius-Smith, as they were killed in action, whilst he brought about his own demise.

By December 1916, he had entered the Indian Army and after six months training, he was gazetted to the Gurkha Rifles and stationed in Quetta. He was then sent out to Mesopotamia and reached Basra in February 1917. He took part in the expedition up the Euphrates as far as Abu Hemal and was present at the engagement at Khan Baghdadi, when the British overwhelmed a Turkish force and took some 5,000 prisoners. Having survived the rigours of battle, Reggie Plunkett was accidentally drowned while bathing in the Euphrates River on 6 September 1918, aged 20. His body was lost and he is now remembered on the Basra Memorial, alongside two other Oundelians, Donald Milne and Alan Scarth. His younger brother Humphrey, who was in New House for four years, also served in the Empire, also with the Gurkha Rifles and survived the war.

As the boys returned to Oundle in late September 1918, at the start of the fifth

Reginald Frederick Desmond Plunkett, School House 1912-16.

year of the conflict, it was far from clear that the war was nearing its conclusion. Sixty-five more Oundelians had perished during the fourth school year of fighting and for most of that time it looked as though Britain and her Allies might lose the war. The Russians had been defeated by the Germans and Austrians; submarine warfare had brought Britain to the brink of starvation; the French army had mutinied; the German Spring Offensive had seen the greatest gains on the Western Front yet and the Americans, who had arrived in April 1918, had not yet had any major military impact. Though the great German advance though Belgium and France had been halted in mid-August, it was by no means clear that Germany and her Allies were on the brink of defeat. With winter approaching once again, many assumed that the end would come, if it came at all, during 1919.

13

Year 5 Away: The Close of the War – September 1918 to December 1922

He is dead and gone, but still his fame remains as bravest of the brave.

One more in Macedon

The first death of the fifth school year of the conflict, occurred back in Macedonia. **William John Board** was the eldest son of a family from Nottingham. Born in Cardiff, where his father was Deputy Town Clerk, the family then moved to Nottingham, when his father reached the top job. William came up to Dryden in September 1914, having previously attended Wolverley School in Worcester and King Edward's School in Stratford-upon-Avon, like his fellow Oundelian, Geoffrey Donaldson. He made little impact on the School in terms of the written records left behind, apart from playing in one cricket house match, where Dryden were soundly beaten by Crosby.

He left Oundle after just two years, in July 1916, aged 17 and went to Nottingham University, where he joined the OTC. The Commanding Officer there reported favourably on his abilities: "Son of the town clerk. Excellent boy, remarkably good at details. Good word of command. Suitable for artillery." He then trained with the Royal Field Artillery at bases at Weedon and Lark Hill. In March 1918, just after his 19th birthday, he received a commission and was in a reserve battalion in Ireland.

In August 1918, he was sent rather further afield, to Salonika, to fight the Bulgars. With the Bulgarians in disarray, the British, French and Greeks had built up large forces by the late summer of 1918, ready to finish off their opponents. William Board arrived in Salonika in late August and was killed in the Third Battle of Doiran. He suffered gunshot wounds on 18 September 1918 while taking ammunition up to the fighting line and died four days later. He had been in Greece just three weeks and was still only 19 years old. On his headstone his parents wrote: "In loving memory of our dear son. He giveth his beloved sleep." Later, they erected a tablet and holy table in their local church, St. Jude's in the Mapperly district of Nottingham.

William John Board, Dryden House 1914-16.

Although the Bulgars were victorious in the Third Battle of Doiran, (the British and Greeks suffered over 7,000 casualties) they decided to retreat in the face of advancing French and Serbian forces. On 30 September 1918, to avoid invasion and occupation, Bulgaria surrendered and the first of Germany's props had fallen away. Looking back, Bulgaria's suing for peace was the first clear sign that the war would soon be over. For contemporaries, who had seen the dread conflict drag on for so long, it was not so clear-cut.

Battle of Cambrai-St.Quentin, 27 September to 9 October 1918

Back on the Western Front, in the early autumn of 1918, there occurred a series of titanic engagements which helped to carry the Allies through to victory. Although the 'Hundred Days' was successful in terms of ground gained, the losses were still enormously high. For the first time, there were serious American casualties, as the U.S. troops under Pershing took on a major role in these autumn offensives. In the end, the Allies won the war because they had apparently limitless fresh supplies of men and resources, while the German forces, undermined by exhaustion, waning supplies, discontent at home and the loss of their allies knew that the end was near. Nonetheless casualties on all sides remained high. The Battle of Cambrai-St. Quentin was launched by the Allies on 27 September 1918, attempting to break through the German's still well fortified Hindenburg Line. It was to be the third costliest day of the war for Oundle deaths – four more Oundelians perished in the service of their country.

Austin Provost Baldwin was brought up by his widowed mother in Peterborough. His father died when Austin was just nine. He came up to Oundle School as a Day Boy in September 1893, the beginning of Sanderson's second year and stayed until July 1899. At school he was a violinist, helped the *oppidans* (town) team to third place in the inter-house gymnastic competition and was fourth in the quarter-mile handicap race in his final year. Being a Day Boy from Peterborough seems to have qualified him to play on two occasions for Barnwell against the School's 2nd XI cricket team. And there were enough Day Boys at that time for them to raise a cricket team to play Laxton School.

Two years after leaving school, he was living with his uncle in Suffolk, employed as a clerk to a wine and spirits merchant. By 1911, he was in Market Harborough as auctioneer, valuer and surveyor and had joined the local lodge of the freemasons. He joined the Artists' Rifles in July of 1917 and was gazetted second lieutenant in June the next year. By August 1918, he was in France and was killed on 27 September 1918, at Flesquières, when the Suffolks attacked German held positions on the east bank of the Canal du Nord near Cambrai. Killed by machine-gun fire at the age of 35, it was his first time in action.

The attacks that day and subsequently were very important in maintaining British momentum against the retreating Germans and especially in beginning the breaching of

Austin Provost Baldwin, Day Boy 1893-99.

the Hindenburg Line. Unless this massive German defence system were pierced, static trench warfare might well start up again, delaying the end of the war. The attack where Austin Baldwin was killed, helped to pave the way for the crossing of the Canal du Nord and the St. Quentin Canal by early October. As both waterways were integral parts of the Hindenburg Line, their capture was crucial to allied success on the Western Front.

One of Austin Baldwin's opponents in the House gymnastics competition was **John Vercoe Rogers**, a youngster in the Sydney team. As fate would have it, these two boys, who had competed together in March 1899, died on the same day, in the same battle on the Western Front nineteen years later. John Rogers was the second son of a family from Canonbury Park, London. He arrived in Sidney House, accompanied by his older brother in January 1898, aged 11 and left in December 1900, after exactly three years, still only 14 years old. As an U14, Rogers ii, as he was known, won the 100 yards and the quarter mile on Sports Day 1898, competing against rather older boys and he was also one of a winning team in Association Sixes (presumably six-a-side football) in his first year. He played house cricket with some success and won a French prize in his last year.

John Vercoe Rogers, Sidney House 1898-00.

At some stage, he lived at Waterloo Farm in St.Mawes in Cornwall and then emigrated to Canada with his future wife in 1906, sailing from Falmouth. They lived out west in Birch River, Manitoba and he came over to France in the Winnipeg Grenadiers, rising to the rank of lieutenant. 5 feet 9 inches tall with dark brown hair and brown eyes, he described himself as a lumberman when he joined the Canadian Army in May 1916. His wife, Susie was his next of kin and he had at least one son. He fought first at Vimy Ridge near the Somme and fell in action on 27 September 1918 at Bourlon Wood, and was buried in Quarry Wood Cemetery in Sains-Les-Marquion, eight miles north-west of Cambrai.

Another who fell that same day, part of the same battle was **Rayner Harvey Johnson**. After Oundle, he went to the Royal Military Academy in Woolwich, won a commission in the Royal Regiment of Artillery, and arrived on the Western Front in June 1915. By February 1916, he was Observation Officer for his battery and promoted to the rank of captain by December of that year and acting major less than two months later. The Commanding Officer of his brigade commented that Rayner Johnson "was the best officer I had." His gallantry was noted by the Australians in July and August 1917, at Passchendaele. The 1st Anzac Corps recommended him for an award in the following terms: "For such a young officer [he was 20] he has shown great skill in handling his guns and men, and considering the losses sustained by the battery and the conditions involved, this Officer's organising powers have proved of high value."

Rayner Johnson was duly awarded the Military Cross in January 1918 but was killed eight months later. Aged just 21, he was making a forward reconnaissance for his battery when he met his death. He was universally respected by fellow officers and by the men. One officer commented: "When we learnt we were to have a new Major, we wondered whether we should get a man who would lead us in a way worthy of the past history of the Battery. It soon became evident that we had got our work cut out if we were to be worthy of the Major we got." He was buried at Louverval Military Cemetery in Doignies, 10 miles south-west of Cambrai. "He being made perfect in a short time, fulfilled a long time" is inscribed on his headstone, and in his local church, St Mary's, Long Ditton, his grieving parents raised a plaque with a heart-felt tribute ending with these words: "A devoted son and brother, a true friend and a gallant soldier. As the shining light that shineth more and more unto the perfect day."

A Surrey boy, Rayner Johnson was born in Surbiton, and lived in Ditton Hill just south of the Thames. He arrived in Grafton House in May 1911, leaving in the fateful summer of 1914, aged 17. He played rugby for the House along-side John Hebblethwaite and Stewart Ridley, both killed within four days of each other in 1916 and played house cricket with Freddie Butcher and Eddie Stevens, two more victims of the war. Neither Grafton team enjoyed success.

The fourth Oundle boy to perish on that fateful day near Cambrai was **Reginald Bourne Seaton**. During the war, he enlisted in the King's Own Royal Lancaster Regiment and was killed that same 27 September 1918 when his battalion, like Austin Baldwin's, attacked the village of Flesquières, west of Cambrai. He has no known grave and his name is inscribed on the memorial panel in the cemetery of Vis-en-Artois. He was 25 years old at the time of his death.

Born on May Day 1893, Reggie Seaton attended Laxton School for two years, leaving in the summer of 1907. His father had moved from Lincolnshire to Woodnewton and then to Oundle where he ran a butcher's shop in North Street. Close by the family shop in Oundle, lived Ralph Lilleker, Bertie Loakes, James Roughton, Herbert Sharpe and Ernest Cottingham who would all be killed in the war. What young Reggie did at school is not really known. He attended Laxton School Old Boys' dinners in the town and there is a splendid signed photo-graph of him posing in his football kit. After school, he worked in his father's shop, presum-ably hoping to take over the business when his parents retired.

Rayner Harvey Johnson, Grafton House 1911-14.

Reginald Bourne Seaton, Laxton School 1905-07.

With four deaths on the 27 October 1918, the next day added a fifth. **Lieutenant Frank Gale Berrill** was one of that rather large number of Oundle boys whose fathers had died before the war. Frank's father had been a military man, rising to the rank of major in the Queen's Regiment. Though born in Streatham in London, on the last day of 1896, Frank was brought up at Pytchly Manor near Kettering. He was sent to a prep school in windswept Cromer and then on to Oundle and Sidney House in September 1910. He was a school prefect in his last year and Head of House in his last term, Michaelmas 1915, when he also played for the XV. At the same time, he was Captain of the Gymnasium and OTC section commander for Sidney, with the rank of sergeant. In the Lent Term of 1915, he spoke up in favour of Belgium in an important school debate about Germany's invasion of that country in 1914. "Is the gentleman opposite me so dulled to all feelings of common decency," he wondered, "that he can gaze upon the spectacle of devastated Belgium without a pang?" Frank Berrill also had a good bass voice and sang several solos in Sidney's house concert in July 1915.

Frank Gale Berrill, Sidney House 1910-15.

Leaving Oundle in December of that year, he joined the Inns of Court OTC in London and trained at Artillery Schools in Exeter and Larkhill, before receiving his commission in the Royal Field Artillery in October 1916. He was sent out to the Lens area of northern France, serving for nearly a year before being invalided home in the winter of 1917-18 with gas poisoning. In June 1918, he joined a battery near Arras, and on 28 September he was mortally wounded near Bailleul, dying on the way to a casualty clearing station. Aged just 21, he was buried in Duisans British Cemetery. His Brigade Commander spoke very highly of his keenness and conscientiousness in all his work.

James Stuart Ricketts, one of the proud Dryden platoon photographed in the summer of 1912 and the sixth member of the Dryden Seven to die, perished one week after Frank Berrill, probably of wounds received in the same battle. Born in Kent and losing his father, a doctor, before the outbreak of war, he lived in St. Leonards-on-Sea in Sussex and came up to Dryden House in May 1909, leaving in 1913. He was part of that doughty Dryden rugby team, which won the senior house rugby cup in both 1911 and 1912. The latter final was notable for being won by Dryden after a replay, the first match, against School House, having resulted in a 0-0 draw. He was also a keen debater supporting Eric Yarrow and Mrs Sanderson in speaking up for women's suffrage. Apparently he answered those against women's rights "in no uncertain fashion". He said that "if he allowed his boots to be blacked by a woman, he ought to be ashamed of himself." James Ricketts was OTC platoon leader in Dryden with the rank of sergeant and was clearly a decent shot. He also represented Oundle at the Schools' Fencing Championship at Aldershot.

After Oundle, he went to the Royal Military Academy in Woolwich and was gazetted to the Royal Field Artillery. He went to France in June 1918 and died of wounds in Rouen, aged 24 on 5 October 1918, after great suffering, and having won the affection of all who saw him by his cheerfulness and patience. Most likely, he was seriously wounded during the fighting around Cambrai as the Allies pushed the Germans back towards the Hindenburg Line.

Two days before Ricketts' death, on 3 October 1918 an attack was launched against the village of Beaurevoir, which soon created a 10 mile breech in the German defences, an astonishing victory in the context of World War I and a testament to the weakness of the German position at this time. Ten days after this, another Grafton boy perished in the area around Cambrai, yet another second lieutenant leading his men into action. **William Donald Raby**, born in May 1899, was from Didsbury in Manchester and came up to Oundle in September 1913. We know little of his school career apart from a photo in rugby kit with his friend William Woodeson, probably taken in the autumn of 1916. The only reference to him in the Laxtonian is a listing as Philostrate, master of the revels to Duke Theseus in *A Midsummer Night's Dream*.

James Stuart Ricketts, Dryden House 1909-13.

On leaving school in 1917, he joined the Manchester University OTC and then an officers' cadet battalion in Cambridge. Completing his training in May 1918, he joined the Royal Welsh Fusiliers and was killed on 8 October 1918 at the head of his men. He and his company attacked the village of Villers Outreaux from one side, while others attacked from the other side. Tanks were being used at this stage "to mop up the village." He was just 19 years old.

Three days later, in the same sector of the Front, **John Harvey Jacobs** was also killed. Like William Raby, he was killed during the successful capture of a French village near Cambrai. John Jacobs came from Cricklewood and was in New House from 1907-09. In April 1909, he won the high jump on Sports Day, with a height of 4 feet 9 inches. He represented New House in fives and gymnastics, though, truth be told, they achieved little in either competition. In the gym, one of his team-mates was Geoffrey Donaldson, who would be killed in July 1916. Captain John Jacobs of the Royal Fusiliers was killed on 11 October 1918. His unit attacked and took the village of St. Aubert, nine miles east of Cambrai but their Captain did not survive. Aged 26, he was buried in the cemetery there, which was started the next day. He won the Military Cross for his valour.

William Donald Raby, Grafton House 1913-17.

The next to die would be **Major Maurice James Miskin**, who won the Military Cross not once but twice. He was on the school staff as a classics master for just one term (Michaelmas 1914) before joining the 9th North Staffs. in December 1914. He went out to France and then Belgium in July 1915 and was involved in some of the heaviest fighting there. He transferred to the Tank Corps in January 1917 and was involved in the great success at Messines. He did so well in the Cambrai Push of 1917 that he was awarded the Military Cross, for conspicuous gallantry and devotion to duty in an attack:

> Though he had mechanical trouble with his three tanks, he successfully overcame it, and was the first to arrive at the objective. He secured the crossing of the [St.Quentin] canal, and went forward to reconnoitre on foot. He gave valuable information to the infantry commander and was instrumental in getting a battalion across the canal. He set a splendid example of courage and initiative.

Maurice James Miskin, Classics Master 1914.

In February 1917, he became Major Miskin and seven months later he was again commended for his bravery. On 29 September at Bellicourt and a week later at Beaurevoir: "he rallied a number of tanks and directed them to the enemy machine guns which were holding up the infantry, and by his skilful leading, he contributed largely to the success attending those operations." Both villages were taken by British, Australian and American forces and their capture was crucial in breeching the Hindenburg Line. For his actions that day, Maurice Miskin won his second MC. Twelve days after these successes, the young classics master was killed, leading his tanks once more into action with the utmost gallantry, in the capture of the village of Honnechy. Sensing that the war would soon be over, his letters show that he was eagerly looking forward to returning to Oundle. It was not to be.

Major Maurice Miskin (who preferred to be called by his second name, James) was born in Bedford in 1892 and spent most of his childhood in Rochester in Kent. He attended the King's School there from 1903-10 where he enjoyed an outstanding school career. A scholar of the school, he was appointed Head of School, Captain of the XI and played for the XV. He went up to University College, Oxford to study classics and history and was appointed to the staff of Oundle School in September 1914. He had little time to make an impact but he helped his fellow young classicist, George Williamson coach the XV and he was credited with helping New House win the Football Shield at the end of his only term at Oundle.

Miskin and Williamson were both enthusiastic officers in the School's OTC, both would join up together at the end of the Michaelmas Term 1914 and both would be killed in the war. Maurice Miskin served throughout the war and was killed less than four weeks before the Armistice. He is commemorated on war memorials (town and church) in Oundle and also in Rochester Cathedral, the King's School, Rochester and on the Roll of Honour in York Minster, as his parents were living in the city when the war ended. Maurice James Miskin was 26 years old at the time of his death, just a few years older than the boys he had taught, all too briefly, at Oundle School.

Three more airmen killed

Two more Oundelians were killed 11 days later on 28 October 1918, both airmen but with differing functions. **Nicholas Greaves** once of Dryden House (1912-14) was involved in the final push for victory in France and Belgium. He had a semi-exotic background as his family lived in Berdiansk in Russia, with their own steel works (the family originally came from Sheffield) called John Greaves and Co. At that time, the city lay in Southern Russia, on the Sea of Azov, east of the Crimean peninsula. Nicholas Greaves came up to Dryden with his elder brother John. The two played together in Dryden's winning rugby teams of 1912, beating New House after a replay, and 1913, where they overcame School House. A useful gymnast, Nicholas Greaves helped Dryden to 2nd place in the house gymnastics and went on to represent Oundle in boxing at the Public Schools' Championships at Aldershot. He also won a German prize in his last year.

On leaving Oundle, aged 16, he returned to Russia as an apprentice at the family firm. During the war, he was entrusted with important munitions work and created a special department making Hotchkiss quick firing shells, managing a shop of 700 workers. He was then caught up in the first Russian Revolution of 1917 (the overthrow of the Tsar) and somehow made the arduous and long journey back to England – some 3,000 miles – to join the Royal Flying Corps early in November of that year. During his training, he showed himself to be a skilful boxer. He was posted to France in August 1918 and was involved in much dangerous and difficult work until he was killed on 28 October 1918, just two weeks before the Armistice, as Allied troops advanced towards Tournai in Belgium. He was 20 years old and lies buried in the Tournai Communal Cemetery Allied Extension in Belgium. The town had been occupied by the Germans throughout the war but was recaptured by the British on 8 November 1918.

Killed on the same day as Nicholas Greaves was another airman but one who was involved in bombing missions over Germany itself. **Peter Hopcraft** was a New House boy from Cheltenham in Gloucestershire, born in January 1899. He came up to Oundle, aged 16, in January 1915 and stayed only for the calendar year. In December 1916, still only 17 years old, he joined the RFC and was sent to fly Handley Page machines in France in the autumn and winter of 1917. In the spring of 1918, he returned to England to act as an instructor.

By August 1918, he was attached to the recently created Independent Air Force near Nancy, close to the German border and became acting captain. His group of strategic bombers was affiliated to the RAF and was designed to carry out strategic bombing missions on German targets. During the last five months of the war, this group under 'Boom' Trenchard, engaged in a series of

Peter Hopcraft, New House 1915.

bombing raids, mostly at night, most often over Germany itself. One of its more famous pilots was W. E. Johns, the creator of the *Biggles* stories, who wrote excitedly about Oundle's VC airman Alan Jerrard. He was stationed with Hopcraft, so the two must have known each other. Peter Hopcraft was killed while returning from a successful bombing mission on 28 October 1918. His Commanding Officer wrote: "He was a skilful and reliable pilot." Hopcraft attained a record in night bombing over the enemy's positions, carrying out 30 night missions in 30 nights. He was 19 years old at the time of his death. On his headstone, his mother inscribed a simple tribute to her son: "Rest after Toil".

Two days after this double Oundle tragedy, a third Oundle airman was killed, probably in a dog-fight. **Alan Luis Pink** was from Horsham in Susssex, having been born in London in August 1898. He came up to Sammy Squire's Laxton House in 1911 but after two terms was transferred to Henry Hale's New House. He was a speedy three-quarter for the 2nd XV and helped New House, captained by Freddie Milholland to win the house competition in December 1914. He was also a promising athlete, winning the half and quarter-miles and the 100 yards dash on Sports Day when he was still an U16. He left school in April 1915, still only 16 and gained a commission in the Rifle Brigade. Later he was attached to the Royal Air Force and was killed in action in aerial combat on 30 October 1918, over Belgium. Earlier his mother attended the meeting of parents in Grocers' Hall in 1917 to approve the building of a new chapel to commemorate the fallen.

Alan Luis Pink, Laxton House and New House 1911-15.

They died in November 1918

Edward John Hassard was another Londoner. He followed in his future Headmaster's foot-steps by attending Dulwich College, before coming to Oundle and Dryden House in 1910. At Oundle, he was notable and very rare as he never appeared in a sports team! Instead, he spoke in a school debate in favour of building a Channel Tunnel but the motion was narrowly lost by 28 votes to 24. He also seconded the opposition to a motion deploring the government's will-ingness to give Home Rule to Ireland. In his Oundle years, he also trod the boards in scenes from two Molière plays. As a junior he was a young lady called Lucinde and later he was a less lovable miser, expressing "the miserliness" of his character "in very pure French." And in a school concert, he contributed one of the "lighter items" with a spirited performance, apparently much appreciated by the audience, of *Galloping Dick*.

He left in March 1914, determined on an army career and went to Woolwich just as the war broke out. By February 1915, he had a commission in the Royal Field Artillery and served in Gallipoli that year, being invalided home after three months. In July 1916, he was sent to France and served for two years, being awarded the Military Cross, before being wounded in August 1918. He was recovering from his wounds when he contracted influenza, and this was followed by septic pneumonia. He died on 7 November 1918 at the Prince of Wales' Hospital in Marylebone.

An officer noted: "We had been together twelve months, and we were all very fond of him. He never complained and was always cheerful, and was such a pleasant companion in the Mess. Under fire, too, he was coolness itself, and I shall never forget how he carried on at Messines and Ypres." Edward John Hassard was 23 years old at the time of his death.

Killed in action on the same day, just four days before the end of hostilities was one of the greats amongst the School's teaching staff. **George Arthur Tryon** was the son of Rev. Arthur William Tryon, Vicar of Middle Rasen, Lincs. and only grandson of Major General Samuel Tryon. He was educated at Uppingham School and from there obtained a mathematical scholarship at Pembroke College, Cambridge. After taking his degree as a Wrangler (first-class honours in his finals), he came straight to Oundle in September 1908. Attached to New House and living in Cottesmore on West Street, he played for the Masters in a fives match against the boys in the autumn of 1909, alongside Francis Norbury and George Williamson, both of whom would also be killed in the war. In January 1910, he succeeded Walter Paine (who was later killed at Gallipoli) as Housemaster of Crosby.

The House could not have had a keener guardian of its welfare or one with a fuller sense of his responsibilities and many of his old boys testified to the close and kindly interest with which he followed their careers both at school and after they had left. In June 1911, as Lieutenant Tryon, he took a detachment of 12 cadets to attend the Coronation of George V. And in March 1914, he lectured to the Science Society about the possibility of life on Mars and seems to have come down in favour of the idea.

He had become an energetic member of the OTC soon after his arrival in Oundle and by 1914 had attained the rank of captain. When the war broke out, he joined up at once and in September succeeded in getting a commission as a captain in the 6th Battalion of the King's Royal Rifles. He went out to France at the end of November 1914 and apparently was nearly killed when a German aeroplane dropped its payload of bombs just yards away, killing 31 men.

He arrived in France about the same time as his great friend and fellow housemaster, Captain Francis Norbury, who was attached to the 1st Battalion of the same regiment. The two had played hockey together for the Masters in a thrilling 5-3 victory

Edward John Hassard, Dryden House 1910-14.

George Arthur Tryon, Mathematics Master 1908-14, Crosby Housemaster 1910-14.

against the School XI in March 1909. A few months later they appeared together playing cricket for the Masters but were soundly beaten by the XI. In March 1912 there was another defeat, this time in hockey, this time a 9-0 drubbing by the school team, with George Tryon in goal!

Three years later, the sport was rather more deadly. Now, Tryon and Norbury saw service together near Béthune in the first awful winter of the war. George Tryon was wounded by a shot through the left forearm on New Year's Day 1915 and his good friend Captain Norbury was killed a week later by a British shell. After about five months recuperation in England, during which time he came back to Oundle and helped with the House he loved, he went to France again and remained there, chiefly on the Front opposite Amiens, during the summer. Meanwhile, back in Oundle, he handed on the running of Crosby to George Brewster, though the school Blue Books continued to show him as the Housemaster. We have one brief note he wrote to young Brewster, which gives interesting details about the amount of pocket money boys were allowed each week. For the rank and file, the figure was sixpence a week, whilst prefects were allowed twice as much.

In September 1915, Tryon's battalion was moved to the Salonika front, near the mouth of the Struma River. He remained there for nearly three years with only one leave. On more than one occasion, he commanded his battalion for two months at a time and was finally promoted major in the spring of 1918. His letters home record some interesting features of his life in northern Greece. He commented that his men were trying to make a decent highway of the road once travelled on by St. Paul on his last missionary journey. He also noted that if the old saint had passed by in 1918, he would probably have been arrested as a spy!

One of the most important and moving pieces he wrote whilst in Salonika was, as we have seen, a poem in memory of one of his boys, Christopher Gell, killed on the Somme in 1916. In 1885, his father had penned a similar poem lamenting the death of General Gordon at the hands of the Mahdi at Khartoum, bidding England take revenge. Clearly Tryon senior was something of an imperialist, whose views of the importance of war, to back up Britain's imperial pretensions, may have influenced his son:

> He is gone – the Christian hero -
> We have lost him: never more
> Shall the voice of Britain welcome
> Gallant Gordon to her shore.
> In her might old England rising,
> As she rose in days of old;
> Will be lavish of her bravest,
> Will be lavish of her gold:
> Till the Mahdi's barb'rous power
> And his fierce fanatic horde
> Shall no longer threaten Egypt,
> Crushed by Albion's victor sword.

Transferred back to the Western Front in July 1918, Arthur Tryon's son George was now acting lieutenant colonel. In October 1918, he came home on leave and was eagerly anticipating a speedy end to the war and a longed for return to his work at the School. At the time, he could have applied for extension of leave, for he had much overdue but he refused to do this, feeling that his men still needed him. Aged 32, he was killed in France, close to the Belgian border by a chance bullet whilst visiting his leading troops, just four days before peace came. He lies buried in the St. Remy-Chausée Communal Cemetery. News of his death reached Oundle only after the Armistice. One of his colleagues there quoted Euripides' words on the death of Hector:

He is dead and gone, but still his fame remains as bravest of the brave.

Perhaps, George Tryon wrote his own epitaph. This verse from his poem in honour of all the boys killed in the war surely applies to him in full measure:

> T'was not in vain; they've played their part,
> Example set of highest worth:
> Their country took from them new heart,
> It saw the Sons of God on Earth.

He was twice mentioned in despatches and was awarded the MC in January 1918. The sympathy of the School he served so faithfully and of the generation of old boys who knew him there, went out in full measure to his widowed mother in the loss of her only son. In Oundle, he is commemorated on the town's war memorial, and in the parish church. There is also a plaque in nearby Bulwick church, where his family were once lords of the manor. With his death, the Laxtonian noted that "all four officers who left the corps in 1914 to take combatant commissions, have now been killed – a sad record but one to be proud of." At the same time, the deaths of George Tryon and Maurice Miskin, so close to the end of the affair, was made more poignant by the fact that "both these gallant officers met their deaths through staying on in the front line when their spell of duty was over and they were entitled to leave."

The day after George Tryon's sad but proud death, **Lionel Russell Wilford** OO also died, this time from disease rather than action in the field. He was the son of an Old Oundelian vicar and came from Wisbech, being born in 1892. In 1906, he arrived at his father's old House (School) and stayed for 5 years. He was a member of the XV in his last two years, playing at full back. He was described as "a great source of strength to the side...a fearless tackler, a safe field and kicks well with either foot." Lionel Wilford also captained the strong School House team but in the 1910 final, they were swept aside by a very talented Sidney side which included Edward MacBryan and the fearsome Gulliland twins. Six months earlier it had been the same story for Lionel in the final of the house cricket. Sidney (with MacBryan and one Gulliland) beat School House by 9 wickets!

Playing only occasionally for the XI in his last year, he missed the chance to play against his father (Rev. H. H. Wilford) who reappeared at his old school to play for the Oundle Rovers. On Sports Day, Lionel Wilford's speciality was throwing the cricket ball. 2nd in his penultimate year at the School, he came through to take the title in his last year with a throw of over 95 yards.

He enlisted in the Public Schools' Battalion in September 1914 and gained a commission with the South Staffordshire Regiment in January 1915. Early in the following year, he was appointed Supervisor of Physical Training and Bayonet Fighting in a reserve Infantry Brigade and posted to Rugeley. In 1918 he was sent abroad as part of the Italian Expeditionary Force. He was killed by influenza, contracted on active service and died in Marseilles on 8 November 1918. He was one

Lionel Russell Wilford, School House 1906-11.

of that small group of Oudelians who died on active service and who was married. Lionel Wilford was 26 years old at the time of his death.

Two days later, another Oundle lad died, possibly of the same disease. **Herbert George Miles Markham**, once of Laxton School has the distinction of being the boy who died closest to the Armistice. He passed away on Sunday 10 November 1918 in a German hospital in Namur, Belgium and the scanty records note simply that he died rather than 'died of wounds'. It is believed that he was a prisoner of war and that he was another victim of the influenza pandemic which was then sweeping through Europe with renewed vigour. The mild strain of the summer had by this time developed into a rather more deadly bacterial version which would eventually carry off more individuals than the war itself.

Herbert Markham was the only son of parents Herbert and Charlotte. His father sold newspapers, books and stationery from his shop in the Oundle market place and was a well-respected local businessman. Young Herbert attended Laxton School from January 1909 until December of 1914, when he was 16. He was conscripted into the army and was on active service in France and Flanders, before being captured and made a PoW. He was reported to be a prisoner in the July 1918 issue of the Laxton School Journal, so must have been incarcerated by the Germans for at least five months. He was just 20 years old at the time of his death.

Cecil Lewis and the Armistice

The next day, Monday 11 November 1918, the Armistice came into force and the war was officially over. For Cecil Lewis, Oundle airman, it was all something of an anti-climax. His squadron was on a remote airbase in Belgium, north of Ypres, where he was in charge of his own Flight for the first time. Arriving there in early November, he noted that the area around 'Wipers' was far more devastated than the Somme. He had time for only one more patrol before the Armistice and then had no means of celebrating the advent of peace, because his airfield was so remote. Later, reflecting on the transition from war to peace, there was no sense of rejoicing. It was a huge anti-climax. The war had been his life. What would he do now?

And so the Great War was over and after the initial surge of rejoicing, which was not universally felt by any means, men and women grappled with the meaning of the most terrible conflict that the world had ever seen. From his vantage point high above the battlefield, Cecil Lewis, no longer a combatant, reflected on what he had witnessed and on the total futility of the whole war effort. From the skies, he had seen the devastation and the slow painful movement of troops from one objective to the next, in what was a war of apparently endless objectives. The war, he thought was "a prodigious and complex effort, cunningly contrived, and carried out with deadly seriousness, in order to achieve just nothing at all." And writing his account of this most dreadful conflict and his part in it in the 1930s, Lewis also foresaw that a new war was looming on the horizon. Just as one Oundelian, Justin Willis, had foreseen the coming apocalypse in 1912, so another Oundelian, Cecil Lewis, writing in 1936, saw that there was even worse to come.

After the War was over

With the war over, the parents of the two Grummitt boys, once of Dryden, might have been celebrating the survival of their sons, who had both been on active service. But events were to disabuse them of any sense of relief. By a cruel twist of fate, both of their boys, Joseph and Hugh, fine sons of Yorkshire, would die within weeks of each other after the Armistice. **Joseph Roland Grummitt** was born in 1894 and came up to Dryden in 1907, leaving four years later just before his seventeenth birthday. He represented the House in rowing, in the gym and at cricket. In his last year, he helped Dryden to an easy win over New House in the first round of the cricket by an innings and 17 runs. Joe Grummitt was not a major contributor with bat or ball but he took the important wicket of Tom Warner with a catch. In the next round however, Dryden were beaten equally easily by School House. They lost by an innings and 42 runs, being bowled out in their first innings for just 18!

In August 1914, Joe Grummitt was in Canada and immediately joined the first Canadian Contingent to help the motherland in her hour of need. He fought with them during 1915 and 1916 at Ypres, Givenchy and Festubert, where he was wounded. In October 1916, he took a commission in the East Yorkshire Regiment, where no doubt, he felt more at home as he had been brought up in Hornsea, in that part of the county. In January 1917, he was on the Continent once again, acting as signalling officer for his battalion. At the end of February, he returned for six months home service. He died from pneumonia, brought on by influenza in Colchester Military Hospital on 14 November 1918, aged 24.

Four months later, the grief of Joseph's parents was doubled when their younger son **Hugh Cecil Grummitt** also died of heart failure probably brought on by flu. He was by four years the younger of the two boys, so they didn't overlap in Dryden. Like his older sibling, he does not appear to have played sport for the School but rather at house level. In cricket he was a handy bowler whose wicket taking helped Dryden reach the senior final. Unfortunately, they lost in that match to the all-conquering Grafton side by an innings and 175 runs. Hugh Grummitt took the all-important wicket of Philip Silk (future Captain of Cricket) but the damage was done, he had already scored 95! Hugh served in the Queen's Westminsters for eight months before taking a commission in the East Yorkshire regiment like his brother, in May 1918. In August he was wounded in France and invalided back to Blighty. He apparently recovered and re-joined the East Yorks. before dying of heart failure on 25 March 1919 in Hull. He was just 20 years old at the time of his death. Now the Grummitt brothers lie side by side in Hornsea Cemetery, their home close to the sea.

Joseph Roland Grummitt, Dryden House 1907-11.

Hugh Cecil Grummitt, Dryden House 1913-15.

Clive Burrell was the last of the Dryden Seven to die. Of the seven boys standing in that unassuming Dryden group photograph of 10 boys taken back in 1910, six were already dead. Now nearly two weeks after the official end of hostilities, the flu pandemic removed a seventh member of the group. For Llewellyn Jones, former Dryden Housemaster and now back in Oundle in charge of the new Bramston House, it was another bitter blow.

Clive Burrell was in Dryden for three years (1907-10) and coxed the School Crew in his last two years. After leaving school, he entered his father's business (he was described as a colour manufacturer) and became a director. A late-comer to the war, he joined the Honourable Artillery Company in March 1917 and, after training at Finsbury Park and Leeds, went to France in September of that year, attached to one of the batteries as a driver. He saw much fighting in 1918, as the Allies pushed the Germans back on the Western Front but the regimental diary serves to remind us that, in its last year, the war had lost nothing of its murderous intensity. In early April 1918, the diary claims that "there was day and night bombardment by H[igh]

Clive Burrell, Dryden House 1907-10.

E[xplosive] gas shells, containing three types of gas, therefore inflicting burns, loss of sight and breathlessness. The area was so saturated by gas that often reinforcements were affected before they reached the battery." Having survived this carnage and just as victory was being celebrated, Clive Burrell contracted influenza and died on 23 November 1918 in a Canadian Hospital in Valenciennes, aged 25. He was the third Burrell brother to die as a result of the war.

And then the real **Captain Gilbert Kennedy** died. Back in April 1917 the Laxtonian reported the death in action of Captain Gilbert Stuart Kennedy, once of School House but this was not the Oundle boy, though in some ways similar, as Oundle's Gilbert had no middle name. Now, in December 1918 the Oundle Kennedy, who was a professional soldier and had served throughout the war, died in France from influenza. Ironically, now that his obituary could be written, it was not and it was the false Kennedy – alias G. S. Kennedy – whose name and two initials found their way onto the marble memorial plaques later erected in the new Memorial Chapel.

The School House Kennedy was the second son of Robert Muirhead Kennedy, who was an important member of the Indian Civil Service. They lived in Rajkot, Cathiawar, Bombay and Sutton in Surrey. Gilbert Kennedy was born in Kaira in India in February 1885 and came up to School House in January 1899, leaving in December 1903. In November 1901, playing amongst the forwards, he was in the all-conquering School House rugby team which defeated Laxton easily in the final. This feat was repeated in his last term (Michaelmas 1903) when again Laxton were surprisingly defeated. The final was postponed that year until mid-December because Gilbert Kennedy amongst others had to sit their army exams. He was clearly a keen photographer and won commendations for his work whilst at school. After Oundle, he went to Sandhurst and then joined the Indian Army and saw active service with the 4th Gurkhas on the North-West Frontier in 1907 and 1908.

In 1914, before the war began, he was with the North Staffordshire Regiment and engaged the Mahsuds tribe at the Battle of Bannu in India. At the outbreak of the European War, he transferred to the Royal Munster Fusiliers. He fought at Loos, the Somme and the Aisne in 1916 and Cambrai in 1917. He was then attached to the 1st American Corps School as an instructor in 1918. He died on 11 December 1918, from influenza and is buried at Les Barques Military Cemetery, Sangatte, France. The real Gilbert Kennedy was 33 years old at the time of his death.

And the flu claimed one more Oundle victim, early in 1919. **Geoffrey Clifford Calvert** was the fourth son of his parents' marriage. Born in 1894 and brought up in Leeds, he attended Sedbergh School before coming up to Oundle at the age of 16 in May 1910. He was in New House for just four terms and was a useful rugby player, appearing regularly for the XV. In the winter

Geoffrey Clifford Calvert, New House 1910-11.

of 1910, he was described as "a great acquisition to the side." Playing at half-back and teaming up with Colin Gulliland, the School's rugby correspondent was quite complimentary: "he gets the ball away well and is very difficult to stop. His dribbling is an example to the side." The XV of 1910 was very successful and young Calvert played a major part in that. He ran well, found openings, linked up with the three-quarters and scored many tries. Possibly, his finest hour was in the match against the Old Boys, which the School won by 15-9. After Oundle, he joined the Headingly Rugby Club in Leeds, won his cap for Yorkshire and in December 1913, played in the English trial matches, representing the North. As for career, he had, by this time, served two years of his pupillage with the Leeds legal firm of John Fowler and Co.

Like his fellow Yorkshiremen, the Grummitt brothers, he joined the East Yorkshire Regiment and went with them to France in 1915. He was in the Battle of Loos but after serving in the Ypres Salient, he was invalided home for six months in hospital. He then transferred to the King's Own Yorkshire Light Infantry and returned to the front. Whilst there and probably after the Armistice, he contracted typhoid and pneumonia and died in a casualty clearing station on 15 January 1919, aged 24. He was buried in Maubeuge (Sous-Le-Bois) Cemetery in France, just south of Mons. The British and Geoffrey Calvert had taken the town of Maubeuge just before the Armistice but while so many of his fellow soldiers returned home afterwards, Geoffrey Calvert remained in France.

Two flying accidents

Then, within five days of each other, two more boys, both airmen, lost their lives in flying accidents. **Arthur Howard Bartlett Stace** like Geoffrey Calvert died near Mons. A Crosby boy and an only son from Brackley in Northamptonshire, he was a member of the XV, "showing great promise at the beginning of the season, but got rather stale perhaps in the last part of the season." He was also Captain of Boating. In house matches, his finest hour was probably in the cricket final of 1916, where Crosby unexpectedly beat Grafton, with young Stace taking 10 wickets over the two Grafton innings. Grafton needed just 81 runs in their second innings to win the match but Stace and his friend Brown skittled them out for just 68.

After Oundle, Arthur Stace joined the Air Force and went to France in September 1918. He enjoyed just six weeks of active service before the Armistice, where his job was chiefly reconnaissance and photography. Having survived the war, he was accidentally killed whilst flying on 3 May 1919. His Commanding Officer spoke of him as a most efficient officer and a keen sportsman. Ironically, the last Oundelian to die on the Continent, was killed near the town of Mons, where the Britain's War in Europe had started in earnest back in August 1914. No Oundelians had been killed in that first encounter but Stace's burial place in Mons Communal Cemetery is one more reminder perhaps of the futility of war. The British at the war's end were no further forward than when it began.

Just five days later, another of Oundle's airmen was killed in another tragic accident but this time on home soil, near the aerodrome at Northolt in Middlesex. **Bernard Paul Gascoigne Beanlands** (always known as Paul) was a Canadian by birth, the only surviving son of Canon Beanlands, Rector of Christ Church Cathedral in the city of Victoria, on Vancouver Island in British Columbia. Paul was born there in September 1897 but the family then returned to England, living at Wickhurst Manor in Weald, near Sevenoaks in Kent and young Beanlands was sent to Oundle in 1909, first to the Berrystead and then to School House. He was on the losing side of the house rugby final of 1913, when School House failed to score against Dryden. He played just once for the XV, at full-back in the Lent Term of 1914, where the School won an apparently titanic encounter with Stamford by a single point. He was also a drummer in the OTC's Drum, Fife and Bugle Band.

He left in the summer of 1914 and just 18 days after war had been declared, entered Sandhurst, leaving there in the following December when gazetted to the Hampshire Regiment. He joined the Hampshires just two days before Xmas in 1914, still only 17 years old. Just a month later he was in 'Plug Street' – actually the village of Ploegsteert, in the Ypres Salient – where he fought in the Second Battle of Ypres. He was a good shot and was employed as a sniper. Had he stayed at Oundle, he would have shot for the School at Bisley.

Arthur Howard Bartlett Stace, Crosby House 1913-17.

Bernard Paul Gascoigne Beanlands, Berrystead and School House 1909-14.

While in the trenches, his Canadian roots were not forgotten. He was detailed to help train the newly arrived 1st Battalion of the British Columbian Regiment and was recognized by Canadian friends from Victoria. In June 1915, he was badly wounded in the hand and had ten weeks leave. By December of that year, only a few weeks after his eighteenth birthday, he was seconded to the Royal Flying Corps and sent to Shoreham to learn to fly. Like his contemporary and School House chum, Cecil Lewis, Paul Beanlands, at over 6ft. 3 inches, was too tall for the training aircraft, so he had to fly in more complicated machines. Later, on the day of the Battle of Jutland in 1916, he was deployed to an RFC squadron in England and, as we have seen, famously landed on the school playing fields on 8 July 1916 (Speech Day) much to the delight of the boys. He claimed that he had just popped over to see the Speech Day cricket match!

Adventure and close calls were never far away. On one occasion, he was flying at 15,000 feet when the 'interrupter gear' in his plane froze and he managed to shoot off one of his propeller blades. He managed to land behind British lines when the whole plane promptly fell to pieces. The damaged propeller, later made its way, via Paul's sister, to the School only to be lost at a later stage. On one day in November 1917, he was credited with shooting down no less than three German planes, in a dog-fight over Belgium. One of the German pilots, Friedrich Heine was wounded and captured by the British. Beanlands won the Military Cross for his endeavours that day but was then seriously wounded near St. Quentin in March 1918 at the start of the German Spring Offensive. He was returning to base, when he noticed British soldiers being hard-pressed in their trenches. He flew low over the German lines and was wounded in both legs by a German bullet. Bleeding heavily, he managed to land in the grounds of an Allied hospital and was placed on the last train out of the area before it was overrun by the enemy.

On his recovery, some months later and still aged only 20, he was promoted to the rank of captain. After the war, in December 1918, he was appointed Examining Wing Officer. By a cruel twist of fate, he was accidentally killed while test-flying a plane near Northolt on 8 May 1919. Paul Beanlands was 21 years old at the time of his death and was buried in Sevenoaks. He was Oundle's premier fighter pilot being credited with 18 kills during his career.

India, Egypt and Russia

But still the war was not finished with Oundelians. Three would die, rather further from British shores than France or Belgium; three more would die after long and painful suffering from wounds acquired in the war and a further three would die in unknown circumstances on unknown dates.

Gordon Harry Edward Sanders died in India. He was another only son, born in February 1898 and coming up to Crosby just shy of his fifteenth birthday in January 1913. He was another of those Oundelians who cut short their education, in order to go off to war, leaving school in August 1914. As his school

Gordon Harry Edward Sanders, Crosby House
1913-14.

career in Oundle was so short and as he left at the age of just 16, there are few mentions of his exploits in the school magazines. All that is known is that he was confirmed by the Bishop of Peterborough and that he and the Crosby House cricket team were soundly beaten by School House in the first round of the 1913 competition, with young Sanders scoring a total of 1 run in his two innings!

A Leicester boy, he joined the Leicestershire Yeomanry in December 1915, still only 17 years old, in December 1915. Given a commission in the 21st Lancers (Empress of India's Regiment) in April 1917, he saw action in Palestine whilst attached to the Lincolnshire Yeomanry. He later served in France before being sent to join the Lancers in India, just before the end of the war. He died in Meerut Station Hospital on 15 May 1919 from an attack of dysentery. His Colonel wrote: "By the death of your son, the regiment has lost a most promising young officer, who…had endeared himself not only to the officers, but also to his men, and by his many sterling qualities had become a great favourite in the regiment." Gordon Sanders was 21 years old at the time of his death. Although originally buried in Meerut, north-east of Delhi; as late as 1951, his body was moved to the military cemetery in India's capital city.

The next death happened in England but was caused in Egypt. **Captain James Allan Ross Armitage** was the third son of Dr and Mrs Armitage from Wolverhampton and Hastings and the third of their sons to be killed in the war – Douglas having been killed at Loos in September 1915 and Frank, the eldest, at Passchendaele in 1917. Their second son, Charles had died of natural causes in 1912 and now the war, even though officially over, claimed their last surviving boy. James, like his brothers, was in Laxton House and like them, was a talented sportsman. He was Captain of Fives and a member of the XV of 1907. Like his brothers, he also became Head of House in his turn and a school prefect. In the XV, James seems to have played hooker in a young team, which often included both of Sanderson's sons and was captained by the elder son, Roy. In house

rugby, he played alongside younger brother Douglas, only to be beaten in the semi-final by Grafton. In fives, the School enjoyed success though it played relatively few matches. James Armitage's team beat the Masters by 10 games to 8 in an exciting encounter. The Masters' team was captained by Francis Norbury, who would be killed as early as January 1915. As well as rugby and fives, James Armitage was a useful hockey player, scoring several goals. He was described as "conspicuous amongst our forwards" and was on the winning side twice against the Masters.

He left Oundle in 1907 and when the conflict began, took a commission in the 15th West Yorkshire Regiment. He served in Egypt and had been promoted to the rank of captain, when, in February 1916, he was recalled to England to take charge of the Farnley Ironworks in Leeds which was run by the Armitage family. He married in 1918 but his health had been undermined by his service in Egypt and broke down seriously in the autumn of 1918. He retired to St. Leonards near Hastings, where his father lived and died there on 19 July 1919, aged 30.

James Allan Ross Armitage, Laxton House 1901-07.

And so we move to Russia. **Gerald Wallace Adam** was another of those only sons killed on active service. He was born in Stockport but the family were living in Buxton when he came up to Grafton in May 1914. He left in December 1916, aged 17 and joined the Manchester University OTC the next month. In May 1918, he gained a commission in the Leicestershire Regiment. The next month, he was attached to the 13th Battalion of the Yorkshire Regiment and then went with them to Murmansk in Northern Russia, arriving in late November 1918. Perhaps not surprisingly, the British troops were apparently unenthusiastic. There was a near mutiny after they embarked on the ship for Russia, when the troops were told where they were going. After all, fighting in a civil war in Russia was not what they had signed up for. The ship then spent three weeks in the Orkneys, after a boiler burst and two weeks in the Shetlands, at

Gerald Wallace Adam, Grafton House 1914-16.

which time the Armistice came into force. The men finally arrived in Murmansk and were then based in Archangel in the middle of the Russian winter. There was then an actual mutiny amongst the British troops in February 1919 as some of the men, being exposed to such terrible weather and knowing that the war in Europe was over, demanded to be taken home.

Since the Bolshevik Revolution, in November 1917, civil war had broken out in Russia between Reds and Whites. Britain and her allies were aligned on the White side against the forces of the new Bolshevik government led by Lenin. In truth, allied forces could do little to influence events in a war which raged widely across Russia. The mutiny amongst British troops was later hushed up but it seems that Colonel Lavie, in charge of the Yorkshire battalions had to use force to restore order. Presumably Gerald Adam, as an officer, had to help in this and in May 1919, he was appointed Intelligence and Code Officer on Colonel Lavie's staff.

Gerald Adam died on active service in Northern Russia, on 10 August 1919, aged 20. The Manchester Guardian reported that he died of dysentery but if he had then he would surely have been buried in Archangel Cemetery. In fact he is only commemorated in the cemetery, his name inscribed on stone panels dedicated to 'the Missing'. It therefore seems more likely that he died on active service, fighting against Bolshevik forces at Seltsoe, where the Reds were successfully pushed back by British soldiers on the day in question. Thus the last Oundelian to die on active service was not killed in the Great War at all but in the Russian Civil War. Could there be a more poignant symbol of the futility of war than 'no known grave' somewhere in the barren wastes of Northern Russia?

Three die of wounds

But the story of Oundle's war does not end in Russia. There were to be three further deaths from wounds sustained in the war, the last one occurring on Xmas eve 1922, by which time Sanderson himself was dead.

Walter Gibson Marsden was in School House from January 1898 until 1905, the elder of two brothers. Always known as 'Billy', in March 1904, as Captain of Hockey, he organized a team to play a side gathered together by Dr Turner, the school physician which resulted in an exciting five-all draw, with young Marsden scoring one of the goals. In his last two years, he was a regular in the XV, playing sometimes as a forward and sometimes as a back, and he captained the victorious School House rugby team for two seasons, a team that included his younger brother Cyril and Roy Sanderson. The two Marsden boys also helped their House win the athletics competition in 1905, with Billy Marsden again taking charge. And his sporting prowess did not end there. He also played regularly for the XI in a pretty successful season, as a bowler. Returning figures of 3 for 8 in a good win over Oakham was perhaps his greatest achievement and, during the 1905 season, he was the most economical bowler in the Oundle attack, returning figures of 11 for 109.

Not surprisingly, he was also a school prefect and Head of House in his last year. Academically gifted as well, he won the Langerman Prize on his final Speech Day in 1905 and an exhibition in natural sciences at Emmanuel College in Cambridge. Whilst there he also won a college science prize and won his college 1st XV cap. He also represented the university 'Freshers' at rugby in his first year. He returned to Oundle with an Emmanuel College Cricket XI but scored only two runs as his old school triumphed over his new college. Ironically, this was a reversal of fortune for the School in this fixture. When Walter Marsden was in the XI, they were thumped by Emmanuel! After Cambridge, where he obtained a degree in medicine, he went to St Bartholomew's in London and qualified as a doctor. He also found time to captain Barts' rugby team 1910-11 and won a cap for Middlesex. Then in 1913, he returned to Oundle to assist the school doctor, Dr Turner, who had got together that hockey team back in 1905. He spent a very happy year back in Oundle until the war intervened. At Xmas 1914, he joined the Red Cross Hospital at Netley (near Southampton) which was expanded during the war until it had some 2,500 beds.

In May 1916, he was sent out to Egypt and from there to Deolali in India, a hospital and a military barracks not far from Bombay which took casualties from the Mesopotamian campaign and elsewhere. Dr Marsden, now a captain in the Royal Army Medical Corps, was in charge of a hospital for officers. The conditions seem to have been harsh there and the small town may have given its name to our word 'doolally' meaning mad. Apparently, the boredom and unhealthy air there led to what was termed locally as Deolali or 'Doolally' fever, signifying insanity. Marsden worked tirelessly there but the effort and the climate took their toll on his health which broke down completely during a severe influenza epidemic and he was evacuated to Egypt. There he did not receive proper treatment for his illness and a delay in finding a ship home meant that he did not return to England until July 1919.

In August 1920, he underwent a serious operation at St. Thomas' Hospital in London, which merely confirmed the doctors' worst fears. He died "after a long and painful illness contracted on active service" on 19 December 1920. At the time he was on the committee of the Old Oundelian Club which had helped to bring the great Memorial Book to fruition. Writing in December of 1920, the president of the Newcastle OOs reported that Walter Marsden, "has come across from Manchester several times recently on business" but concluded with the ominous remark "but he has not been heard of for the last few months."

His Colonel wrote afterwards: "I have had a very great regard for 'Billy' ever since I knew him and so appreciated him as a comrade and so valued all the good and hard work he did when he was with me abroad." The obituary in the Laxtonian commented: "He enjoyed the respect and affection of Masters and schoolfellows in an unusual degree and was possessed of a never-failing power of drawing all men to him." His obituary in the St. Thomas' Gazette noted: "His last few months were a wonderful example of almost constant suffering most cheerfully borne." Shortly before his death, he married Esmé, sister of his late friend Arthur Chevasse. The Laxtonian's account of his life and death concluded with these words:

By his sunny disposition and supreme unselfishness and constant care for the feelings and happiness of others, he endeared himself to all who came in contact with him...To meet him was to like him and to know him was to love him. Those of us who were numbered amongst his friends should be grateful for such a privilege and proud of such a memory.

Billy Marsden was 34 years old at the time of his death.

Cyril Renals Woodward also died of wounds long after the war. A Nottingham boy, born in 1894, he resided in Sidney from 1908 until 1910, so was just 15 when he left Oundle. He rated no mentions in the Laxtonian magazines of his day. The grant of probate made after his death stated that he was an actor. According to the School's Memorial Book, he was gazetted as a second lieutenant in the Sherwood Foresters in January 1917, started his military service in France the next month and was wounded in May of that year. He was awarded the silver wound badge (SWB) but does not seem to have been in receipt of an army pension. He died in a nursing home in Weston-super-Mare on 27 October 1922 "of a wound received in the war." Aged 28, he was unmarried and left his estate to his sister Eva.

Walter Edwin Knight Brindley was a South African, the younger brother of Victor Brindley, a soldier turned pilot who was killed on the Somme in 1918. Like his brother, Knight Brindley was also in Dryden (1906-09), where he played some house rugby and cricket but with limited success. In the war, he served with South Africa's Imperial Light Horse mainly in East Africa. In 1916, having captured German South-West Africa with few casualties, South African Forces under General Smuts, agreed to help the British fight against German East Africa. This campaign was much more costly in terms of casualties, which included Knight Brindley. By 1917, South African troops withdrew from the area leaving the British largely in control. Despite British success there, the German Commander Paul von Lettow-Vorbeck evaded capture and only surrendered in November 1918, when news of the Armistice was confirmed.

Knight Brindley survived the war but died four years after the end of the conflict. He passed away on Christmas Eve 1922, aged 30, "after terrible suffering since his service in East Africa during the war." On his headstone in South Africa, his grieving parents recorded the names of their two lost sons. He appears in the index of the Oundle School Memorial Book as wounded only, as this volume was published in 1920, two years before his death. Only his brother's name appears on the memorial tablets in the School Chapel, since Knight's name was not included in the list of Oundle's dead for the consecration of the Chapel in November 1923, even though this was nearly a year after his demise. However his death and its cause were recorded in the Laxtonian magazine published the next month. Knight Brindley has the distinction of being the last Oundelian to die as a result of the war and ironically or perhaps fittingly, the wounds that killed him were inflicted in the same country which saw the death of the very first Oundle victim, Sam Edmonds, eight years before. Both came to grief not in France or Belgium but in East Africa. In those eight years, East Africa and the world had changed almost beyond recognition.

Three with unknown dates of death

Three more Oundelians are known to have died in the conflict but details, including dates of death are not known. **John Greaves** was the elder brother of Nicholas Greaves, who was killed in late October 1918. They were both born in Berdiansk in Southern Ukraine and both attended Dryden House at exactly the same time (January 1912 – July 1914) despite the fact that John was two years older than his sibling. He was 16 when he arrived and sang bass in the School Choral Society. He won a maths prize in July 1912 and that same term, the two brothers played together in the house cricket competition, reaching the semi-final. They enjoyed better fortune playing together in the house rugby final of 1912, the one which went to a replay before Dryden emerged victorious. In 1913, John Greaves was beaten in the second round of the fives competition by Gervase Spendlove, who would be killed in the war just eighteen months later. In the School Memorial Book, John Greaves is not even listed as serving in the armed forces, let alone dying for his country. His name, unlike that of his brother is not on the official printed list, which appeared when the Memorial Chapel was consecrated in November 1923 but his name is inscribed on the memorial tablets in the Chapel which were consecrated in May 1926. He had a younger brother, George, at school until 1924, so news of John's death could have reached the School in that time. The most likely explanation is that he died after the war had finished, perhaps as a civilian in the Russian Civil War? It is possible that he went back to Russia after the outbreak of war, like his younger brother Nicholas to help run the steelworks in the Ukraine, which would explain why he did not join up. Overall, the exact circumstances of his inclusion on the memorial tablets still remains a mystery.

Lastly, there are two more Laxton School boys, whose names appear on the wooden plaque put up in the Laxton Long Room to honour the fallen. **Cecil Lawrence** was born in June 1893 and seems to have lasted just two terms in Laxton School, they being the Lent and Summer Terms of 1908, when he was 12. He may have been born in Rushden, the son of George and Nellie Lawrence, working in the boot trade by the time of the census of 1911. This Cecil Ernest Lawrence joined the navy but there is no record of him being killed. The Laxton School Journal claimed that Cecil Lawrence joined the (Northants?) Yeomanry and was killed in 1917 aged 23 or 24 but the Commonwealth War Graves Commission has no record of him.

Similarly, there are reports that **John Bryan Ward** also of Laxton School (from 1904-1906) was likewise killed in the war but again, there are few details about him and not even a year when he might have died. He was born in June 1891 and left Laxton School at the age of 14. He was born in Upper Benefield and may well have lived there as well. As for military record, none has been found.

So there is some doubt about what happened to these three men and it may reveal that the great bureaucracy within the armed forces was always likely to lose track of some men in the confusion of war or that some records were later destroyed or lost. Perhaps it is surprising that only three boys out of the 263 Oundelians killed have left no track in the official records.

Two more discoveries – one more war death

And then there is at least one other Old Oundelian whose early death could be attributed to the strain of war work. **Harold Swithun Morton**, assistant bursar at King's College, Cambridge died in April 1919. A Fellow of King's by 1915, he threw himself into work at the War Office because his health "did not allow him to serve abroad." In the Royal Army Service Corps, he attained the rank of staff major and received an O.B.E. and died, shortly after his return to Cambridge, after a short illness. As a man with health problems, it is certainly possible that his war work hastened his demise. He was in Grafton House from 1904-08 and then went up to Corpus Christi College, Cambridge as a scholar and took a first in natural sciences in 1910. He was born on St Swithun's Day in 1889 and so was still only 29 when he died. He is registered in the Cambridge University list of those who served but his death is not officially linked to the war.

By contrast, **William Oliver Redman King**, who was another Cambridge man, can now be seen as having died in the course of his military duties, even though the School failed to link his death to his active service in the war. He was attached to the Royal Army Medical Corps when he died in February 1919. He was in School House from 1900-06 and was another very talented schoolboy. Aged 14, he played 'pretty' piano pieces in the Xmas term entertainment and the next year played four numbers from Schumann's *Kinderscenes*, "playing with such expression and showing considerable promise." He also trod the boards being cast in 1903 as Starveling in *A Midsummer Night's Dream*. As a senior, he took on the more taxing role of Sir Andrew Aguecheek in *Twelfth Night*. The Laxtonian later reported that "King could not have entered into his part better." William King was also a very good sportsman. The only picture we have of him is in the photograph of the XV of 1905 but he also won the Challenge Cup for shooting. Academically, he was very much to the fore and though he would go on to study science at Cambridge, he won the Latin Prose prize in 1905. Not surprisingly, he was Head of House and a school prefect.

From Oundle, he went up to Sidney Sussex, Cambridge where he gained a double first in 1909. He then travelled to California to work with the distinguished German biologist, Jacques Loeb. After that, he worked in the Marine Laboratory in Naples to begin his independent research. After a short spell at St. Andrews in Scotland, in 1912, he took up a post teaching zoology at Leeds University. A year

Thought to be William Oliver Redman King, School House 1900-06.

later he married Annie Peniston who held an M.Sc. from Leeds and who was also engaged in biological research work.

When war broke out, he threw himself into the work of the University OTC. From 1915-18, he worked in the Medical Research Committee on Dysentery and then went out to France to carry out further research into the disease amongst the troops. Whilst there he caught influenza and travelling from London to Leeds before he was fully recovered, he suffered a relapse which turned to pneumonia, with fatal consequences. He was 32 years old at the time of his death. Both Sidney Sussex College and Leeds University now count him among their war dead, with Leeds adding him, with 24 others, to their war memorial. Perhaps it is now time that Oundle School did likewise.

Fourteen Oundelians died after the Armistice as a result of their involvement in the war, the last one over four years after the conflict was officially brought to an end. Two hundred and fifty-nine old boys of Oundle School and Laxton School plus five highly valued members of staff (Francis Norbury being in both categories) had perished because of the conflict. Though the vast majority were old boys, none of them was old. They had "given up the years to be" in the service of their country.

14

Year 5 Home: War and Peace – Oundle School 1918-1919

> Their lives were long enough to leave
> A trail of blessing in their wake,
> And so we have no right to grieve
> Nor count them lost – 'tis but a break –

The final Laxtonian of the war, published in December 1918 makes clear that the end of the war came as something of a shock. The grisly conflict had ground on for so long and false hopes of a swift termination had been so frequently dashed, that the Armistice when it came was unexpected: "When we came back at the end of September, even the most sanguine optimist could hardly have hoped that peace was as near as it proved to be; since then, however, events have moved rapidly, perhaps too rapidly for us to realize them fully, secluded in a backwater of the Midlands."

Term as usual

So for much of the Michaelmas Term 1918, it was wartime business as usual. The footballers noted that their efforts had again been handicapped "by agriculture at the beginning of the term, and by the claims of munitions all through." The XV still played against the RFA Cadet School from Weedon and an RAF team from Stamford. The house rugby matches produced a replayed semi-final in which Dryden eventually overcame New House, only to lose narrowly in the final to Laxton.

Debating was as lively as ever. A motion that the fagging system was "highly desirable in public schools" was carried easily. As well as being good for discipline, it was believed that the system was good for new boys. It "shook down new boys who had been important in their preparatory schools" and gave a fag "prestige from being employed by one of the leading lights of the House." It was also claimed that "ill treatment of fags was unknown," and that the system, "introduced the conception of the dignity of labour." And the mood was even more light-hearted on October 12th when the House considered whether "Modern Social Functions are positively deadly" or not. In a well-attended debate, Mr Matchett (Gethin Matchett of Dryden, who proposed the motion) "painted in strong colours the perils of that time-honoured torture, the Drawing-Room tea." He also asserted that in countries more primitive and less artificial, "such as Wales," there was no place for such deadly functions, instead they preferred to focus on more fundamental matters "such as the price of cabbages". He concluded that school debating chambers themselves witnessed a particularly deadly Social Function: "He did not wish to hear Mr Hindley (Clement Hindley of New House, Head of School) nor, he trusted did anyone else." Mr Little (Alan Little of School House) also supported the motion, painting a very droll and wholly Dickensian picture of modern weddings where, "the bride wept incessantly, the bridegroom was in what is colloquially termed a 'blue funk', and the best man, primed with concentrated alcohol, did his best to prevent the bridegroom from running away." He concluded by examining the photo of the wedding group "somewhat upset," he averred, "by the untimely efforts of one of the bride's sixteen fat aunts to get more of her person into the picture than her other relations thought desirable." The war did rate one passing mention in the debate when Ian McCracken noted that "the King's visits to munition works were now quite informal."

At the same time, the last term of war saw the revival of the Science Society with lectures on X-rays, aircraft and their engines, the cinematograph and the eye. All the lectures were given by pupils. The one on eyes was the last before the Armistice, delivered on 31 October 1918, by George Wells, elder son of the writer H. G. Wells. The Choral Society reported good attendances that term but noted that the basses, whilst having several safe and sound singers amongst them, still lacked "the heavies of pre-war times."

OTC before the Armistice

For the OTC, some disruption was caused with the enlargement of the school armoury, required by the increase in OTC activity during the war. This meant that the corps moved temporarily into a warehouse in the market square. Though this had "disarranged the parades to some extent," it did mean that the field house contingents had "some useful practice in marching." A Field Day had been arranged with Rugby near Market Harborough for Wednesday 6 November but Rugby apparently "had to cry off", so Oundle boys decided "to have a show of our own," since all the arrangements including tea and a "special train" had been made. And the day proved quite successful, with groups of cadets involved in attack and defence whilst the November weather, luckily, "was excellent."

Meanwhile the war still took its toll amongst the OTC officers. The deaths of Maurice Miskin and George Tryon were enormous blows but Oundle's OTC was still losing officers who were still joining up. In the summer of 1918, Lieutenants Kingham and Woodall both joined the real army.

Oundle School OTC parading in 1919.

And even after the Armistice, it seemed to be a matter of business as usual for the Oundle military. The Laxtonian's OTC correspondent noted: "We have not even noticed any marked falling off in the number of our parades since hostilities ended."

Meanwhile, the recently formed Cadet Sixth continued to work hard, embodying Sanderson's ideas on education to the full. Members of the form helped in the teaching of junior forms and carried out exciting historical research in the library. The results of their investigations were printed to help Oundelians in the future. As well as promoting historical research, Sanderson would have been encouraged by one project which looked at "various Education Bills and Labour Problems in Town and Country, suggested solutions being added." The report on this research project concluded with an invitation to hear the Head speak on the topic of 'Industry and Educational Reconstruction" at the Industrial Reconstruction Council the following March. Clearly the war had made such reconstruction and reshaping of both education and industry more necessary than ever.

The Roll of Honour

And the final term of warfare was certainly no different to others in terms of the list of killed and wounded. The last wartime Laxtonian would not be the last to include Oundle war deaths and now recorded 25 more Oundelians killed, including the irrepressible Justin Willis, his enthusiasm now stilled for ever. Three more were reported missing, two of whom Jaime Brown and John Emtage were also dead. Four more were prisoners of war, all of whom survived, though two were wounded. At the same time, there were more awards for valour – five DSOs, fourteen MCs, three DFCs, one Italian Bronze Medal and two Orders of the Crown of Italy.

Charitable Giving

Throughout the war Oundle School raised money for a variety of charities, many of them related to the conflict. The total given during the war was an impressive £1,530. Nine charities, which were all given more than £50, were the main beneficiaries of this largesse, with much of the money raised in fortnightly collections in chapel. The recipients of the money show that Oundle's charitable giving did not begin and end at home. While Duston Military Hospital in Northampton received £52 and the Prisoners of War Fund £75; the Belgian Victims' Fund was granted £60 and the Serbian Relief Fund £105. The biggest grant by far however went to the Public Schools' Red Cross Hospital with a spectacular £450 donated over the course of the war.

The end of the War

Poetry

One poem, entitled *IO! SATURNALIA*, celebrated the doubling of the meat ration by the government one week after the Armistice. The verse, in suitably heroic style, took up the news with gusto:

> Lo! The word has gone forth to the uttermost North,
> To Cambrian and soulful Celt;
> For a sennight's[1] pause in Rational Laws,
> And the Briton may loosen his belt.

---

1   Sennight – abbreviation for seven nights or a week.

So the nation dines to the health of Clynes[2]
And pledges its friends in peace;
And, D.O.R.A.[3] my dear, come Christmas Year,
We'll drink to your ripe decease.

Actually, D.O.R.A. took a little while longer to die. By the end of term the only outward sign "of the decease of the obnoxious Dora and other wartime inconveniences" was "the charm of being able to disperse the works of darkness with a stray beam of light unchecked by special constables."

Thanksgiving and Commemoration

The Laxtonian of December 1918 talked little of how the end of the war was celebrated, merely recording that on Wednesday 13 November, "there was a Thanksgiving Service in the Great Hall to mark the cessation of hostilities and another in the Chapel the following Sunday." On Sunday 8 December, just before the end of term, a Memorial Service was held in the Great Hall for all "the old boys and masters who have fallen."

The editor of the magazine noted that though influenza had returned that term, it mercifully "abated as quickly as it came." Then he writes eloquently of the hopes of the new age: "And so, with every hope for the increased prosperity of the school in the forthcoming era that is to usher in a new heaven and a new earth, we wish our readers a Merry Christmas in the old-fashioned sense, trusting that in the general rejoicings, our own imperfections may be treated with the indulgence that springs from peace and plenty."

Bramston House 1918 with Llewellyn Jones back in harness.

---

2   John Robert Clynes was a labour politician and Minister of Food Control, July 1918-January 1919.
3   D.O.R.A. was the Defence of the Realm Act passed on 8th August 1914 giving the government wide-ranging powers in time of war.

In reality, the ending of the war brought Oundle School to the brink of revolution. Thanks to the chance survival of one letter written by a junior boy in Bramston House to his mother, we know that Sanderson's reaction to the Armistice caused consternation and outrage amongst the boys and staff alike. The Head claimed that the war was not over, that there was no cause for rejoicing and he refused to give the boys a holiday:

> There is so much to tell you, I don't know where to begin. On Monday [11 November 1918] at 12.30 we heard the news. The town was all beflagged and there were demonstrations and flag-waving. However we had work as usual in the afternoon. Then the church bells pealed for hours and the clock struck the hours after 7 which it has not done since the war began for fear of raids. The whole place was lighted up. In the evening the townspeople had a meeting in the Market Place [outside Bramston] and Beans tried to stop it, declaring that they ought not to rejoice! Beastly Cheek. But they took no notice of him. Willie Cole [the new Bramston Housemaster] called for cheers for the soldiers and sailors after lunch.

Sanderson's attempt to stop the town rejoicing was just the start of the trouble. The next morning, he tried to explain his feelings and was met with rebellion:

> Tuesday 12th. Beans made a most peculiar speech, saying he wished [for] no rejoicing and that the war was not over. Masters and boys furious. He gave us no work off or anything and was very annoyed with the Major [Nightingale], because he refused to have a parade.

The boys' disgruntlement boiled over by the afternoon:

> 2p.m. The Cadet Sixth in the munition workshops, with all the men, struck, refusing to work! They chalked a great notice on the doors, '30,000 munition girls get £1 each and 3 days holiday. N.B. STRIKE'. As Beans has often said, 'the Cadet Sixth is the highest form in the school.'

This notice reflected the government's decision to reward all the munition workers with an extra pound and a three day holiday. Boys at Oundle, who had toiled for over four years providing materials for the war effort, were outraged that they could apparently claim no reward for all their unpaid efforts. What they wanted was some sort of holiday to mark the Armistice.

By 4:30 p.m. that Tuesday afternoon, matters had got worse for the Headmaster as the school prefects, led by the editor of the Laxtonian, Gerald Rittener and the Head of Sidney, Ian McCracken (brother of Angus McCracken who served in Gallipoli and provided the School with his war diary), organised a mass demonstration to parade round the boarding houses ending up outside Sanderson's study in School House. Our Bramston correspondent takes up the story:

> Returning from footer, we heard there was to be a demonstration in front of School House at 5pm. We had a collection in the house and the gardener went and bought 2 Union Jacks and about 20 yards of red, white and blue ribbon, which we cut up in strips. At 5pm we rushed out (I carried one of the Union Jacks and [Reginald] Sapey the other) up to the Science Block and down to the road from the station [presumably North Street] where we found all the field houses. In front was a house common room table-cloth used as a banner with the inscription:
> 'God save the King
> And damn the Kaiser'
> Some chaps wore their corps hats, others their Sunday Straws, others their caps inside out, and many their coats inside out. You never saw such crowd. The whole time we kept a roar of cheering.

More worrying for the Head was the covert or overt support for the 'demonstration' by members of staff, including at least two housemasters:

> Upon reaching Laundimer we were joined by the whole of Laundimer who came out before the very eyes of Mr Ault, he making no effort to stop them. At Dryden, Mr Hale [the bird] appeared and never did anything. Thence we proceeded through the market place where we met Mr Chadwick, Miss Edge and Mr Bray cheering us.

The boys then reached School House and it was time for Sanderson to act:

> When we got to the School the cheering stopped and…McCracken called for three cheers for Marshal Foch, Sir Douglas Haig and the Head-Master!!! We then sang the National Anthem, Rule Britannia and the Marseillaise. Then fireworks were let off. Out came Beans perfectly furious! Took out his watch and said very quietly, 'I want you boys to report to your housemasters within 10 minutes! Go away.' More cheers and fireworks. Off we went in a body and returned to the houses. We all reported to Willy Cole, who said he sympathised with us and told us to go back to the common room. Whereupon we cheered him loudly.

Jane Sanderson, 'Ma Beans' to the boys, taken in 1912.

Though the demonstration had been quelled, rumours began to spread:

> The rumours we heard were wonderful. Beans was said to have declared that he would resign and the Head of School, Hindley, had to try and calm him. Also McCracken, Williams and Hirst of the Cadet Sixth were said to have been expelled.

None of the rumours proved well founded, instead Sanderson called the school prefects together to explain his outrage. He said that the demonstration was "most inconsiderate to him and to his wife and broke down." The root of the problem was thought to be his son Roy's death, the previous April:

> His son's death seems to have completely unnerved him, poor chap! But it was rather selfish not to allow others to rejoice. As a matter of fact Ma Beans seems to have been the trouble. She, poor lady, weeps copiously at every service and as she did not want a holiday, Beans did not give one. That evening he lectured School House expressing surprise that 'Ma orne harse [my own house] turned against me'.

Clearly Sanderson and his wife were very distressed but the letter gives a real insight into the boys' perspective both on Jane Sanderson as the power behind the throne and on Sanderson's 'geordie' accent! The drama continued the next day:

9.45 Prayers. Enter the Head. You could have heard a pin drop. He said he was very sorry it had happened; he had some sympathy with it, but it was not the right thing. He was melted by the fact that when 'I asked you to go away, you did so. Well boys, we are going to have a Thanksgiving Service in the Hall, and after that there will be no more work today' (cheers) 'If the Head of the School had asked me to give you a holiday, I think I should have done so. I am not sure but I think so, boys...I think so. Well boys, I don't know whether you deserve it (Laughter) But whether you do or not, boys, you shall have it!' (Cheers). He took it awfully well, poor old chap, but it was a very hard pill to swallow. What a poor excuse! A holiday on an occasion like that surely ought to have needed no asking for! He said afterwards he was sorry he had not taken a more lenient view. Fireworks, concerts and all sorts were arranged in the Houses...

But this happy resolution of the boys' grievances was then undermined by another bombshell as the Head later countermanded his permission for celebrations:

The Head specially asks that there be no rejoicing to-night, as news has just been received that Colonel Tryon M.C. (House Master of Crosby, who has been out for 4 years and had been in Oundle just 3 weeks before) was killed on Thursday.

So everything was off. The next day, Sanderson was able to revert to his opposition to any rejoicing to mark the end of hostilities. As our correspondent makes clear:

George Tryon and Crosby House 1911. The Housemaster was killed four days before the Armistice.

Thursday Beans jawed the whole School; about Major Tryon, saying that 'Many of us knew intuitively that the time had not come for rejoicing'. What had happened in the School was what might be expected from youth.

Having dealt with the great crisis of Sanderson's headmastership, our anonymous Bramston boy reverts to more normal news, which his mother probably heard about pretty often – sport – though even this still had a war-time feel: "On Thursday the XV played the New Zealand Machine Gun corps and they won. One of their chaps put his leg out during the game. Yesterday, Laxton beat School House in the semi-finals of the cup."

Ironically then, the ending of the war brought about the biggest crisis of Sanderson's 30 years in charge of Oundle School. Though he seemed out of touch with the feelings of the boys, one can understand his hostility to their celebrations. Though a dramatic four days in the history of the School, it was not a real crisis, there was no chance of Sanderson actually resigning but it did reveal, at Oundle as at so many other schools, the length and breadth of the country, the conflicting emotions unleashed by the Armistice. On the one hand relief and joy that it was finally over and victory secured but at the same time, an enduring shock and grief at the cost of the war in terms of so many young lives prematurely ended or permanently scarred. Sanderson and his family continued to mourn for their son Roy and masters and boys alike mourned for all the old boys and masters – eventually some 263 of them – who had died because of the conflict. For the boys currently at the School, some of course mourned for lost siblings or other relatives, some might have felt cheated that the war had ended before they could serve but most looked forward to a brighter future. For old boys, particularly amongst those who had served, there were also mixed emotions. For many relief that they had survived and that they had played their part in the defeat of the enemy. At the same time, the sights they had seen, the mental and physical scars inflicted upon them would not be easily, if ever erased. Many also endured survivors' guilt. Why had they 'come through' when their friends and comrades had not? And could they really believe that the war had been worth it? In addition, they had to live with an uncertain and on the whole bitter legacy of the war. For Cecil Lewis, as no doubt for many other young men suddenly demobilized, there was the feeling that the great adventure was over and that their lives would never be as meaningful again. Lewis was still only 20 when the war ended and felt that suddenly he had no place in the world.

Shavian Plaudits

A high watermark of school drama production came in the April of 1919. With the war over, the School decided to put on a production of George Bernard Shaw's *Arms and the Man*. Though a witty comedy, written in 1894, the play nonetheless underlines the futility and destructiveness of war, so it was very much *a propos* a few months after the ending of the Great War. In a peculiar Oundle twist, the performances came about through some staff and senior pupils meeting informally to read the play, when someone suggested that they should actually put it on! There were nerves before the production: "A clear fortnight left. It could not be done. It might be tried." But at least the School now had ladies to play the ladies' parts. "Miss Nayler played the part of Catherine with convincing force… Miss Edge showed high dramatic instinct… Miss Hough displayed unfailing judgement and flair for stage effect… Miss Denison played with intelligence and charm…" Margaret Denison was now working at the School because of the war. Her brother John, an Oundelian pilot had been killed the year before and Margaret asked if she might work at Oundle to help her through her grief. She had often visited her brother in his school days and now hoped that living in the town and working for the School he loved, would ease her pain. She wrote to Sanderson with her request and he was only too happy to oblige. John Denison had been killed just four days before his own son. Though Miss Denison was apparently enthusiastic about the play, her mother was worried. At one point, Winifred Naylor tells us, "there was a terrible fuss because she was involved in the bedroom scene in Act 1." Her mother wrote to say that her daughter must not be seen in bed and that "she would have to come out of the play." Luckily a compromise was found, whereby young Miss Denison appeared lying on a divan!

Though confidence was high, Margaret Denison and the rest of the cast of *Arms and the Man* were apparently alarmed by the news that the playwright himself, a friend of Sanderson, as well as H. G. Wells (whose son George took one of the main parts), would be in the audience. "The blood of the unhappy company was frozen by the news that Mr Bernard Shaw had not only courteously allowed them to attempt his play and given them hints upon its staging but had accepted the Headmaster's invitation to see them perform it." As if Shaw's presence was not enough to unnerve the cast, also in the front row of the balcony that night was the Headmaster, H. G. Wells of course and also another famous contemporary writer, Arnold Bennett!

Though the Laxtonian drama critic was self-deprecating about the outcome, it is clear that the play was triumph. "Mr Bernard Shaw, in response to enthusiastic calls for the author was brought before the curtain by the Headmaster. He mercifully spared the company the castigation they had anticipated and delighted the audience with a typical speech, full of the subtle and pungent wit with which he is associated." The taking of a 'call' by the author was, as it turned out, a historic moment for the School and for George Bernard Shaw. It was "the first to which he had acceded since the original production of the play 25 years ago."

Writing later to his friend Lady Augusta Gregory, who was another Irish playwright of some distinction, George Bernard Shaw expressed his admiration for the performance at Oundle, particularly the shooting: "H. G. Wells…took me down [to Oundle] to see a school performance of Arms and the Man, the fusillades in which, performed by the entire School Rifle Corps behind the scenes, surpassed anything I have ever heard either at a professional performance or at the front." Shaw was clearly very impressed by everything he saw at Oundle as the real purpose of his letter was to tell Lady Gregory where she should send her young grandson to school. The boy's father, Lady Gregory's son, had been shot down in Italy by an Italian pilot in 1918, who mistook him for the enemy. Now Lady Gregory, a fairly formidable woman at the best of times was charged with finding a school for her grandson. His father had attended Harrow, a school which did not meet with Shaw's approval. Instead, he recommended Oundle in glowing terms:

> I really cannot have Richard sent to that obsolete and thrice accursed boy farm which is an evil tradition in the family. Richard has a right to choose his fate. Show him the picture postcards of the workshops, and tell him that the boys repair all the cars in the countryside, and test the farm seeds, and pick-up Latin and Greek for fun in their spare time with such success that they beat all the other public schools at examinations, Eton and Harrow being nowhere, and Rugby, which has been modernised, the only feared competitor. Or, if you like, don't mention the Latin and Greek and mention only the workshops. You may mention, though, that there are no punishments [!], and that Sanderson, the headmaster, is rather like Granny in respect of calmly doing everything he wants to do, however subversive of established institutions, by simply walking in his heavy amiable way through every prejudice. It would be a crime to deliver Richard over to some imbecile don when there are men like that about. Intellect is respected, and athletics tolerated with due kindness, but no more…Harrow is in the old tradition: Oundle is in the new.

Sadly, his advice was not heeded and Richard Gregory was sent to Harrow in 1923. Nonetheless, these were glowing plaudits indeed for Oundle – on the strength of just one visit.

Part of the School Workshops c1920.

Peace dividends

Meanwhile, the Lent Term of 1919 gave more signs that peace had arrived. The Laxtonian editor noted that, "The hand of militarism has lain light on us, and our field day luckily fell in an isolated period of fine weather." An even clearer sign of the peace dividend was "the occasional appearance of chocolate at the tuck-shop." But although peace had been declared, Oundle boys were acutely aware that the post-war economic slump had led to widespread strikes and demonstrations as men returned home to face unemployment. There were some 36 million strike days during 1919 as miners, engineers, transport workers and even the police went on strike. Sanderson, as a socialist was of course much exercised about the problems faced by working men at this time. On Speech Day 1919, he opined that the great work of reconstruction after the war needed above all "the man who could create peace and mutual confidence between employers and employed, persuading them that each is vitally necessary to the existence of the other."

The Debating Society had taken up the theme the previous November, just two days before the Armistice, with a motion "That Strikes are justifiable." Edwin Hedley, who would apparently lose an arm the following year, yet still captain the Cambridge University Shooting Team in later life, proposed the motion. He lamented "the lack of sympathy between capital and labour" and that strikes were the inevitable response of "the workers" against "bad housing and the lack of education." The opposition on this occasion was led by George Wells (son of H. G.) who claimed that "men struck for an increase in their wages, whereas they should confine their attention to the removal of the more fundamental causes of their discontent." After that promising start, apparently, this fine actor and scion of a great literary father was less convincing: "Mr Wells then rendered the tenor of his speech totally unintelligible to the more cultured part of his audience by introducing slang phrases into his discourse, until, apparently overcome with mortification at having employed such diction, the honourable gentleman resumed his seat."

As well as industrial unrest, the Lent term of 1919 was notable for truly shocking weather as reported in a poem entitled:

The Middle of a Perfect (?) Term

It rained. The school looked on with joyous eyes.
There's no parade in rain.
It rained. Lieutenants vainly heaved forth sighs,
The Major[4] cursed in vain.

It rained. The floods grew larger. Boating ceased
And Rugger was no more;
And though a school from all parades released
Should sing – it only swore.

It stopped! At half-term one parade we tried.
Went on the river twice,
One game of Rugger, and one day we 'fived,'
And then – It rained – how nice!

As the weather closed in, the Choral Society cheered itself up pursuing patriotic themes, so characteristic of the war years. By April 1919, they had reportedly "learnt something" of *Land of Hope and Glory* and had chosen this moment to perfect their singing of Eaton Faning's lesser known but equally stirring *We love our Island story*. Eaton Faning was a distinguished composer who, ironically enough given his name, had taken up the post of Director of Music at the 'thrice accursed boy farm', Harrow School in 1885!

One notable rugby fixture of the Lent Term 1919 was the return, almost, of the match between the XV and the OOs. Last played in November 1913, the match in the spring of 1919 was between the XV and Cambridge OOs:

> The Cambridge Old Oundelians brought over a team, which contained a number of strong players, and some who were not in practice. Naturally, the School team, accustomed to one another's play, won by a good many points, but the game was a pleasant reminder that the war is over and we may look for the restoration of this match to the list.

OTC after the Armistice

While the Choral Society sang patriotically, the OTC adjusted to a new world of peace. Despite the outbreak of peace and the interruptions caused by the weather, it was still very much in evidence in the Lent Term of 1919 and looking forward to taking charge of its new armoury after the Easter break. A Field Day in March, with Uppingham and Rugby, enjoyed fine weather as Oundle and Uppingham, co-operating for once, attempted to blow up a railway line defended by Rugby. One peace-time bonus for the Oundle cadets was assistance from three demobilized officers, who had all seen prolonged active service in France. Then came the official thanks to the School's OTC from the War Office:

> I am commanded by the Army Council to express their appreciation of the great work carried out by the Contingents of the Officers' Training Corps during the recent war...The list of those who have fallen and those who have been mentioned in despatches and decorated show how

---

4   Major Nightingale, Head of the School's OTC.

School Chapel in 1905, the 'Tin Tab', another victim of the War.

grandly the ex-Officers' Training Corps cadets have fought for King and Country and form a record of which the Schools may justly be proud.

News from Old Oundelian soldiers at peace and at war

In April 1919, the Laxtonian also gave a timely reminder that many OOs had still not been demobilized. The OO Club was keen to hold a meeting as soon as possible but noted that "as a number of OOs are still serving abroad, it is not certain if this will be feasible in the coming summer, as was hoped." The theme was taken up by an OO who was currently based in Cologne as part of the Army of Occupation: "The number of O.O.s in the Army of Occupation must be prodigious, and who am I that I should presume to stand out from them all, and hold forth on the subject of life in occupied German territory?" The reason for the letter, it seems was to correct views expressed in the press that relations between the British military and German civilians was a powder-keg waiting to explode:

> The writer speaks of the British garrison being 'butchered out of hand,' if 'reinforcements, ammunition and supplies' were not 'readily available.' This is indeed a startling statement to one with the smallest acquaintance of the German population of Cologne and its neighbourhood, where a bar of soap or a stick of chocolate will purchase good-will, even servile adoration from a whole village.

At least one OO soldier was still in Belgium in the summer of 1919. His views on the country were hardly encouraging. He regretted that he could not pen "a breezy article on Belgium." Instead he affirmed that if he should write about the country and its inhabitants he would "be shot under D.O.R.A. for disturbing the harmony of the League of Nations. Remember Belgium? – shall we ever forget it?"

At the same time, in May 1919, came news that another old boy had been wounded on active service. 25 year-old Captain Sidney Scott of 109th Indian Infantry, part of a force of some 3,000 men, found himself defending an Indian fort at Thal when it was attacked by over 12,000 Afghans armed with German guns. Scott himself, who left New House in 1912, was in command of an exposed picket and "had rather a hot time" but he managed to carry on, despite being wounded and "finally drove off the enemy." He was last heard of in hospital and "doing well." Despite the presence of German arms (Krupp howitzers and field-guns), this encounter was not the death throes of the Great War but a reversion to older imperial conflicts so familiar in pre-war days. Indeed Scott's experiences were actually the start of the Third Anglo-Afghan War, which lasted some three months. It followed the Second Afghan War of 1878-80. The third in the series, despite its brevity and successful outcome, was also of course a pre-echo of the decline of the British Empire in the inter-war period. While Scott survived, the Laxtonian of July 1919, still carried the obituaries of seven more Oundelians killed by the war. Here was Beanlands and Rogers, Sanders and Stace and the two Grummitt brothers of Dryden. The seventh was James Armitage.

Meanwhile the Laxtonian also reported that there were still Oundelians on active service as some were still fighting in Russia! One of those was Victoria Cross winner Alan Jerrard. He had been released by the Austrians when the war ended and had gone to Buckingham Palace to receive his VC from King George in April 1919. Although granted a disability pension, he stayed with the RAF and joined the North Russian Expeditionary Force in Murmansk in July, staying there until the end of the year. His health was further undermined as result of this excursus and he had to retire from the RAF in 1933.

Summer Term 1919

By the end of the Summer Term 1919, the editor of the Laxtonian was in little doubt that while the world was on the brink of a new era, the School was very much back to normal. And the primary indication of 'normal' to him was, of course, the resumption of normal games: "It is extremely gratifying to note that the general prosperity of the School is reflected in the flourishing condition of every branch of its games." That term, the School once again sent representatives to the Public Schools' Boxing Competition and the XI, boosted by the return of their coach Freddie Holland from the fighting, was the best that could be remembered since before the war. The shooters shot at Bisley once again and the School Crew, without any races during the war, had a notable victory over Durham School. The OTC won plaudits on Inspection Day and the old school gym, restored to its former glory, after its wartime existence as a carpenters shop, was a gym once again.

A successful gathering of OOs Oundle in mid-June 1919 "incomplete though it necessarily was [!]," had the school looking forward to further gatherings as an annual fixture, as in the old days: "As many as possible were put up in their old houses, where all had meals; the remainder had lodgings provided for them in the town." Certainly there was a rush of OOs on offer to play in the newly revived cricket match against the XI on 14 June that year: "This match, was quite a revival of pre-war conditions, over 100 OOs being present, so that it was easy to select a good side from so large a number." In fact there were so many old boys eager to play that the School's 2nd XI was also called into action.

Despite the great gathering of old boys anxious to renew their ties with their *alma mater* now that peace had come, the OO 1st. XI still made room for the Housemaster of Laxton, Sammy Squire, and he played a large part in the OOs victory that day. The School XI started well with Campbell and Marshall putting on 84 for the first wicket but then slumped to 166 all out with Mr Squire's slow bowling taking 9 for 50! This feat was all the more remarkable as he had been knocked for 31 runs before taking his first wicket! When the old boys batted they reached 199 all out to claim victory, with

Squire scoring a useful 26 of the total. This match was one of thirteen played by the XI that year, a clear improvement on just seven matches the previous year, when the war was still to be won.

Peace Day

On 19 July 1919, some three weeks after Speech Day, the town of Oundle, aided by its two famous schools, held an official 'Peace Day'. There was much bunting and many flags in evidence around the town and the day started at 10:30 a.m. with a parade from Milton Road, involving various public bodies of the town, the OTC and the rest of the School. The parade ended in the market place where a joint service of thanksgiving was held. In the afternoon there was a cricket match on the field and the Band of the London Fire Brigade (no less) marched and played. However, perhaps foreshadowing future developments across the land, the Peace Day afternoon came to a premature close after 4:00 p.m. when it started to rain heavily. Cricket was abandoned, tea was taken "under the trees" and a water polo match, House tugs-of-war and even 'crocodile races' had to be abandoned.

Spirits lifted in the evening however, when a dance was held in the Great Hall for school employees and in the houses there were sing-songs and dances and some even had fancy dress parades. The climax of the evening came with a firework display from 10:15 p.m. until midnight, (a lot of fireworks!) given by the generous Messrs. Pain who not only supplied the pyrotechnics but also provided operators to set them off. The whole school thoroughly enjoyed them "in spite of the pouring rain."

Speech Day 1919

And then there was Speech Day, back to its pre-war best and held on 28 June, five years to the day since the Archduke and his wife were assassinated in far-off Sarajevo and the very day on which the Peace Treaty of Versailles was signed. Although the day thus marked "the definite beginning of a new phase in the life of the School" the packed programme precluded any "special celebrations" to mark the day on which peace officially broke out. A record number of parents came down "more than the town could accommodate" so that some had to find beds as far away as Peterborough. Unlike 1914, Speech Day weather 1919 was "not all that could be desired." It was cold and windy, though rain kept off.

On the Saturday morning came the Commemoration Service in the parish church, attended by the Master and Wardens of the Grocers' Company in their robes, after which came speeches in the Great Hall. After the no doubt full-throated singing of Jerusalem, Sanderson rose to his feet and a hush descended on the Great Hall. He turned first to the important work of reconstruction that lay ahead. "The most pressing problem at the present moment," he averred, "was reconstruction, the rebuilding of the nation and of its schools." The workers who had gone off to war did not intend, he claimed "to go back to their old life and conditions – slums, mines, factories;" they were "unwilling to return to dull mechanical work" and schools like Oundle "must take part in the active work of the world, because it was a dull kind of thing only to go to school to learn."

He recounted how Oundelians had taken an active part in the war effort with "munitions and agricultural work." He went on to thank masters and boys who had carried out various investigations into contemporary issues such as "the League of Nations and labour problems, including profit-sharing and syndicalism." After doing this kind of work "boys left school in closer touch with the life of the community." Finally he referred to the new Yarrow Museum opened the year before in memory of Eric Yarrow killed in May 1915. He was often asked what it was for and his response was that "it was somewhere for a distracted headmaster to go and rest." But, "In the future, it was hoped that its walls would show the history of the work of the great and lofty souls who had made the world." Replying to the Headmaster, the Master of the Grocers' Company, Mr

Speech Day 1920, inside the Great Hall.

Egerton Hensley, made much of the virtues of an Oundle education, which he had no doubt were particularly relevant and crucial in the forthcoming work of reconstruction. He told his audience that the Grocers:

> were proud of Oundle, proud of being associated with a system of teaching animated by such high ideals and giving such good results; and they looked to the members of the School to carry into the world not only the knowledge they had gained, but the spirit and ideals of Oundle.

Like Sanderson, he believed that the key to future social peace and harmony lay in creating a better and more co-operative working relationship between workers and employers:

> At present, our greatest benefactor would be the man who could create peace and mutual confidence between employers and employed, persuading them that each is vitally necessary to the existence of the other. Men were wanted to impart into our industrial life high religious and patriotic ideals, such as were an essential part of the Oundle training.

In this regard, he concluded that the boys before him must:

> never forget those who had nobly died that we might live.

Lord Bledisloe, a conservative politician who was in charge of sugar supplies during the war, gave the vote of thanks to the Grocers' Company. He also sang the praises of the School. He suggested that Oundle was producing just the right men for the future:

The nation required men who were alive to the lessons of the war, and to the needs of our great Empire, and men of unblemished integrity to promote those ideals, of which they, as Englishmen, were most proud. Oundle was pointing the way amongst British public schools to the best method of producing such men and other great public schools would be compelled to follow her lead.

For the Laxtonian editor, there was a clear feeling that this was indeed a landmark Speech Day:

As for Speech Day…no-one could have been present without feeling a thrill of pride at their connection with the School; and surely what we have achieved during the war may be considered as merely an earnest of what may be accomplished in the new epoch to which we can look forward with confidence and hope.

After the speeches came the traditional garden party at which the Northants. Volunteer Band played. After tea in the Great Hall, parents could wander round and enjoy all the scientific experiments laid on by the boys, in what was clearly a bumper year: "We were fortunately able to show a large number [of experiments] that had not been seen here before, extending over every department of Science." The evening saw the traditional Speech Day concert. An immense audience of over a thousand had gathered for the occasion, such that "those who could not find seats in the Hall found them in School House garden or wandered about on the lawns and listened to the music from outside." The orchestra set the tone with three dances from Edward German's less well-known operetta *Nell Gwyn* and were joined by the chorus in a stirring rendition of Eaton Fanings's *We love our Island Story*, in preparation since the previous term. The chorus' singing was praised in these terms: "pleasing in expression, attack, sonority, and freshness…" The Junior School Singing Class was also a decided success, singing not only in French but also in Spanish. Their voices were, "of clear and resonant quality, and their singing and pronunciation of the French and Spanish denoted the careful training they have had: in fact, their diction, generally, was very good and the whole effect of their singing was admirable." Pupil soloists that evening included Theodore Collet and Bernard Robinson on violin, John Graham and Fynes Peirson-Webber pianists and the singers Charles Brown and Walter Hattrell, with stirring patriot numbers – *The Sea Road* and *The Yeomen of England*. As so often in the past, (though not in 1914) the School was pleased to welcome a professional singer, to add a little extra quality to the proceedings. In 1917, it was Oundle parent, Lady Maud Warrender, in 1918 the celebrated tenor David Ellis fresh from singing at one of Sir Henry Wood's promenade concerts, the previous September and in 1919, on the day Peace was signed, Oundle welcomed the famous Irish baritone Frederick Ranalow, whose singing "gave us all genuine delight." The next day, morning service was held in the Great Hall as there was not enough room for everyone in the Chapel and in the evening there was a Memorial Service at which Ranalow sang *O God, have mercy* from Mendelssohn's oratorio *St Paul*.

Whether God would have mercy in the future was an open question in the summer of 1919, whether He had shown mercy in the last five years was even more open to question. Just five years separated Speech Day 1914 from its successor in 1919. On the surface, someone who visited the School only on those two days would have thought that little had changed and in some ways they would have been right. On the other hand, for those who lived through those years, masters and boys alike, it was clear that much had changed. The progressive and optimistic School of 1914 had been swept away in the carnage of war. Two hundred and sixty-three of her sons had been slaughtered in all parts of the world at their country's behest. Their lives, apparently freely given for the nation, had enriched the school, its heritage and its history in ways which would have been unimaginable before 1914. Their example of sacrifice and selfless heroism would live on to inspire and guide the boys and girls who would come after them – the future generations of Oundelians. It was time to build their memorials.

Epilogue: Memorials, Commemoration and the Death of Sanderson

> For humbly we may dare to think
> Each death but means one friend the more
> Who when 'tis ours to cross the brink
> Will greet us on the further shore.

Oundle at the Front

A letter to the Laxtonian from Gilbert Hoole OO, two weeks after the Armistice, noted that in the old front line between Hulluch and La Bassée Canal in northern France there was a place officially called Oundle Post. He did not know how it had acquired that name and wondered if anyone reading the magazine might have the answer. "There might be an interesting story attached to the name," he wrote. Probably no-one now knows why it was so called but it is surely good to know that Oundle School did make its own small mark on the military maps of the conflict, as a small reminder of the contribution of so many Oundelians to the terrible struggle which was played out in these years of war. The conflict had been a huge test for the great reforms of Sanderson and his determination that boys should understand and contribute positively to the world around them. The conditions and carnage had also been a huge test of the resolve, courage and determination of that particular generation of Oundelians, born in the 1880s and 1890s for the most part and shaped by the School's progressive ethos and by its idiosyncratic headmaster. The war had shown that Oundle School, Home and Away, had passed that test with flying colours.

The wounded

For many Oundelians, their wounds were the most notable memorial of the war and their part in it. A letter from one old boy to the Laxtonian magazine of April 1919, reminded everyone that though the dead were gone, the wounded remained. Writing in the summer of 1918, "O.O. Blackpool" as he signs himself, records meeting up with six other wounded Oundelians in a hospital in that Lancastrian town. All seven were wounded on the Western Front: "Looking along the North shore during the morning, one finds Lieut. T.K.Clifford – having missed a tramcar – violently waving his crutches to a passing taxi." Then he espied J.M.Dyson "taking his morning promenade but should this prove too energetic for him, he may be seen indulging in a 'Dry Ginger' or a game of bowls at Squires Gate." He also noticed Lieutenants Frederick Golding and William McGeoch who, "despite their leg and arm disabilities, were usually found rowing or yachting at Fairhaven." Meanwhile another wounded old boy, Captain Leslie Wall was to be heard lecturing other convalescents, while Thomas Brocklehurst and Captain Cecil King were also known to be in the hospital there at that time. These were all less seriously wounded Oundelians, whose tales could be safely told in the school magazine.

The Memorial Book records that some 151 Oundelians were wounded (most likely a serious underestimate); 14 were wounded at least twice, with Major Walter Gray, of the Royal Field Artillery and Captain John Burrell, of the Royal West Surreys both wounded three times. Captain

William Carslake, also with the West Surreys and once of Laxton House, had the misfortune to be wounded on no less than four occasions.

How serious these wounds were is impossible to say. Humphrey Bostock lost his right arm but his injury is the only one given specific details in the Laxtonian reports of the wounded. A letter from Professor Thomas Preston reported that his father George, once of New House and serving with the Yorkshire Regiment, lost a leg in Flanders, not in combat but from an accident during a hand-grenade training exercise. Leaving Oundle, he had won a scholarship to Caius College, Cambridge but joined up before he could go up. Now, aged 19, George came round only to see one of his legs "some distance away." He was taken to hospital and given a bottle of brandy a day to help ease the pain. His mother was sent for, and had him transferred to a convent where his wounds were washed in salt water twice a day. He said afterwards that he then knew what the pains of St. Ignatius were like! George Preston then convalesced in the agreeable climate of the West Indies at the home of the parents of Clarence Lyon-Hall, his exact contemporary in New House, who had been killed on the Somme in July 1916. No doubt, caring for a seriously wounded Oundelian helped to ease their own grief and suffering. The chances are that many more Oundelians lost limbs and suffered serious injury so that their lives were never the same again. And we know from the fate of Knight Brindley, who died of his injuries four years after the war was over and from the death of Hugh Turnill, at home in Warmington, six months after being wounded on the Somme that such wounds might be long lasting and lead to an early death.

And then there were the mental scars. Firstly amongst those 28 Oundelians we know about who were prisoners of war, some for years. Their loss of liberty, feelings of guilt at being unable to fight alongside their fellows and their treatment at the hands of the Germans must have hit them all hard. Certainly, John Binder reports on Oundle men coming back from captivity being emaciated and hungry. Those imprisoned for long periods of course were just a small fraction of the hundreds of Oundelians for whom the sights and sounds of the war left indelible mental scars. Again, it is impossible at this distance to be specific about the scale and seriousness of the mental impact of the war on survivors, even those who came through physically unscathed. Most did not wish to talk about their experiences but few could hope to blot out the war's inhumanity. Insomnia and nightmares were recurrent problems for so many of those who survived. We know more generally of those whose character and temperament were changed for the worse by what they experienced at the front, many became depressed at the futility of the war and the suffering, and a number committed suicide. Others, though not outwardly wounded physically or mentally, still felt guilty that they had survived when so many of their comrades had not. And always, there was the continuing uncertainty of whether the war had been worth the fighting. Even Sanderson's optimism through the suffering might have been seriously tested if he had lived longer and seen the bitter legacy of the conflict.

Graves in foreign fields

Meanwhile, for most Oundle war victims, one permanent memorial has been their headstone in a foreign field, lovingly tended to this day by the Commonwealth War Graves Commission. Oundelians lie in over one hundred cemeteries across the globe and in ninety-five of those cemeteries, they are the only Oundelian present. Most, of course, lie on the Western Front across the battlefields of the Somme, Arras and Ypres but others lie further from home. Norman Edmonstone in Israel, Stewart Ridley in Cairo, John Atkinson and Geoffrey Bull in Alexandria. Gordon Sanders' last resting place is in Delhi, Stanley Marlow's in Gaza, while George Needham and Hugh Hopkinson overlook Suvla Bay, not far from John Rhodes and Arthur Goodfellow and Walter Paine. Richard Irwin and William Board are in Greece, Moira Maclean in Singapore, Lionel Wilford in Marseilles, Basil Watts in Quebec, Rivers Begg in Otranto, Noel Money in Malta.

Of course, many Oundelians had no known grave, indeed nearly ninety of the fallen boys were in this category, over one third of the total. One of those denied proper burial was Reggy Secretan but the lack of a grave did not deter his mother from finding some way to commemorate him, close to where he fell. The idea, typically, had come from Reggy himself, nearly a year before he was killed on the first day of Passchendaele. In August 1916, 'Old Sec.' (as he was known) advised his mother that she should come out to the Front when the war was over to "see these places where such hundreds of men have given up their lives." She duly visited the Ypres area in 1920 but was unable to find her son's grave, as he had none. So, in the autumn of that year, she decided to send a young rambler rose to a Belgian family who lived close to where he had fallen. The next year she visited again and took further roses to distribute to local people:

> My daughter and I have just returned from a visit to Ypres. We found my rose growing strong in the little garden, it will be a mass of blooms next year. I took some more plants from another mother whose son was also killed there. We took young rose plants and cuttings to various people on the Yser Canal banks and at Watou, Poperinghe, Vlamertinghe and Zillebeke, about fourteen lots altogether; everyone received us with great kindness, and understood at once. I like to think that the roses from the home he loved so dearly, will bloom along the ways he used to pass those last three years of his young life.

The names of Oundlians who have no known grave are displayed across the globe from Nairobi to Archangel, Basra to Arras, Ypres, Thiepval, Cambrai and Chatham, Macedonia and Mombasa, Helles, Loos, Neuve Chapelle, Ploegsteert and Plymouth, Savona, Tyne Cot and Vimy. Most are remembered, naturally enough, on the Western Front. Four at Tyne Cot, eight on the Arras Flying Services Memorial, ten on the Menin Gate and seventeen on the Thiepval Memorial.

And then there were the tangible memorials in their awards for bravery in the field from a number of countries as well as Britain. The large number of awards is impressive by any standards, particularly bearing in mind that the average age at death was just 23. Many junior officers barely had time to impress before being swept away in the maelstrom of war. As well as the three Victoria Crosses, there were 115 Military Crosses and 6 Bars, 29 Distinguished Service Orders and three Bars, together with 23 foreign decorations.

Memorials in Oundle

Yarrow Gallery 1916

The war changed the Oundle landscape, most visibly with two new buildings and a statue of a small boy volunteering to serve. In November 1915, six months after the death of Eric Yarrow, the Laxtonian reported on the beginnings of the 'Yarrow Museum' enterprise: "through the munificent generosity of Mr A. F. Yarrow we are being provided with a new Art Museum…In a letter to the Headmaster enclosing a cheque for £2000, Mr Yarrow refers to the great affection his boy had for Oundle, and suggests a suitable inscription." By the end of the school year 1915-16, the building was nearly ready:

> The building of the Yarrow Museum is now approaching completion and we feel sure that some worthy use will be found for it. It is to be feared that the majority of the School do not sufficiently appreciate the advantages we enjoy from the possession of all these numerous aids to a liberal education and we would urge that the scheme for making the new building into a complete museum in miniature should be carried out to the fullest possible extent.

The report echoes some concerns about the exact purpose of the building, which Sanderson himself liked to refer to as a 'Temple of Vision'. By Speech Day 1918, Sanderson was able to give the assembled dignitaries a tour of the new building. Inside, in pride of place was a fine picture of Eric Yarrow in military uniform and on the opposite wall an inscription explaining Sir Alfred's Yarrow's gratitude to the school which moulded his son's character:

> This building has been erected by Sir Alfred Yarrow in appreciation of the good influence of this School on the character of his son, ERIC YARROW, who died fighting for his country May 8th 1915 near Ypres in the cause of right and true civilization.

The main purpose of the building in its early years was as an exhibition space with charts and maps and graphs and the work of great men, all designed and made by the boys, with a view to putting the carnage of the war in its proper long-term context. The exhibits would focus on the progress of mankind over the centuries, so that the war might be seen as only a temporary set-back in the inexorable rise of man and of mankind. In the fullness of time, of course, men might see that the war had actually been an engine of change and social improvement.

Here Am I, Send Me

The statue of the little naked boy, created by Captain Scott's (now re-married) widow, Kathleen, Lady Hilton Young, was bought by Sanderson in 1922 after it was exhibited in the Royal Academy. It was one of the last things he did before his death in June of that year. It was often claimed that the boy was modelled on the sculptress' son Peter Scott, who came up to School House in 1923, just before the consecration of the chapel. With the statue on full view outside the new building, it is easy to see why the boys would believe that young Peter was the model and no doubt he was teased accordingly. Though his mother always denied this, David Campbell O.O. claims that Peter Scott himself, when giving a lecture at Oundle, admitted that he was the model for the young boy. Whatever the truth about the statue, Kathleen Scott clearly created it as a powerful war memorial and for Sanderson, its message about the volunteering spirit of youth clearly mirrored that spirit of service and selfless sacrifice displayed by all those Oundle boys who had volunteered to fight in their country's cause.

Though now situated outside (and facing) the Yarrow Gallery, for Sanderson, it was intended to site the figure in or near the new Chapel which, in 1922, was under construction. In a sermon before the OOs, he confessed that he had done "a very dreadful thing: he had bought a statue of a little naked boy: and he intended to place it so that everyone entering the new Chapel should see it." And indeed, it was placed on its plinth next to the south door, towards the eastern end of the

Here Am I, Send Me, statue by Kathleen, Lady Hilton Young, formerly Kathleen Scott 1922.

building, in front of the foundation stone laid in 1922. The fame of the little figure soon spread and the Archdeacon of Huntingdon, Kenneth D. Knowles was inspired to write a poem:

AT OUNDLE
Within the chapel precincts of the school,
Beside the path, you who pass may see
(Old boy and young, the genius and fool)
A naked little statue stand
All eager, with uplifted hand
To answer venture's blind demand
By silent gesture – "Here am I, send me."

Here dwells the cradled spirit of our youth,
Offspring of age-long Christianity,
The reflex of the great incarnate Truth,
Prepared to meet whate'er befall,
Begrudging nothing, giving all,
Flashing the answer to the call
For ready service – "Here am I, send me."

Memorial Book 1920

In the summer of 1917, it was proposed to print a memorial book containing brief biographies and photographs of those old boys who had fallen in the war. Naturally, an appeal went out to parents to assist in making the record as complete as possible. The old boys who fell are arranged chronologically, not in the order in which they died but the order in which they arrived at Oundle. Thus Charles Edward Andrews is the first entry because he came to Oundle as early as 1887, some five years before Sanderson's appointment. The last in the sequence of increasingly younger faces is Walter Maynard Hoyle who arrived in Laxton House as late as May 1915. There are then biographies and pictures of the three members of the teaching staff who were not old boys (Tryon, Williamson and Miskin) and then an index of all the boys who served with the names of the dead highlighted in bold. Finally there are seven pages detailing the awards won by Oundle boys ranging from Victoria Crosses and Distinguished Service Orders to the Order of St. Vladimir and the Serbian Gold Medal! The two masters put in charge of collecting together the material were H. M. King and E. E. Yeld. Officially entitled Oundle Memorials of the Great War and published by the Medici Society, the book duly appeared in 1920 and the Headmaster decreed that every house should be presented with a copy, so that current and future pupils would know what their predecessors had suffered in the cause of freedom. The Latin dedication read:

Haec monumenta suis posuit pia mater alumnis, vivere quos docuit, nec minus illa, mori.

(A pious mother [the School] has set forth these monuments to her sons. She taught them how to live and no less, how to die.) Two pages later, a further inscription appears, this time in English, attempting to deny the fact of death:

They do not die
Nor lose their mortal sympathy
Nor change to us, although they change.
Death's truer name

is "Onward," no discordance in the roll
and march of that Eternal Harmony
whereto the worlds beat time.

Memorial Chapel 1923

With the rise in Oundle School numbers to 350 in 1914 (compared to just 90 when he was appointed), Sanderson had been talking about the need for a new chapel before the war began. And as that war ground on and the death toll rose, Sanderson believed that a new chapel in honour of those killed would be the perfect permanent memorial for the School to build. A meeting of parents in the Great Hall on 1 July 1917, pledged its support for the idea of building such a chapel. It was suggested that perhaps parents and old boys might fund the chancel while the Grocers would fund the rest. A few weeks later, another meeting of some 67 parents was held at Grocers' Hall. Mr Summers Hunter, who had had six sons at Oundle took the chair and reminded his audience of Oundle's international reputation in the teaching of science, as well as the importance of a fitting memorial for all those who had served in the war and especially those "who have given their lives to the country." Here the remit of the fundraising was widened: "It was finally decided that a special Old Boys' Fund should be formed to provide some part of the proposed memorial sanctuary and choir, and, when their needs were known, for the education of sons of old boys killed in the war."

Funds were quickly raised, Arthur Blomfield was again engaged as architect and construction work on the site on Milton Road, just along from the field houses, soon began in earnest. Architecturally, its simple Gothic revival style fitted in well with the Great Hall, Yarrow Gallery and Science Building, all designed by the same architect. Arthur Blomfield was the son of one famous architect, Sir Arthur Blomfield and cousin of another, Reginald Blomfield, who designed the Menin Gate and the Cross of Sacrifice in the British cemeteries on the Western Front.

By Speech Day 1920, Blomfield had drawn up a plan for a larger building than first thought because of the continuing increase in school numbers since the idea was mooted back in 1917. The total cost was now estimated at £50,000 – £60,000. Building work began early in 1922 and the foundation stone laid in a ceremony held in July of that year. The procession to the chapel site started at the Yarrow Memorial. Led by the Bishop of Peterborough and the Master of the Grocers' Company, who laid the foundation stone (still visible on the south-east corner of the building) and watched by staff, boys and many old boys, the ceremony was judged "most impressive." They sang the hymn, *Christ is our corner-stone*; the Captain of the School read a lesson from Corinthians and the occasion ended with the singing of *Jerusalem*.

The Laxtonian correspondent noted that the new memorial chapel "is not only a memorial to personal service in the past, but a call for such service in the future." For all present at this important ceremony, there was an extra reason for sadness and reflection. The Headmaster was not there. Frederick William Sanderson had died just thirty days earlier. This chapel was to be his memorial as well as a memorial for his lost boys. At the ceremony the school chaplain, Sanderson's great friend Malcolm Brown (also a Christ's College man like the Head) said simply:

Grant, O Lord, that we may all use this time of work while it is called to-day, remembering gladly those who have gone before, who have stood by us and helped us in past days, who have cheered us by their sympathy and strengthened us by their example, especially Thy servant Frederick William Sanderson.

Death of Sanderson

Sanderson died in harness on 15 June 1922, aged 65. He had not been in the best of health for some little while. He was overweight and took little exercise. In 1920 he was affected by heart trouble but his death was still sudden and unexpected. 1922 had been a good year for him. He was about to complete his thirtieth year as Headmaster of his beloved school. In February, his daughter, Mary Dorothea (known as 'Dolly Beans' by the boys!) married an old boy, indeed a School House old boy, Francis Marshall, in the parish church. That year, he also purchased that statue of a little naked boy of volunteering spirit, to beautify the school grounds and by June, he was looking forward to the laying of the foundation stone for the new chapel, fixed for mid-July. The new building had taken up much of his time in recent years, in terms of planning and fund-raising and it was, of course, a project close to his heart. On 10 June 1922, he addressed a meeting of old boys and appeared to be in excellent health and spirits. Five days later he was gone.

Fittingly, he died after delivering yet another lecture on his life's work and his life's mission – the vital importance of education and progressive educational ideas in the future development of society. It was 15 June 1922. In the morning, he enjoyed a long visit to the experimental farm at Rothamsted and in the afternoon he went to the opticians to get a new pair of spectacles. It was a hot and close afternoon. There was a large audience in the semi-circular Botanical Theatre of University College, London. Sanderson was addressing the National Union of Scientific Workers and he told them of his work and ideas and of his aspirations for the future, in a world free of warfare. He stood throughout the lecture. Although he had made nearly seven drafts of his speech back in Oundle, his lecture was a little hard to follow. Sanderson had never been very good at expressing himself with clarity; it was something his pupils noticed from his very first days at Oundle. Now he was clearly tired and out of sorts. The lecture finished, he sat down. There was applause. H. G. Wells, who was the chairman that day, rose to propose a vote of thanks:

> Then I heard a little commotion behind me and turned round to see what was the matter. Sanderson had slipped from his chair on to the platform and was lying on his back breathing hoarsely…I thought it was an epileptic fit…I could not believe it when they told me he was dead.

Later, it was Wells who was waiting for Jane Sanderson at her London hotel, the Welbeck Palace. She had been out shopping that afternoon. In a further twist of fate's knife, she and her husband had been staying at the same hotel when news of their son Roy's death came through, four years earlier.

And so the tributes to the great Headmaster rolled in. In July there appeared an 'In Memoriam' supplement to the Laxtonian magazine with essays by some who knew him well. It was decided that H. G. Wells would edit a volume of such essays for publication but arguments between him and Jane Sanderson meant that when it was published in 1923 under the title 'Sanderson of Oundle', Wells had withdrawn his name and none of the individual contributors were named. The next year, Wells, chairman at the fateful last lecture, produced his own biography of Sanderson. Perhaps his was the most fulsome in its praise of the great man. In his book, *The Story of a Great Schoolmaster*, he wrote:

> I think him beyond question the greatest man I have ever known…He was himself a very delightful mixture of subtlety and simplicity, generosity, adventurousness, imagination and steadfast purpose, and he approached the general life of our time at such an angle as to shed the most curious and profitable lights upon it. To tell his story is to reflect upon all the main educational ideas of the last half-century, and to revise our conception of the process and purpose of the modern community in relation to education. For Sanderson had a mind like an octopus, it always seemed to have a tentacle free to reach out beyond what was already held,

and his tentacles grew and radiated farther and farther. Before the end, he had come to a vision of the school as a centre for the complete reorganization of civilised life.

Consecration of the Memorial Chapel

Immediately after the laying of the Chapel's foundation stone, days after his death, the School launched a Sanderson Memorial Fund to pay for the interior fittings of the new building. Eighteen months later, on 22 November 1923, the new centre for school worship was formally consecrated by the Bishop of Peterborough. At noon that day, the ashes of Sanderson were carried by his surviving son Thomas from the old chapel to the new and placed in the niche at the eastern end prepared for them. Present at the ceremony were Sanderson's widow, Jane, their two surviving children Thomas and Dorothea and Sanderson's daughter-in-law, Margaret, his son Roy's widow, and the new Headmaster, Dr Kenneth Fisher. Later a slate plaque was put up to guard the ashes of the great man.

> Here rest the ashes of Frederick William Sanderson
> Headmaster 1892-1922
> To whom God Granted Grace to revive this ancient
> school, which is itself his memorial.

In the official consecration service, which began at 2:15, the new Head read out the Roll of Honour now comprising some 223 Oundle School names. In his address, the Bishop of Peterborough quoted Sanderson himself:

> If we are to see a new world arise out of this conflict and strife, we must go up into the mount – the new mount of vision. See, boys, that you make it after the pattern which hath been shown you on the Mount...The fact is that some new freedom, some new principle of life, some new desire to grow, has for a long time been taking root in the minds and souls of men. The urge to become more creative – the urge to gain more of life and to give more of life – becomes at last intense. And there is an immense desire to satisfy the great urge of nature. The old order passes. The gathered forces seek release. The pangs of birth are upon us. May I explain it in this way?

Procession to consecrate the Memorial Chapel, 22 November 1923.

In this School we do not believe in suppression. We believe in the creative urge. Our belief is that every one of the boys in the School has a tremendous desire to do something, and to do it well.

Fittingly, the bishop also quoted Rupert Brooke as he reflected on the sacrifices made by Oundle boys in the recent war:

Blow out, you bugles, over the rich Dead!
There's none of these so lonely and poor of
    old,
But, dying, has made us rarer gifts than gold.
These laid the world away; poured out the red
Sweet, wine of youth; gave up the years to be
Of work and joy, and that unhoped serene,
That men call age; and those who would
    have been,
Their sons, they gave, their immortality.

Frederick William Sanderson in 1920.

At the end of the service, the school prefects were presented to the bishop and the Captain of the School, Hubert Child of New House presented him with a silver key to Oundle School's new memorial for her fallen sons.

It was not until May 1926 that five memorial tablets with the names of the fallen were finally consecrated in the chapel. They were placed in the ambulatory area and entitled *Sacrifice, Faith, 1914-18, Hope* and *Service.* A new bishop of Peterborough appeared and many old boys, who had

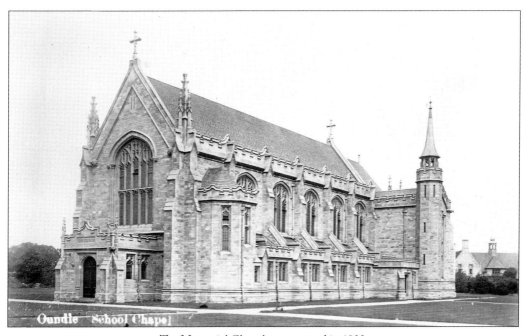

The Memorial Chapel, consecrated in 1923.

Interior of the Memorial Chapel 1923.

served in the war, joined the official procession behind the school prefects and stood in the ambulatory whilst the bishop consecrated them:

> Vouchsafe, O God, of thy goodness, to bless these Memorials now set in this hallowed place, that those whose names are here recorded, who answered the call of duty and gave their lives for us, may by their example inspire in all who worship here a like readiness to serve Thee, their King and country, and all mankind.

Just two of the fallen are remembered individually in the chapel's ambulatory. Major Geoffrey Spencer Bull, who died in unexplained circumstances in Alexandria and Captain Moira Francis Allan Maclean, victim of the Singapore Mutiny are both remembered on brass plaques. Two further, touching memorials were also added to the growing stock in the new chapel. Jane Sanderson, whose ashes would later rest with those of her husband, presented a wooden chapel stall for the use of future headmasters, in memory of her son Roy and a splendid oak pulpit, in memory of her husband. One other memorial to Roy Sanderson was the planting of an avenue of oak trees up on the playing fields.

Other memorials

In Laxton School only a wooden plaque was erected to the dead in the Long Room but not until May 1950. At such a date, it could include those killed in the second great conflict of the century as well as the names of the thirty boys known to have died in the Great War. A number of schoolboys and masters are commemorated both on the town war memorial (erected in 1920) and in the parish church, on a beautifully carved stone memorial complete with gothic tracery and the figure of Christ upon the cross. Both memorials have the names of four Laxton School boys (Curtis, McMichael, Markham and Seaton) two day boys at Oundle School (Coombs and Siddons), one Oundle School boy (Roy Sanderson) as well as four members of the Oundle School staff (Miskin, Norbury, Tryon and Williamson).

As we have seen, many more Oundelians from both schools were commemorated up and down the country in the villages, towns and cities that they called home. As well as names on war memorials, a number were also remembered in stained glass or other church furnishings, especially wall plaques. And the hundredth anniversary of the outbreak of the war has clearly prompted many around the country to do their bit to keep these memorials in good order. Church memorials to Gervase Spendlove and Harold Walton have been recently repaired with money from Old Oundelians. Others, like Stewart Ridley, Basil Coates and Christopher Gell, have their memorials in poems written in their honour, inspired by their lives and deaths. Elsewhere relatives of Oundelians killed have posted biographies, letters and military records in the school archive and on the internet. A more unusual memorial was Beanlands' damaged propeller. As we have seen, after his death, his sister was keen that the School should have this rather dramatic memorial to Oundle's most successful fighter pilot of the war. Unlike the more enduring memorials, the propeller was sadly lost at some point after the Second World War.

The school archive has done much to publicise documents and artefacts linked to Oundle's First World War experience with exhibitions, booklets and special classes. Recently it has acquired the war medals of two of Oundle's many second lieutenants, those of Randall Mason killed at Neuve Chapelle in the spring of 1915 aged 20 and those won by Norman Negretti killed at 19 near Ypres at the start of 1917. And recently, Robin Apthorpe has kindly donated the silver matchbox adorned with the School's coat of arms which his uncle, Guy Apthorpe of Sidney House (1911-15) took with him to the Front.

Commemoration

Specific acts of commemoration in honour of all Oundle's fallen sons have been a regular feature of school life both during the war – with the reading out of the lengthening Roll of Honour and the obituaries in the Laxtonian magazine – and thereafter. Remembrance Day services have been held every year in chapel

Stained Glass Window , with School Crest and Motto, in honour of Alexander Line, Laxton House 1910-14.

and the School's marching band has been a regular feature in the town's Remembrance Day service at the war memorial. Equally, for many years now, the school community has gathered in the Cloisters at 11am on 11th November itself, Union Jack at half-mast fluttering over the tower, to observe the two minutes silence, listen to the Last Post and to hear the familiar words of Binyon's poem.

One hundred years on

As the year 2014 approached, the School, partic-ularly the History Department, determined to commemorate the fallen, one hundred years on. A special memorial screen was installed in the Cloisters, near the old workshops area, to display pictures and citations of those who died. Here, on the 100th anniversary of each death, in a part of the School which would have been entirely familiar

Silver Matchbox belonging to Guy Apthorpe, Sidney House 1911-16. (Ivan Quetglas)

to them, each Oundelian is remembered in a special ceremony. On each occasion, the citation is read out by a pupil from the same House, who then places a framed picture of the deceased in the 'Memorial Archway' in the Cloisters. Another copy of the picture is then displayed in the chapel. As time passes, so the 'Memorial Archway' fills with row upon row of Oundle boys in military uniform. When the process finishes on Armistice Day 2018, both walls of the archway will be full.

In September 2014, a blue plaque was unveiled in St. George's Memorial Chapel in Ypres to commemorate the boys of Oundle School and Laxton School who fell in that sector during the war, to sit alongside plaques commemorating those who fell from other British public schools. On Armistice Day 2014, the whole School gathered for a spectacular and moving Drumhead Remembrance Service. Before the ceremony, pupils gathered in their houses to be given a special briefing on Oundle School and the War. Laxton School met in the Chapel, emphasising that all pupils are now Oundelians and that the 30 Laxton School boys killed in the conflict are equally to be remembered as their counterparts at Oundle School. The moving ceremony which followed involved the whole school community and culminated in pupils casting their poppies on the area of lawn on the south side of the chapel, where a forest of crosses, one for each life lost, had been positioned.

Also in 2014, the School commissioned a play about the wartime experiences of Cecil Lewis. *In the Shadow of Wings*, written by Old Oundelian and playwright Eddie Elks, (really Eddie Holmes) ran for three performances in the school theatre in March 2015 – a dramatic and moving tribute to one of Oundle's most famous war heroes. Two months later, the School unveiled a life-size statue of Eric Yarrow, sited on the grass to the west of the chapel, created by Oundelian Alex Johnsen (Fisher House) whilst still an Oundle pupil. It is a poignant and entirely fitting addition to the chapel grounds, to show that the current incumbents of Oundle School, still remember the sacri-fices of the First World War generation.

On 13 October 2015, a special ceremony was held in the School Cloisters to remember the five Oundelians killed that day, one hundred years before, at the Battle of Loos. Citations were read out by pupils, pictures held aloft, the last post sounded and five more Oundelians were added to the Memorial Archway. And a similar ceremony took place again on 1 July 2016 to remember the five Oundelians killed on the first day of the Somme. On at least two occasions then, large numbers of current Oundelians have gathered to remember individual pupils who made the supreme sacrifice.

Then in autumn of 2016, the entire Fourth Form, together with the CCF Marching Band visited Ypres and the Somme, holding remembrance services for Oundle's boys at the Menin Gate and the Thiepval Memorial. Each one of 17 groups of Oundle pupils visited a different cemetery on the Somme where at least one Oundelian was buried. Graves were found, citations read out and wreaths, centred on the school crest, were laid. At each cemetery a second Oundelian, whose name is on the Thiepval Memorial, was similarly remembered. For many, this was the emotional high point of the visit. Discovering and surveying an Oundle grave and finding out about the Oundelian there buried made a real connection between past and present for these pupils. Revisiting, some of the cemeteries a few weeks later, most of the pictures, wreaths and messages were still in place, pinpointing the remembered Oundelians. On the cards attached to the wreaths current pupils had left messages of thanks. On some they had signed their names in gratitude and some groups had made their presence known with similar messages in the visitors' book.

At Harponville Communal Cemetery, just 34 British soldiers lie buried. One of them is Edward Stevens, once of Grafton House. The wreath laid in late September by current pupils was gone but his connection with Oundle remains proudly proclaimed on his headstone:

God Grant Grace
Oundle School

This memorial volume, which began with Housman's poem about heroism, duty and sacrifice ends with Wilfrid Gibson's lines about the impact of the war, not only on the dead and wounded but also on all those contemporaries who survived and on all of us who were not there but who remember the sacrifice and the lives cut short. Published in 1918 and entitled simply *Lament*, it is now a testament to the enduring need we feel to commemorate the loss of all those young men

The Yarrow Statue (unveiled 2015) stands to the west of the Memorial Chapel. (Author)

Headstone of Edward
Stevens, Grafton House
1913-16. (Author)

Wreath placed at the
headstone of Harold
Coates, Dryden House
1909-14, by Oundle
pupils, September
2016. (Author)

who marched away to play their part in the Great War, amongst whom, the boys of Oundle School and Laxton School can proudly take their place.

> We who are left, how shall we look again
> Happily on the sun, or feel the rain
> Without remembering how they who went
> Ungrudgingly, and spent
> Their all for us loved, too, the sun and rain?
>
> A bird upon the rain-wet lilac sings –
> But we, how shall we turn to little things
> And listen to the birds and winds and streams
> Made holy by their dreams
> Nor feel the heartbreak in the heart of things?

Cloisters Memorial Archway 2016. (Ella Ingram)

Appendix I

The Fallen

	House/dates	rank/regiment at death	date of death	age	where died/fatally wounded/where buried/commemorated
GERALD WALLACE ADAM	G 1914-16	2 Yorkshire Regiment	10 August 1919	20	Archangel/Archangel Memorial, Russia
JOHN HIRST AINLEY	S 1913-16	2 Rifle Brigade	21 June 1918	19	Béthune/Le Vertannoy Cemetery, Béthune, France
DOUGLAS JAMES AITCHISON	D 1911-13	2 RFC/Royal Air Force	17 April 1918	21	Blood poisoning, Hampstead/Beckenham, Kent
JOHN TURNBULL ANDERSON	L.S. 1909-16	2 Machine Gun Corps	5 October 1917	19	Passchendaele/Tyne Cot Memorial, Ypres, Belgium
CHARLES EDWARD ANDREWS	Lx 1887-89	M Highland Light Inf	25 October 1916	45	Fricourt, Somme/Peake Wood Cemetery, Fricourt, Fr.
EDWARD NORMAN ANDREWS	Sch 1911-16	2 East Kent Regiment	23 August 1918	19	Albert, Somme/Daours Cemetery, France
*DOUGLAS WILLIAM ARMITAGE	Lx 1906-12	2 Royal Sussex Regiment	25 September 1915	22	Loos/Loos Memorial, France
*FRANK RHODES ARMITAGE	Lx 1896-02	C Royal Army Medical Corps	30 July 1917	34	Ypres/Brandhoek Cemetery, Ypres, Belgium
*JAMES ALLAN ROSS ARMITAGE	Lx 1901-07	C West Yorkshire Regiment	19 July 1919	30	Disease, Egypt/St Leonards, Sussex
HAROLD WILFRED ASBREY	L.S. 1908-12	P Royal Sussex Regiment	13 August 1917	20	Passchendaele/Klein-Vierstraat Cemetery, Ypres, B.
EDWARD LEICESTER STUART ASTWOOD	D 1910-11	2 Royal Fusiliers	20 September 1916	21	Flers-Courcelette, Somme/St. Sever Cemetery, Rouen, Fr.
JOHN BROADWOOD ATKINSON	G 1909-13	L Royal Irish Fusiliers	24 December 1915	21	Gallipoli/Chatby Military Cemetery, Alexandria, Egypt
LANGLEY LATTON ATTWOOD	D 1906-10	2 Royal Garrison Artillery	12 August 1917	24	Passchendaele/Vlamertinghe Cemetery, Ypres, Belgium
HENRY KENYON BAGSHAW	N 1908-09	L Duke of Wellington's Reg.	13 April 1918	26	Lys, Ypres/Tyne Cot Memorial, Ypres, Belgium
ARNOLD RENNIE BAKER	N 1908-12	2 Royal Flying Corps	16 August 1917	23	Lille/Lincelles Cemetery, Lille, France
AUSTIN PROVOST BALDWIN	Day 1893-99	2 Suffolk Regiment	27 September 1918	35	Flesquières, Cambrai/Lowrie Cem. Havrincourt, Fr.
ROBERT FRANCIS COOPER BALLARD	D 1911-13	2 Bedfordshire Regiment	30 July 1916	20	Trônes Wood, Somme/Thiepval Memorial, France
MAURICE BARBER	G 1907-10	C York and Lancaster Reg.	26 November 1917	25	Cambrai/Cambrai Memorial, Louverval, France
THOMAS BEECH BARTON	G 1913-16	P King's Liverpool Regiment	30 June 1918	18	Pneumonia, Oswestry/Gresford Churchyard, Wrexham
*HUGH WILLIAM EAMES BARWELL	S 1907-11	C Royal Flying Corps	25 March 1918	25	Somme?/Air Services Memorial, Arras, France
*HUMPHREY EAMES BARWELL	S 1912-16	2 Royal Flying Corps	3 February 1918	19	Albert, Somme/ Doullens Cemetery, France
JOSEPH BAXTER	L.S. 1907-11	LS Northants. Regiment	26 September 1915	20	Loos/Loos Memorial, France
BERNARD PAUL GASCOIGNE BEANLANDS	By/Sch 1909-14	C RFC/Royal Air Force	8 May 1919	21	Accident, Northolt/Sevenoaks Cemetery, Kent
*HENRY BERNERS BEGG	Sch 1907-13	2 Royal Flying Corps	23 November 1916	22	Bapaume, Somme/Flying Services Memorial, Arras, Fr.
*RIVERS GORDON BEGG	Sch 1910-15	2 Royal Naval Air Service	17 July 1917	20	Otranto/Otranto Town Cemetery, Italy
CHRISTOPHER DOBREE BENSON	G 1908-13	2 Royal Fusiliers	18 February 1917	22	Miraumont, Somme/Varennes Military Cemetery, Fr.
FRANK GALE BERRILL	S 1910-15	L Royal Field Artillery	28 September 1918	21	Bailleul, Arras/Duisans British Cemetery, Arras, France
MICHAEL BEVERLEY	Sch 1890-91	P Australian Infantry	27 March 1918	44	Spoil Bank, Ypres/Bedford House Cemetery, Ypres, B.
GERALD MAURICE GOSSET BIBBY	Xby 1911-14	2 Royal Flying Corps	6 March 1917	19	Vimy Ridge/Barlin Cemetery Extension, Béthune, Fr.

	House/dates	rank/regiment at death	date of death	age	where died/fatally wounded/where buried/commemorated
JOHN HOBART BIRD	Lx 1903	L West Surreys	26 October 1914	25	1st Ypres/Menin Gate, Ypres, Belgium
WILLIAM JOHN BOARD	D 1914-16	2 Royal Field Artillery	22 September 1918	19	Doiran, Salonika/Sarigol Milit. Cem. Kriston, Greece
PAUL BOND	Lx 1887-88	P Royal Fusiliers	30 April 1916	44	Loos/Tranchée de Mecknes Cemetery, Aix-Noulette, Fr.
FRANK BOOTH	G 1915-17	2 Royal Naval Air Service	3 January 1918	18	Arras/Cabaret-Rouge Cemetery, Souchez, France
GUY EDWIN BOSTOCK	D 1909-13	C Royal Munster Fusiliers	30 January 1916	21	Loos/Mazingarbe Cemetery, France
CHARLES BAILEY BOUCHER	S 1905-09	L Lancs. and Yorks. Reg.	9 August 1915	24	Hooge, Ypres/Menin Gate, Ypres, Belgium
ROBERT CHARLES BRAGG	D 1909-11	L Royal Field Artillery	2 September 1915	22	Gallipoli/buried at sea/Helles Memorial, Turkey
FRANK BRAY	Sch 1912-16	2 Royal Naval Air Service	15 July 1917	18	Arras/Arras Flying Memorial, France
*VICTOR GEORGE BRINDLEY	D 1905-09	2 South African Inf./RAF	30 August 1918	27	Aerial combat, Somme/Villers Bretonneux Mil. C. Fr.
*WALTER EDWIN KNIGHT BRINDLEY	D 1906-09	T S. African Imp. L. Horse	24 December 1922	30	Wounds, British East Africa/South Africa
CECIL HOYLE BROADBENT	Sch 1895-00	L Yorkshire Light Infantry	1 March 1916	34	Accident, Somme/Warloy-Baillon Cemetery, France
JOSEPH HUGH TURNER BROCKLEBANK	G 1906-07	T Lincolnshire Yeomanry	3 November 1915	24	Western Mediterranean, U-boat/Oran, Algeria
JAIME CAVEL BROWN	Lx 1912-15	Argyll/Suth. Highlanders	24 March 1918	21	Pozières, Somme/Pozières Memorial, France
WILLIAM JOHN HENRY BROWN	D 1906-09	L Norfolk Regiment	4 September 1916	24	Guillemont, Somme/Thiepval Memorial, France
CHARLES RALPH BUCKMASTER	S 1905-08	Returning home to enlist	4 April 1915	24	Drowned off Shetland Isles/Lost at sea
GEOFFREY SPENCER BULL	Lx 1891-98	M Vaughan's Rifles	25 March 1916	35	Alexandria/Chatby Military Cemetery, Alexandria, Egypt
HOWARD CHURCH BURBIDGE	S 1900-02	2 East Yorkshire Reg.	13 September 1916	26	Chocques/Chocques Cemetery, Béthune, France
*CLIVE BURRELL	D 1907-10	D Royal Horse Artillery	23 November 1918	25	Influenza, Valenciennes/Valenciennes Cemetery, France
*PERCY EDMUND BURRELL	D 1896-99	2 South Wales Borderers	21 August 1915	33	Chocolate Hill, Suvla, Gallipoli/Helles Memorial, Turkey
*SIDNEY BURRELL	D 1897-00	2 Middlesex Regiment	20 July 1916	32	Somme/Heilly Station Cemetery, Méricourt-L'Abbé, Fr.
FREDERICK WILLIAM BUTCHER	G 1909-15	R Royal Irish Rifles	9 August 1917	20	Passchendaele/Menin Gate, Ypres, Belgium
GEOFFREY CLIFFORD CALVERT	N 1910-11	L King's Own Yorkshire L.I.	15 January 1919	24	Typhoid, pneumonia/Maubeuge Cemetery, France
CHALMERS CARMICHAEL	S 1901-04	2 South African Army	15 July 1916	29	Delville Wood, Somme/Thiepval Memorial, France
EZRA HOWARD CARTER	L.S. 1907-09	P Northants. Regiment	27 September 1915	21	Loos/Loos Memorial, France
ERIC CHALKER	D 1909-12	L Royal Field Artillery	19 July 1916	23	Caterpillar Wood, Longueval, Somme/Thiepval Mem. Fr.
RONALD CHRISTIE	Sch 1911-13	C Royal Garrison Artillery	12 April 1918	22	Vailly-sur-Aisne, Soissons/Vailly British Cemetery, Fr.
WILLIAM MICHELL CLARKE	G 1911-15	2 S. Midlands Royal Eng.	12 November 1916	19	Martinpuich, Somme/Martinpuich Cemetery, France
CHARLES CLAYSON	Bandmaster	CSM Northants. Reg.	22 October 1915	U	Disease, Gallipoli/Alexandria Military Cem. Egypt
BASIL MONTGOMERY COATES	N 1910-12	2 Rifle Brigade	7 September 1915	21	Ypres/Ploegsteert Memorial, Ypres, Belgium

	House/dates	rank/regiment at death	date of death	age	where died/fatally wounded/where buried/commemorated
HAROLD BREARLEY COATES	D 1909-14	2 Yorkshire Regiment	1 July 1916	20	Somme/Dantzig Alley Cemetery, Mametz, France
JOHN COATES	D 1904-06	2 Yorkshire Yeomanry	15 August 1918	29	Hazebrouk/Grand Hasard Cem. Morebecque, France
BERNARD VALENTINE COLCHESTER	Lx 1903-05	2 Bedfordshire Regiment	24 April 1917	27	Greenland Hill, Arras/Arras Memorial, France
THOMAS COOK	Lx 1902-05	L Essex Reg. (att. Lincolns)	2 October 1915	28	Green Knoll, Suvla, Gallipoli/Helles Memorial, Turkey
ARTHUR ERSKINE GURNEY COOMBS	Day 1898-02	L HMS *Hawke*	15 October 1914	26	*Hawke* sunk by U-boat/Lost at sea, North Sea
HENRY HAYR COX	Lx 1910-14	2 Royal Field Artillery	16 May 1917	20	Vimy Ridge/Chocques Cemetery, Béthune, France
ALEXANDER BASIL CRAWFORD	Lx 1903-08	C West Yorkshire Regiment	10 May 1916	24	Neuve Chapelle/Richebourg L'Avoue, France
CLIFDEN JAMES CROCKETT	S 1909-11	L Royal Warwickshire Reg.	18 August 1916	22	Somme/Pozières British Cemetery, Pozières, France
JOHN COLIN CROSBIE	D 1911-15	L Royal Flying Corps	7 September 1917	20	St. Omer/Aire Cemetery, St. Omer, France
HENRY NEVILLE CURTIS	L.S. 1909-14	2 Royal Flying Corps	25 July 1917	18	Lille/Mouvaux Cemetery, Lille, France
SYDNEY GUY DAVEY	N 1908-12	M Machine Gun Corps	25 March 1918	24	Ervillers, Bapaume/Arras Memorial, France
IVOR THEOPHILUS DAVIES	By/Lx 05-13	L Ox. and Bucks. L.I.	22 June 1915	20	Hooge, Ypres/Menin Gate, Ypres, Belgium
HUGH COURTNEY DAVIS	N 1911-15	2 Royal Flying Corps	5 August 1916	19	St. Omer/Aire Cemetery, St. Omer, France
JOHN DENISON	S 1913-17	2 RNAS/Royal Air Force	13 April 1918	18	Lys, Armentières/Pernes British Cemetery, France
CLAYTON HOWARD DE VINE	D 1900-02	L Canadian Infantry	3 June 1917	32	Avion, Vimy/Vimy Memorial, France
JOHN DICKINSON	G 1906-09	L Royal Field Artillery	8 April 1917	25	Vimy/Ecoivres Military Cemetery, Mont-St.Eloi, Fr.
JAMES EVELYN BEVAN DIXON	Lx 1907-13	C Royal Warwickshire Reg.	1 July 1916	22	Somme/Serre Road Cemetery No. 2, Serre, France
GEOFFREY BOLES DONALDSON	N 1907-12	C Royal Warwickshire Reg.	19 July 1916	22	Neuve Chapelle/Ploegsteert Memorial, Ypres, Belgium
JOHN MILES DUNWOODY	Lx 1911-13	2 Royal Dublin Fusiliers	4 May 1917	20	Drowned, Ligurian Sea, U-boat/Savona Mem. Savona
SYDNEY TRUMAN DUROSE	S 1907-10	C Sherwood Foresters	2 April 1917	24	Le Verguier, Somme/Jeancourt Cemetery, Péronne, Fr.
CHARLES BERTRAM DYSON	G 1909-14	L East Lancashire Regiment	26 March 1918	21	Gommecourt, Somme/Beaulencourt Military Cem. Fr.
SAMUEL FRANK EDMONDS	Lx 1893-98	T East African Rifles	25 September 1914	35	British East Africa/British Memorial, Nairobi
NORMAN STUART EDMONDSTONE	D 1913-14	L Queen's Westmin. Rifles	7 November 1917	21	Kauwukah, Gaza/Beersheba War Cemetery, Israel
JOHN EDMUND EMTAGE	S 1912-17	L Royal Air Force	9 August 1918	19	Arras/Flying Services Memorial, Arras, France
ALFRED CECIL ENGLISH	D 1900-03	2 Artists' Rifles (London R.)	30 December 1917	30	Marcoing, Cambrai/Thiepval Memorial, France
DONALD EWEN	S 1901-05	P Royal Army Medical Corps	13 October 1915	28	Loos/Loos Memorial, France
GEORGE JOHN FENCHELLE	N 1908-10	2 Royal Sussex Regiment	30 June 1916	21	Neuve Chapelle/Cabaret-Rouge Cemetery, France
MAURICE FRANK FOULDS	L.S. 1909-15	2 London Regiment	30 October 1917	20	Passchendaele/Tyne Cot Memorial, Ypres, Belgium

	House/dates	rank/regiment at death	date of death	age	where died/fatally wounded/where buried/commemorated
WILFRED HENRY GANN	L.S. 1907-08	P Australian Infantry	19 October 1917	22	Passchendaele/Nine Elms Cemetery, Ypres, Belgium
GEOFFREY ATKINSON GAZE	Lx 1896-00	C London Regiment	15 September 1916	35	Longueval, Somme/Caterpillar Valley Cemetery, Fr.
CHRISTOPHER STOWELL GELL	Xby 1911-15	2 W. Yorkshire Regiment	18 September 1916	19	Serre, Somme/Thiepval Memorial, France
STANLEY OSWYN GEORGE	L.S. 1908-09	LS Bedfordshire Regiment	3 May 1917	28	Arras/Arras Memorial, France
ARTHUR GODFREY-PAYTON	S 1904-06	C Royal Warwickshire Reg.	29 August 1916	27	Thiepval, Somme/Puchevillers Cemetery, France
ALAN GODSAL	By/Sch 05-13	2 Rifle Brigade	30 July 1915	21	Sanctuary Wood, Ypres/Menin Gate, Ypres, Belgium
COLIN HAROLD GODWIN	Xby 1909-11	2 York and Lancaster Reg.	1 July 1916	22	Serre, Somme/Thiepval Memorial, France
EDWARD DERMOT LEDLIE GONNER	Sch 1907-11	L Royal Warwickshire Reg.	2 July 1918	25	Influenza, Newcastle/Willaston, Cheshire
ARTHUR JAMES GOODFELLOW	Sch 1902-04	C Lancashire Fusiliers	7 August 1915	28	Gallipoli/Pink Farm Cemetery, Helles, Turkey
ERIC ANTONY ROLLO GORE-BROWNE	S 1906-08	M King's African Rifles	3 July 1918	28	Portuguese East Africa/Mombasa British Mem. Kenya
DUNCAN HEPBURN GOTCH	S 1905-10	2 Worcestershire Regiment	11 March 1915	23	Neuve Chapelle/Le Touret Memorial, France
*CHARLES SHORTLAND GRAY	N/Xby 06-09	C Lincolnshire Regiment	13 October 1915	23	Loos/Loos Memorial, France
*JOHN PARNWELL GRAY	Xby 1911-15	L Royal Field Artillery	13 September 1918	20	Accident, France/Stamford Cemetery, Lincolnshire
*JOHN GREAVES	D 1912-14	Unknown	Unknown	U	Unknown
*NICHOLAS GREAVES	D 1912-14	2 Royal Air Force	28 October 1918	20	Shot down, Tournai/Tournai Communal Cemetery, B.
GERALD HENRY GREENFIELD	S 1910-15	2 Royal Field Artillery	17 August 1917	20	Passchendaele/Lijssenthoek Cemetery, Ypres, Belgium
HUGH CHARLES GREENHALGH	G 1904-06	2 Middlesex Regiment	5 May 1917	26	Fins, Somme/Fins New British Cemetery, France
DOUGLAS HOWARD WILSON GREENWAY	Lx 1906-07	2 Worcestershire Regiment	17 October 1915	24	Gallipoli/Azmak Cemetery, Suvla, Turkey
*HUGH CECIL GRUMMITT	D 1913-15	2 East Yorkshire Regiment	25 March 1919	20	Influenza, Hull/Hornsea, Yorkshire
*JOSEPH ROLAND GRUMMITT	D 1907-11	L East Yorkshire Regiment	14 November 1918	24	Influenza, Colchester/Hornsea, Yorkshire
JOHN HUTCHISON GULLILAND	S 1906-11	C Essex Regiment	18 July 1916	23	Ypres/Lijssenthoek Cemetery, Ypres, Belgium
ROBERT AINSLIE HAMILTON	Sch 1909-12	L King's Own Light Infantry	28 March 1918	23	Pozières, Somme/Pozières Memorial, France
JOHN ARMITAGE HARTLEY	D 1908-10	2 Duke of Wellington's Reg.	19 December 1915	22	Ypres/Lijssenthoek Cemetery, Ypres, Belgium
WILLIAM EDWIN HARTLEY	L.S. 1899-05	2 Artists' Rifles (Lond. Reg.)	1 October 1915	27	Loos/Loos Memorial, France
ROBERT CLIVE HARVEY	By/Xby 08-12	L Leicestershire Regiment	13 October 1915	19	Loos/Loos Memorial, France
EDWARD JOHN HASSARD	D 1910-14	L Royal Field Artillery	7 November 1918	23	Influenza, Marylebone/Norwood Cem. London
*LAWRENCE COLLIER HATCH	Sch 1907-11	L Durham Light Infantry	27 September 1915	21	Loos/Loos Memorial, France
*PHILIP RANDALL HATCH	Sch 1906-10	L East Kent Regiment	7 October 1916	24	Le Sars, Somme/Thiepval Memorial, France

	House/dates	rank/regiment at death	date of death	age	where died/fatally wounded/where buried/commemorated
JOHN CHRISTOPHER HEBBLETHWAITE	G 1911-14	L Royal Field Artillery	22 June 1916	20	Ypres/Vlamertinghe Cemetery, Ypres, Belgium
GUY STEVENSON HEWITT	G 1912-15	2 Artists' Rifles (London Reg.)	8 March 1918	19	Ribecourt, Cambrai/Arras Memorial, France
ROBERT WILLIAM HOARE	L.S. 1899-04	C Worcestershire Regiment	9 October 1917	31	Passchendaele/Poelcapelle British Cemetery, Ypres, B.
HERBERT EDWARD HOBBS	Lx 1909	2 Northumberland Fusiliers	25 May 1915	20	2nd Ypres/Menin Gate, Ypres, Belgium
JOHN HOLLICK	S 1913-17	2 RNAS/Royal Air Force	18 May 1918	19	Sailly-sur-Lys, Armentières/Flying Services M. Arras, Fr.
COLIN HOLT HOOPER	D 1907-11	L London Regiment	28 September 1915	22	Loos/Le Tréport Military Cemetery, France
PETER HOPCRAFT	N 1915	L RAF/Independent AF	28 October 1918	19	Shot down, Nancy/Charmes Milit. Cem. Essegney, Fr.
EDWARD FAVILL GEORGE HOPKINS	D 1912-14	2 Royal Field Artillery	30 March 1917	19	Hendecourt, Arras/Aizecourt-le-Bas, Somme, Fr.
HUGH JAMES PEARSON HOPKINSON	S 1906-09	L Royal Engineers	5 November 1915	23	Gallipoli/Hill 10 Cemetery, Azmak, Turkey
WILLIAM HORSFORD	L.S. 1905-09	P Lincolnshire Regiment	4 October 1917	21	Passchendaele/Tyne Cot Memorial, Ypres, Belgium
WALTER MAYNARD HOYLE	Lx 1915-16	2 Norfolk Regiment	11 May 1917	18	Pneumonia, Weybridge/Golders Green Memorial, Lond.
EDWARD HUNT	L.S. 1908-10	G Royal Field Artillery	3 July 1917	23	Achiet-le-Grand, Arras/Achiet Cemetery, Arras, France
ALFRED JOHN AVALON HUTCHINS	Lx 1912-15	2 Royal Sussex Regiment	22 March 1918	20	Boesinghe, Ypres/Harlebeke New Military Cem. B.
RICHARD NYNIAN IRWIN	S 1911-14	L Gloucestershire Regiment	6 March 1917	19	Salonika, Macedonia/Karasouli Cemetery, Polykastro, Greece
CEDRIC ARTHUR JACKSON	G 1908-10	L Royal Flying Corps	5 November 1917	24	Accident, Dover/Christchurch Churchyard, Dore, Yorks.
JOHN MONTAGUE HAMMICK JACKSON	By/Xby 1907-13	L Ox. and Bucks. Light Inf.	18 August 1915	20	Ypres/Littleham, Devon
JOHN HARVEY JACOBS	N 1907-09	C Royal Fusiliers	11 October 1918	26	St. Aubert, Cambrai/St. Aubert British Cemetery, Fr.
FRANK PASS JOHNSON	L.S. 1910-14	G Tank Corps	5 December 1917	19	Unknown/Rethel French National Cemetery, Rheims, Fr.
RAYNER HARVEY JOHNSON	G 1911-14	M Royal Reg. of Artillery	27 September 1918	21	Cambrai/Louverval Milit. Cem. Doignes, France
KENNETH CHAMPION JONES	Sch 1904-09	L East Lancashire Regiment	14 July 1916	25	Beaumont Hamel, Somme/Thiepval Memorial, Fr.
JOHN HARVEY BAINBRIDGE KAYSS	Sch 1908-10	P Princess Patricia's Can. L. I.	25 March 1918	23	Accident, Shorncliffe, Kent/Wigton, Cumbria
LEONARD SHELDON KENCH	D 1902-06	C Royal Warwickshire Reg.	29 June 1916	27	Neuve Chapelle/ Longuenesse Cemetery, France
GILBERT KENNEDY	Sch 1899-03	C Royal Munster Fusiliers	11 December 1918	33	Influenza/Les Barques Military Cem. Sangatte, Fr.
PHILIP CHABERT KIDD	Xby 1905-06	L Yorkshire Regiment	30 October 1914	22	1st Ypres/Menin Gate, Ypres, Belgium
WILLIAM OLIVER REDMAN KING	Sch 1900-06	L Royal Army Medical Corps	28 February 1919	32	Influenza, pneumonia, Leeds/unknown
GEORGE NELSON KINGTON	L.S. 1909-10	P Northamptonshire Reg.	10 July 1917	20	Nieuport/Nieuport Memorial, Belgium
ALBERT EVELYN FAIRFAX KYNASTON	Lx 1895-98	Ship's Surgeon, HM.S Devonshire	13 October 1914	33	Dunskaith House/ Naval Cemetery, Cromarty, Scotland

	House/dates	rank/regiment at death	date of death	age	where died/fatally wounded/where buried/commemorated
JOHN LAUGHTON	S 1906-09	U South African Volunteers	19 July 1918	26	Long illness, South Africa/unknown
CECIL LAWRENCE	L.S. 1908	U Northants. Yeomanry?	1917?	23?	Unknown
AUDLEY ANDREW DOWELL LEE	N 1908-14	C Leicestershire Regiment	1 October 1917	22	Passchendaele/Tyne Cot Memorial, Ypres, Belgium
CECIL DARLEY FARRAN LEECH	Xby 1906-09	L North Staffordshire Reg.	2 March 1918	25	Accident, Attoc, India/Karachi Memorial, Pakistan
JOHN YOUNG ALEXANDER LINE	Lx 1910-14	2 North Staffordshire Reg.	13 March 1915	20	Neuve Chapelle/Merville Cemetery, France
SEISYTH HUGH LLOYD	Lx 1912-16	2 Royal Naval Air Service	14 August 1917	19	Passchendaele/Flying Services Memorial, Arras, France
CLARENCE ESPENT LYON-HALL	N 1909-14	L South Wales Borderers	7 July 1916	20	La Boisselle, Somme/Bécourt Cemetery, France
EDWARD CROZIER MacBRYAN	S 1908-12	2 Somerset Light Infantry	1 July 1916	22	Beaumont Hamel, Somme/Thiepval Memorial, France
WILLIAM JOHN MacCOMBIE	G 1906-10	C King's Own Scottish Bord.	17 July 1916	24	Longueval, Somme/Thiepval Memorial, France
MOIRA FRANCIS MACLEAN	Sch 1897-00	C Malay States Guides	15 February 1915	31	Singapore Mutiny/Kranji War Cemetery, Singapore
DOUGLAS WILLIAM McMICHAEL	L.S.1902?-12	L Bedfordshire Regiment	20 April 1916	23	Ypres/Essex Farm Cemetery, Ypres, Belgium
ROBERT LEONARD MANN	N 1910-14	2 Royal Welsh Fusiliers	9 October 1916	19	Ypres/Essex Farm Cemetery, Ypres, Belgium
HERBERT GEORGE MILES MARKHAM	L.S.1909-14	P Royal West Surrey Reg.	10 November 1918	20	Influenza?PoW Namur/Belgrade Cemetery, Namur, Bel.
STANLEY JOHN MARLOW	N 1910-12	L Northamptonshire Reg.	19 April 1917	21	Gaza/Gaza Military Cemetery, Palestinian Territory
WALTER GIBSON MARSDEN	Sch 1898-05	C Royal Army Medical Corps	19 December 1920	34	Illness, India, London/Bromsgrove, Worcestershire
RANDALL STEWART MASON	Xby 1907-12	2 Rifle Brigade	14 March 1915	20	Neuve Chapelle/Neuve Chapelle British Cemetery, Fr.
ALEXANDER PERCIVAL MATHESON	D 1910-12	L Royal Flying Corps	13 July 1917	22	Oudenaarde/Oudenaarde Cemetery, Belgium
WILLIAM REGINALD MATTHEWS	S 1895	2 South African Rifles	April 1916	37	Accident/South Africa
IAN MOREHOUSE METCALFE	Xby 1910-14	L Worcestershire Regiment	1 November 1917	20	Festubert/Loos Memorial, France
FREDERICK RAYMOND MILHOLLAND	N 1909-14	C Yorkshire Regiment	27 February 1918	22	Chocques/Chocques Military Cemetery, Béthune, Fr.
DONALD FARROW MILNE	G 1910-12	L Manchester Regiment	5 November 1917	22	Tikrit, Mesopotamia/Basra Memorial, Iraq
MAURICE JAMES MISKIN	Staff 1914	M N. Staffs. Reg./Tank Cor.	17 October 1918	26	Honnechy, Cambrai/Honnechy British Cemetery, France
NOEL CAMPBELL KYRLE MONEY	Sch 1897-00	M Connaught Rangers	7 September 1915	32	Gallipoli/Pieta Military Cemetery, Malta
RICHARD HENRY MOORE	Lx 1913-16	2 Royal Field Artillery	21 March 1918	19	Bapaume, Somme/Grevillers Brit. Cem. Bapaume, Fr.
CHARLES FREDERICK WILLIAM MORBEY	S 1903-05	C Suffolk Regiment	9 August 1917	28	Monchy, Arras/Monchy-le-Preux, Arras, France
JAMES OUTRAM MORRIS	S 1902-05	Cp Artists' Rifles (London R.)	30 October 1917	31	Passchendaele/Tyne Cot Memorial, Ypres, Belgium
GEORGE WILLIAM MOUNTNEY	L.S. 1904-09	LC Northamptonshire Reg.	14 July 1916	25	Trônes Wood, Somme/Thiepval Memorial, France
KENNETH JOHN WHARTON MOWBRAY	D 1910-14	2 Suffolk Regiment	9 April 1917	20	Arras/Tilloy British Cemetery, Arras, France
HENRY COLLISTER MULOCK	N 1907-08	L Royal Flying Corps	15 February 1917	25	Somme/Grove Town Cemetery, Meaulte, Somme, Fr.

⁇⁇⁇⁇

	House/dates	rank/regiment at death	date of death	age	where died/fatally wounded/where buried/commemorated
GEORGE GEOFFREY NEEDHAM	Sch 1907-13	L Lancashire Fusiliers	22 August 1915	20	Gallipoli/Hill 10 Cemetery, Suvla, Turkey
NORMAN CHARLES ACHILLE NEGRETTI	Lx 1911-14	2 Middlesex Regiment	30 January 1917	19	Ypres/Dickebusch Military Cemetery, Ypres, Belgium
THOMAS STANLEY NEWELL	By/D 1906-14	2 Cheshire Regiment	5 July 1915	19	Dickebusch, Ypres/Bailleul Communal Cemetery, Fr.
JOHN SHERWOOD NEWMAN	N/G 1908-12	2 East Yorks. Regiment	9 August 1915	21	Suvla, Gallipoli/Helles Memorial, Turkey
FRANCIS CAMPBELL NORBURY	Lx 96-01	C King's Royal Rifles	8 January 1915	32	Béthune/Le Touret Cem., Richebourg, Béthune, France
ALFRED VERNON OLIVER-JONES	Xby 1906-10	2 Royal Flying Corps	21 July 1916	24	Beaulencourt, Somme/Flying Servs. Mem. Arras, Fr.
WALTER LIONEL PAINE	Sch 1894-00	C Lancashire Fusiliers	4 June 1915	34	Gallipoli/Twelve Tree Copse Cemetery, Helles, Turkey
ROBERT WILLIAM PEARSON	D 1894-97	C Durham Light Infantry	15 May 1915	34	2nd Ypres/Ypres Reservoir Cemetery, Belgium
FRANCIS GIFFORD PERKINS	L.S. 1910-13	P Royal Fusiliers	10 October 1916	20	Le Transloy, Somme/Thiepval Memorial, France
ALAN LUIS PINK	Lx/N 1911-15	L Royal Air Force	30 October 1918	20	Shot down near Ypres/Kooigem Cem., Kortrijk, B.
*ARTHUR LESLIE PLATTS	Lx 1904-10	L Suffolk Regiment	20 July 1916	25	Delville Wood, Somme/Thiepval Memorial, France
*REGINALD HARDY PLATTS	Lx 1901-05	L (Royal Garrison Artillery)	31 May 1918	31	Accident, Whiffen Labs. London/Wandsworth, London
REGINALD FREDERICK DESMOND PLUNKETT	Sch 1912-16	L Gurkha Rifles	6 September 1918	20	Accident, drowned, Mesopotamia/Basra Mem. Iraq
JOHN ERIC STIRLING PRITCHARD	S 1910-15	2 Royal Field Artillery	27 October 1917	20	Passchendaele/Lijssenthoek Cemetery, Ypres, Belgium
NORMAN FELLOWES PRYNNE	D 1913-15	2 Devonshire Regiment	24 April 1917	19	Petit Couronne, Salonika/Dorian Mem. Macedonia
WILLIAM DONALD RABY	G 1913-17	2 Royal Welsh Fusiliers	8 October 1918	19	Villers Outreaux, Cambrai/Prospect Hill Cem. Gouy, Fr.
ARTHUR TEMPLETON RAILTON	Xby 1906-09	L Seaforth Highlanders	9 May 1915	24	Aubers Ridge/Cabaret-Rouge Cemetery, Souchez, Fr.
DONALD WYAND RAMSAY	Sch 1911-15	2 Royal Naval Air Service	7 July 1917	20	Lille/Bousbeques Cemetery, France
OLIVER FRANCIS RANDS	Lx 1909-13	P Royal Fusiliers	3 May 1917	22	Monchy-le Preux, Arras/Arras Memorial, France
WILFRID REDFERN	Sch 1898-04	C East Yorkshire Regiment	22 March 1918	30	Beaulencourt, Somme/Beaulencourt Milit. Cem. Fr.
WILFRED DEXTER REES	L.S. 1909-12	P Machine Gun Corps	29 May 1918	20	Aisne/Soissons Memorial, France
ERIC GEORGE RENTON	G 1913-17	2 RFC/Royal Air Force	14 August 1918	18	Rosières, Amiens/Heath Cemetery, Harbonniers, Fr.
JOHN HENRY WILCOCK RHODES	D 1894-97	P Australian Imperial Army	4 October 1915	34	Gallipoli/Lone Pine Memorial, Anzac Cove, Turkey
JAMES STUART RICKETTS	D 1909-13	2 Royal Field Artillery	5 October 1918	24	Beaurevoir, Cambrai/St. Sever Cemetery, Rouen, Fr.
STEWART GORDON RIDLEY	G 1910-14	L Royal Flying Corps	18 June 1916	19	Libyan Desert/Cairo War Memorial Cemetery, Egypt
JAMES TREVOR RILEY	N 1908-11	L Duke of Wellington's R.	3 September 1916	22	Guillemont, Somme/Thiepval Memorial, France
GUY HEPWORTH ROBERTS	N/G 1907-11	C King's Own Yorks. L.Inf.	22 November 1917	25	Cambrai/Rocquigny-Equancourt C. Manancourt, Fr.
JOHN APPLEBY ROBSON	L.S. 1912-14	C Northants. Yeomanry	13 April 1917	18	Arras/Duisans Military Cemetery, Etrun, France

	House/dates	rank/regiment at death	date of death	age	where died/fatally wounded/where buried/commemorated
RICHARD IVAN ROBSON	Sch 1904–09	C Royal Irish Rifles	18 August 1917	26	Passchendaele/Lijssenthoek Cemetery, Ypres, Belgium
JOHN VERCOE ROGERS	S 1898–00	L Winnipeg Grenadiers	27 September 1918	32	Bourlon Wood, Cambrai/Quarry Wood Cem. Arras, Fr.
LESLIE ERIC RUNDELL	Sch 1910–13	L London Regiment	11 December 1917	21	Bapaume, Somme/Ruyaucourt, Bapaume, France
EVAN WILMOT HARLEY RUSSELL	S 1907–09	P Honourable Artillery Co.	16 June 1915	22	Hooge, Ypres/Menin Gate, Ypres, Belgium
JOHN WILLIAM BINFIELD RUSSELL	By/Sch 08–14	2 Duke of Wellington's Reg.	7 July 1916	19	Mametz Wood, Somme/Thiepval Memorial, France
GORDON HARRY EDWARD SANDERS	Xby 1913–14	L 21st Empress of India's Lancers	15 May 1919	21	Dysentry, Meerut/Delhi War Cemetery, India
ROY BROUGHTON SANDERSON	Sch 1898–08	L Royal Garrison Artillery	17 April 1918	29	Mont Noir, Ypres/Haringhe Military Cem. Ypres, B.
EDWIN WALTER SAUNDERS	Xby 1906–10	L Cambridgeshire Regiment	5 May 1915	22	2nd Ypres/Menin Gate, Ypres, Belgium
JOHN RAYMOND BOSCAWEN SAVAGE	N 1912–14	2 Royal Flying Corps	18 June 1916	17	Sallaumines, France/Bully Grenay Cemetery, France
ALAN EDWARD SCARTH	Xby 1911–13	L Imperial Indian Army	22 April 1917	21	Istabulat, Mesopotamia/Basra Memorial, Iraq
HERBERT SELWYN SCORER	Lx 1901–03	C Lincolnshire Regiment	13 October 1915	29	Loos/Loos Memorial, France
REGINALD BOURNE SEATON	L.S. 1905–07	P King's Own R. Lanc. R.	27 Sept. 1918	25	Flesquières, Cambrai/Vis-en-Artois Memorial, France
REGINALD HERBERT SECRETAN	S 1909–14	L Hertfordshire Regiment	31 July 1917	22	Passchendaele/Menin Gate, Ypres, Belgium
GEOFFREY EDWARD SEWELL	D 1912–15	2 Royal East Kent Reg.	2 September 1917	19	Loos/Noeux-les-Mines Cemetery, France
PHILIP EDMUND SHARPLES	By/Lx 09–12	L York and Lancaster Reg.	7 June 1917	21	Ypres/Railway Dugouts Cemetery, Ypres, Belgium
BRUCE LIONEL SIDDONS	Day 1898–02	S Australian Imp. Infantry	1 September 1918	32	Péronne, Somme/Péronne Communal Cem, France
RUSSELL HARRY LOUIS SIMMONS	D 1909–13	2 Royal Berkshire Reg.	25 September 1915	20	Ypres/Ploegsteert Memorial, Ypres, Belgium
STANLEY HAROLD SLATER	L.S. 1914–16	P Royal Fusiliers	24 August 1918	19	Somme/Bagneux British Cemetery, Gézaincourt, Fr.
MARCEL FRANCIS CONRAN SMITH	Sch 1892–94	Civilian on SS *Persia*	30 December 1915	39	Drowned off Crete, U-boat/Lost at sea
THOMAS SPENCER	L.S. 1899–00	LC Northamptonshire Reg.	17 November 1914	31	Passchendaele/Perth Cemetery, Zillebeke, Belgium
GERVASE THORPE SPENDLOVE	S 1909–13	2 South Lancashire Reg.	31 July 1917	18	1st Ypres/Ypres Town Cemetery, Belgium
EDWARD REGINALD SPOFFORTH	Sch 1906–08	L Yorkshire Regiment	2 March 1916	25	Ypres/Poperinge New Military Cemetery, Ypres, Belg.
HENRY STEPHEN SPURLING	G 1910–12	2 East Surrey Regiment	21 August 1916	20	Guillemont, Somme/La Neuville Cemetery, Corbie, Fr.
ARTHUR HOWARD BARTLETT STACE	Xby 1913–17	L Royal Air Force	3 May 1919	20	Accident, Mons/Mons Communal Cemetery, Belgium
ALEXANDER JEWELL STANNARD	S 1905–08	M Royal Garrison Artillery	19 August 1917	26	Passchendaele/The Huts Cemetery, Ypres, Belgium
NORMAN STEEL	N 1911–15	2 Gloucestershire Regiment	16 August 1917	20	Passchendaele/Tyne Cot Memorial, Ypres, Belgium
EDWARD ALFRED MURTAGH STEVENS	G 1913–16	2 East Kent Regiment	18 June 1918	19	Albert, Somme/Harponville Cemetery, Somme, France
TALBERT STEVENSON	Xby 1910–12	C Black Watch	14 November 1917	22	Polderhoek, Ypres/La Clytte Military Cem. Ypres, B.

	House/dates	rank/regiment at death	date of death	age	where died/fatally wounded/where buried/commemorated
JOHN CROCKETT STIMPSON	Sch 1911-13	2 West Yorkshire Reg.	1 July 1916	19	Thiepval, Somme/Thiepval Memorial, France
HENRY BERRY STRANGER	L.S. 1903-07	P Northants. Yeomanry	9 August 1915	25	Poperinge, Ypres/Poperinge Cemetery, Belgium
PERCY STRICKLAND	S 1900-05	L Royal Navy, HMS *Dublin*	31 May 1916	25	Jutland/Old Kinloss Abbey, Moray, Scotland
RONALD CHRISTIAN SUNDIUS-SMITH	N/Sch 09-12	L West Yorkshire Regiment	12 March 1915	20	Neuve Chapelle/Neuve Chapelle Memorial, France
JOHN EGREMONT THIMBLEBY	Lx 1902-06	L Lincolnshire Regiment	28 August 1915	26	Motorcycle accident, St. Albans/Spilsby, Lincolnshire
FREDERICK ALFRED TRENCHARD	Lx 1902-06	L Royal Field Artillery	24 May 1915	27	2nd Ypres/La Brique Military Cemetery, Ypres, B.
ROLAND WILLIAM TRUBRIDGE	Xby 1912-15	L Royal Air Force	6 May 1918	20	Somme/Crouy British Cemetery, Amiens, France
GEORGE ARTHUR TRYON	Staff 08-14	LCol King's Royal Rifles	7 November 1918	32	Maubeuge/St. Remy-Chaussée Cemetery, France
HERBERT KERSEY TURNER	Sch 1905-08	C Suffolk Regiment	15 July 1916	24	Somme/Flatiron Copse Cemetery, Mametz, France
HUGH VICTOR TURNILL	L.S. 1909-14	P Honourable Artillery Co.	15 April 1917	20	Ancre, Somme/Warmington, Oundle, Northants.
WILFRED ULYATT	L.S. 1908-09	B HMS *Lion*	1 June 1916	20	Jutland, North Sea/Buried at sea
EDWARD WILMOT VAUGHAN	S 1910-13	2 Royal Field Artillery	15 July 1916	19	Somme/Quarry Cemetery, Montauban, France
WEDGWOOD VAUGHAN	D 1896-99	L Red Cross Driver	12 April 1918	36	Pneumonia/ unknown
JOHN SHERARD VEASEY	G 1904-06	L Worcestershire Regiment	12 March 1915	26	Neuve Chapelle/Le Touret Memorial, France
CHARLES VIPAN	L.S. 1905-08	P Royal Berkshire Regiment	17 October 1917	26	Passchendaele/Prowse Point Military Cem. Ypres, B.
FREDERICK MAXWELL WAITE	G 1909-12	2 Leicestershire Regiment	7 June 1915	20	Messines Ridge/Packhorse Farm Cemetery, Ypres, B.
JESSE EUGENE WALLIS	L.S. 1908-14	P London Scottish Regiment	28 March 1917	20	Agny, Arras/Agny Military Cemetery, France
HAROLD HENRY WALTON	Lx 1908-12	C Sherwood Foresters	13 October 1915	20	Loos/Loos Memorial, France
LIONEL BERNARD RAY WANSBROUGH	G 1903-05	L HMS *Monmouth*	1 November 1914	25	Battle of Coronel, off Chile/Lost at sea, Pacific Ocean
JOHN BRYAN WARD	L.S. 1904-06	Unknown	Unknown	U	Unknown
THOMAS LOVELL WARNER	N 1908-13	M Leicestershire Regiment	27 December 1917	23	Appendicitis, Somme/Tincourt British Cemetery, France
JAMES BOOKER BROUGH WARREN	G 1903-07	L Border Regiment	26 October 1914	25	1st Ypres/Menin Gate, Ypres, Belgium
BASIL HERBERT WATTS	S 1894-98	P Canadian Infantry	18 April 1915	36	Ypres/Mount Royal Cemetery, Montreal, Canada
ALAN HERBERT MANWARING WEST	Sch 1911-15	L Indian Army	7 January 1918	20	Accident, Amara, Mesopotamia/Amara War Cem., Iraq
WALTER MONTAGU WEST	Sch 1910-13	L Cambridgeshire Regiment	6 May 1915	19	Ypres/Klein-Vierstraat British Cemetery, Ypres, B.
PHILIP SELWYN WHISTON	Xby 1905-08	2 Sherwood Foresters	21 March 1918	27	Loos/Loos Memorial, France
LIONEL RUSSELL WILFORD	Sch 1906-11	L South Staffordshire Reg.	8 November 1918	26	Influenza/Mazargues War Cemetery, Marseilles, Fr.

	House/dates	rank/regiment at death	date of death	age	where died/fatally wounded/where buried/commemorated
LAWRENCE ARNOLD WILKINS	Lx 1908-13	C York and Lancaster Reg.	25 August 1918	24	Ervillers, Somme/Mory Abbey Military Cemetery, Fr.
EDWARD MAURICE WILLIAMSON	Xby 1906-11	L Sherwood Foresters	1 March 1915	21	N. Chapelle/Royal Irish Rifles Cemetery, Laventie, Fr.
GEORGE HAMILTON WILLIAMSON	Staff 1913-14	C King's Royal Rifle Corps	12 April 1917	27	Arras/Warlincourt Halte Cemetery, Saulty, France
JUSTIN CHARLES WILLIS	N 1909-13	M Royal Engineers	6 August 1918	23	Vignacourt, Amiens/Vignacourt British Cemetery, Fr.
OSWALD COKE WINSTANLEY	S 1901-04	2 Welsh Regiment	10 August 1915	27	Suvla, Gallipoli/Helles Memorial, Turkey
ERNEST WALTER WINTON	G 1911-14	2 Royal Garrison Artillery	15 December 1917	19	Ypres/Bleuet Farm Cemetery, Ypres, Belgium
CYRAL RENALS WOODWARD	S 1908-10	2 Sherwood Foresters	27 October 1922	28	Wounds from war/Weston-super-Mare, Somerset
ARTHUR ERNEST WYNN	G 1910-12	2 Royal Flying Corps	1 November 1916	20	Bapaume, Somme/Flying Services Memorial, Arras, Fr.
ERIC FERNANDEZ YARROW	G 1909-13	L Argyll/Suth. Highlanders	8 May 1915	20	2nd Ypres/Essex Farm Cemetery, Boezinge, Ypres, B.
COLIN TURNER YOUNG	D 1903-07	C Duke of Wellington's Reg.	24 April 1917	26	Somme/Fins New British Cemetery, Péronne, France

Key to Ranks

LCol – Lieutenant Colonel
M – Major (10-4%)
C – Captain (40-15%)
L – Lieutenant (79-31%)
2 – Second Lieutenant/Sub-Lieutenant (87-34%)
CSM – Company Sergeant Major
S – Sergeant
LS – Lance-Serjeant
Cp – Corporal
LC – Lance-Corporal
P – Private
R – Rifleman
G – Gunner
B – Bombardier
T – Trooper
D – Driver
U – Unknown

The Fallen by Age

Average Age of those killed – 23.6 years
Oldest: Charles Andrews aged 45
Youngest: John Savage aged 17

  1 aged 17
  9 aged 18
33 aged 19
47 aged 20
23 aged 21
24 aged 22
14 aged 23
20 aged 24 = 171/263 (65%) aged 17-24

The Fallen by House (number in House and Housemaster Michaelmas 1909)

Berrystead (By)	8	(21 – Mr Brown)
Crosby (Xby)	21	(41 – Mr Paine)
Day Boys	3	(1)
Dryden (D)	40	(38 – Mr Jones)
Grafton (G)	32	(45 – Mr Wagstaff)
Laxton (Lx)	37	(45 – Mr King)
Laxton School (L.S.)	30	(42 – Mr Ross)
New House (N)	26	(38 – Mr Hale)
School (Sch)	38	(54 – The Headmaster)
Sidney (S)	37	(43 – Mr Nightingale)

Staff killed   5

MAURICE MISKIN
FRANCIS NORBURY (OO) Hsm Grafton
GEORGE TRYON Hsm Crosby
GEORGE WILLIAMSON
CHARLES CLAYSON Bandmaster

The Fallen by Service

Army	224	86%
Airmen	31	12%
Royal Navy	5	2%

The Fallen by Geography – places of burial/commemoration

France	133 = 51%
Belgium	57 = 22%
Eastern Mediterranean+Middle East	23 = 8%
U.K.	21 = 8%
Africa	10 = 4%
Lost at sea	5 = 2%
India	2 = 1%
Canada/Italy/Malta/Russia/Singapore	5 = 2%
Unknown	7 = 2%

The Fallen by cause of death

Killed	230	88%
Disease	19	6.5%
Accident	14	5.5%

*Brothers in Arms – 10 sets of brothers amongst the Fallen

Armitage 3
Barwell 2
Begg 2
Brindley 2
Burrell 3
Gray 2
Greaves 2
Grummitt 2
Hatch 2
Platts 2

The Fallen at Cambridge and Oxford   45 = 12%

(includes those who gained places but did not matriculate)

CAMBRIDGE (39)

Christ's College	Philip Hatch
Clare College (5)	John Anderson, Christopher Benson, Sydney Davey, Douglas McMichael, Ernest Winton
Downing College	John Line
Emmanuel College (4)	Guy Bostock, Walter Marsden, James Morris, George Williamson

Gonville and Caius College (9)	William Clarke, Harold Coates, Ivor Davies, Geoffrey Donaldson, Duncan Gotch, John Gulliland, William MacCombie, Arthur Platts, Thomas Warner,
Jesus College (2)	Edward MacBryan, Randall Mason
Pembroke College (4)	Douglas Armitage, Frank Armitage, Lawrence Hatch, George Tryon
Queens' College (2)	Basil Coates, Roy Sanderson
St. John's College (2)	Geoffrey Gaze, Francis Norbury
Selwyn College	Norman Prynne
Sidney Sussex College (3)	Samuel Edmonds, William King, Walter Paine
Trinity College (4)	Robert Bragg, Cecil Broadbent, James Dixon, Eric Yarrow
Trinity Hall	Frederick Trenchard

OXFORD (6)

Balliol College	Frederick Milholland
Keble College	Herbert Hobbs
Lincoln College (2)	Charles Buckmaster, Audley Lee
University College (2)	Maurice Miskin, John Russell

Something in the order of 1200 boys from Oundle School and Laxton School joined up. At least 35 were prisoners of war and perhaps 350 were wounded. 263 were killed = 22% of those who joined up.

Appendix II

The Fallen by Month/Three Months/School Year

	Year 1 1914-15		Year 2 1915-16		Year 3 1916-17		Year 4 1917-18		Year 5 1918-19		Years 6-9 1919-22	
September (term time)	1		6		0		0		6		0	Total
October	5	*8	10	*21	4	*13	9	*18	7	*22	1	83
November	2		2		3		7		6		0	
December	0		3		0		5		1		2	
January	1	*2	1	*4	1	*3	2	*9	1	*3	0	23
February	1		0		2		2		1		0	
March	5		4		4		13		1		0	
April	2	*14	3	*9	11	*21	6	*23	0	*4	0	71
May	7		2		6		4		3		0	
June	4		6		2		3		0		0	
July	2	*15	20	*30	10	*22	3	*14	1	*2	0	83
August	9		4		10		8		1		0	
September (holidays)	3		6		2		3		0		0	Date Unknown
Totals	42		67		55		65		28		3	3

Death Toll: 263 Staff and Old Boys of Oundle School and Laxton School
*3 monthly figures: Sept.–Nov./Dec.-Feb./March-May/June-Aug.
(September holidays added to September term time.)

Appendix III

Awards & Decorations

205 in total

British awards   182

Victoria Cross	3
Distinguished Service Medal	2
Military Medal	1
Military Cross	115
Bar to Military Cross	6
Distinguished Service Cross	3
Air Force Cross	2
Distinguished Flying Cross	4
Distinguished Service Order	29
Bar to D.S.O.	3
C.B.E.	2
O.B.E.	6
M.B.E.	2
Victorian Order (M.V.O.+C.V.O.)	2
Companion of the Order of St. Michael and St. George	2

French Awards

Croix d'Officier	1
Croix de Chevalier	2
Croix de Guerre	7

Italian Awards

Bronze Medal	1
Chevalier	2
Croce di Guerra	1
Croce al Merito di Guerra	1

Russian Awards

Order of St. Stanislas	1
Order of St. Anne	2
Order of St. Vladimir	1

Belgian Awards

Chevalier de l'ordre de la Couronne	1
Ordre de Léopold	2

Serbian Award

Gold Medal	1

Appendix IV

Senior and Junior House Results during the War[1]

	Football	Cricket	Rowing	Athletics	Fives	Shooting	Section Drill	Gym.	Swimming
Senior									
1914-15	New	School	Dryden	Dryden	School	Laxton	Laxton	Dryden	Dryden
Junior		Grafton			Grafton				
1915-16	Grafton	Crosby	Laxton		Grafton	Crosby	New	Dryden	Sidney
Junior		Sidney			Sidney				
1916-17	Sidney	Sidney	Dryden	Laxton	Sidney	Crosby	Dryden		Dryden
Junior		Sidney			Sidney				
1917-18	Laxton	Dryden	Dryden	Sidney	School				
Junior					Grafton				
1918-19	Laxton	Laxton			School	Grafton	Dryden		Dryden
Junior		School			Grafton				
TOTALS	Crosby 3	Dryden 12	Grafton 7	Laxton 7	New 2	School 5	Sidney 9		

1 From W.G.Walker, *A History of the Oundle Schools*.

Bibliography

Primary Sources

David Angus (ed.) 'Diary Extracts of William B.G. Angus', presented to Oundle School Archive 1988. Unpublished.

Hamish Bradley (ed.), 'Old Oundelian obits from the Great War', CDRom 2010 presented to Oundle School Archive.

R.C.Bragg 1892-1915 unpublished original letters and transcriptions of Robert Bragg, deposited in Oundle School Archive by Lady Adrian.

Avalon Eastman (ed.), *Oundle School Memorial Book of the First World War 1914-1918* (Exeter: Short Run Press 2006).

Friends and Associates of F.W.Sanderson, *Sanderson of Oundle* (London: Chatto and Windus, 1923).

Geoffrey Hamilton and Keith Hamilton (eds.), *Diary and Letters of Geoffrey Donaldson* (Blurb creative publishing service, 2007) donated to Oundle School Archive.

H.M.King and E.E.Yeld (eds.), *Oundle Memorials of the Great War MCMXIV-MCMXIX* (London: Philip Lee Warner, publisher to the Medici Society, Ltd, 1920).

The Laxtonian: The Oundle School Chronicle published termly 1906-1928, printed by Alfred King and Son, printers to Oundle School.

Cecil Lewis, *Sagittarius Rising* (London: Greenhill Books 2006, first published 1936 by Peter Davies).

Peter Ling, 'Lieutenant Roy Sanderson' (Unpublished photocopied essay, deposited in Oundle School Archive by Mike Ling).

Lyn Macdonald, *They Called It Passchendaele* (London: Penguin Books 1993).

Florence Muckley (ed.), *Letters of Justin Willis* (self-published 1926), bound by Frank Garrett for Harold J. Willis. Deposited in Oundle School Archive by John Clark in 2007.

Jane Orde and Charlotte Farmer (eds.), *Gallipoli Diary – Letters of A. M. McCracken* self-published/ photocopies 2000. Available in Oundle School Archive

Oundle School Blue Books 1892-1928, printed by Alfred King and Son, printers to Oundle School. (School Lists)

Oundle School Commemoration 1900-24, booklets printed by Alfred King and Son, printers to Oundle School.

Richard John Palmer, 'The Life of F. W. Sanderson (1857-1922) with special reference to his work and influence at Oundle School (1892-1922)' unpublished D.Phil. thesis for the University of Hull 1981. Donated to Oundle School Archive.

Ray Rundle, *Shadows of the Past – the Oundle War Memorial Men 1914-18* (Barnwell: Inkwell Printing, 2014).

J.W.Russell, 'Selections of diary and letters of Lt. J.W. Russell' published in *The Iron Duke, the Regimental Magazine of the Duke of Wellington's Regiment* (June 1928 and February 1929) (Weston-super-Mare: Lawrence Bros).

Mrs. H. Secretan (ed.), 'Life and Letters of Reginald Herbert Secretan', unpublished and donated to Oundle School Archive.

Alice Thomas (ed.), *Diary of John Coleman Binder* (Oundle Museum Trust, 2013).

Sue Warner, 'Thomas Lovell Warner', an article for the Hoby and District History Society available at http: www.hobyanddistricthistory.co.uk (accessed 9 September 2016).

H.G.Wells *The Story of a Great Schoolmaster* [biography of Frederick William Sanderson] (New York: Macmillan 1924).

Sir Alfred Yarrow (ed.), 'Eric 1915 – A Memoir', Life and letters of Eric Yarrow compiled by his father Sir Alfred Yarrow. Available on Oundle School website: http: www.oundleschool.org.uk Unpublished

Secondary Sources

Barry Blades, *Roll of Honour – Schooling and the Great War 1914-19* (Barnsley: Pen and Sword, 2015).

Alexandra Churchill, *Blood and Thunder – The Boys of Eton College and the First World War* (Stroud: The History Press, 2014).

Alan Clark, *The Donkeys* (London: Pimlico, 1991).

Stephen Cooper, *The Final Whistle – The Great War in Fifteen Players* (Stroud: The History Press 2012).

Reginald Fair and Charles Fair, *Marjorie's War – four families in the Great War 1914-18* (Menin House 2012).

John Laffin, *British Butchers and Bunglers of the First World War* (Stroud: Sutton Publishing 1988)

Martin Middlebrook, *The First Day on the Somme* (London: Allen Lane 1971).

Richard Pearson, *The Boys of Shakespeare's School in the First World War* (Stroud: The History Press 2010).

Anthony Seldon and David Walsh, *Public Schools and the Great War – The Generation Lost* (Barnsley: Pen and Sword 2013).

Sue Smart, *When Heroes Die* [Gresham's School and the Great War] (Derby: Breedon Books Publishing Company Ltd. 2001).

William George Walker, *A History of the Oundle Schools* (Hazell, Watson and Viney Limited, London 1956).

Index

INDEX OF PEOPLE

INDEX OF PLACES

INDEX OF GENERAL & MISCELLANEOUS TERMS

INDEX OF MILITARY FORMATIONS & UNITS